PRAISE FOR THE RIGHT THING TO DO

"Tom Shanahan has always been ahead of the curve when it comes to writing about race relations in sport—dating to the great, integrated Duffy Daugherty teams of the 1960s. *The Right Thing to Do* is another example of his unique ability to go inside stories that need to be told in rich detail."

—John Feinstein, best-selling author of 44 books, most recently *Raise a Fist, Take a Knee*

"John Hannah and Duffy Daugherty turned Michigan State football into a beacon that showed the world how athletes from disparate racial, socioeconomic and geographical backgrounds could not just coexist but thrive alongside one another, and Tom Shanahan continues to shine a light into the Spartans' impact in integrating major college athletics in the 1950s, '60s and '70s. Shanahan masterfully spotlights the zeitgeist that made East Lansing the epicenter of an evolving college football landscape in the decades that followed and would push the sport forward to its more racially inclusive present form."

—Chris Solari, *Detroit Free Press* Michigan State beat writer

"Tom Shanahan's *The Right Thing to Do* is an important, timely and well-researched contribution to the study of sports and race in America. In breaking the 'conspiracy of silence' that has existed since the days of segregation, Shanahan elevates the stories of the players and coaches who changed the face of college sports into their rightful place in history."

—Andrew Maraniss, *New York Times*-bestselling author, *Strong Inside: Perry Wallace and the Collision of Race and Sports in the South*

"Much has been written or broadcast about inclusion in big-time college football, but this book carefully credits innovators and contributors whose accounts are far more essential and intriguing than apocryphal locker-room speeches and latter-day efforts."

—Bijan C. Bayne, Author, *Martha's Vineyard Basketball: How A Resort League Defied Notions Of Race & Class*

"Jimmy Raye has been called a trailblazer. I consider him a treasure. Under the most trying circumstances, he carried himself with grace and class. And when he never got the opportunity to climb to the top of the coaching ladder because of discriminatory hiring practices, he continued to blaze a trail by working behind the scenes to create opportunities for minority coaches coming behind him. Soft-spoken, his words carried an impact. Few in the NFL were as respected as Raye."

—Jim Trotter, *NFL.com*, formerly of *Sports Illustrated* and ESPN and author of *Junior Seau: The Life and Death of a Football Icon*

"The flood of extraordinary Black athletes in the NCAA and NFL today may seem as inevitable as a river rushing to the sea. But it took singular men digging precarious channels back in the 1960s…and Tom Shanahan's relentless spadework in *The Right Thing to Do* six decades later to understand who and what it took to make water run downhill."

—Gary Smith, *Sports Illustrated* writer and National Sports Media Hall of Famer

"One of the great beauties of *The Right Thing to Do* is author Tom Shanahan unflinchingly names names. He shows us the good people and hidden figures who did the important work of integrating college football and calls out the obstructionists who were on the wrong side of history. The glory and the shame of it all is here, researched in painstaking detail."

—Johnette Howard, author of *The Rivals* and co-author of *All In: An Autobiography* by Billie Jean King

"Such an important chapter of American sports history, one that was in grave danger of being lost forever if not for Tom Shanahan's dogged reporting and insightful analysis."

—Mike Jensen, *Philadelphia Inquirer*

"With *The Right Thing to Do*, Tom Shanahan continues his heroic efforts to fill in the huge gaps in our understanding of how college football went from being barely integrated in the 1950s to thoroughly integrated by the 1980s. This is a story that has long needed telling."

—Michael Oriard, Oregon State professor emeritus whose books on football and American culture include *Bowled Over*; he played at Notre Dame and four years in the NFL with the Kansas City Chiefs

"The right thing for all of us to do—immediately—is to read Tom Shanahan's newest epic tome, *The Right Thing to Do*. This riveting saga of the struggle to triumph with innate and powerful goodness, embodies the best of humanity's efforts to right the wrongs of an immoral history. Shanahan shines the most powerful of lights on a tragically bleak past and then finds the bright side of our human highway. We cannot, or will not, be able to move forward to a better tomorrow, unless we know and learn from what went down. Failing to engage on this most important topic will only eternally mire us in the deepest depths of denial. *The Right Thing to Do* is a beacon of hope that makes us believe that a world as it can, could and should be is attainable. And the efforts to make it so, are essential, and totally worthwhile. Read on. Learn on. Know on. Act on. It's the right thing to do."

—Bill Walton, *BillWalton.com*

"The Right Thing to Do…was for someone to dig deep and tell the whole story of one of the most important fights in college football history. That someone was Tom Shanahan, a gifted storyteller who knows what Duffy Daugherty did as well as anyone outside the Michigan State football locker room. His work, a labor of love, is more than impressive. It's equally important. As the author of eight books, it isn't often I say, 'I wish I'd written that!' And I won't say that here….I couldn't have it as well as Tom did."

—Jack Ebling, host of "The Drive with Jack" and "Press Pass" and MSU sports historian

"In yet another groundbreaking book, chock-full of gumshoe reporting, Tom Shanahan introduces us to the unsung heroes of the 1960s college football integration movement, young Black athletes who excelled on the gridiron but received no credit for their exploits by a white press that chose to look the other way. *The Right Thing to Do* has the heart of a good sports story and the journalistic backbone to finally set the historical record straight, shedding light on a chapter of college football that has shamelessly been long left in the dark."

—John Glionna, former *Los Angeles Times* writer whose work was featured in the 2019 edition of *The Best American Sports Writing* and the author of *Outback Nevada: Real Stories from the Silver State*

"We are a country that often blindly embraces historical myths, but fortunately Tom Shanahan proves with *The Right Thing to Do* that it's never too late to set the record straight. His strong reporting ensures that these important stories can now be told with accuracy, not mythicism."

—David Little, Chico (Calif.) *Enterprise-Record* editor and former NFL beat writer

"In the long run this world cannot be a good place for anybody or anything until it is a good place for everybody and everything. Tom Shanahan's book, *The Right Thing to Do*, underscores the history and truth of this statement in the world of college football."

—Joe Romig, Colorado All-American lineman, College Football Hall of Famer, Rhodes Scholar

"Tom Shanahan continues to do a masterful job uncovering and reporting an incredibly important point of time in the game of football when it comes to integration and inclusion for all. No one does a better job than Shanahan at finding the accurate information so we can all have a better understanding for how we have gotten to the present and to be aware that there is still a lot of opportunity to improve even further."

—Corey Robinson, 247Sports/CBS Sports/Co-host Spartan Spotlight

"They call it 'big-time' football, but it's amazing how many overlooked people made it happen during the crucial years of the modern civil rights movement. *The Right Thing to Do* includes the famous names you know but also a myriad of players, coaches, and families you should."

—Lane Demas, Central Michigan University Ph.D history professor and author of *Integrating the Gridiron: Black Civil Rights and American College Football* and *Game of Privilege: An African American History of Golf*

"In order for us to move forward it is important to understand our past. I appreciate Tom Shanahan for helping us frame the past and point us toward the future."

—Herman Edwards, former Arizona State and NFL head coach

"More than 50 years after Duffy Daugherty rose to the top of college football, helped by the recruitment of outstanding Black players, most casual American sports fans would not be able to identify Duffy or Michigan State as pioneers in the integration of national college football.

This is similar to how the 1963 Loyola-Chicago basketball team gets overlooked in a discussion of the integration of college hoops. It's not that the 1966 Texas Western team wasn't hugely important; of course, it was. It's just that the story of 1963 Loyola needs to be told and given credit as a central shaper of our society.

"So, it also is in college football with Duffy Daugherty and his Underground Railroad in the 1960s, from the Deep South and Texas to East Lansing.

"Daugherty was a great coach regardless of anything else he did, but the fact that he integrated college football and mentored both elite players and great assistant coaches (such as Bill Yeoman, who became an icon at Houston) makes him a hugely important figure in college football history. Not enough people know about him. Tom Shanahan is telling a sports story younger generations of Americans need to read."

—Matt Zemek, college football editor and writer since 2001

"Each paragraph, each chapter provided me a fresh new perspective and understanding of the college football integration movement. These are heroes whose stories needed to be told."

—Jeff Fann, publisher of *All-Sports Discussion.com* and *TalkinACCsports.com*

"Tom Shanahan's *The Right Thing to Do* is the right book at the right time. By telling us about Duffy Daugherty and Michigan State, he makes the point—one that sadly still needs to be made—that our football teams and our country is better when it is integrated."

—Chris Lamb, author of *Stolen Dreams: The 1955 Cannon Street All-Stars and Little League Baseball's Civil War*

"Tom tackles an important topic head on. Integration in college football mirrors our nation's path toward racial equality. Too often incremental progress has been sidetracked by maddening steps backward. Tom Shanahan looks beyond the myths and half-truths to tell the story of how this truly American sport slowly came closer to inclusion of our entire population."

—Steve Wiseman, *Raleigh News & Observer* Duke beat writer

"When James Owens signed with Auburn University as the first African-American player, it was not only a learning curve for me but for all

Auburn people. James Owens could not have been a better football player, person, father, husband, humanitarian and friend. He was courageous and the best choice Auburn ever could have made is signing James Owens first. He fit right in with all of us, and we learned a lot from James in the four years we played together and in the friendship that we carried for so many years until his passing. I'm so proud he became an Auburn Tiger. I'm even more proud to call him my friend for life. In *The Right Thing to Do* you'll learn about my friend and teammate and other 1960s pioneers."

—Terry Henley, Auburn running back and Sr. Vice President, Palomar Insurance Corporation

THE RIGHT THING TO DO

THE TRUE PIONEERS OF COLLEGE FOOTBALL
INTEGRATION IN THE 1960S

TOM SHANAHAN

August
Publications

CONTENTS

Acknowledgments	xv
Foreword	xxiii
Ruffin McNeill	
Preface: Filling the Gaps	xxvii
Sherman Lewis: A Coaching Legacy	xxxi
Part I: Michigan State's Pioneering Role in College Football Integration	xxxvii
1. Duffy's Leadership and Coaching Tree	1
2. Jimmy Raye's Black Coaching Network	22
3. Two Games of the Century	36
4. Arizona State's Dan Devine and Frank Kush	48
5. Dan Devine and Missouri's Desegregation	65
6. Colorado, Sonny Grandelius and the Orange Bowl	77
7. Oklahoma, Chuck Fairbanks and Barry Switzer	90
8. Success in Nebraska, Engineered by Bob Devaney	105
9. Houston's Bill Yeoman Pioneers Texas Integration	117
10. Earle Edwards Rebuilds N.C. State	131
11. Wyoming: Challenges for Bob Devaney and Lloyd Eaton	146
12. Dan Devine at Notre Dame: Image is Everything	154
13. The 1967 NFL Draft That Changed the Face of the League	166
14. Polynesian Pioneers: Charlie Wedemeyer and Bob Apisa	169
15. Gideon Smith, Ferris State, Michigan State and Statues	180
16. Willie Ray Smith Sr., the Chief Engineer	188
17. Michigan State as the North Star for Southern Pioneers	198
18. A Mississippi Kid's Sixth-Grade Dream, 1963	210
Part II: The True 1960s Pioneers at Southern Schools	223
19. Blazing a Trail Through the ACC	224
20. MLK, SMU's Jerry LeVias and SWC integration	230
21. Gary Steele Blazes West Point Path	240
22. Kentucky's Wilbur Hackett and Tennessee's Lester McClain	249
23. James Owens' "Quiet Courage" Blazed Auburn Trail	259
Part III: Examining the 1970 USC-Alabama myths and fiction	265
24. The Blackout and Blank Canvas	266
25. UCLA and Jim Murray Battle 'Bama, Bryant	276
26. Michigan State at Segregated North Carolina, 1964	295
27. Duffy and The Bear	299
28. The Time Cover That Launched a Thousand Bear Bryant Myths	308

29. Deconstructing the 1970 USC-Alabama Fiction	323
Part IV: Voices From the Next Generation	339
30. The Next Generation: Families Impacted by Football Scholarships	340

The Right Thing to Do: The True Pioneers of College Football Integration in the 1960s

August Publications
5115 Excelsior Blvd., #734
St. Louis Park, MN 55416
augustpublications.com

Copyright © 2024 by Tom Shanahan. All rights reserved.

No part of this book may be reproduced in any form or by any electronic or mechanical means, including information storage and retrieval systems, without written permission from the author, except for the use of brief quotations in a book review.

All trademarks are the property of their respective owners.

Visit the author's website at *tomshanahan.report*.

Cover photo courtesy Michigan State University.

An index is available from the publisher. Please send a request to *info@augustpublications.com*.

Library of Congress Control Number: 2022950453

ISBN 978-1-938532-73-3 (Print)
ISBN 978-1-938532-74-0 (eBook)

9 8 7 6 5 4 3 2 1

Designer (cover): Natalie Nowytski

To the true 1960s pioneers of college football integration, Black and white, North and South. You all played a Jackie Robinson-like role, but your courage and legacies have been unjustly overshadowed by myths and fiction crafted around the 1970 USC-Alabama game. The true 1960s pioneers include Michigan State coach Duffy Daugherty's teams and players opening doors; Duffy's assistant coaches following his blueprint at their new schools; Duffy's pioneering Black coaches; Duffy's Chief Engineer for the Underground Railroad, Willie Ray Smith Sr.; and the first Black players on their Southern campuses. The 1960s barriers they broke down cleared the way for the 1970 USC-Alabama game to be played without incident.

ACKNOWLEDGMENTS

John Meadows told me a Duffy Daugherty story that for a moment had me thinking—"ah, this is it." I thought the Colorado football alum from Royal Oak, Michigan, was revealing the first "yeah, but" Duffy story.

In a decade of research for *Raye of Light* and now for *The Right Thing to Do*, I've only heard about him as a trustworthy leader. In *Raye of Light*, Michigan State All-America tight end Billy Joe Dupree explained if Daugherty said something, players could count it as "true 99.9 percent of the time."

Daugherty had recruited Meadows in 1960 out of Dondero High in suburban Detroit, but Meadows committed to Colorado coach Sonny Grandelius, a former Duffy assistant. Meadows, though, soon felt homesick. While he was home for Christmas break, he drove to East Lansing to ask Daugherty if he could transfer to the Spartans.

Meadows continued in a grim tone: "Duffy said, 'We'll take you because you're a Michigan boy. But you have to promise me you'll return to school, go through spring ball and not flunk any of your classes.'"

I thought this was the moment Meadows opened a closet door to a Daugherty skeleton, but he shifted tones and laughed.

"Duffy knew what was best for me better than I did. Once I got back to school, I realized I wanted to finish what I started with the guys in my class. I stayed at Colorado."

All these years later he was instrumental to me understanding the backstory of Colorado's players threatening to boycott the 1962 Orange Bowl (Chapter 6). The Buffaloes said they wouldn't travel to segregated Miami unless their five Black teammates were guaranteed the same accommodations as the rest of the team.

If you're reading this and suddenly thinking you never heard about the 1961 Big Eight Conference champions threatening to boycott the Orange Bowl played on January 1, 1962, read on. That's one of many unreported moments about race in sports that athletes, coaches, family members, historians and others have helped me assemble to write this book.

The dozens of unknown college football integration events seem individually disjointed, but they combined by the end of decade to turn the sport into a game that reflected America. At the center of it was Duffy Daugherty's 1960s teams—college football's first fully integrated rosters.

Meadows' Colorado teammates Joe Romig and Bill Harris also offered great insight. I told Romig I've interviewed Hall of Famers and Olympic champions, but he was the first Rhodes Scholar. Colorado associate athletic director Dave Plati, who I've known since Colorado quarterback's Sal Aunese's promising career turned tragic with his death, generously helped. Bobby Anderson from the 1969 team provided great insight on the Buffaloes' win over Alabama and Bear Bryant's all-white team in the Liberty Bowl.

Chuck Fairbanks Jr. and Bill Yeoman Jr. were so close to their late fathers, I felt like their quotes came directly from their dads. Also helpful on those two schools were two College Football Hall of Famers, Oklahoma's Greg Pruitt and Houston's Elmo Wright.

When Wright and I discussed the 1970 USC-Alabama myths and fiction, Wright told me, "I love it. Tom Shanahan setting everybody right."

I knew Barry Switzer and Daugherty were friends, but I didn't know they were so close. Switzer was preaching to the choir when he told me no coach did more for college football integration than Daugherty. Oklahoma historian Michael Brooks was a big help breaking down the year-by-year increases of Black players under Fairbanks and Switzer, from the single digits they inherited to fully integrated rosters in the 1970s.

The NCAA didn't collect such diversity data until the 1980s. And those surveys were partly a response to college coaches exploiting Black athletes without concern for graduation rates. Standards were put in place.

The numbers I cite on Black scholarship athletes on teams are based on information from talking to school historians, players on the teams and current administrators. The National Football Foundation's Phil Marwill provided me with the organization's list of the first Black players at each school. Black History Month stories, a relatively new trend, also helped identify previously overlooked figures.

Team photos also reveal the lack of Black faces on the 1962 and 1967 USC national title teams. USC was not a model program on integration. As late as the 1950s, USC didn't list Black alumni in its football media guide, omitting All-American lineman Brice Taylor.

My research from interviews, archives and books are cited directly in the stories I tell. You don't have to look to the bottom of the page for notations and then thumb to the back of the book.

Retired Wisconsin coach and athletic director Barry Alvarez was generous with his time. Alvarez played at Nebraska under Bob Devaney and knew Devaney admired Daugherty. I feared he would be hard to get on the phone, but Wisconsin Director of Football Brand Communications Brian Lucas and Alvarez's secretary Linda Wilkins got me in touch while he was in Florida.

Nebraska players Rich Glover and Johnny Rodgers were also a delight to talk with about playing for Devaney, their careers and an overlooked aspect of the 1971 Game of the Century.

Wyoming associate athletic director Tim Harkens dug up information for me on Devaney's Wyoming years. Better yet, in this age of sports information people letting their phone go to voice mail, Harkens picked up. As I recall, it was after the first ring.

Dan Devine turned out to be a far more fascinating story than I expected, forcing me to reshuffle his contributions. I wrote three separate chapters covering his years at Arizona State, Missouri and Notre Dame. Arizona State senior associate athletic director Mark Brand connected me with then-head coach Herman Edwards, who considers Michigan State's Jimmy Raye a mentor. Norm Bryant, the founder of the Greater Flint Afro American Sports Hall of Fame, told me the backstory on Michigan State's Burt Smith helping him and Leon Burton make their way from Flint to ASU under Devine and Frank Kush. Leon's daughter Lynnae Pickens, a Wall Street executive, added greatly to the chapter.

Michigan State's Athletics Communications office, keepers of the Fred Stabley/Nick Vista flame, was again immensely helpful. Matt Larsen and Paulette Martis have helped on both my books. Ben Phlegar, since joining the staff, dug into the rich files from the Stabley-Vista years.

Other schools may have downplayed the presence of Black athletes, but Stabley and Vista, like Daugherty, were ahead of their time. There is no better example than the iconic photo of Duffy with his five All-American players, with four African Americans (Bubba Smith, George Webster, Clinton Jones and Gene Washington) and one Samoan (Bob Apisa).

Missouri associate athletic director Molly O'Mara double-checked Devine facts for me and connected me with two Missouri players, Phil Snowden and Russ Sloan. I was given a number for another player, Jim Miles. I didn't know he had passed away when I called his wife, Mary

Lou. But she graciously and proudly shared stories about her late husband's contributions to Missouri's desegregation years.

Devine also had an impact on Notre Dame. The 10 Black players he signed in 1976 was the largest such class in school history. One of them was Vagas Ferguson. Vagas is the first All-American athlete I've had working for me. He volunteered to dig into his files, which was especially helpful considering Notre Dame's communications office isn't eager to help.

North Carolina State historian Tim Peeler saved me a lot of time researching Earle Edwards' years in Raleigh that included the Wolfpack's first Black players. Charley Young told me about his days playing for N.C. State with his friend, the late Willie Burden. Willie Burden Jr. was also a big help with his father's story.

As you'll read in the Foreword, Ruffin McNeill has intersected with Michigan State in unique ways. I didn't know that until I introduced myself to Ruff at a National Football Foundation-Bill Dooley chapter Pigskin Preview annually held in Cary, North Carolina. Ruff and I had more to talk about regarding Michigan State than I expected. Small world.

Over the years I had written about young Black coaches who consider Michigan State pioneer Jimmy Raye a mentor. I realized I can take all those quotes from Willie Taggart, Herman Edwards, Tony Dungy, Pep Hamilton, Tyrone Willingham and Charlie Baggett and blend them into a chapter.

If you watch the NFL Network and Big Ten Network, you'd think the only successful Black head coaches are Tony Dungy and Dennis Green. BTN producers, editors and writers don't understand that Jimmy Raye and Sherman Lewis—players and coaches for Daugherty—contributed major roles mentoring young coaches in the 1980s, 1990s and into the 21st century. When I gave an NFL Network producer a brief bio on Jimmy, suggesting a story idea, he replied, "I know who Jimmy Raye is." I should have replied, "If so, why haven't you done a story?" (Since then, a documentary aired on the NFL Network, *NFL 360: The Indelible Legacy of Jimmy Raye*, won an Emmy Award for Outstanding Edited Special.)

Raye and Lewis deserved to be head coaches, but they were ahead of their time. Don't hold that against them, BTN and NFL Network. They were victims of "sham" interviews. It's an absolute disgrace the NFL Network and Big Ten Network haven't produced a feature story on Lewis and Raye as pioneering Black athletes from the segregated South and pioneering coaches in college and the NFL.

I also included a chapter on Daugherty leading the way recruiting

Hawaiian talent in the 1950s and 1960s long before the state was producing a Heisman Trophy winner and contenders. The timing was right with Charlie Wedemeyer inducted into the Polynesian Football Hall of Fame in 2022, joining previous inductee and MSU teammate Bob Apisa.

Wedemeyer's inspiring life grew into a national story as he coached high-school football in the San Francisco Bay Area while battling Amyotrophic Lateral Sclerosis. Wedemeyer's wife, Lucy, a saint, patiently told the story about their life together as high-school sweethearts in Hawaii to Michigan State to supporting Charlie's desire to continue coaching despite the ravages of ALS. You can hear it in a video on my website, *TomShanahan.Report*.

Former San Francisco 49ers coach Steve Mariucci was generous with time to discuss why he felt it was important to establish a Bay Area Coach of the Week and Coach of the Year awards sponsored by the 49ers in Wedemeyer's name.

One regret I had after finishing *Raye of Light* was not focusing more on Bubba Smith's father, Willie Ray Smith Sr., a legendary Texas high-school coach during segregation. He was the Chief Engineer of the Underground Railroad. I checked that box in this book.

Hopefully, this better explains the significance of Daugherty offering scholarships to Bubba Smith and George Webster was more about opportunity for Black athletes than it was about these two immensely talented athletes. They would have received scholarships if they were polka-dotted or from Mars. They could have come out of Grambling in the 1960s, but 10 or 20 years earlier we might never have heard of them.

Another chapter worthy of *Raye of Light* that didn't make it was on Eric Marshall. What a remarkable story from the riots of Oxford, Mississippi to Vietnam to San Francisco high-school principal. His daughter Erica Marshall Lee, a Ph.D at Emory University, assisted me.

I have chapters in Part II on true 1960s pioneers at Southern schools. Wake Forest's Bob Grant and SMU's Jerry LeVias were generous with their time.

Auburn's James Owens had passed away, but teammate Terry Henley told Owens' story and also expressed Auburn's regret the school didn't do more for desegregation. You won't hear that kind of apology from anybody at Alabama about Bear Bryant dragging his feet. The myths and fiction surrounding the 1970 USC-Alabama game are like pulling out obstinate weeds. No matter how many times the tale has been debunked, the weeds grow back.

Army West Point and Gary Steele isn't a Southern tale, but Steele gave me his time for a story that needed to be included. Race wasn't discussed in the 1960s, but I quote Army West Point coach Jeff Monken on the importance of a football team understanding diversity.

Writing about race is a difficult subject. People are quick to misinterpret things. One reason is many Americans don't understand or won't accept the challenges of being Black in America. The great Arthur Ashe once said, "Being a Black man in America is like having another job." And when we do make progress as a nation, there is inevitable pushback. Donald Trump destructively inflaming passions is the latest manifestation.

A turning point for me eventually writing *The Right Thing to Do* was interviewing Kentucky's Wilbur Hackett and Paul Karem, and Tennessee's Lester McClain and Chuck Rohe. I learned they also are upset about the 1970 USC-Alabama game receiving too much credit as a tipping point for college football integration. People at Kentucky and Tennessee want you to know their schools were far ahead of the 1970 USC-Alabama game. Kentucky assistant athletic director Tony Neely was a big help on reaching athletes and providing background on Kentucky's statues of their four Southeastern Conference pioneers.

My criticism of the 1970 USC-Alabama myths and fiction and shining a light on the true 1960s pioneers is far deeper than my status as a Michigan State graduate.

I also need to thank others for the development of the manuscript. First is Rick Gosselin, the veteran NFL writer. He connected me with Kevin Reichard of August Publications when I was having trouble finding a publisher for *Raye of Light*. Gosselin's book, *Goodfellows: The Champions of St. Ambrose*, is now in its third edition with August Publications.

Although we're still looking for that national tripwire to push *Raye of Light* into wider recognition, Reichard encouraged me when I proposed *The Right Thing to Do* as a project. Maybe we'll find the tripwire this time.

I also want to thank retired U.S. Army Colonels Herman Bulls and Rick Steinke and veteran journalists David Little, Johnette Howard and Lynn Henning. Bulls provided a Black voice in my research for all the chapters. I'm fascinated researching the subject, but in the end I'm a white guy. Bulls lived such experiences. He was the first Black quarterback at his Alabama high school in the fall of 1973. He was recruited by Steele to play at West Point at a time there were still few Black cadets. He graduated, retired as a Colonel and has been recognized as one of the country's top African-American executives with the international firm Jones Lang LaSalle.

I met Bulls through Col. Steinke, Bulls' West Point classmate. Steinke has been my friend dating to our Little League baseball days in Big Rapids, Michigan, a great Midwestern town befitting a Rockwell cover.

David Little was a veteran NFL writer from my San Diego days who shifted his career to become closer to his favorite fishing holes in his hometown of Chico, California. His provided an editor's eye from his days as editor of the *Chico Enterprise-Record*. Howard and Henning provided encouraging feedback on my conclusions from selected chapters.

College professors and authors Chris Lamb (Indiana University-Purdue University Indianapolis), Lane Demas (Central Michigan) and Louis Moore (Grand Valley State) also offered great insight. Lamb helped on the media not covering race prior to the 1970s, Demas on credit misdirected to Bear Bryant, and Moore on the value of statues to Black football pioneers on campuses.

I spent extensive time researching archived stories—digital versions make it a less daunting task than the microfilm days as recently as when researching *Raye of Light*.

Upon researching *Los Angeles Times* sports columnist Jim Murray's showdown with Bryant over eight UCLA Black players threatening to boycott the 1962 Rose Bowl, I was stunned. I learned no other writers addressed the issue between mid-November and the game's kickoff. More evidence Murray was a giant. The library staffs at the North Carolina State and UCLA libraries were patiently helpful assisting me as a technology-challenged person. Diana King at UCLA went above and beyond the call of duty helping with the *Los Angeles Sentinel* archives.

I'm also proud to include in Part IV voices from the Next Generation. A player doesn't have to be a first-round draft pick showered with millions of dollars to lift his family's trajectory. A football scholarship is enough. Thanks to the Next Generation voices that contributed to Part IV.

Thanks to all the media members that contributed book cover blurbs. I'm humbled by their praise.

Thanks to the many journalists who provided book cover blurbs. I'm humbled by their praise. Bill Walton was my favorite basketball player growing up, so his endorsement is a life's full-circle moment. As a high-school basketball player, I once mimicked a Walton response to a jeering crowd. If we'd won the game, I'd tell you more about it.

But most of all, thanks to the true 1960s pioneers, North and South, for their fortitude to toil in anonymity. They deserve far more credit than they've received for changing the game and America. The media, too eager to play along with Bear Bryant as a crusader, has failed you. This is my effort to shine a light, even though I know it will fall short in such a complicated world.

A motivating echo ever present in the back of my mind to finish the book was a line I once read from Pulitzer Prize-winning biographer David Maraniss: "History writes people out of the story. It's our job to write them back in."

And there was no stopping me once the great Ken Burns, the great historian and award-winning producer of documentaries, told me, "… just keep plowing ahead."

—Tom Shanahan
May 2023

FOREWORD
RUFFIN MCNEILL

Ruffin McNeill. *Photo courtesy N.C. State University.*

The fight for equality, inclusion, diversity and social justice in our lives and the world of athletics is a continuous process, to say the least. A 1960s starting point came when individuals and teams of pioneers displayed courage and unrelenting perseverance. They combined it with unconditional love.

For me, the 1960s journey began in Lumberton, North Carolina, where my parents, Ruffin and Bonnie McNeill, were both teachers, and I was attending all-Black schools through my middle-school years. My parents and I were a part of the first classes of teachers and students to begin integration in Lumberton. Thanks to the pioneers taking on sacrifices and challenges so that paths were in the process of being cleared for all races and ethnic groups.

I earned and received a football scholarship to East Carolina University, 1976-80. I began my career as a high-school teacher and coach until joining the college coaching ranks. I eventually became the head coach at my alma mater from 2010-2015. When I was a 12-year-old kid cropping tobacco during hot North Carolina summers for $10 a day, to think such a path would become available was an unthinkable hope and dream.

This book researches the history of the when, where, who and why college football broke down racial barriers. It's about the people who gave African-American athletes and coaches opportunities. The pioneers made personal decisions, commitments and huge sacrifices for diversity. The athletes took advantage of their opportunities in the academic arena and as major contributors in athletics and, in particular, the world of major college football.

The breaking down of color barriers began in the 1960s at integrated schools. Coaches such as Michigan State's Duffy Daugherty began to expand opportunities for Black athletes beyond the unwritten roster limitations of single digits. As the numbers grew, segregated Southern programs began to recruit their first Black football players. The dominoes continued to fall until rosters in the 1980s evolved to healthy numbers of Black athletes successful on the field as well as in the classroom.

If you were a Black kid growing up in North Carolina in the 1960s and 1970s, you knew the legend of Jimmy Raye. He was from a segregated area of Fayetteville, not far from my hometown and where my father and uncles grew up and participated in sports with Jimmy. Jimmy Raye boarded Daugherty's Underground Railroad in 1963. He was one of only two Black starting quarterbacks in the nation in the 1966 season. The Spartans played Notre Dame in the Game of the Century.

Daugherty also influenced coaching opportunities for African Americans. He added Jimmy Raye to his staff in 1972 along with Sherman Lewis. Michigan State had two Black coaches when many schools were hiring their first Black assistant. Jimmy and Sherman continued down another pioneering road as NFL assistants and NFL offensive coordinators.

My path to becoming a head coach has another uncanny Michigan State connection. In 2009, I was the defensive coordinator at Texas Tech as we prepared to play the Spartans in the Alamo Bowl. The day we began bowl preparations, I was suddenly thrust into the role of interim Texas Tech head football coach. One of my first decisions was to make Lincoln Riley, our receivers coach, the offensive coordinator.

In a game that drew high TV ratings, we had an exciting win versus Michigan State, 41-32. Spartans coach Mark Dantonio said in his post-game press conference that he felt I deserved to be named the next head coach for Texas Tech. We felt, I felt, we had 10 successful years and after one of the memorable games in Texas Tech history we would get the job. Unfortunately for the staff and I, the school went in another direction.

I was 51 years old, and I felt that may have been my last chance to become a college head football coach. I later accepted a job under then-Stanford head coach Jim Harbaugh as his defensive coordinator. As I flew back home a few nights later I had a flight layover. Unexpectedly, I received a call from then-East Carolina athletic director Terry Holland. He said he wanted to interview me for the Pirates' vacant head-coach position. I was very cautious, especially after not getting the Texas Tech job. I was not going to put myself or my family through another emotionally challenging moment, and I definitely did not want to become just a token interview! I informed Coach Holland that I had accepted the Stanford coaching position, but I added if they were serious about me coming to interview for the football head-coaching job to take some time and call me back—but only if they were serious.

Terry did call me back and assured me this was a legitimate interview. Sure enough, I got the job: I became the first-ever African-American head coach in any sport ever hired at East Carolina. I was honored to be part of history. It was a great experience to return to East Carolina University as the head football coach. I brought Lincoln Riley with me as my offensive coordinator, and I was able to hire a great staff. We had a lot of "first to ever" success experiences on the field and in the classroom, teams of amazing young men and won a lot of games against tough schedules. The wins included beating Atlantic Coast Conference neighbors North Carolina, N.C. State, Virginia Tech. We earned four bowl games.

When our 2014 team played Florida in the Birmingham Bowl, I put on my high-school teacher's hat. We held history lessons and visited museums, and I told the players we were at the center of the civil rights movement. This was where many people paid a price to create equal rights. Martin Luther King's civil rights movement is recent history, not ancient.

As time marched on, Terry Holland retired and a new athletic director was hired, and I endured one of my most challenging experiences, with my alma mater letting me go after the 2015 season. Bronco Mendenhall had just accepted the job as Virginia's head coach and called me immediately to join his staff at Virginia. A year later, my coaching career came full circle. By then, Lincoln Riley was Oklahoma's head coach. He hired me to join his staff as Assistant Head Coach and Defensive Line coach.

I like to jokingly compare our relationship as a boss, a brother, a dad and a son. Our coaching bond also represents our sincere love, appreciation, trust and mutual respect we have for one another. Lincoln and I represented a hiring process where we both based it on character, professionalism and trust. We will always be family, **first-last-always**!

I'm 63 years old now, enjoying my position as a special assistant to North Carolina State head coach Dave Doeren—but I'm also young enough to have experienced the segregated South. We've come a long way. I'm thankful for men like Duffy Daugherty who opened doors for Jimmy Raye and for Jimmy Raye subsequently opening more doors. I'm thankful for Terry Holland viewing me as a man and a coach who could and would inspire and lead the football program with discipline, love and professionalism.

We have to continue down the path of fighting for inclusion, diversity and equal rights until there are more men like a Duffy Daugherty and a Terry Holland making hiring decisions.

I say "Much Love and Thank You" to the pioneers that cleared a path for me and others as a player and a coach. Brave and selfless people forged, fought and created a "TEAM" of courageous pioneers. They are what I affectionately call, "GOD WINKS AND DREAM MERCHANTS."

—Ruffin McNeill, April 2022

PREFACE: FILLING THE GAPS

Let's be clear: Black Historiography and Critical Race Theory are necessary instructional tools to understand American history. That includes recognizing that college football integration successfully spanned the tumultuous 1960s while blending with the civil rights movement.

Black Historiography, put simply, is what *was* and *wasn't* recorded. In football, the gaps were a consequence of the 1960s media avoiding race in sports stories. CRT helps us understand past perceptions compared to previously overlooked Black milestones and filling in the holes.

Here is a simple example:

When I researched *Raye of Light: Jimmy Raye, Duffy Daugherty, The 1965-66 Michigan State Spartans and the Integration of College Football*, I realized Raye was the South's first Black quarterback to a win a national title. Michigan State coach Duffy Daugherty recruited him aboard his Underground Railroad out of segregated Fayetteville, North Carolina. The 1960s Spartans featured college football's first fully integrated rosters and won shares of the 1965 and 1966 national titles.

Once *Raye of Light* was published, the National Football Foundation's Phil Marwill, Director of Communications, verified the milestone. Marwill included Raye's newfound place in history in a 2015 NFF newsletter. Raye's moment in time is now recognized as part of his bio as a Michigan State Hall of Famer.

It didn't take a Woodward and Bernstein moment for me to realize

Raye's achievement had been overlooked for decades. He was a member of two small clubs. That narrowed the research.

The first club—exclusive for the wrong reasons—reminds us how few Black athletes played major college football well into the late 1960s. Black Historiography and CRT teach us that even "integrated" football programs followed unwritten quotas, limiting rosters to a half-dozen or so Black players. USC won the 1962 national title with five Black players, and the Trojans won their 1967 national championship with only seven. In the 1966 Game of the Century, Notre Dame had one Black player, Alan Page. Meanwhile, in that same game, Michigan State featured 20 with 11 Black starters and two Black team captains, College Football Hall of Famers George Webster and Clinton Jones, and Raye playing quarterback.

Raye's second club is even smaller. He was one of only two starting Black quarterbacks in major college football in the 1966 season.

Understanding timelines in the 1960s helps us comprehend how USC went from single-digit Black players in the 1960s to winning its next national title in 1972 with 23 Black players. Fans don't learn that from accepted college football lore, but Black Historiography and CRT shine a light on hidden figures.

MARKING THE MILESTONES

Each chapter of this book covers previously unappreciated milestones. They range from the 1961 UCLA and Colorado football teams threatening boycotts of major bowl games to increasing the number of Black players in college football in the late 1960s. By 1970, 33 of the 37 major college football programs had recruited their first Black football player. You could win bar bets on that trivia question.

Each chapter in Parts 1, II and III address a row of dominoes that were tumbled. The dominoes started falling separately, but undercurrents connected them. By the end of the decade the tributaries flowed together with force of the mighty Mississippi spilling into modern football's predominantly Black rosters.

Michigan State represented rows of tumbled dominoes as a fully integrated program and the unprecedented leadership positions of African Americans. Michigan State assistant coaches from Daugherty's 1950s coaching tree tumbled more rows spanning the continent. As new head coaches, they followed Daugherty's blueprint that ignored the quota limitations.

Martin Luther King's civil rights movement provided a backdrop to push over the first Southern dominoes. One by one the brave 1960s figures included Maryland's Darryl Hill and Wake Forest's Bob Grant in the Atlantic Coast Conference; Houston's Warren McVea in the state of Texas; Southern Methodist's Jerry LeVias in the Southwest Conference; and Kentucky and Tennessee athletes in the Southeastern Conference.

By now many readers might be wondering where the 1970 USC-Alabama game factored into college football integration. It doesn't. There were no true 1960s pioneers on USC's 1970 roster or Alabama's all-white team despite the myths and fiction crafted in the 1990s. There was no overnight impact. All of the above tumbled dominoes cleared a path to integrated teams playing in Southern stadiums without incident in the 1960s.

America doesn't solve racial problems overnight. MLK successfully launched the Montgomery Bus Boycott in 1955, but it wasn't until 1964 and 1965 that President Lyndon Johnson signed two Civil Rights acts.

Nevertheless, the national sports media fell for the 1970 USC-Alabama myth hook, line and sinker and has regurgitated it for 30-plus years. A media flaw is one writer following another when they think they've latched onto a good story. Worse, a cottage industry of books and films based on myths and fiction profited at the expense of the true 1960s pioneers.

The media has continued to sell the myth, even though USC fullback Sam Cunningham, RIP, punched a major hole in the story as early as 2003. He has repeatedly said he was never taken into the Alabama locker room by Bryant to show his players what a football player looked like. That fictional scene is the lynchpin to the tale spreading rapidly. Good ole boys chuckle about the big, bad Black man overpowering the skinny white guys.

In 2016, Cunningham was quoted in the *Los Angeles Times* regretting "the sauce" that was added to the story. I believe Cunningham realized the true 1960s pioneers did the dirty work before him in the 1960s, and he was used by the 1970 USC-Alabama mythmakers: All Cunningham did was carry the ball through huge holes opened by five white offensive linemen. Another overlooked fact: Cunningham was only one of only five Black starters at a school with a campus located in heavily populated and diverse Los Angeles.

In 1980, *Time* Magazine published a 5,100-word cover story reflecting on Alabama coach Paul "Bear" Bryant's career as it was winding down.

There wasn't a single word on the 1970 USC-Alabama game. Nor was there a single word in Bryant's 1974 autobiography, *Bear*, with John Underwood.

Why? USC mythmakers crafted the fiction two decades after the game to embellish USC's role in college football integration. Bryant's apologists embraced the tale to obfuscate Bryant dragging his feet on integration until the 1970s—long after the campus desegregated in 1963.

The opportunity of a college football scholarship and the success of the athletes is at the heart of this book, but education also underscores their stories of the athletes. They provided a foundation for The Next Generation. Those stories are told in Part IV.

I'll put my research and conclusions up against anybody, anytime, anywhere.

—Tom Shanahan

SHERMAN LEWIS: A COACHING LEGACY

Two trailblazing coaching careers launched by Duffy Daugherty were those of Sherman Lewis and Jimmy Raye. He had recruited them both out of the segregated South as players, then hiring Lewis as an assistant in 1969 and Raye in 1972.

In 1972, Daugherty's final season upon retirement, Michigan State numbered two Black assistants at a time other schools were hiring their first Black coach.

Lewis and Raye were pioneers in college and the NFL who should be perched on Duffy's head-coaching tree, but the 1980s and 1990s were a time when attitudes of male white athletic directors and NFL owners dictating hiring.

Given an opportunity, no doubt they would have followed Duffy's blueprints similar to other Duffy assistants whose stories are detailed throughout this book.

Lewis and Raye are long retired from their NFL careers, but the Pro Football Hall of Fame has honored them in a manner that also extends Duffy's legacy.

Raye was honored in the inaugural class of NFL Awards of Excellence, sponsored by the Pro Football Hall of Fame in 2022. Lewis joined him in the second class honored on June 29, 2023 at the Hall in Canton, Ohio.

Sherman Lewis accepting his NFL Award of Excellence, 2023. *Courtesy Pro Football Hall of Fame.*

Pro Football Hall of Fame quarterback Dan Fouts, the event's Master of Ceremonies, cited Daugherty's leadership. He noted Raye was in the audience and asked Lewis about Daugherty's influence on them.

"Duffy is one of the greatest guys of all-time in coaching," Lewis said. "He was also one of the funniest guys. We worked hard, but he made sure coaching was fun. He wanted us to understand other things in life are important. I enjoyed my time with Duffy, and I'm thankful to him for this day for hiring me."

Their Michigan State coaching days were springboards to their NFL careers as offensive coordinators. Raye was the second Black coordinator in the NFL in 1983 as the Los Angeles Rams' offensive coordinator. Lewis also was an early Black coordinator when Green Bay Packers head coach Mike Holmgren hired him in 1993.

Daugherty recruited Lewis out of segregated Louisville in 1960 as a halfback. He was Michigan State's first Underground Railroad All-Big Ten choice in 1962 as a junior and first Underground Railroad All-American pick as a senior in 1963. He also was third in Heisman Trophy voting to Navy's Roger Staubach.

Lewis coached four seasons with Daugherty until the College Football Hall of Fame coach's retirement following the 1972 season. Lewis was retained by Daugherty's successors, Denny Stolz (1973-75), Darryl Rogers (1976-79) and Muddy Waters (1980-82). But even when MSU passed over Lewis for then-57-year-old Waters, a coach with a small-college background, Lewis remained loyal to his alma mater. He held together the recruiting class and then served under Waters.

After Waters was fired at the end of the 1982 season, Lewis moved onto the NFL under San Francisco 49ers coach Bill Walsh, who, like Daugherty, was a leader of racial equality.

When Raye joined the 49ers under then-coach Ken Meyer six years earlier, there were only seven other Black assistants in a 28-team league.

Lewis began filling his jewelry box with Super Bowl rings in the 1984, 1988 and 1989 seasons, coaching the 49ers' running backs (1983-90) and wide receivers (1991). When 49ers Mike Holmgren landed the Green Bay Packers job in 1992, he brought Lewis with him as Green Bay's offensive coordinator (1992-99). Lewis earned a fourth Super Bowl ring in the 1996 season when the Packers defeated the New England Patriots, 35-21.

"He didn't achieve the ultimate goal as a head coach, but that doesn't negate he was a great teacher and great coach in the business of pro football," Raye said. "His selection for this award proves it."

Both Lewis and Raye endured sham interviews that teams conducted to comply with the punchless Rooney Rule, which required franchises to interview a Black candidate.

Jimmy Raye accepting his Award of Excellence, 2022. Courtesy Pro Football Hall of Fame

Offensive coordinators from Super Bowl teams are typically hot candidates for open head-coaching jobs, but Lewis didn't land one of the 11 vacant positions in 1997 after the Packers' Super Bowl XXXI title. The Packers won the 1997 NFC title to return to Super Bowl XXXII on January 25, 1998, but Lewis again wasn't a hot commodity.

Holmgren endorsed Lewis as a head-coach candidate and noted he often turned play calling over to Lewis for a change of pace. But as Lewis met with the media during the week leading up to the Super Bowl game in San Diego, he was told one knock against him was that Holmgren called the plays.

"That's just another excuse," Lewis said during the Super Bowl media session. "When Bill Walsh was the coach, Sam Wyche didn't call plays, Paul Hackett didn't call plays and Denny Green didn't call plays. What's more important in the game is the game plan."

Wyche and Green became NFL head coaches, and Hackett ended up as USC's head coach. Green was Black, but he had gained a reputation as a head coach for his success reviving Northwestern's moribund program.

Of the four head-coaching vacancies for the upcoming 1998 season, Lewis was interviewed for the Dallas Cowboys job. But Lewis described being set up by the Cowboys on Page 272 of *Raye of Light, Jimmy Raye, Duffy Daugherty, the Integration of College Football and the 1965-66 Michigan State Spartans.*

"I was coming in for an interview that I thought was under cover and all of the sudden these television camera lights flashed on me." Lewis said. "There were TV cameras everywhere. Everyone knew I was coming. I think that interview was just for show."

The Cowboys hired Pittsburgh Steelers OC Chan Gailey. And fired him after two seasons.

Lewis continued as Green Bay's offensive coordinator in 1998 and 1999. He finished his career as an offensive coordinator with the Minnesota Vikings (2000-01) under Dennis Green and the Detroit Lions (2003-04) under Steve Mariucci. He retired from coaching until Washington needed an offensive coordinator at midseason in 2009, when general manager Vinny Cerrato appointed Lewis.

The pattern of a Black offensive coordinator passed over for not calling plays has continued into the 2020s. The knock against Kansas City Chiefs offensive coordinator Eric Bieniemy was that head coach Andy Reid called plays for the Super Bowl champions. But that didn't stop two white KC offensive coordinators, Doug Pederson and Matt Nagy, from landing head-coaching positions, prior to Bienemy's promotion to OC. NFL owners dismiss the lack of Black head coaches as an issue.

Another role Lewis played off the field was guiding future Underground Railroad passengers. Southern Black athletes faced a different challenge adapting from the Jim Crow South than did the Spartans' long history of Black athletes from the north.

"He was a great influence on all of us on and off the field with the way he carried himself," Raye said. "He shared with us advice about academics, making sure we got our degrees and the pitfalls to avoid getting caught up in the social climate."

Daugherty recruited Lewis out of Louisville's duPont Manual High based on a tip from a white coach at rival Flaget High, the Catholic school alma mater of 1956 Heisman winner Paul Hornung.

Raye arrived on campus from segregated Fayetteville, North Carolina, in the fall of 1964 when Lewis was playing with Toronto in the Canadian Football League (1964-65), but Lewis returned to Michigan State in the spring. Lewis put up Raye to join the Black fraternity, Omega Psi Phi.

"You wanted to be associated with anything involving Sherman Lewis," said Raye.

The Pro Football Hall of Fame illuminates Lewis' college and NFL careers.

"Sherman was a mentor of mine," Raye said. "He was a college football integration forerunner as a player and as a Division I coach. I'm very happy he's receiving recognition. He was a tremendous football coach and excellent teacher. It's a great honor to be on that stage recognized by the true football minds who have followed the game."

Raye also went on to be a leader among Black coaches in the NFL, identifying promising young coaches and helping them gain an opportunity. His story is told in a later chapter.

Tony Dungy, the Pro Football Hall of Fame coach, considers Raye a mentor. Raye says Lewis was his mentor.

Enough said.

PART I: MICHIGAN STATE'S PIONEERING ROLE IN COLLEGE FOOTBALL INTEGRATION

CHAPTER 1
DUFFY'S LEADERSHIP AND COACHING TREE

FACT: Of the Black college football players in the 1960s to earn a national championship ring from the Associated Press or United Press International, 41 percent played at Michigan State.

"Duffy did more for integration than any other coach in college football. He had players from all over the South. There were great Black players in the state of Texas that were passing over Oklahoma to play for Duffy. He had all those players from the Houston area. And Duffy also was the first one to recruit Samoan players." —Barry Switzer, Oklahoma's College Football Hall of Fame coach.

"That's *BULLSHIT!*"

Oklahoma coach Barry Switzer was never accused of being at a loss for words, dripping passion while winning three national titles in 1974, 1975 and 1985. The College Football Hall of Famer liked to tell his Sooners, "Let's go hang a half-a-hundred on them!"

Switzer is now in his 80s, but many subjects still trigger his passion. They include defending the record of his old friend, Hugh "Duffy" Daugherty, as the leader of college football integration. Such notice from Switzer is significant for the simple reason Switzer possesses his own prominent place championing college football integration with his 1970s teams. Yet he points to Daugherty for pushing the largest rock uphill in the 1960s.

Switzer, in the 2020s, is one of the few living figures from the 1960s and 1970s who can validate Daugherty's leadership.

"Duffy was ahead of his time," Switzer said. "He was doing the right thing. That's what I tried to do when I recruited Black players at all the positions.

"Duffy did more for integration than any other coach in college football. He had players from all over the South. There were great Black players in the state of Texas that were passing over Oklahoma to play for Duffy. He had all those players from the Houston area. And Duffy also was the first one to recruit Samoan players."

Duffy Daugherty with Jimmy Raye. *Courtesy Michigan State University.*

In 1962, the Associated Press reported Michigan State's 17 Black players represented "the largest delegation of Negro athletes in major college football history." His 1965 and 1966 national-title teams numbered in the twenties, with double-digit Black starters during a decade many schools followed an unwritten quota limiting their rosters to half-dozen or so Black athletes.

The most startling measuring stick, though, was Michigan State's overwhelming *41 percent share* of Black players throughout the nation to win a 1960s national championship ring, according to the titles voted upon by the AP (writers) and United Press International (coaches, now USA Today) polls. There were 23 Spartans with rings and a combined 30 from all other schools for the decade.

This 41 percent figure is new research, but the numbers are easy to break down for two reasons: 1) Segregated Alabama and Texas won multiple titles; 2) USC and Notre Dame won titles while following an unwritten quota of only a half-dozen or so Black players on their rosters.

The overall breakdown:

- Michigan State: 23, 1965 UPI national champion.
- Rest of college football: 30, AP and UPI champions representing six schools spanning 1960 to 1969.

The breakdown by schools and titles:

- 1960, University of Minnesota (8-2-0), AP and UPI national champions, five Black players.
- 1961, University of Alabama (11-0-0), AP and UPI, zero on a segregated roster.
- 1962, University of Southern California (11-0-0), AP and UPI, five Black players.
- 1963, University of Texas (11-0-0), AP and UPI, zero, segregated.
- 1964, Alabama (10-1-0), AP and UPI, zero, segregated.
- 1965, Michigan State (10-1-0), UPI, 23 Black players and 10 Black starters; Alabama (9-1-1), AP, zero, segregated.
- 1966, University of Notre Dame (9-0-1), AP and UPI, one Black player.
- 1967, Southern California (10-1-0), AP and UPI, seven Black players.
- 1968, Ohio State University (10-0-0), AP and UPI, 12 Black players.
- 1969, Texas (11-0-0), AP and UPI, zero, the last segregated national champion.

The glaring contrast between Daugherty's role in college football integration and inaction from other schools has been largely unrecognized. Historical memory was lost to the 1960s media custom of avoiding race in sports stories. The practice went back to the 1930s and the "Conspiracy of Silence," a term used by Black sportswriters. They claimed the mainstream media was complicit maintaining Major League's Baseball's color line by failing to write about segregation in the National Pastime.

MARKING THE MILESTONES

Black Historiography and Critical Race Theory are related. The Black athletic milestones that weren't reported in the 1960s prevented the public from understanding and appreciating the progress taking place in real time. CRT, a new view with the holes filled in, helps us understand perspective then and now.

Daugherty's 1960s leadership was changing the landscape, and other coaches began to recognize the future. USC coach John McKay, for example, soon grew his number of Black players from single digits into the 20s. By 1972, when the Trojans won their next national title, there were 23 Black players on the team. This was a significant jump from 1967, when O.J. Simpson was one of only seven Black players.

McKay's 1970 team had only four Black starters for the game at Alabama, although that game that has been misleadingly presented as a tipping point in college football integration. Four Black starters on a 1970 football team was a residue from the Trojans limiting their rosters to the unwritten quotas of the 1960s. The myths and fiction surrounding the 1970 USC-Alabama game and embellishing USC as a college football integration leader are dissected elsewhere in this book.

But it was more than Daugherty, his players and other 1960s pioneers, Black and white, who were failed by the incomplete Black Historiography of the 1960s. History also failed to pick up on Daugherty's coaching tree. As his assistants spread out across the country to jobs as head coaches, they followed the Daugherty blueprint of equal opportunity.

Four assistant coaches on his 1954 staff became head coaches: Dan Devine, Bob Devaney, Sonny Grandelius and Bill Yeoman. Two former players entered coaching and climbed the ladder to a head coaching spot: Frank Kush and Chuck Fairbanks. Earle Edwards was a Daugherty colleague when they were assistants under Biggie Munn.

They all followed Daugherty's blueprint of mining Pennsylvania surplus talent (which at the time that resembled 21st century excess talent in Florida and Georgia) and ignoring unwritten quotas for Black athletes. Add to that recruiting the segregated South aboard his Underground Railroad and attracting great players from the Midwest, and the die was cast.

"There was a different attitude at Michigan State," said Chuck

Fairbanks Jr., whose father shared many conversations with him about football and race while growing up and before Chuck Sr.'s death at age 79 in 2013. "The Michigan State coaches were open and progressive toward advancing African-American opportunities. If you look at the number of Black athletes at Michigan State in the 1950s and 1960s, they were pioneers at accepting Black athletes. It was more than they were good athletes. They were treated equally on the team."

The 1954 Michigan State coaching staff. Front row (from left): John Kobs, Hugh "Duffy" Daugherty, Bob Devaney and Dan Devine. Back row (from left): Everett "Sonny" Grandelius, Burt Smith, Don Mason and Bill Yeoman. *Courtesy Michigan State University.*

Duffy's Disciples, with chapters on each coach later in this book:

- **Dan Devine, Arizona State, Missouri and Notre Dame; Michigan State assistant, 1950-54:** Devine increased the number of Black athletes at Arizona State (1955-57) and Missouri (1958-70) as well as in the 1970s at Notre Dame (1975-80). One of Devine's first Black recruits at Arizona State was Leon Burton, a

1,000-yard rusher in 1957 for the Sun Devils. He hailed from Flint, Michigan.
- **Frank Kush, Arizona State; Michigan State player, 1950-52:** Kush followed Devine to Arizona State as an assistant coach. When Devine left for Missouri, Kush was promoted to head coach (1958-79). Kush's fully integrated rosters elevated the program to a level that earned a membership in the Pac-10 in 1978.
- **Bob Devaney, Wyoming and Nebraska; Michigan State assistant, 1953-56:** Devaney recruited increasing numbers of Black athletes at both Wyoming (1957-61) and Nebraska (1962-72). Nebraska's first fully integrated rosters were under Devaney, highlighted by back-to-back national titles in 1970 and 1971.
- **Sonny Grandelius, Colorado; Michigan State assistant, 1954-58:** A Michigan State All-American halfback in 1950, he was an assistant coach five seasons on Daugherty's staff, 1954-58. Grandelius was only at Colorado three seasons (1959-61), but he helped increase the number of Black athletes on the roster. He also supported his 1961 team when 69 white players led a decision to decline an Orange Bowl invitation unless they were assured their five Black teammates were spared Jim Crow laws in Miami and able to stay in the same hotel and eat at the same restaurants.
- **Bill Yeoman, Houston; Michigan State assistant from 1956-61:** Yeoman desegregated Houston's program as the Cougars' head coach (1962-86). He signed Warren McVea in 1964 as the first major Texas college to recruit a Black athlete. His last recruiting class upon retirement included a freshman on his way to becoming the first Black quarterback to win the Heisman Trophy: Andre Ware.
- **Chuck Fairbanks, Oklahoma; Michigan State player, 1952-54.** Fairbanks climbed the coaching ladder through Michigan State connections—Kush at Arizona State and Yeoman at Houston. As the head coach at Oklahoma (1967-72), Fairbanks improved numbers from single digits to fully integrated rosters, including a showdown in the 1971 Game of the Century against Nebraska.
- **Earle Edwards, North Carolina State; Michigan State assistant, 1949-53:** Edwards' span as the North Carolina State head coach

(1954-70) included desegregating the program. The first two Black players were walk-ons in the late 1960s, and Edwards signed the Wolfpack's first two scholarship Black recruits in 1970.

Four of the eight coaches have been enshrined in the College Football Hall of Fame; they have combined for a career record of 884-438-29 (.664), five national titles, 24 major bowls and 48 bowls overall.

- **College Football Hall of Fame:** Daugherty, 1984; Devaney, 1981; Devine, 1985; and Yeoman, 2001.
- **Career records**: Daugherty, 109-69-5; Devaney, 101-20-2; Devine, 172-57-9; Yeoman, 160-108-8; Fairbanks, 59-41-1; Grandelius, 20-11-0; Kush, 176-54-1; and Edwards, 77-88-8.
- **National titles (5):** Daugherty, 1965 and 1966; Devaney, 1970 and 1971; and Devine, 1977.
- **Major bowls (24):** Daugherty (2), both Rose; Devaney (7), five Orange, one Cotton, one Sugar; Devine (7), three Sugar, two Orange and two Cotton; Yeoman (4), all Cotton; Fairbanks (3), two Sugar, one Cotton; and Grandelius (1), Orange.
- **All bowls (48):** Daugherty, 2; Devaney, 10; Devine, 10; Yeoman, 11; Fairbanks, 5; Grandelius, 1; Kush, 7; and Edwards 2. (Note: The Fiesta Bowl was a fledgling bowl during Kush's career that wasn't yet in the major bowl rotation.)

The Spartans' 1960s Underground Railroad teams transported talent from the segregated South, adding these players to the school's long history of Midwest-based rosters. The roster included Black players when Biggie Munn was head coach (1947-53) and Daugherty his top assistant and line coach. Then, Daugherty pushed the needle further as Munn's successor in 1954-72. The 1950s teams, with Black players from Michigan factory towns, gained notice on TV while winning the 1954 and 1956 Rose Bowls in an era when few games were televised.

LeRoy Bolden (Flint), Ellis Duckett (Flint) and Jim Ellis (Saginaw) played on the 1953 Big Ten champion that beat UCLA in the 1954 Rose Bowl. Clarence Peaks (Flint), James Hinesly (Detroit) and John Lewis (Fremont, Ohio) played on the 1955 No. 2-ranked team that defeated UCLA in the 1956 Rose Bowl.

Bolden shared the team captain role in the 1954 season with a white player, Don Kauth. Bolden, Duckett, Peakes, Hinesly and Lewis were all NFL draft picks.

The Hinesly family also represented progress as an example of second-generation Black athletes. James Hinesly was an end from 1954-56 out of Detroit Miller. He was the team MVP as a senior in 1956. The 1956 season also marked Daugherty's first win over Michigan in three tries as head coach. Hinesley forced and recovered a fumble to set up the Spartans' only touchdown in a 9-0 victory.

Two decades later, his son James A. Hinesly, an offensive tackle from Detroit Country Day, helped head coach Darryl Rogers to his first win over Michigan in his third try. The Spartans won 24-15 on the way to the Big Ten co-title with the Wolverines.

Other early Black players included Willie Thrower of New Kensington, Pennsylvania. He was a popular backup quarterback on the 1952 national title team behind Tom Yewcic, an All-American two-sport athlete in football and baseball who later played for the AFL's Boston Patriots. Thrower was the first Black quarterback in the modern era of the National Football League with the Chicago Bears in 1953. His place in history has been recognized at the Pro Football Hall of Fame in Canton, Ohio.

Daugherty's late 1950s and early 1960s teams had been consistent contenders for Big Ten titles, but the influx of Southern talent lifted Michigan State's 1965 and 1966 roster atop the college football world. The Spartans won back-to-back unbeaten Big Ten titles and national titles.

One year after Yeoman signed McVea at Houston, Southern Methodist University coach Hayden Fry signed Jerry LeVias as the now-defunct Southwest Conference's first Black scholarship player in 1965. LeVias endured isolation on campus, feeling ostracized by students and even teammates.

"They only needed me on Saturdays," he said.

By contrast, Michigan State's white players learned through relationships what their Black teammates faced growing up in America with institutionalized racism. Ed McLoud and Drake Garrett were teammates on the mid-1960s Spartans, recruited from high schools in the Dayton, Ohio, area. McLoud was a white backup offensive lineman from Fairborn, Garrett a Black starting defensive back from Dayton's Black neighborhood school, Dunbar. During a school break their freshmen year, they rode a bus home together from East Lansing to Dayton.

"I grew up in a totally segregated town outside Dayton, Ohio, and race never seemed something I thought about until Drake Garrett rode home with me on the bus when we were freshmen," McLoud said. "I told him that my mother would get us at the bus station, then we'd go to my house for dinner and then I'd take him home. He asked me if I was sure that it would be OK. Lesson learned."

Michigan State's three-sport All-America athlete Gene Washington, a College Football Hall of Famer, had a similar experience with his white track and field teammates. Washington was an indoors and outdoors track All-America athlete, including a 1965 NCAA indoor 60-yard hurdles title.

Bob Steele, one of Washington's classmates who went on to win back-to-back NCAA 440-yard hurdles titles in 1966 and 1967, told a story about the Spartans' freshman season in the spring of 1964 while attending the Ohio State Relays. During a break in the competition, they looked for a restaurant. As they walked off campus and approached a restaurant, Washington stopped Steele.

"Do you think they'll let me in?" Washington asked.

Steele, who had grown up a suburban Detroit, said the thought of a problem arising over Washington's skin color never crossed his mind.

"There were 18 of us, and we were all in our track blazers," Steele said. "The manager in the restaurant looked at us and didn't want to let us in. I told him, 'It's all 18 or nothing.' He left and sent a waitress over to serve us. These kinds of things would happen in Columbus and Iowa City, they never happened in East Lansing."

Daugherty didn't overtly talk about race on the team, which was a product of the times when race was an unspoken subject, but Daugherty's leadership set a tone the team followed. However, one night at a team dinner Daugherty was upset to see the Black and white players eating in separate groups.

"There are only two colors on this team, green and white!" said Daugherty, telling the players to reshuffle the seating arrangements.

Daugherty leaving race as an unspoken subject might not have worked in other environments. Certainly, it hasn't in other situations across the spectrum of American life. But unspoken leadership from the right kind of leader trickles down.

MISSION FIRST, PEOPLE ALWAYS

Herman Bulls is a West Point graduate, Army Ranger and retired U.S. Army Colonel. The vice-president at JLL, a Washington, D.C.-based international company, has been honored many times as one of America's top Black executives. Retired Duke coach Mike Krzyzewski invites him as a speaker to his annual Coach K Center on Leadership and Ethics.

"During my military career I learned the motto, 'mission first, people always,'" Bulls said. "This simply means it is important to understand the objective—in war it is to defeat the enemy and in sports it is to win the game. However, you achieve success in team endeavors by focusing on the people. You need to know that you can depend on the person to your left and right during crucial moments. Spending time together and learning about one another instills trust and a feeling of belonging. A feeling of trust and belonging produces winning teams."

Michigan State's Pat Gallinagh, an Academic All-America defensive lineman in 1966, wrote a poem in his about the Spartans, Black and white, and the players' pride in their groundbreaking seasons.

Here is a stanza from "What is a Spartan?"

"A Spartan is an artist, a creative soul and muse
An architect of beatify song and verse for common use
A Spartan is an activist who speaks out when they see wrong
Who combats ignorance and hatred with truths buried far too long"

"We never had discussions about race at all, but anytime you get a bunch of guys together, things happen," Gallinagh said. "But it was nothing more than, 'Who took my soda?' Or somebody pulled a practical joke. It was never racial."

Clinton Jones, a College Football Hall of Fame running back, labeled them family squabbles.

"We had people from all over the world at Michigan State," Jones said. "It's a testament to Michigan State's history. We came together. We never had racial overtones on our team. We had Black guys from the South with no association with white players and white players with no association with Black players. When we squabbled, it was like a family—like brothers. It wasn't racial."

There was no better example than a fight between Gallinagh and Bubba Smith, Michigan State's 6-foot-7, 285-pound College Football Hall of Fame defensive end. It started out frightening and ended up comical.

The Spartans were on the last leg of their march to the Game of the Century against Notre Dame on November 19, 1966 at Spartan Stadium, needing one more victory over the Hoosiers on November 12 to remain unbeaten. In the locker room after a Friday afternoon walk-through practice on the Memorial Stadium turf, Gallinagh, who is white, and Smith, one of the Black Underground Railroad recruits from Texas, exchanged words. Masculinity was questioned. Testosterone comes in all colors and body sizes. The confrontation escalated to swings before the players were broken up.

Indiana team managers in the locker room viewed the confrontation through a stereotypical lens. They ran to inform the Hoosiers coaches, "Michigan State's Black guys and white guys are fighting."

Daugherty was furious when he learned about the tussle. He called Smith and Gallinagh into a locker-room office. He told them they were both wrong and to apologize at the team dinner than night.

"Bubba got up and said he was sorry," Gallinagh said. "I was a little more long-winded. I said I was sorry and lucky I wasn't killed. I didn't hear it, but I was told later guys were saying to 'shut up and sit down' so they could eat. That was probably (offensive tackle) Jerry West saying that."

That's how quickly the "fight" was put behind the Spartans. A racial issue would have lingered and possibly derailed the season. The Spartans rolled to their ninth straight victory, a 37-19 victory the next day. The win marked the first time a school won back-to-back unbeaten Big Ten titles.

Michigan State's campus life was inviting for the Spartans' Underground Railroad passengers. George Webster, a College Football Hall of Famer from Anderson, South Carolina, wrote a paper in one of his freshman classes explaining that attending classes was the first time in his life he sat in a room with white people and didn't feel tension.

Gene Washington, a College Football Hall of Famer from La Porte, Texas, preferred to stay in East Lansing and attend summer school rather than go home.

"It was so much nicer at Michigan State than in the segregated South," Washington said. "You knew when you went home what it would be like, and it wasn't like it was at Michigan State. After my freshman year, I didn't go home often. There was no way I wanted to go back to Texas. We didn't really talk about it that much when we got to Michigan State because you knew that's the way it was in the segregated South. As I got older and looked back on it, though, it was disgraceful."

Michigan State's integration policies extended throughout the campus. When Washington arrived from Texas to check into his dormitory room, his roommates were two white swimmers, Gary Dilley and Ed Glick.

"It was my first integrated housing experience," Washington said, and it was the same for Dilley and Glick. "We lived together, studied together and supported each other in our sports."

Dilley, from Huntington, Indiana, won multiple NCAA titles and was a 1968 Olympic silver medalist in the 200-meter backstroke.

"I had a great time at MSU," Dilley said in a 2008 MSU newsletter. "Having traveled to every campus in the Big Ten, I can tell you there was not a friendlier place than MSU. It was probably a reflection of President John Hannah, because that was his personality."

Contrast the ground-level integration with what happened at Alabama, where football coach and athletic director Bear Bryant opened a dormitory in 1965 built exclusively for the football and basketball players. His teams were not only all-white, but they were also isolated from the rest of the student body. By the 1990s, the NCAA outlawed athletic-specific dorms. They must include 51 percent non-athletes.

Hannah pushed integration policies throughout his time as president, 1941 to 1969. In 1965, he invited Martin Luther King to speak at the MSU Auditorium. The event was a fundraiser for Michigan State students to travel in the summer to Mississippi to aid with voter registration campaigns.

"It meant a lot to me to see Dr. King speak," Washington said. "I was impressed with the turnout—the students, the whole university. I was enjoying how nice it was at Michigan State during integration."

One of the MLK's memorable lines from his speech: "Time is neutral. And the time is always right to do right."

The Spartans' success and popularity spread around the community. Bubba Smith, long before his famed Miller Lite beer commercials with Dick Butkus and *Police Academy* movies playing the role of Moses Hightower, was a presence who transcended race.

The bond between the players eventually crossed into life-and-death chapters. In 2010, Don Japinga, a team captain in 1965 with quarterback Steve Juday, was dying from lung cancer. The East Lansing businessman was hospitalized in Lansing for three weeks until he died at age 66.

Japinga's son, Steve, said many teammates called to express support. He was answering the phone and speaking to Michigan State legends, including Bubba Smith. Steve, a senior vice-president for the Lansing Regional Chamber of Commerce, was only 26 years old at the time.

"Bubba called me several times," Steve said. "He'd say, 'How's your dad? Tell him I'm praying for him. That's my captain.' It was surreal to

Bubba Smith and Don Japinga.
Courtesy Michigan State University

talk to him. I had heard stories about him from my dad and seen him in the *Police Academy* movies."

Don Japinga, a 5-foot-7, 160-pound defensive back, was a foot shorter than the 6-7 Smith. The Sports Information Department's Fred Stabley and Nick Vista, long ahead of the country in sports information work, had them pose for a photo together on picture day at the stadium. Steve said his father told him a story about one night he was shooting pool at Coral Gables, a bar near campus that remains an institution.

"The guy my dad was playing wanted to fight him," Steve said. "Bubba was there and came over and said, 'Don't mess with my Donnie.' The guy said, 'Uh, yeah, OK. I'm out of here.'"

Another time Japinga invited his teammates, white and Black, home to Holland to enjoy the beach on Lake Michigan. Years later, Steve said a cousin of his father told him a story about the community buzzing when it heard the news, "Bubba Smith is walking around downtown with Donnie Japinga!"

BUILDING BONDS

The locker-room culture of Duffy's Spartans was carried forward by Duffy's assistant coaches as head coaches across the country. Barry Alvarez, Wisconsin's College Football Hall of Fame coach, played for Devaney at Nebraska as a linebacker, 1965-67.

"I don't remember Bob ever talking about race," Alvarez said. "The coaches treated everyone the same."

For coaches like Daugherty and Devaney, whose leadership trickled down to the players without expressively discussing race, that was sufficient for the times. But modern coaches recognize the need for awareness among their players on race and other issues in the country.

Army West Point coach Jeff Monken sets aside time in his program's structure for the players—recruited from the across the nation's borders and spectrum—to discuss.

Duffy Daugherty with five returning All-American players in 1966. (L-R) Clinton Jones, Bob Apisa, Bubba Smith, Gene Washington and George Webster. *Courtesy Michigan State University.*

"That's become part of the culture of our program," Monken said "Our guys are very open, and we continue to have conversations about how we can develop a better team, stronger bonds across racial lines and religious lines and political lines. We come from every walk of life, and they all have different thoughts and ideas and values."

J.B. Hunter, a senior offensive tackle in the 2020 season, said the discussions were especially valuable in Spring 2020 following the death of George Floyd while he was in the custody of Minneapolis police. His death, captured on video, sparked Black Lives Matter protests. The cadets had been sent home during the spring pandemic, but they still communicated through Zoom calls.

"I'm from California, and I didn't know what was happening in Alabama and Georgia," said Hunter during the 2020 fall season. "I would have never met these guys if I hadn't come to this institution. I'm very grateful for that. It's created understanding in other aspects. When I become a platoon leader, it's going to help me understand people."

Monken's awareness is connected to Duffy Daugherty's legacy. When he was a graduate assistant coach at Hawaii, 1989-90, he got to know then-Hawaii strength coach, Kale Ane. Daugherty had recruited Ane as one of his Hawaiian Pipeline members, 1972-74. Ane went on to play seven seasons in the National Football League.

"Duffy Daugherty was way ahead of his time," Monken said. "When he was building his teams at Michigan State, he had a very diverse football team.

"Kale was a great guy, and he talked about how Duffy had those great teams with guys that came from all over the country, and they really felt at home there. It's fantastic to have a guy like that who worked in our profession, who really paved the way for everybody else and was a model we can still follow today."

Monken became a head coach at Georgia Southern from 2010-13 and has been Army's head coach since 2014.

"Sharing those discussions and being able to talk through those issues are really important to our program," Monken said. "And that's been led by our players. They do a great job with that. I'm really proud of their efforts and what those guys put into it on a daily basis. We've continued to have people that come in and talk to our team about those things and the importance of including everyone."

Race may have been unspoken on Daugherty-influenced teams, but it was front-and-center in the South as football coaches resisted the civil rights movement. Alabama's campus was desegregated in 1963, but Alabama coach Paul "Bear" Bryant didn't have a Black player on his varsity roster until 1971.

Bryant didn't avoid the subject of race before Alabama met Nebraska in the Orange Bowl with a national title possibly in play. Alvarez said he and Jackie Sherrill, Alabama's fullback in 1965 who went on to a long-time career as a head coach at Washington State, Pitt, Texas A&M and Mississippi State, talked about their Orange Bowl game later in life.

"Jackie Sherrill told me Bryant used that as motivation—they were all white and we were integrated and so forth," Alvarez said. "We weren't even made aware of it. I don't think we even realized they were segregated going into the game."

Bryant's motivational ploy included explaining how a string of upsets could land Alabama atop the Associated Press rankings, thanks to a one-year AP experiment conducting the final vote after the bowl games rather than the traditional end-of-regular-season tally.

The 1965 regular season ended with No. 1 Michigan State (10-0-0), 35 first-place votes; No. 2 Arkansas (10-0-0), 10 first-place votes; No. 3 Nebraska (10-0-0), zero votes; and No. 4 Alabama (8-1-1), one first-place vote.

As the bowl games played out, No. 5 UCLA upset Michigan State, 14-12; unranked LSU upset Arkansas, 14-7; and Alabama upset Nebraska, 39-28.

The folksy Bryant knew how to play up to the media, and the writers rewarded his one loss, one tie team over the one-loss Spartans and one-loss Razorbacks. The AP's first experimental postseason vote was No. 1 Alabama, 37 first-place votes; No. 2 Michigan State, 18 first-place votes; and No. 3 Arkansas, one first-place vote. UCLA was No. 4 and Nebraska No. 5. Overall, it was a split national title. Michigan State won the UPI (coaches) and the National Football Foundation awards, and the Spartans and Crimson Tide shared the FWAA.

A SOUTHERN EXODUS

The success of Daugherty's mid-1960s teams featured an Underground Railroad identity with an influx of Southern players escaping segregation. The label was a reverent nod to the bravery of Harriet Tubman leading slaves out of the antebellum South.

In all, Daugherty recruited 44 Black players from the segregated South between 1959 and 1972, but only 10 of them earned All-American or All-Big Ten honors. The 22-percent batting average on stars represent another progression Daugherty set in college football integration. The unwritten quotas of single digits led to coaches offering scholarships to only to Black athletes with a high ceiling. They were the 4-star and 5-star players in today's vernacular.

Daugherty took chances on his Southern recruits, including Jimmy Raye of Fayetteville, North Carolina, a late addition to the Spartans' 1964 recruiting class. By the end of his career, he was a two-year starter and the South's first Black quarterback to win a national title. Raye was one of only two Black starting quarterbacks in the nation in 1966 along with Stanford's Gene Washington. Raye returned as a starter in 1967 as a senior, while Washington was shifted to wide receiver.

"Duffy Daugherty was one of the most courageous persons I've had the privilege to be associated with in my athletic career," Raye said. "I can only imagine the pressure he must been under and received when he made the decision to make me the starting quarterback in the mid-1960s."

Michigan State's Eric Marshall, a Black quarterback on the 1965 and 1966 title teams recruited out of Oxford, Miss., also was a late addition to the 1962 recruiting class. Marshall was never a star, serving in a scout team role, but he was among the 68 percent of Daugherty's Underground Railroad players who graduated. He served in the U.S. Army in Vietnam, rising to Lt. Colonel upon retirement.

The Spartans' 1965 and 1966 teams featured three College Football Hall of Famers from the segregated South: George Webster; Bubba Smith, Beaumont, Texas; and Gene Washington. A fourth College Football Hall of Famer among the 1966 seniors was Clinton Jones from Cleveland, Ohio.

When Jones was enshrined in 2015, it marked the first time four Black players from the same class were inducted into the College Football Hall of Fame. Also, it was the first time four players from any school in the same class were jointly inducted since 1940.

In addition to Raye, other Underground Railroad starters on the 1965 and 1966 teams were linebacker Charlie Thornhill, Roanoke, Virginia; cornerback Jim Summers, Orangeburg, South Carolina; and safety Jess Phillips, Beaumont, Texas. Raye was second-team All-Big Ten to Purdue All-America QB Bob Greise. Thornhill was first-team All-Big Ten and Summers a two-year starter. Summers was an All-American sprinter on the track team. Phillips was an All-Big Ten pick who played 10 NFL seasons.

BUILDING AN UNDERGROUND RAILROAD

Although Daugherty's Underground Railroad was groundbreaking, it developed quite by accident. History hasn't given Daugherty and Southern Black high-school coaches credit for how the tracks were laid.

Popular opinion, mistakenly, features a narrative that Daugherty got lucky with a handful of Southern Black players steered to him by alumni. That's not what happened. It was a network of Southern Black high-school coaches who sent Daugherty talent out of respect for him and their trust in him to treat their players fairly.

Hank Bullough, Daugherty's defensive coordinator before he went on to an NFL coaching career, explained how Daugherty first struck up a relationship with the coaches at a Southern clinic in the late 1950s. Bullough, who died in 2019, told the story in a 2012 interview for *Raye of Light: Jimmy Raye, Duffy Daugherty, the 1965-66 Michigan State Spartans and the Integration of College Football*.

Upon Daugherty's arrival at the clinic, he was angered that Jim Crow policies denied entry to the Black high-school coaches. Daugherty subsequently put on a free clinic for them. The interaction added to the knowledge the coaches already had of Michigan State through its Rose Bowl history with Black stars. Daugherty's engaging personality easily made friends.

The details of that first clinic are fuzzy; Bullough believed it took place in Atlanta. But what mattered was the first clinic was so well received Daugherty continued the practice in the South. He also invited the Black coaches to Michigan State's campus in East Lansing for a clinic.

"I remember Duffy had Jimmy Raye throwing me passes and seeing all these Black coaches," Washington said. "I wondered where they came from."

The most notable Southern Black coach sending Daugherty players was Willie Ray Smith Sr., father of Bubba Smith. Willie Ray was a Texas high-school coaching legend during segregation. He won 235 games and two Black state titles in 33 years at three schools. His story is told in Chapter 16 —a story that includes nine players, including son Bubba Smith, sent by Willie Ray from the Houston area to East Lansing. Daugherty's network was far more sophisticated than getting lucky from a few alums tipping him off to players—the common perception.

"That's just *bullshit*," repeated Switzer, "for anyone to say Duffy only got lucky with Bubba Smith and a few other players."

BIG AUDIENCES, BIG RETURNS

The makeup of the 1965 and 1966 Spartans was apparent on television screens, even if the print media wasn't highlighting the contrast.

The 1965 team played in the Jan. 1, 1966 Rose Bowl, a TV ratings bonanza in the era before the Bowl Championship Series (1998-2013) and the current College Football Playoff (2014-).

The 1966 Game of the Century's 33 million TV viewers outpaced viewers of Super Bowl I two months later. Fans saw the contrast in rosters on their screens. Michigan State lined up 20 Black players, 11 Black starters, two Black team captains (Webster and Jones), and Raye at quarterback. Notre Dame had one Black player on its roster, Alan Page.

The 20-to-1 difference was only one ratio that demonstrated Daugherty was ahead of the nation with his 1966 roster. Willie Ray Smith boarded three Black starters—Bubba Smith, Gene Washington and safety Jess Phillips—on the Underground Railroad. His Houston-area contribution was 3-to-1 compared to Notre Dame's national recruiting base. Not to mention two Black quarterbacks with Raye and Marshall.

By the end of the decade, the rest of the nation began catching on to Daugherty's model. Football coaches are copycats, and the Daugherty was quickly followed. Those schools included USC under coach John McKay.

Despite USC's campus location in heavily populated and highly diverse Los Angeles, the 1962 USC national title team had only five Black players, and the 1967 national championship roster only seven. But by USC's next national title in 1972, the Trojans' roster numbered 23 Black players.

Also overlooked by USC myths and outright fiction embellishing the impact of the 1970 USC-Alabama game on college football integration: the 1970 Trojans had only five Black starters. Most of the 18 Black players on the roster, including sophomore fullback Sam Cunningham, were recruited in the previous couple seasons.

Notre Dame's next two national title rosters listed 10 Black players in 1973 under Ara Parseghian and 17 in 1977 under Dan Devine. Notre Dame, with its national recruiting base, had previously avoided recruiting Black athletes for fear of hurting its recruitment of Southern stars.

But Daugherty didn't limit his trailblazing to Black northern athletes or Black Southern athletes escaping segregation.

RECRUITING SAMOANS, HAWAIIANS AND POLYNESIANS

As Switzer noted, Daugherty was the first coach to recruit Samoan and Polynesian athletes. Daugherty's Hawaiian Express included 10 players from 1955 to 1972. Daugherty like to joke when he divided up the nation for recruiting among his assistant coaches, he took Hawaii—and his golf clubs.

The pipeline was established when Michigan State played at Hawaii in 1947. Head coach Biggie Munn, with Daugherty an assistant, essentially made the trip a bowl game. Daugherty struck up a friendship with Hawaii coach Tommy Kaulukukui, a legend from his days as an All-America honorable mention halfback playing for the Rainbow Warriors in the 1930s.

Hawaii wasn't a Division I program until 1974, so once Daugherty succeeded Munn as head coach, he told Kaulukukui to inform him of Big Ten-caliber players on the islands. Hawaii wasn't a recruiting hotbed back then, with a population of only 642,000 in 1960, as opposed to now, with a population of 1.4 million.

Daugherty's most notable Hawaiian recruit was Bob Apisa of Honolulu Farrington. Apisa was college football's first Samoan All-American pick as a two-time All-American fullback on the 1965 and 1966 teams. He has been long considered the godfather of Polynesian players that now permeate all levels of football, coast to coast.

The Polynesian Football Hall of Fame in Hawaii has enshrined two of Daugherty's recruits, Charlie Wedemeyer and Apisa. Wedemeyer, whose ancestry was German and Hawaiian, was a quarterback and receiver for the Spartans, 1966-68.

Those Hawaiian milestones are lost to historical memory similarly to the lack of recognition for Daugherty's pioneering fully integrated rosters.

INFLUENCING THE COLLEGE WORLD

Daugherty's role pushing college football integration began to influence integrated programs and trickle down to the South, where there were like-minded coaches. Maryland's Tom Nugent recruited the first Black player in the Atlantic Coast Conference, Darryl Hill, a transfer from Navy, 1962; Southern Methodist's Hayden Fry the first Black player in the Southwest Conference, Jerry LeVias, 1965; and Kentucky's Charlie Bradshaw, who recruited the first two Black players in the Southeastern Conference, Nate Northington and Greg Page.

Wake Forest's Bill Tate recruited the ACC's first three Black players out of high school, 1964; Baylor's walk-on John Westbrook made his varsity debut as the SWC's second Black player, 1966; and Tennessee was the second SEC school to recruit a Black player, Lester McClain, 1967.

The ACC's last holdout teams with a Black athlete on the varsity were Clemson and Virginia's 1971. The Southwest's last holdouts were Texas and Arkansas, 1970. The SEC's last three were Georgia, LSU and Mississippi, 1972. They followed Alabama (1971) by one year.

A popular myth about Bryant: he once said he might not be the first in the SEC, but he wouldn't be the third. That's true. He was the seventh out of what was then a 10-team league, trailing Kentucky, Tennessee, Florida, Mississippi State, Auburn and Vanderbilt.

However, many progressive moments continued to be overlooked by the 1960s sports media's failure to properly record Black Historiography.

In 1966, Houston junior running back Warren McVea was the first Black player to score a touchdown in a Southeastern Conference Stadium. The Cougars routed Kentucky 56-18 on Nov. 12 before 32,000 fans at McLean Stadium. McVea scored on a 63-yard run in the first quarter and 32 and 11 yarders in the second period. He finished with 14 carries for 148 yards and three touchdowns.

Officials had their choice of three balls to secure, package and send to the College Football Hall of Fame for display. But anyone in such a position was oblivious to the significance.

Compare the 1966 oversight to the 2020 college football season. When Vanderbilt's Sarah Fuller was the first women to score in a major college football game with two extra points, one of the footballs she scored with was sent to the College Football Hall of Fame.

In the modern media, milestones of pioneers are properly recognized. In the Tokyo Olympics contested in 2021 due to the COVID-19 virus, news reports heralded Tamra Mensah-Stock's gold medal at 68 kilograms as the first Black women to win an Olympic wrestling medal. The same was true at the 2022 Winter Olympics when Erin Jackson was the first Black woman to win an individual Olympic speedskating gold medal.

History left behind a treasure trove of 1960s milestones unreported and still unappreciated. Daugherty's pioneering in the 1960s has suffered at the expense of the aggressive and embellished promotion of the 1970 USC-Alabama game.

The revisionist history to sell a story has overshadowed the true 1960s pioneers. But the milestones Daugherty, his players, his assistant coaches that branched out and the Southern athletes who broke segregation barriers are out there to be found by anyone looking for them.

CHAPTER 2
JIMMY RAYE'S BLACK COACHING NETWORK

FACT: Michigan State's Duffy Daugherty hired Jimmy Raye as a pioneering Black assistant coach (1971-75) along with Sherman Lewis (1969-82). Raye moved on to the NFL in 1977, developing an early network and fulfilling a decades-long mentoring role for young Black coaches.

"As I grew in my career, I appreciated more the guys who came before me and how hard they worked to open doors. You learn to appreciate the example and the foundation they set for those of us who have followed them." — Willie Taggart, head coach at Western Kentucky, South Florida, Oregon, Florida State and Florida Atlantic.

The University of South Florida's 2013 trip to play Michigan State was a routine nonconference contest, but the Bulls' Willie Taggart wasn't your usual college football head coach. He was a 37-year-old Black head coach. He understood the significance of leading his team onto the field at the school that drove college football integration.

He called Spartan Stadium "hallowed ground."

Charlie Baggett with Jimmy Raye, 1973, after the QB transferred from North Carolina. Baggett ended up coaching at his alma mater. *Courtesy Michigan State University.*

Taggart traced his 2013 moment through Jimmy Raye to Michigan State coach Duffy Daugherty. Raye was a groundbreaking Black quarterback in the 1960s—the first from the South to win a national title. After Raye's brief National Football League career, Daugherty hired him as a pioneering Black assistant coach—part-time in 1971 and full-time a year later.

Raye joined an MSU coaching staff that already included Sherman Lewis, Daugherty's first Underground Railroad All-American pick in 1963 as a halfback. Lewis was hired in 1969 and Raye joined the staff full time in 1972.

"Jimmy Raye and those guys worked hard to overcome a lot—and not just in football," Taggart said in a 2013 preseason interview. "They worked hard to prove it could be done, and they had to work a lot harder to do it then than we do now."

Daugherty's Underground Railroad teams added talent from the segregated South to traditional Midwest-based rosters. Lewis of Louisville, Kentucky, was Daugherty's first Underground Railroad All-American player as a senior halfback, in 1963. Raye was the South's first Black quarterback to win a national title as the Spartans' starter in 1966 and frequently used backup in 1965. Daugherty steered both into coaching.

Daugherty receives even less credit for opening doors to Black coaches. He had two Black assistant coaches on his 1972 staff at about the same time many schools were just getting around to hiring their first Black coach. Raye moved onto the NFL and began to establish a fledgling network of opportunity for young Black coaches.

One of those coaches who benefitted from doors opening wider was Ruffin McNeill. He was an assistant at eight schools spanning 25 years until he finally got his chance as a head coach at East Carolina, his alma mater, in 2011-15. McNeill grew up in Lumberton, North Carolina, not far from Raye's hometown of Fayetteville. Segregation had ended during his school years, but he was aware of Raye's legend as a groundbreaking Black quarterback and coach.

"It was important that older coaches with experience reached out to younger coaches," McNeill said. "What was important was when Jimmy started coaching, he exhibited professionalism on the job the entire time. That helped to erase any doubts that may have arisen."

Pep Hamilton, a long-time college and NFL assistant, is a more direct Raye protege. He grew up in Charlotte, North Carolina, two decades after McNeill, but Raye's name was still an important name in his football circles. In 1999, Hamilton was Howard University's offensive coordinator when Raye, then with the Kansas City Chiefs, visited campus. Raye was scouting talent for the upcoming draft, but he also saw in Hamilton a young coach with a future.

"I sat in on a couple of offensive meetings and watched him work on the field," Raye said. "I thought he had a future in coaching and needed an opportunity."

Raye arranged for Hamilton to work with the Chiefs in the 2000 offseason intern program sponsored by the NFL. The NFL's intern program, inspired by the late Bill Walsh as the 49ers' head coach in the 1980s, helps young Black coaches gain entrée to a network that otherwise might be hard to crack.

Hamilton filled similar roles in 2001 with Washington and 2002 with Baltimore. By 2003, the Jets hired him as a quality control coach. Hamilton was soon ascending in coaching circles, both in college and the NFL. He was the offensive coordinator at Stanford from 2011-12, Indianapolis Colts in 2013-15 and Houston Texans, 2022. He's also been an assistant head coach of the Cleveland Browns and University of Michigan.

"I feel like the game of football is the greatest meritocracy in our society," Hamilton said. "The sport has been great to me and my family, and Jimmy Raye helped paved the way."

Raye was paying forward what Daugherty paid to him.

"I was always cognizant of young talent that was coming along after I started," Raye said. "It was different when I started coaching. I was looking for and helping the next group of guys. A lot of what I learned about mentoring and serving I got from Duffy. He's the one that got me started coaching and steered me to the first two or three jobs I had."

Lewis remained a Michigan State assistant until 1982 before moving to the NFL and the 49ers under Bill Walsh. Lewis won three Super Bowl rings and a fourth, then Mike Holmgren brought him to Green Bay as his offensive coordinator. He and Raye worked together mentoring young coaches.

The contrast between Daugherty at Michigan State with two Black assistant coaches in 1972 at a time when many schools were still hiring their first Black assistant coach can't be understated. As late as November 1970, *Harper's Magazine* exposed Texas coach Darrell Royal's reluctance to hire a Black assistant. Royal, who had been having trouble recruiting Black athletes until Julius Whittier signed in 1969 and made his varsity debut as a sophomore in 1970, was asked about it by a *Harper's* reporter.

"Is it important to you that you have Negro players on the team?" Royal replied "No." He added, "A bunch of Negro boys came to me a while ago and said I could solve all possible difficulties by hiring a Black coach. Now that would be fine for them, but I've got to look at the other side. I'd have a lot of white boys on the team coming to me saying they couldn't play for a Black coach. The family atmosphere of the team would be destroyed....Once the club harmony and spirit begin to deteriorate, I don't care what kind of talent you have, you won't win."

But even Daugherty needed to be pushed into hiring his first Black coach.

A STUDENT-LED CHANGE

The late 1960s was a time for Black activism on college campuses. Soon enough, sports weren't immune to the civil rights movement.

At Alabama, that meant the Alabama Afro American student association suing Bear Bryant in July 2, 1969 for failing to recruit Black athletes. Bryant caved by finding Wilbur Jackson of Ozark, Alabama, signing Jackson in the 1970 class as his first Black recruit.

At Michigan State, the newly formed Black Student Alliance (BSA) protested the lack of Black people working in the athletic department, from administrators to coaches to secretaries. Daugherty's players didn't complain about their treatment on the team, but the problem affected the team when some players supported the BSA, and the BSA asked them to boycott spring practice. Daugherty was ahead of his time in many ways, but he was still an old-school coach about missing practice. The issue was about to explode with the players caught in the middle.

Michigan State president John Hannah headed off problems. Hannah, who pushed for integration throughout his time as Michigan State's president, set in motion changes in the athletic department that satisfied the BSA. Spring drills went on as planned.

Clarence Underwood, a Michigan State graduate, was hired as assistant ticket manager. He was promoted to assistant athletic director in 1972 and eventually served as the school's AD from 1999 to 2002. Jim Bibbs was hired as an assistant track coach and promoted to head coach in 1977.

Daugherty hired Don Coleman in 1968 as the Spartans' first Black football assistant coach. When Daugherty later hired Lewis and Raye as Black assistants, he indirectly influenced the coaching careers of Tyrone Willingham and Charlie Baggett. They were both mentored by Lewis and Raye.

The cycle of opportunity for Black coaches was underway.

Don Coleman was the Spartans' first Black All-America player as a senior lineman and the team's MVP, in 1951. He was the school's first Black College Football Hall of Famer when he was enshrined in 1975. His 1951 season also nearly set another precedent when he finished second in the Outland Trophy voting. The first Black Outland Award winner didn't come until 1962, when the University of Minnesota's Bobby Bell snared the honor. Coleman was a teacher in Flint when he accepted Daugherty's offer to join his staff. However, he coached only one year, deciding coaching wasn't in his blood. He continued to work at the school in several roles, including assistant dean of the graduate school.

Sherman Lewis was hired in 1969 to replace Coleman. He coached with Daugherty though his final season in 1972 and was retained in 1973 by Denny Stolz, 1976 by Darryl Rogers and 1980 by Muddy Waters. He left for the NFL in 1983 with Bill Walsh and the San Francisco 49ers. Lewis won four Super Bowl rings in his career, three with the 49ers and one as the offensive coordinator with the Green Bay Packers under Mike Holmgren. Like Raye, he was a victim of sham head-coaching interviews and denied a chance.

Jimmy Raye was hired fulltime in 1972. Denny Stolz retained him, but when Stolz was fired after the 1975 season, Raye moved on to Wyoming under Fred Akers, after Daugherty advised him to take the Wyoming job over an offer from San Jose State. He said Akers was a coach on the rise and was expected to be named the head coach at either Texas or Arkansas. When Darrell Royal resigned after the 1976 season, Akers was hired by Texas and brought Raye with him. He was with Akers recruiting in the offseason until he was hired by the 49ers, launching an NFL career spanning five decades.

Fred Akers died in 2020 at age 82, but in a 2014 interview Akers spoke about hiring Raye as his offensive coordinator at Wyoming in 1976 and then bringing Raye with him to Texas in the same role in 1977, although Raye landed a job with the San Francisco 49ers prior to the start of the 1977 season.

"I'll tell you right now, Jimmy Raye would have been a great head coach," Akers said. "He was dedicated, and he told it like it is. He was a coach who could lead and inspire young men. He was a perfectionist who left nothing undone. You can't find a better coach than Jimmy Raye."

Charlie Baggett and Tyrone Willingham, 1974. *Courtesy Michigan State University.*

Tyrone Willingham was recruited by Raye out of Jacksonville, North Carolina, in Daugherty's final recruiting class, in 1972. He began coaching as a graduate assistant under Darryl Rogers in 1977 when Lewis was still on the staff. After stints at other schools and in the NFL, Stanford named Willingham its head coach (1995-2001). He was the first Black head coach to take a team to the Rose Bowl with Stanford in the 1999 season. He was later the first Black coach in any sport at Notre Dame (2002-04). Although Notre Dame fired him with an overall record of 21-15, he was one of the first examples of a fired Black head coach getting another chance when he accepted an offer from Washington (2005-08).

Second chances for Black coaches aren't handed out as readily as for white coaches, but here was another road cleared through the Daugherty coaching tree.

Recent Black head coaches receiving a second chance include Karl Dorrell at Colorado after he was a head coach at UCLA, though Dorrell was fired mid-2022 season after a miserable start; Maryland's Mike Locksley after he was a head coach at New Mexico; Kevin Sumlin at Arizona after he was a head coach at Houston and Texas A&M; and Taggart at Florida Atlantic after he was fired by Florida State.

Willingham, addressing the sham interviews Raye and Lewis were subjected to in the NFL, says he is embarrassed he was a head coach and not his mentors. "No. 1, they both deserved to be head coaches," Willingham said. "The system malfunctioned by not allowing them that opportunity. There were many young men—Black, white, brown, green… whatever—that were deprived an opportunity to be tutored by these two men. And that's the shame that it is. That's segregation or racism. It costs the overall public opportunities for a lot of very talented people."

Charlie Baggett was recruited by Daugherty in his 1971 class, but Baggett signed with North Carolina with trailblazing ambitions as a Black quarterback at the ACC school. However, after playing on the Tar Heels' freshmen team, he was told he was being switched to wide receiver as a sophomore in 1972. Baggett instead transferred to Michigan State. He had to sit out the 1972 season by NCAA rules, but he was a three-year starter, in 1973-75.

Following his playing days, he enrolled in an IBM executive training school in New York with no plans for coaching. That changed when he got a call from Bowling Green State University coach Denny Stolz, Daugherty's successor when Baggett played, about joining his staff as a graduate assistant. Baggett, tired of wearing a tie and sitting in an office, took the job offer.

Stolz later hired Baggett as a full-time coach, but in 1981 he made the first of several coaching moves. Tony Dungy, then a University of

Minnesota assistant, called to tell Baggett he had recommended him to Minnesota coach Joe Salem. Dungy was leaving his alma mater for the Pittsburgh Steelers. Baggett eventually coached 35 years, 24 in college and 11 in the NFL. He had two stops at Michigan State under George Perles (1983-92) and Nick Saban (1995-98). His second stint overlapped with a Saban-hired graduate assistant destined to become a Spartans' head coach, Mel Tucker.

"As adults we look back at how we developed and things we could have done differently," Baggett said. "I look back at how Duffy recruited me, and it had to be a godsend that I left North Carolina and transferred to Michigan State. I don't think I'd be where I am today. Michigan State was an integral part of my growth and maturity. I'm blessed with how college and my life turned out."

JIMMY RAYE'S LEGACY

Raye moved on as a college coach under Fred Akers at Wyoming and then followed Akers to Texas. He went through offseason recruiting and conditioning leading up to spring football when he spoke at a clinic in San Antonio. A chance meeting between Raye and Los Angeles Rams assistant coach Ken Meyer played out for Raye similar to how Raye's chance meeting benefited Hamilton.

Rams head coach Chuck Knox was originally set to speak at the San Antonio clinic, but he was forced to cancel over a scheduling conflict. Knox sent assistant coach Ken Meyer in his place. Meyer was impressed by Raye's session in the clinic.

In a sudden twist of fate, Meyer was named the San Francisco 49ers' head coach on April 19, 1977. He succeeded Monte Clark, who was fired after a conflict with newly named general manager Joe Thomas. Meyer invited Raye to join his staff. At the time, there were only seven other Black assistant coaches in a 28-team league.

"I've always said I was lucky Chuck Knox didn't make that clinic," said Raye with a laugh, "and Ken Meyer stuck around to hear me talk."

Raye also was a mentor to Tony Dungy, the second Black coach enshrined in the Pro Football Hall of Fame behind Fritz Pollard. Dungy, the first Black coach to win a Super Bowl in 2006 with the Indianapolis Colts, was inducted in 2016. During his speech, Dungy mentioned Raye among other pioneering Black coaches.

He closed his speech saying, "I'd like to say a special thank you to 10 men: Willie Brown, Buck Buchanan, Earnel Durden, Bob Ledbetter, Elijah Pitts, Jimmy Raye, Johnny Roland, Al Tabor, Lionel Taylor and Allan Webb.

"Without those 10 coaches laying the groundwork, the league would not have the 200-plus minority assistant coaches it has today. And we would not have had Lovie Smith and Tony Dungy coaching against each other in Super Bowl 41. So, tonight, as I join Fritz Pollard as the second African-American coach in the Hall of Fame, I feel like I'm representing those 10 men and all the African-American coaches who came before me and paved the way. And I thank them very, very much."

Of those 10 Black coaches Dungy mentioned, Raye arguably played a larger role than any other establishing a network among Black coaches that carried on into the 1980s, 1990s and 21st century based on his longevity and time with multiple teams as an offensive coordinator. Raye coached 37 continuous seasons between 1977 and 2013, longer by more than a decade than the others. That's not to diminish the pioneering roles of the other coaches Dungy mentioned. It's to point out Raye broke many barriers except being given a chance as a head coach.

Raye was the NFL's second Black coordinator when Rams head coach John Robinson named him as his OC in 1983. Robinson, who largely brought his staff from USC with him, said he needed Raye's NFL experience on the staff. He especially valued his memory for recalling plays in the years long before computers and analytics took over game planning.

"He had an encyclopedic knowledge of the NFL," Robinson said in an interview years later. "We would talk about trying something and he'd say, 'Well, Detroit did that in 1978...or he'd say, if we try this, they'll cover it this way.' These days you can call everything up on a computer, but in those days, it was mostly in a coach's mind how a team would react. He was a very smart guy and knew the ins and outs of every team."

In all, Raye coached with 11 franchises, including two stints with the Rams, Tampa Bay Buccaneers, New York Jets, Atlanta Falcons and San Francisco 49ers. After the Rams, he was an OC with Tampa Bay, New England, Kansas City, Washington, Oakland and San Francisco.

That's a lot of jobs, but in coaching it's a badge of honor. The coaching profession may be the only one that values recycled employees as a stamp of credibility. But Raye's career marked a barrier crossed as a Black coach like recycled white coaches.

Among the 10 Dungy mentioned, only Lionel Taylor (14 years) was a coordinator. He was the first Black offensive coordinator with the Rams for two seasons (1981-82) under head coach Ray Malavasi. Taylor, unfairly or not, wasn't hired as an OC again. Raye broke that ground as a coordinator rehired as an OC.

Roland (26) and Pitts (24) were the only others with at least 20 years in the NFL, but they weren't coordinators. Pitts, though, was an assistant head coach for the Buffalo Bills from 1992-97. Earnel Durden coached 16 years and Willie Brown 10.

The entire time Raye was working on X's and O's and teaching techniques, he had his eye out for promising young coaches who needed the opportunity Daugherty provided him.

"I just hope I set an example for them about coaching," Raye said. "I told them to do the best job they could coaching and don't worry about the next job. The best job is the job you have. I hope some of that rubbed off."

Raye was in his second stint with the Jets (2007-08) when Jason Michael began coaching the Jets' tight ends. Michael had been Western Kentucky's quarterback in 2002 when Taggart was an assistant coach, and the Hilltoppers won the NCAA Division I-AA title.

"Jason was my quarterback, and we're good friends," Taggart said. "Jason and Jimmy got to be good friends, and I got to know Jimmy through him."

Herman Edwards, a Black head coach with the New York Jets and Kansas City Chiefs and later head coach at Arizona State, also was influenced by Raye. Edwards was first a scout for the Chiefs until coaching on the same staff with Raye under Kansas City head coach Marty Schottenheimer. Edwards said he learned through Raye in their time together about Daugherty's influence on Raye's career as a quarterback and coach.

"Duffy was way ahead of the curve—there is no doubt about that," Edwards said. "Jimmy has told me a lot about him. You didn't see Black quarterbacks in the 1960s. Duffy didn't care about color. The best players played. Football teams are a collection of all types of players from different walks of life. That's what makes a team."

By 2002, their relationship came full circle. Edwards was hired as the head coach of the Jets. Raye was looking for work after Marty Schottenheimer was fired as Washington's head coach at the end of the 2001 season. Edwards hired Raye as a senior offensive assistant.

Herm Edwards leading his 2019 Sun Devils at Spartan Stadium. *Courtesy Arizona State University.*

"Jimmy Raye had a lot of knowledge—an excellent coach and a really good friend," Edwards said. "He helped me a lot in the coaching profession. He had the knowledge to be a head coach, but he didn't get a head coaching job. Tony (Dungy) and I often reflect on those guys that came before us. I always say we stood on their shoulders."

Edwards also educated his players about Raye as a trailblazer.

"A lot of our players didn't realize Jimmy played quarterback in college before he got into coaching," Edwards recalled. "I remember him telling them that.

"They'd say, 'Wha-a-a-t? Where?'

"…'Michigan State…'

"'No, you didn't!'"

That included teaching them overcoming segregation was recent history, not ancient.

"It's amazing. They think the '60s was a long time ago. I lived in that era! I grew up in the '60s—the civil rights movement."

As Edwards' coaching life progressed, he enjoyed his own day leading his 2019 Arizona State team on to the hallowed ground of Spartan Stadium. Michigan State coach Mark Dantonio needed one more win to break Daugherty's career record of 109 wins, but Edwards forced him to wait another week. The Sun Devils won 10-7 in an upset of the No. 18-ranked Spartans.

MOVING PAST THE OLD BOYS

McNeill eventually set an example of Black coaches adding to the old boys' network. White coaches had long been recycled into jobs through coaches they had worked for or with in the past. When McNeill landed the East Carolina job, he brought with him Lincoln Riley as his offensive coordinator. They had been assistant coaches at Texas Tech.

Over the next few seasons, Riley's star rose as an offensive coordinator. When Oklahoma coach Bob Stoops called to interview Riley, McNeill not only granted permission, he endorsed Riley. It was a step up in pay and prestige.

The calendar continued to flip when McNeill was fired in a controversial move in 2015, with many ECU fans rallying to his support. Then-Virginia coach Bronco Mendenhall was quick to put in a call to add McNeill to his staff.

"Ruffin McNeill is a larger-than-life figure, and I loved having him on our staff," Mendenhall said. "He's an amazing leader of men, a family man and great person. He has had so many unique life experiences. When he was fired by East Carolina, I thought, 'Who and why would anyone fire Ruffin McNeill?'"

After McNeill coached at Virginia for a year, Riley called to have him join his staff.

"Our relationship has been as a boss, a brother, a dad and a son," said McNeill, "but it's not just Lincoln and me. It's our families. It's my wife Erlene and his wife Caitlin. We're all close."

Riley is now the head coach at USC, but McNeill has remained in his home state. He has moved into a different coaching phase now that he's in his 60s—the wise advisor. North Carolina State coach Dave Doeren hired McNeill in 2020 as Special Assistant to the Head Coach. McNeill took a break from coaching in 2019 to care for his ill father, but he remains one of the most respected coaches in the nation among his peers.

The lack of Black head coaches in college and the NFL remains a glaring problem in a sport with more than 50 percent Black athletes, but Raye's career path was the first step toward building the network of Black assistant coaches.

Raye summed up what progress has been made: "It's very gratifying for me to see some of the younger guys take advantage of opportunities without some of the anxiety and turmoil that existed when I came along," Raye said.

Six years after Raye attended Dungy's Hall of Fame enshrinement and heard his speech, he was honored during the August 2022 week of induction festivities. He was named among five assistant coaches in the inaugural class to be awarded with the Pro Football Hall of Fame's Awards of Excellence. Raye, Ernie Zampase, Alex Gibbs, Fritz Shurmer and Terry Robiskie were honored at the 2022 Pro Football Hall of Fame induction week festivities.

"They've honored commissioners and owners in the past, but this is the first time for this category of assistant coaches, public relations people, athletic trainers and equipment manager, so I'm very humbled to be a part of this group as an inaugural class," Raye said. "It's something I didn't expect, and I'll always cherish. A lot of it goes to my (late) wife, Edwina, for all the years of her sticking by me while I was coaching through all the ups and downs. I'm honored to be one of the recipients."

CHAPTER 3
TWO GAMES OF THE CENTURY

FACT: The 1966 Game of the Century was the first epic showdown to include Black athletes and first with a fully integrated roster on one side of the field. The 1971 Game of the Century was the first with two fully integrated rosters. Both classics have Duffy Daugherty's fingerprints.

"What puts a real Game of the Century over the top is when it has great meaning or context beyond football. Michigan State coach Duffy Daugherty has 20 African-American players and Jimmy Raye as an African-American quarterback. There is not one singular thing you can point to that says, 'Hey, college football is integrated but what Duffy Daugherty did with the 1966 team is a tremendous part of the evolution of race in college football." —Jerry Barca, author and filmmaker, 2019 ESPN film.

ESPN produced *College Football 150: The American Game* as a 2019 series recognizing the 150th anniversary of the sport. The engaging series included an episode entitled, "The Games of the Century." Note the "s" on *games*.

Basic math says the 1900s can have only one Game of the Century, but sports passion tosses math out of bounds. X = various opinions. Ivan Maisel, formerly of ESPN, was the editor at large for the series. He commented on what qualifies as a Game of the Century along with other media figures invited to appear.

"The term Game of the Century is not thrown about willy-nilly," Maisel said on the film. "There have only been a handful. And that phrase has only been used in the history of college football. That's pretty cool."

Another media member said there needs to be a season-long build up with a national title on the line.

ESPN's Paul Finebaum added, "A Game of the Century has to have certain elements. It can't just have a great finish."

Really, though, there are only two worthy Games of the Century, and they were staged in 1966 and 1971. They both impacted sports and America beyond the final score. Their rosters reflected an inclusive America. They were college football's first contributions to living up to a nation's ideals stated in Thomas Jefferson's 1776 document.

And both games have Duffy Daugherty's fingerprints. He was the head coach of Michigan State's 1966 team, and the two head coaches of the 1971 Game of the Century came from Daugherty's coaching tree: Nebraska's Bob Devaney and Oklahoma's Chuck Fairbanks.

Devaney was a Michigan State assistant under Daugherty from 1953 to 1956. He moved on as the head coach at Wyoming (1957-61) and then Nebraska (1962-72). Fairbanks played for the Spartans under Daugherty, 1952-54. His path to head coach was through two Daugherty disciples. Arizona State head coach Frank Kush, Fairbanks' MSU teammate, hired Fairbanks as a Sun Devils assistant, 1958-61. Houston head coach Bill Yeoman, a Daugherty assistant, added Fairbanks to his Cougars staff, 1962-65.

The 1966 and 1971 Games of the Century stand apart thanks to the leadership of the Spartans' College Football Hall of Fame coach. His 1950s and 1960s teams led the college football integration into the 20th century.

THE 1966 GAME OF THE CENTURY

November 19 before 80,011 fans at Spartan Stadium, East Lansing: Notre Dame 10, Michigan State 10.

The epic showdown marked the first time Black athletes took the field in a Game of the Century. Daugherty's 1960s teams were college football's first fully integrated rosters. Notre Dame, with Alan Page its only Black player, resembled the old-world order of white privilege when integrated programs followed unwritten quotas limiting Black athletes on the roster.

"What puts a real Game of the Century over the top is when it has great meaning or context beyond football," said Jerry Barca, an author and film producer said in the ESPN Game of the Century episode. "Michigan State coach Duffy Daugherty has got 20 African-American players and Jimmy Raye as an African-American quarterback. There is not one singular thing you can point to point to that says, 'Hey, college football is integrated but what Duffy Daugherty did with the 1966 team is a tremendous part of the evolution of race in college football.'"

The Irish and Spartans played to a head-to-head tie and finished with identical 9-0-1 records, which prompted the National Football Foundation to name co-national champions. The NFF is one of four organizations the NCAA sanctioned as naming an official national champion from the poll era prior to the Bowl Championship Series and current College Football Playoff. Notre Dame claimed the other three: Associated Press (writers), United Press International (coaches) and Football Writers Association of America.

Michigan State coach Duffy Daugherty and team captains George Webster and Clinton Jones and Notre Dame coach Ara Parseghian and team captain Jim Lynch represented their schools when the NFF presented the MacArthur Bowl Trophy representative of the national title. The NFF's Vincent DePaul Draddy was quoted in *The New York Times* article covering the event.

"The reasons are rather obvious why we divided the award," he said. "It seemed the only fair thing to do with a couple of excellent teams like Notre Dame and Michigan State."

THE 1971 GAME OF THE CENTURY

November 25 before 62,884 fans at Oklahoma Memorial Stadium, Norman: Nebraska 35, Oklahoma 31.

Five years passed from Michigan State's groundbreaking roster until two fully integrated rosters faced off in a Game of the Century. A primary reason was Devaney and Fairbanks followed Daugherty's blueprint of ignoring quotas.

The rosters they inherited with single-digit numbers Black athletes were no different than USC's 1962 national championship team with five Black players and the Trojans' 1967 national title roster of only seven, despite USC's location in heavily populated and diverse Los Angeles. USC's Black athletes in high-profile positions, including 1965 Heisman

Trophy winner Mike Garrett and 1968 Heisman winner O.J. Simpson, gave a misleading impression of USC's actual rosters of Black athletes limited to single digits.

Nebraska's Rich Glover, an All-Big Eight defensive lineman in 1971 who went on to 1972 All-American honors and the 1972 Outland Trophy, said the Cornhuskers' appreciation of the moment grew with time. One reason the milestone didn't hit them until later was the media avoided race in 1960s sports stories. There was little, if any, analysis of the game's evolution spurred by Daugherty and his disciples and the 1966 game's impact on 1971.

"Looking back, the number of Black players on both teams is something we're proud of," said Glover in an interview for this book. "At the time we were only thinking about winning the game. We wanted to win the Big Eight to go to the Orange Bowl and then win the national championship. We had a tight group of Afro-American brothers, and we came along at the same time Oklahoma had some great Afro-American brothers. We helped changed the game."

Much of the game's anticipation was generated by Oklahoma's wishbone offense leading the nation and Nebraska's Blackshirts defense leading the nation. *Sports Illustrated's* November 22 edition prior to the game featured a cover photo with Nebraska linebacker Bob Terrio and Oklahoma running back Greg Pruitt spliced together face-to-face. The headline: **"Irresistible Oklahoma meets Immovable Nebraska."**

Oklahoma offensive coordinator Barry Switzer never played for Daugherty or coached under him, but he was in the middle of a game connected to Daugherty's legacy. He knew Daugherty well through Fairbanks and retired Oklahoma coach Bud Wilkinson, Daugherty's partner in the Kodak All-American Coaches Clinics. Switzer also knew and respected Devaney as a rival coach. Devaney remained at the center of the rivalry once he retired to Nebraska's athletic director chair. He had been serving in the dual role of AD and coach from 1967 through 1972 and then continued as AD from 1973 to 1992.

TWO FOUNDATIONAL GAMES FOR INTEGRATION

Before the 1966 and 1971 games, no other college football integration moment measured up as a tipping point. Anything afterward was built on the foundation the two games set.

Michigan State's 20 Black players and 11 Black starters in 1966 doesn't sound like much compared to today's rosters unless stacked against the rosters of their era. The same is true of the 1971 game, with Nebraska numbering 15 Black players and seven Black starters and Oklahoma's 16 Black players, also with seven Black starters.

Glover was a year away from All-American honors, but two Nebraska teammates named to the 1971 All-American team were receiver/return man Johnny Rodgers and defensive end/tackle Willie Harper. Glover was from Jersey City, New Jersey and Harper from Toledo, Ohio, but Devaney faced a tougher task securing a commitment from the home-state prospect, Rodgers of Omaha Tech.

"The primary reason Coach Devaney got me to come to Nebraska was he told me he was going to recruit more Black players and they were going to let them play," Rodgers said. "That pretty much did it for me. I was trying my best to go to USC, because when I was in high school Nebraska was 6-4 and 6-4.

"Bob was a players' coach. He really got you believing in him. We would rather slide bare ass on a razor blade than disappoint Coach Devaney."

Oklahoma's Black players included junior running back Greg Pruitt as an All-American pick recruited out of Houston. Two other Black stars in 1971 were All-Big Eight defensive end Ray Hamilton and defensive back Glenn King, the Sooners' first Black team captain as a 1971 senior.

In the ESPN "Games of the Century" episode, the first epic showdowns highlighted were 1935 Notre Dame-Ohio State at Ohio Stadium in Columbus and 1946 Notre Dame-Army at Yankee Stadium in New York. The four teams featured stars and the two games dramatic moments, but the four rosters lacked Black athletes. Ohio State's first Black players were Arthur Carr in 1904 and William Bell from 1929-31, but the 1935 team didn't have a Black member. A backlash against civil rights progress led to many 1930s teams not having Black athletes. Notre Dame's first Black letterman wasn't until Wayne Edmonds (1953-55) and Army's not until Gary Steele (1966-68).

A Game of the Century can't be limited to just white privilege. The Declaration of Independence should be about more than expressing ideals. Even the American Revolution's first casualties included people of color. Crispus Attucks, who was African and Native American, has gone in history widely considered the first person killed at the Boston Massacre.

As for buildup, the 1966 Game of the Century had an excess. The preseason poll listed Michigan State ranked No. 2 and Notre Dame No. 6.

On the first poll of the regular season, September 19, Michigan State was No. 1 and Notre Dame dropped to No. 8 despite not playing a game. MSU/ND were 1-4 on September 26, 1-3 on October 3 and 1-2 on October 10.

But in the Monday, October 17 poll, the Spartans and Irish flip-flopped, even though Michigan State won its game at Ohio State two days earlier. The Spartans survived an upset bid on October 15 with an 11-8 score played on a muddy field in heavy rain. But on the same Saturday Notre Dame routed North Carolina 32-0. Margin of victory counted with the voters.

"I always thought the object of the game was to win," Daugherty said after the poll was announced.

Notre Dame and Michigan State remained unbeaten and 1-2 the next four weeks until they met in East Lansing. When the November 19 game finished in a 10-10 tie, Parseghian was criticized for having Notre Dame run out the clock.

BIG IMPACTS FROM MODEST CHOICES

Interestingly, Parseghian's decision to play for a tie also touched on Daugherty opening ethnic doors. He had been recruiting Hawaii since the 1950s, forming a Hawaiian Pipeline when the islands were lightly recruited. Daugherty's 1966 roster included fullback Bob Apisa, the first Samoan All-American player; bare-footed Dick Kenney, who was Irish-Hawaiian; and all-purpose player Charlie Wedemeyer, German-Hawaiian decent.

"Kenney had kicked a 47-yard field goal earlier," Parseghian told reporters after the game. "We were placed in a difficult position. Our field position was such that an error on our part would have given Kenney an opportunity to kick a field goal to beat us. We were not going to give them that opportunity."

A kicker with 40-plus range in the 1960s equates to kickers in the modern game with 50-plus range.

But as the game turned, the mere presence of Notre Dame's only Black athlete may have decided the game. Early in the fourth quarter, with the game tied 10-10, Michigan State quarterback Jimmy Raye, an elusive runner, broke off a 20-yard gain to the Notre Dame 46-yard line. The play began with him spotting Page and running and cutting right, where he was eventually tackled by Notre Dame All-American linebacker Jim Lynch.

"I look back on that play as a missed opportunity," Raye said years later. "If I would have cut hard to right and then to the left, I might have taken it to the house. I thought I would get another chance, but I didn't."

In the November 21 poll two days later, Notre Dame remained No. 1 in the AP poll, while UPI returned Michigan State atop the poll. The coaches apparently responded to Parseghian playing for a tie. At the time, the Spartans' season was complete with a 9-0-1 record. Michigan State was unable to return to the Rose Bowl due to the Big Ten's no-repeat rule. Michigan State also couldn't accept another bowl bid due to the Big Ten's exclusive contract with the Rose Bowl.

Notre Dame, though, had one game remaining on November 26 in Los Angeles. The Irish routed No. 10 USC, 51-0. The UPI coaches returned Notre Dame to No. 1. Parseghian's calculation that settling for a tie against Michigan State wouldn't cost the Irish the national title if they defeated USC proved correct.

Lynch also won the Maxwell Award as the nation's top player. The Heisman Trophy voting including three players in the Top 10 voting. Notre Dame running back Nick Eddy was third, Spartans' halfback Clinton Jones was sixth and Notre Dame quarterback Terry Hanratty was eighth.

"I still say to this day those are the two best teams to ever play each other," Hanratty said. "You look at the amount of talent on both sides of the field."

The 1971 Nebraska-Oklahoma game also had a year-long buildup in the polls, although Notre Dame began the year ranked No. 1 over defending national champion Nebraska. The Cornhuskers were No. 2 and Oklahoma No. 10. After the first week of play, Nebraska moved to No. 1—and remained atop the polls the rest of the season—with a 35-7 win over Minnesota. Notre Dame dropped to No. 2 despite not playing. Oklahoma won its opener over Southern Methodist 30-0 but fell to No. 11. The Sooners next beat Pitt 55-29 and then No. 17 USC 33-20 to move up to No. 8. They jumped to No. 2 after a rout of No. 3 Texas, 48-27. Nebraska and Oklahoma remained unbeaten and 1-2 until their Thanksgiving Day showdown.

The game's drama began early with Rodgers' 72-yard punt return for a 7-0 lead, one of most iconic plays in college football lore. Oklahoma's All-American running back, Greg Pruitt, was on punt coverage and has forever lamented not staying in his lane. Pruitt thought he had a chance for a hard hit, but Rodgers made a quick cut to avoid Pruitt's grasp. He zigzagged between more tacklers in the middle of the field before running untouched down the left sideline to the end zone with just 3:32 elapsed time on the clock.

On the other side of the ball, Nebraska geared its defense to slow down Pruitt, the nation's leading rusher among major schools in 1971 with 1,760 yards and 18 touchdowns. Only Ed Marinaro, playing in the lower division Ivy League, had more yards and TDs with 1,881 and 24.

Rodgers recalled the game plan:

"Our defense made sure we turned Pruitt back into Richie [Glover]. He had a lot of tackles."

Glover was a 6-foot-1, 234-pound defensive lineman with linebacker mobility. He finished with 22 tackles—three unassisted, 19 assisted.

Pruitt was among the Oklahoma players who commented in the 2006 book Rodgers published, *An Era of Greatness*. Pruitt, in his chapter, says Oklahoma All-American center Tom Brahaney, who played nine years in the NFL, needed help blocking Glover.

"My most talented opponent was NU's Rich Glover," Pruitt wrote. "One of the mistakes we made was trying to let Brahaney handle Glover by himself. That was a big part of the outcome of the game. Brahaney needed help with Glover."

But slowing down Pruitt opened the offense for All-American quarterback Jack Mildren to run 31 times for 130 yards and a pair of 3-yard touchdown runs. In the air, he completed 5-of-10 for 137 yards with two touchdown tosses of 24 and 16 yards to Jon Harrison.

In the third quarter, Nebraska running back Jeff Kinney scored on runs of 3 and 1 yards for a 28-17 lead. But Mildren responded with a 3-yard TD run late in the third quarter and a 16-yard TD toss to Harrison for a 31-28 lead with 7:30 left in the game. Nebraska received the ensuing kickoff and began its possession from its 26-yard line. As the Cornhuskers' offense took the field, Rodgers said Devaney's instructions to quarterback Jerry Tagge were simple.

"He said, 'Give the ball to Kinney and if you get in trouble, look for Rodgers.' That's what he did."

Kinney, a third-team All-American pick, finished with 31 carries for 171 yards. He scored the game-winning touchdown on a 2-yard run with 1:38 left.

"I think our game is the Game of the Century," Rodgers said. "It had all the drama, and it came down to the wire."

POST-GAME POLITICS

The usual Fairbanks custom after a home game was to invite coaches and wives over to the house for dinner. Fairbanks' wife, known as Puddy, enjoyed playing hostess. But this was a Thanksgiving Day game. The dinner was a quiet family affair until the phone rang later in the evening. Chuck Fairbanks Jr., a quarterback at Norman High and later at Houston under Yeoman, answered.

"They asked to speak to Chuck Fairbanks, and I said this is Chuck. Then they said, 'This is the White House. Hold on for the President.'"

Chuck Jr. quickly clarified, explaining, "You want my dad." He got his father on the phone to speak with President Richard M. Nixon.

"He told my dad he wanted to call to say he thought both teams had played a great game," Chuck Jr. recalled.

Nixon stayed home for the 1971 Game of the Century after the controversies he caused—one football, one political—his first year in office by attending the 1969 Game of the Century. The showdown matched two all-white rosters, No. 1 Texas at No. 2 Arkansas on December 6 before 47,500 fans at Razorback Stadium in Fayetteville.

When Texas won 15-14 in dramatic fashion, Nixon declared the Longhorns national champion. He had superseded the poll votes to be released two days later. At the time, Texas had been ranked No. 1 only that last week of the season. Ohio State had been No. 1 since the 1969 preseason poll until the Buckeyes suffered a shocking 24-12 loss to Michigan. Nixon ignored that Penn State was 10-0 and USC 9-0-1, and bowl results could impact the final vote. Texas got him off the hook by beating Notre Dame in the Cotton Bowl to finish 11-0, but Penn State (11-0) coach Joe Paterno and his fans still objected.

The other controversy: Nixon was regarded as playing to white Southern voters, who were resisting the civil rights movement. Texas' 1969 roster went down as the last all-white national championship team. In American race relations, there always is a backlash to racial progress. This was Nixon's response to President Lyndon B. Johnson signing the 1964 and 1965 Civil Rights acts.

Erin Tarver, philosophy professor at Emory University with a Ph.D, commented on Nixon attending in ESPN's "Game of the Century" episode. She also is the author of the 2017 book, *The I in Team, Sports Fandom and Reproduction of Identity*.

"President Nixon decided he's going to come," Tarver said. "The election that just recently happened, George Wallace, the segregationist, carried several Southern states. After Nixon was elected, Nixon's team is looking for ways to appeal to Southern whites. So, Nixon, as part of his Southern Strategy, says, 'Oh, good. I'm going to go to this marquee matchup.' And this was an incredibly useful political tool for Nixon."

Nixon's Southern Strategy came just six years after Martin Luther King delivered his "I Have a Dream" speech at the Lincoln Memorial. The Alabama Ku Klux Klan provided its answer to King's speech three weeks later. A bomb was planted at the 16th Street Baptist Church in Birmingham, killing four little girls.

The 1971 Game of the Century was a reaffirmation of the sport's progress generated through the 1966 Game of the Century. Another result of the 1966 and 1971 Games of the Century was Black athletes began to more fairly be considered for All-American honors and awarded the Heisman Trophy for the best player and the Outland Trophy for the best interior player.

Dick Schaap, honored as a Hall of Famer by the National Sports Media Hall of Fame, often spoke later in his career on the injustice of Syracuse running back Jim Brown finishing fifth in the 1956 Heisman voting. Four white players finished ahead of him (in order): Notre Dame's Paul Hornung, Tennessee's Johnny Majors, Oklahoma's Tommy McDonald and Oklahoma's Jerry Tubbs.

The first Black Heisman winner was Syracuse halfback Ernie Davis, in 1961. The previous year, the only Black player in the Top 10 Heisman voting was New Mexico State halfback Pervis Atkins, who was ninth. Throughout the decade Black halfbacks finishing in the Top 10 were Michigan State's Sherman Lewis and Clinton Jones, Syracuse's Floyd Little and UCLA's Mel Farr, as well as Minnesota quarterback Sandy Stephens.

The omission of Black players at other positions was never more egregious than the 1966 season. Three of college football's greatest defensive players were on the Spartan Stadium turf for the Game of the Century: Smith, Webster and Page.

Smith was one of the most famous players in the nation. There had never been a 6-foot-8, 285-pound player with his speed and quickness. But Webster was considered the better player. He had his number retired by the school before Smith's was retired. Page was to Notre Dame what Smith and Webster were to the Spartans.

But when the Heisman voting was tabulated, the trio was left out of the Top 10. The two defensive players in the Top 10 were from segregated schools, Arkansas' Lloyd Phillips (ninth) and Georgia's George Patton (tenth). Phillips also won the Outland Trophy. Arkansas was ranked No. 13 and Georgia No. 4.

Given the TV exposure and drama of the 1966 Game of the Century, if Webster, Smith and Page were white, it's hard to imagine them not gaining Top 10 votes over Phillips and Patton. But the exposure that overlooked them may have helped future Black athletes gain votes. Oklahoma defensive lineman Granville Liggins finished seventh in 1967 and Ohio State safety Jack Tatum tenth in 1969 and seventh in 1970. Prior to their finishes, Minnesota's Bobby Bell's third-place total in the 1962 Heisman was the only time a Black non-offensive backfield player cracked the Top 10. In the same decade, 24 white non-offensive backfield players finished in the Top 10.

The 1971 Game of the Century resulted in more open-minded voting. Nebraska's 1971 success accounted for the first two Black players sweeping the Heisman and the Outland. In 1972, Rodgers was only the fourth Black Heisman winner and the first since O.J. Simpson in 1968. Glover also was the fourth Black Outland winner but the first since Bell in 1962. Interestingly, Iowa's Calvin Jones won the Outland in 1955 and Ohio State's Jim Parker in 1956 but given the lack of TV coverage in the 1950s and media coverage in general, it's fair to wonder how many voters knew Jones and Ferguson were Black athletes. They were anonymous linemen, not running backs that showed up in pictures.

America's game really became America's game after the 1966 and 1971 Games of the Century.

For the record, the ESPN panel highlighted eight games, although two involving Notre Dame—against Miami in 1988 and Florida State in 1993—are dubiously included. They can easily be thrown out. There are also plenty of issues with other Games of the Century. The records in parenthesis below are the marks entering the showdown.

1935, Notre Dame (5-0) at Ohio State (4-0), November 2, 81,038 fans, Ohio Stadium, Columbus: Notre Dame 18, Ohio State 13.

This game doesn't measure up on several levels. Notre Dame lost the following week to Northwestern 14-7 and then played Army to a 6-6 tie for a final record of 7-1-1. Minnesota (8-0) was named the national champion by Helms and NCF. The AP poll didn't begin until 1936 and the UPI poll in 1950.

1946, No. 1 Army (7-0) vs. No. 2 Notre Dame (5-0), November 9, 74,121 fans, Yankee Stadium, New York: Notre Dame 0, Army 0.

The all-white teams played a gritty game, including Notre Dame's Johnny Lujack making a late-game, touchdown-saving tackle of a run from Doc Blanchard, the 1945 Heisman Trophy winner. Another mark against qualifying this game was Notre Dame had three more games to play and Army two. That's too early. AP voted Notre Dame (8-0-1) No. 1 in the final poll.

1969, No. 1 Texas (9-0) at No. 2 Arkansas (9-0), December 6, 47,500 fans, Razorback Stadium, Fayetteville: Texas 15, Arkansas 14.

The last all-white national champion won with a comeback, but the larger mark against qualifying this contest was the lack of buildup. Ohio State was ranked No. 1 from the preseason poll until a suffering a 24-12 upset loss on November 22. ABC, in a stroke of luck, convinced Texas and Arkansas to move the game from the usual midseason date to December 6. Texas (11-0) swept the AP, UPI, FWAA and NFF titles.

1988, No. 1 Miami (4-0) at No. 4 Notre Dame (5-0), 59,075 fans, October 15, Notre Dame Stadium, South Bend: Notre Dame 31, Miami 30.

October is too early in the season to qualify as a Game of the Century. Notre Dame (12-0) eventually swept the AP, UPI, FWAA and NFF titles.

1993, No. 1 Florida State (9-0) at No. 2 Notre Dame (9-0), November 13, 59,075 fans, Notre Dame Stadium, South Bend: Notre Dame 31, Florida 24.

A Game of the Century team can't lose games. Notre Dame lost the next week to Boston College. That led to Florida State claiming the national title despite the loss in the big game. Florida State (12-1) swept the poll titles.

2005, No. 2 Texas (12-0) vs. No. 1 USC (12-0), January 1, 2006, 93,986 fans, Rose Bowl, Pasadena, California: Texas 41, USC 38.

Texas (13-0) won the Bowl Championship Series game 41-38 to claim the title. So far, this game stands alone as the 21st Century's Game of the Century.

CHAPTER 4
ARIZONA STATE'S DAN DEVINE AND FRANK KUSH

FACT: Dan Devine and Burt Smith were colleagues on Duffy Daugherty's 1954 staff. In 1955, Devine was building a roster as Arizona State's new head coach. Smith encouraged Devine to take a gamble on Leon Burton, who had recovered from a near-fatal car accident. In 1957, the former Flint Northern star led the nation in rushing and scoring.

"Burt Smith was a great man. He cared about his players and kept in touch with them. He was always ready to help you."—Norm Bryant, founder of the Greater Flint African American Sports Hall of Fame.

Sometimes Leon Burton smiled, cognizant of why his daughter Lynnae Pickens handed him the latest photo to arrive in the U.S. Mail as an Arizona State halfback. He slid deeper into dementia's murky sea while cared for at a Las Vegas nursing home until his death at 87 in 2022. Yet somehow fans found him with autograph requests.

On the good days, he connected his record-setting career on the field with the requested autograph. He also understood off the field he established a progressive barrier-busting presence. He was Arizona State's first Black star, 1956 to 1958.

Leon Burton in a typical publicity shot of the era. *Courtesy Arizona State University.*

"It's amazing the number of cards and photos that come here, and how they know where to find him," Pickens said. "They write they followed his career and ask him to sign one card or photo, return it and keep the other. My father is a humble man, so I didn't understand he set all these records and what he accomplished at Arizona State.

"It's wonderful people still care and realize the impact he had on the football program and the school. It warms my heart. It's incredible. It truly is. On my father's good days, he's flattered by it all."

Burton was a small, speedy halfback in high school while he played for Flint Northern coach Burt Smith. In post-World War II America, Flint was a thriving Michigan automobile factory city. Burton, as a senior in 1952, ran for 1,050 yards and 10 touchdowns. In the spring, he won the 1953 Michigan High School Athletic Association's state 180-yards hurdles title with a state-record time of 19.1 seconds. "The Flint Flyer" was two-tenths off the national record.

Burton's prowess originally earned him a Michigan State scholarship, but a fateful chapter turned tragic. He was a passenger who survived a near-fatal single car accident. Six Flint Northern buddies piled in Houston McKell's new 1953 Buick Special, a graduation gift from his father, Houston "Mickey" McKell. The elder McKell was a Flint high-school legend who played pro baseball in the Negro Leagues. He was enshrined in the inaugural 1985 class of the Greater Flint African American Sports Hall of Fame.

The fateful night came not long before Burton was to leave for Michigan State. The friends were headed to Saginaw, an automobile parts factory town 36 miles to the north, to go roller skating. They had made the trip in the past, but this time McKell took the curve too fast at the fork in the road between North Saginaw Street and Dort Highway. The car slid off the road into a ditch, severely injuring all six. This, of course, was long before the late 1960s, when seat belts were mandated in the front seat of cars.

Norm Bryant, who founded the Greater Flint African American Sports Hall of Fame, still cringes when retelling the crash story 65 years later. Bryant was a sophomore on the Northern football team during Bryant's senior year.

"Leon nearly had his shoulder sawed off," Bryant said. "No one was killed, but they were all lucky to survive. With them filling the car, people wondered if bouncing into each other saved them."

Burton's other injuries were a punctured lung and internal bleeding. Doctors told him his sports career was over. But with time—a year and a half—Burton defied the odds through rehabilitation. As the 1955 calendar flipped closer to a new school year and football season, Burton felt he eager to return to his sport.

By then, though, Michigan State's recruiters had moved on. After all, Burton had missed the 1953 and 1954 seasons. The Spartans were a national power, winning the 1952 national title and posting a 28-game winning streak that extended into the 1953 Big Ten title season, topped by the January 1, 1954 Rose Bowl victory. The Spartans didn't have to take chances on damaged goods.

GO WEST, YOUNG MAN

Arizona State, by contrast, was a fledgling program with a 30-year-old, first-time head coach building his initial roster. The Sun Devils hired Dan Devine in 1955 based on his five seasons as a Michigan State assistant, 1950-54. Both Biggie Munn and Duffy Daugherty endorsed Devine to Arizona State athletic director Clyde B. Smith.

Devine remained deeply tied throughout his life to Daugherty. Their friendship dated to Devine's entry into coaching as a 23-year-old high-school head coach and teacher in 1948 at East Jordan High. The small school, located in a northern Michigan town on Lake Charlevoix, was coming off a winless 1947 season. Devine led back-to-back unbeaten teams (one tie each season) in 1948 and 1949. To celebrate the stunning 1948 success, school officials called Michigan State, asking to send a speaker to the football team's post-season banquet. Munn sent Daugherty.

Devine and Daugherty hit it off. Devine wrote about that first meeting in his 2000 book, *Simply Devine: Memoirs of a Hall of Fame Coach*. East Jordan is a three-hour-plus drive north from East Lansing, so Devine invited Daugherty to spend the night at his home with his wife Jo and infant twin daughters.

"I don't think there ever was a person who did more for other people, at least in athletics, than Duffy Daugherty," Devine wrote. "Duffy spent the night sleeping on the couch in the living room because we only had one bedroom. When Jo and I awoke in the morning and walked into the living room, he had one twin under each arm. That's how our long and great relationship began."

By 1950, Daugherty invited Devine to join Michigan State's staff as a graduate assistant. Devine finished his degree as Munn and Daugherty added roles each year. By the time Clyde Smith, a former Indiana head coach familiar with the Spartans, was searching for ASU's next head coach, Munn and Daugherty told him Devine was ready.

Devine brought with him two former Michigan State All-American players as assistant coaches, Frank Kush and Bob Carey.

Dan Devine leading the ASU Sun Devils. *Photo courtesy Arizona State University.*

Kush, who later succeeded Devine, was an All-American lineman in 1952. Daugherty had recruited Kush as an all-state player out of Windber, Pennsylvania, a coal-mining town not far from Daugherty's hometown of Barnesboro. Kush committed to Washington and Lee in Lexington, Virginia, which at the time was a Division I program. But after his freshman year, he called Daugherty to ask if he could transfer to play for the Spartans.

Kush died in 2017 at age 88, but in his 2015 book, *Frank Kush: The Incredible Life Story of a Coaching Legend in His Own Words*, he said of Duffy, "I felt a kinship with Duffy because he, too, was a coal miner's son."

Upon graduation, Kush spent 1953 and 1954 as a lieutenant in the U.S.

Army. When Devine offered him a job, he drove straight from Fort Benning in Georgia to Tempe.

Bob Carey was an All-American end in 1951 who played two NFL seasons before a knee injury interrupted his career. He coached one season under Devine and then resumed his NFL playing days.

As Devine and his staff prepared for the 1955 season, Burt Smith, Devine's colleague on the 1954 Michigan State staff, reminded Devine about Leon Burton. Yes, Smith had climbed the ladder to the college ranks, but he wasn't the type to forget about his high-school players.

"Burt Smith was a great man," Bryant said. "He cared about his players and kept in touch with them. He was always ready to help you."

Burton was small—a 5-foot-9, 175-pounder in college—but Devine was aware the Spartans had recruited him. Burton was presumed to be following in the footsteps of two former Smith players at Northern, Michigan State All-American picks Leroy Bolden and Ellis Duckett. Smith turned out talent like the Buicks rolling off Flint factory assembly lines.

Bolden and Duckett played on the Spartans' 1952 national title team and the 1953 Big Ten title team that won the 1954 Rose Bowl. Michigan State beat UCLA 28-20 with Bolden and Duckett both scoring touchdowns—Duckett on a 6-yard return of a punt he blocked and Bolden on a 1-yard run.

ON THE REBOUND

Smith believed Burton could turn his tragic chapter into a phoenix-like rise in the desert. On Smith's advice, Devine gambled on Burton's health. After all, his legs were unscathed from the car crash. The question was his shoulder holding up.

"Football was my father's first love," Pickens said. "To not be able to play because of the car accident devastated him. Through the grace of God, he got healthy again. But when he was able to resume a normal life the only jobs for Black people were working in a factory. When he got the call from Dan Devine to play football and go to college, it meant the world to him."

Soon enough, Devine knew he hit the jackpot. In Burton's first game on the 1955 freshmen team, he ran for 235 yards on five carries against Hardin-Simmons, a Division I school in those days.

During Burton's junior year in 1957 he led the nation in both rushing with 1,127 yards and in scoring with 96 points. The 10-0 record with a

Border Intercollegiate Athletic Association title was the school's first unbeaten team and first national ranking at No. 12. But the season also was significant as Burton became the first Black star leading a previously all-white program. Of his 16 touchdowns—12 rushing and four receiving—five were 75 yards or longer. He was on his way down a path that ultimately led him to join Bolden and Duckett in the Great Flint Area Sports Hall of Fame as well as the Greater Flint African American Sports Hall of Fame.

Prior to Devine's arrival, Arizona State was 4-5-1 in 1953 and 5-5 in 1954. Although Burton played on the 1955 freshmen team, he helped spark Devine's quick turnaround. Devine's 8-2-1 record in 1955 was followed by a 9-1 mark in 1956. Burton joined the 1956 varsity and showed flashes of himself despite playing the season through some nagging injuries. He totaled 60 carries for 532 yards (8.9 per carry) and four touchdowns. He added seven receptions for 75 yards (10.7 per catch).

Then came the magical 1957 title season. In addition to Burton's nation-leading numbers, this time he terrorized Hardin-Simmons' varsity with an Arizona State school-record 243 yards. As a team, the 1957 Sun Devils also led the nation in total offense (444.9 yards per game) and scoring (39.7 points). They finished the season in style, routing bitter in-state rival Arizona 47-7 to win the Territorial Cup game. In the two games prior to Devine coaching the Sun Devils, Arizona embarrassed the Sun Devils, 54-15 and 35-0.

Devine, who died in 2002 at age 77, often paid tribute to Burton's role building Arizona State's foundation. He was quoted in an article printed in the program for the induction ceremonies of the Greater Flint Area Sports Hall of Fame on December 12, 1987, at the Flint Regency Hotel.

"Leon made us at Arizona State," Devine said. "He was very instrumental in building our program, our stadium, and my career. His role in the early growth of Arizona State football tradition was just tremendous."

In *Simply Devine*, he wrote of Burton, "He might have been the best running back I've ever seen. I wonder how good he would have been on a national championship-caliber team, but he was extremely good for us."

Burton was an eighth-round pick by the San Francisco 49ers in the 1959 NFL draft, but his size contributed to him not making the team. A year later, though, former Hardin-Simmons coach Sammy Baugh gave him a shot in the American Football League. Baugh, the College and Pro Football Hall of Fame quarterback who was Hardin-Simmons' head coach from

1955 to 1959, was named head coach of the New York Titans. Burton played one year as a punt and kickoff returner.

Although Devine had arrived in Tempe with plans to follow the Daugherty blueprint—hitting Pennsylvania's fertile recruiting turf and ignoring unwritten quotas limiting rosters to a half-dozen Black players—another reason for the quick transition was Clyde Smith being of the same mindset while he was Arizona State's head coach and as athletic director.

Smith, who was from Pennsylvania, had begun recruiting Keystone State athletes and Black talent in his three seasons as the Sun Devils' head coach (1952-54). Smith was born in Monongahela, near Pittsburgh, played at Geneva College, a Pennsylvania school, and his first coaching job was at Red Stone High in Pennsylvania. He made his way to the desert with stops as head coach at Wisconsin State College-La Crosse and Indiana.

Devine inherited three Black Keystone players from Clyde Smith's roster. Two were brothers from Reading, Pennsylvania: All-BIAA lineman John Jankans, a senior in 1955, and Bart Jankans, a sophomore. Bobby Mulgado was a 1955 sophomore from McKeesport, Pennsylvania; Devine later considered Mulgado one of his top all-around players.

In addition to Devine adding Burton as a late member of the 1955 recruiting class, two more Black freshmen Devine recruited were Joe Belland of Pennsylvania and Al Carr of Phoenix. But as it turned out, Burt Smith wasn't done adding former Northern players to Devine's 1955 class. Norm Bryant was one of three more Black players who joined the freshmen team. Bryant was a halfback, Dave Copeland a halfback and Willie Fields a lineman.

Their roundabout path to Tempe began with Bryant learning from Arkansas A&M his scholarship was withdrawn. The Historically Black College and University in Pine Bluff told him there was a budget shortfall. Bryant, confused on what to do next, called Burt Smith, rather than Smith's successor. Smith had been Bryant's Northern coach as a senior in the 1954 fall season.

"Burt Smith was my coach," Bryant said. "I had problems with the new coach. To him I was one of 'Burt's Boys.' I called Burt, and he said, 'Hold on, let get me back to you.' He called Dan Devine, and Devine offered a partial scholarship—books and tuition."

But Smith didn't stop his lobbying there. Somewhere along the line of the conversation Devine found partial scholarships for Fields and Copeland. Although Bryant, Fields and Copeland didn't finish their careers at Arizona State, their presence helped Devine establish his plan to build fully integrated rosters. In sparsely populated 1950s Arizona, that meant tapping out-of-state talent.

He was transforming Arizona State's all-white rosters, including a 9-2 team in 1950, into a program of equal opportunity. Devine, though, learned to his dismay recruiting Black athletes at his new school was problematic.

"One thing that surprised me in Arizona was the attitude of some of the people toward minorities," Devine says in his book.

MAKING A STAND

Many of Arizona's early settlers in the late 1800s were former Confederates. Arizona wasn't admitted as the 48th state until 1912, and the state's schools were segregated until 1953. The Arizona population in the 1950 Census was only 756,000. Phoenix, the largest city, was growing rapidly, but the 1955 population numbered only 107,000. Among those 1955 denizens, there were few African Americans then as well as now. The 2020 U.S. Census listed the state as 54.1 percent white, 31.7 percent Hispanic and only 5.2 percent African American.

There were exceptions to Arizona State's all-white rosters. The Sun Devils' first Black letterman was Emerson Harvey, 1937-38. Joe Hernandez was a star Hispanic halfback on the 1939 and 1940 teams. By 1957, Devine grew his roster to seven Black players, which was more than most schools in the nation. A decade later, USC's 1967 national title team in diverse and heavily populated Los Angeles had only seven Black players. The Trojans' 1962 national championship roster had only five Black players.

Burton's success as a national star helped a largely white state to accept Black athletes. Winning teams intoxicate fans into making exceptions. Devine might otherwise have encountered more pushback from recruiting Black players.

But in America, race issues are never easily solved. Burton encountered his share of racism even as his star rose. Devine understood he needed to watch out for his Black players in the social climate of Arizona.

"My dad experienced racism," Pickens said. "Being a football star didn't change that for him individually or others as a group. There were times my father and mother would go out and they wouldn't be served. People love athletics, but they don't realize the things Black athletes had to go through despite their significant contributions to the team.

"Dan Devine knew it wouldn't be easy for my dad, and he watched out over him in a parental role. My dad called him, 'Daddy Dan.'"

Devine faced down another racial scene in his second season, when Arizona State was scheduled to play at Hardin-Simmons in Abilene, Texas. Devine learned in the past Arizona State's white and Black players stayed in separate Abilene hotels and ate at different restaurants.

The Lone Star State had fought on the side of Confederacy. It wasn't until June 19, 1865—more than two months after Confederate General Robert E. Lee surrendered to Union General Ulysses S. Grant at Appomattox—the slaves in Texas learned of their freedom. Union troops arrived in Galveston, Texas, informing Texans of the 1863 Emancipation Proclamation and end of the Civil War. Juneteenth began to be celebrated the next year as a Black holiday. President Joe Biden signed the Juneteenth National Independence Day Act on June 17, 2021.

In other words, a 1956 road trip to Texas was like visiting segregated Alabama.

Devine decided to provide Hardin-Simmons and the BIAA membership a lesson in civics and the U.S. Constitution. Devine told his athletic director if his team couldn't stay in the same hotel and eat at the same restaurants, he would put his players back on the bus and return home on the 890-mile one-way trip. Clyde Smith replied Devine had his support.

The trip went off without a hitch, including a win over Hardin-Simmons, 26-13. The message was sent throughout the BIAA, which in addition to Hardin-Simmons included Arizona, New Mexico State, West Texas State and Texas Western (now UTEP). Devine spoke of his "pride" over the change in policy in his book.

Stories like that weren't reported in sports media of the 1950s, but Devine's stance, through word-of-mouth, was enough to establish Arizona State's progressive plan to recruit Black athletes. Devine and Kush had Arizona State on a rapid ascent from the dusty days of the first half of the 20th century to fully integrated rosters.

The unbeaten 1957 season gave Devine a 27-3-1 (.887) record. Missouri was among a half-dozen schools that came calling. For Devine, the Big Eight Conference school represented a step up in national prestige. He also felt comfortable leaving Arizona State, believing Kush, who was only 29 at the time, was ready to become a head coach.

CONTINUITY WITH FRANK KUSH

Kush took the baton and continued to raise the program's profile. He stayed 22 years, compiling a mark of 176-54-1 (.765). He had the same mindset as Daugherty and Devine on integration. In Kush's book, he mentions his teammate Willie Thrower, the Spartans' backup quarterback behind All-America Tom Yewcic, and the first Black quarterback to play in the modern NFL.

Kush's first season started slowly at 2-3, but a five-game winning streak to end the year, including beating Arizona 47-0, left the Sun Devils 7-3 overall. The 3-1 BIAA record was second to Hardin-Simmons. Burton didn't put up another 1,000-yard season, but he made the All-BIAA team for the second straight year with 642 yards (5.9 per carry) and nine touchdowns. His 8.1 yards career per-carry average would rank him third among the NCAA career leaders, but his 285 carries was short of the minimum 300.

Kush continued building the program with BIAA titles in 1959 and 1961. In 1962, the Sun Devils left the dusty BIAA to join the newly formed Western Athletic Conference with fellow members Arizona, Brigham Young, Colorado State, Wyoming, UTEP, New Mexico and Utah. Arizona State won the 1963 WAC title, and then Kush's teams went on a dominant run of four straight league titles, 1969-72.

One of Kush's first hires as the new head coach in 1958 was Chuck Fairbanks, his Michigan State teammate. Fairbanks had been coaching high-school football at Ishpeming High in Michigan's frigid Upper Peninsula, but he quickly found his way to the desert.

"Frank Kush gave my dad a station wagon and a credit card and told him to find some players," recalled Fairbanks' son, Chuck Jr. "Kush told him to head across the desert to Texas."

Chuck Sr. found talent, including a Texas oil gusher in the 1960 recruiting class. He stopped at Grand Prairie's Black high school, Dalworth, and asked the school's coach if he had any college talent. The Dalworth coach threw up a sheet on the office wall and started a projector rolling film. The black-and-white images were fuzzy, but Charley Taylor stood out. He was fleet-footed while standing 6 feet, 3 inches.

Fairbanks offered Taylor a scholarship. Taylor, wanting to escape segregation, accepted without visiting ASU's campus. After all, the University of Texas under Darrell Royal was proud of its all-white rosters, so that option was closed to Taylor.

Taylor played halfback for the Sun Devils, rushing for a career total of 1,997 yards (5.7 per carry) and 25 touchdowns in three seasons, 1961-63. He was named a charter member of Arizona State's Hall of Fame in 1975.

Frank Kush at Arizona State University. *Courtesy Arizona State University Athletics.*

Taylor was the third pick of the 1964 NFL draft by Washington and was NFL rookie of the year. But in 1966, head coach Otto Graham switched Taylor to receiver, and Taylor was on his way to the Pro Football Hall of

Fame. He retired after the 1977 season with the NFL career receptions record—just before the NFL relaxed defensive rules to open up passing games. Taylor's mark stood until Charlie Joiner, playing in the San Diego Chargers' Air Coryell offense, broke it in 1984.

Although Kush's Sun Devils won a BIAA title with Taylor in 1961 and a WAC championship in 1963, All-American honors escaped Taylor. School reputations have plenty to do with All-American choices, especially for a program outside the major conferences. Burton's 1950s numbers and Taylor's 1960s number eventually helped future Sun Devils earn All-American recognition.

Arizona State's first Black All-American player in 1965 was Ben Hawkins, recruited out of Nutley High in New Jersey. His best season was as a junior in 1964 with 42 catches for 719 yards and five touchdowns. Those numbers propelled him onto the 1965 All-American radar. Although his numbers dropped off as a senior with 36 catches for 504 yards with no touchdowns, he made the All-American team.

Kush recruited another immensely talented player with Pennsylvania ties, but his All-American sport turned out to be baseball. Reggie Jackson, the Baseball Hall of Famer known as Mr. October, was from Cheltenham Township just outside of North Philadelphia. Jackson was a football and baseball star who wanted to play both sports in college.

That gave Arizona State an edge for two reasons. The first was Jackson's high-school coach: he and Kush were friends dating back to their days as Pennsylvania high-school athletes.

The second reason was Kush appreciated multi-sports athletes from his Michigan State days. Michigan State football coach-turned-athletic director Biggie Munn was an All-American football player and track and field shot putter. Michigan State track and cross-country athletes knew Munn emphasized that athletes needed to adapt and welcomed participation in multiple sports. For instance, Spartans quarterback Tom Yewcic was the College World Series Most Outstanding Player as a senior in 1954. He later played baseball in the Detroit Tigers' minor-league system and was an AFL quarterback with the Boston Patriots.

Jackson played on the 1964 freshmen team according to the NCAA rules of the era, but as it turned out played only one varsity season, in 1965.

In Arizona State's 1965 season finale, the Sun Devils beat Arizona 14-6 in a game remembered for a Curley Culp interception. Culp was an All-American defensive lineman and NCAA 1967 heavyweight wrestling champion who went on to a Pro Football Hall of Fame career with the Kansas City Chiefs. The interception came at a pivotal moment when ASU was clinging to a 7-6 lead. Kush credits Jackson for Culp's theft.

"Most people don't remember that the play was set up by the aggressive play on the defensive line by a young man named Reggie Jackson," Kush wrote. "The Wildcats were double-teaming Curley, as teams usually did, and that gave Reggie a chance to be very disruptive at the line of scrimmage. He was a valuable member of our team in the time that he was with us. I think he would have been an outstanding football player for a long time if he stuck with it. Unfortunately, he would only be with us for one season before leaving the team in 1966 to play baseball for Bobby Winkles on a full-time basis."

After Jackson's sophomore All-American baseball season in the spring of 1966, the Kansas City A's selected Jackson as the second overall pick of the amateur baseball draft. The franchise moved to Oakland in 1967, and Jackson was in The Show by the end of the 1967 season for 35 games. He was a full-time big leaguer by 1968, hitting 29 home runs out of his 21-year career total of 563.

Arizona State's football loss was the national pastime's gain.

In addition to the four straight WAC titles, 1969-72, the Sun Devils shared WAC titles in 1973 and 1977, sandwiched around a 1975 outright championship. Kush was named the American Football Coaches Association National Coach of the Year. His 1975 team was led by Michael Haynes of Marshall High in Los Angeles, proving Arizona State could draw elite talent out from under USC and UCLA. Haynes has been enshrined in both the College and Pro Football Halls of Fame.

The 1975 Sun Devils finished 12-0 and ranked No. 2. They entered the bowl games at No. 7 and upset No. 6 Nebraska in the Fiesta Bowl. The bowl games resulted in ASU voted No. 2 behind national champion Oklahoma, jumping previous No. 1 Ohio State, No. 2 Texas A&M, No. 4 Alabama and No. 5 Michigan.

The 1970s success ushered Arizona State into the west's premier conference. In 1978, the Pac-8 expanded, adding ASU and Arizona to form the Pac-10. Kush's 1978 Sun Devils proved they were ready for the step up when they upset No. 2-ranked USC 20-7 in a Saturday night, October 14 game played before 70,138 delirious fans at Sun Devil Stadium.

This was no ordinary USC team. Arizona State was the only team to beat the Trojans in a 12-1 season that ended with a national championship. Curiously, USC was forced to share the 1978 national title with

Alabama (11-1), even though the Trojans handed Alabama its only loss with a 24-14 victory on September 23 before 77,313 fans at Legion Field in Birmingham. Alabama coach Bear Bryant was a media darling, and the Associated Press poll (writers) voted the Crimson Tide No. 1. USC, under little-known third-year coach John Robinson, settled for the national title voted upon by the United Press International (coaches) poll.

Arizona State's upset of USC jumped the Sun Devils to No. 12, but after a bye week, the next game in Seattle proved to be Kush's waterloo. Washington routed the Sun Devils, 41-7, but the loss itself didn't spell Kush's doom.

A year later, ASU punter Kevin Rutledge claimed Kush punched him in the face after a poor punt in the Washington game. Rutledge filed a $1.1 million lawsuit against Kush and his staff for emotional and physical harassment.

Kush's 1978 punch took place two months before Ohio State coach Woody Hayes was fired for punching a Clemson defensive player after he was tackled on the sidelines following an interception. The punch happened in the Gator Bowl on national TV. Hayes' story faded with his immediate dismissal, but with the drawn-out tale of the 1979 lawsuit, Kush replaced Hayes as the football face of an abusive coach. He was fired midseason after ASU athletic director Fred Miller determined Kush had interfered with the investigation.

Although Kush had the reputation as a fiery coach prior to the Rutledge punch coming to light, he contended his success was based on preparation he learned from Daugherty.

"Duffy, in particular, always taught me that you can't win a football game by pleading with the team at the last minute or trying to give them an extra-inspirational pep talk moments before a big contest. The focus and the competitive desire are something you have to work on all year."

Kush was only 50 years old when he was fired, but he later coached in the Canadian Football League and the Baltimore/Indianapolis Colts in the NFL. He eventually outlived the ignominious end to his ASU coaching career.

In 1996, Arizona State invited him back as a goodwill ambassador, hosted a "Frank Kush Day" and named the playing surface at Sun Devil Stadium, "Frank Kush Field."

Michigan State honored Kush in 1997 with the Jack Breslin Lifetime Achievement Award. He was nominated for the honor by his old teammate, Hank Bullough, who was Daugherty's long-time assistant coach before he moved on to the NFL.

"Looking back, I was very lucky to end up at Michigan State when I did," Kush wrote. "It affected the trajectory of my life in more ways than one. Although I was going to school for an undergraduate degree at Michigan State, I received a master's degree in game of football."

BURT SMITH'S FORGOTTEN LEGACY

As for Burt Smith contributing behind the scenes to the Devine/Kush legacy, Smith's 29-year, multi-faceted career at Michigan State turned bittersweet. He began as a Daugherty assistant football coach on the varsity, 1954-60. Smith shifted after those seven years to taking on administration duties that included overseeing Duffy's office tasks, monitoring athlete academics and serving as the freshman coach, 1961-64.

Smith's roles were instrumental to the influx of players Daugherty recruited from the segregated South aboard the Underground Railroad. He helped them adjust to the freedom that came with college life above the Mason-Dixon Line and the academics of a Big Ten school.

Bubba Smith benefitted the most from Smith's watchful eye. Smith provided opponents plenty of trouble on the field, but he also was a mischievous headache off it. Nobody knew that better than Bubba's father, Willie Ray Smith Sr., who coached his son at Charlton Pollard High in his career as a legendary Texas high-school coach for 33 years at three Black schools during segregation.

"Bubba's father loved Burt," said Marty Daly, Michigan State's equipment manager at the time. "He knew Burt helped keep Bubba out of a lot of trouble. Burt kept a lot of guys out of trouble and stayed on them academically. When I've gone back for team reunions, the players all talk about how much they appreciated Burt."

When Burt Smith died in 1991 at age 74, Bubba Smith was quoted in the *Lansing State Journal*'s October 17, 1991, article.

"Burt was the guy who took the time with us," said one of college football's greatest defensive players, who died a decade later in 2011 at his home in Los Angeles. "I mean the precious time, the time when you are really lost and don't know where to turn. We all turned to Burt. I have never said this before, but he was the closest thing outside of my family to me."

As the 1960s progressed beyond Daugherty's 1965 and 1966 national championship teams, Burt Smith continued to shift his career into administrative roles. When athletic director Biggie Munn suffered a stroke, Smith was named interim athletic director in 1972. He served in a full-time role from 1973 to 1975.

However, Smith's career went unappreciated in real time. Worse, his career ended under two dark clouds. An NCAA football recruiting scandal resulted in the forced resignation of head coach Denny Stolz and the football program's three seasons of probation, 1976-78. The other cloud was a walkout by Michigan State's Black basketball players, despite head coach Gus Ganakas' popularity among the players, before the Spartans faced No. 2-ranked Indiana and coach Bobby Knight on January 4, 1975. Indiana, with the nucleus of the unbeaten 1976 NCAA champion, won 107-55.

Smith was replaced in the spring 1976 as athletic director and reduced to obscure jobs, including working from a cinderblock office in the basement of Munn Ice Arena.

"Burt's relationship with players was his great gift and probably made him a better associate staffer," said Lynn Henning, long-time *Detroit News* sportswriter and author of two books on Michigan State sports: *Spartan Seasons* and *Spartan Seasons II*.

"As an athletic director, he wasn't as facile, wasn't as dynamic, and his timing was awful as renegade recruiters torched the Denny Stolz era and brought on that terrible, and unnecessarily harsh, stretch of NCAA probation. The fact he and Jack Breslin (MSU vice president) weren't in synch pretty much guaranteed he was finished as AD. And from there he was sent into a kind of oblivion. But his players never forgot how essential he had been to their lives and careers."

Burt Smith has been forgotten at Michigan State, and he likely never stepped on Arizona State's campus unless there was an obscure NCAA meeting he attended as athletic director. But he played a valuable role in helping athletes launch their careers and gain induction into their respective school's Hall of Fame.

From Leon Burton and a roadside ditch in 1955 to Clinton Jones and the College Football Hall of Fame banquet at New York's Waldorf Astoria Hotel in 2015, from the Great Lakes to the desert, they're all connected as Burt's Boys.

CHAPTER 5
DAN DEVINE AND MISSOURI'S DESEGREGATION

FACT: Dan Devine led Missouri to its first Orange Bowl trip in 10 years in the 1959 season, only his second in Columbia. Devine, though, was haunted the rest of his life by a decision he made after the game over a country club's Jim Crow policy.

"Dan said many times over the years it was the worst decision he ever made."
—Phil Snowden, Missouri's Hall of Fame quarterback and former Missouri state legislator.

Dan Devine's background prepared him for the awkward moment, but bigots caught him off guard. A couple hours after his 1959 Missouri team lost to No. 5-ranked Georgia and quarterback Fran Tarkenton in the Orange Bowl, 14-10, the Tigers' team busses pulled into the parking lot of a segregated Miami country club.

The New Year's Day 1960 Orange Bowl was played as an afternoon contest. The two teams gathered for a dinner punctuated by light-hearted player skits in a quaint custom long since outdated by the modern high stakes of college football.

Officials met Devine in the Indian Creek Country Club parking lot to inform him Missouri's two Black players, Norris Stevenson and Mel West, weren't welcome. West and Stevenson were key players. West led the team in rushing and total yards, Stevenson was fourth in rushing and third in total offense. At the time, Missouri was the southernmost integrated program while Georgia, which was all-white until 1972, presented no such problem.

"Dan had a choice to make," said Phil Snowden, Devine's Missouri Hall of Fame quarterback, later a lawyer who served in the Missouri state senate. "He could leave and have us boycott the dinner, or he could take our team inside without Norris and Mel."

Devine was seemingly prepared for the moment, having cut his teeth as a Michigan State assistant coach, 1950 to 1954. In Devine's first job as a head coach at Arizona State (detailed in Chapter 4), he stood up to a previous segregation policy in Abilene, Texas, demanding the whole team stayed in the same hotel or he would turn around the bus and drive back to Tempe, 890 miles. Devine won the standoff, and the Sun Devils the game, 26-13.

The media of the 1960s, which avoided race in sports stories, failed to report the divine story of good winning out over evil. But for anyone hearing the Arizona State backstory, it adds to the puzzlement of what Devine was thinking on that 1960 New Year's night in Miami. He didn't protest, telling a team athletic trainer to take Stevenson and West to dinner elsewhere.

"I don't have an answer," said Snowden, who added the players were unaware of what was happening in the parking lot discussion. "Yes, it is strange."

The Miami decision haunted him the rest of his life.

"Dan said many times over the years it was the worst decision he ever made," Snowden continued. "If he had to do it over again, he would have left with his team. I heard Dan say it at least twice—at a team reunion and at a state legislature event. He said it multiple times to many groups."

Admitting his mistake indicated how much it haunted him. He wasn't pressed to apologize—not then or in future years. When reflective stories were written decades later, Stevenson and West didn't complain bitterly about the humiliation. Yet Devine apparently felt he needed to admit his mistake. It's a story that has gone down in history as little known as what happened in Abilene three years earlier.

For Devine, who died in 2002 at age 77, telling the story on himself may have been cathartic.

"I think that's true," Snowden said. "Dan was a very principled person. He didn't enjoy speaking before groups, but it was part of the job. He certainly wasn't a gregarious, backslapping guy, but he could express his thoughts and make a good speech. He owned up to that decision."

Devine, though, recovered from his mistake. His Missouri legacy featured both championship football and extending scholarship opportunities for Black athletes, just as he did at Arizona State, although he receives little credit for his integration leadership.

Missouri's 1968 roster numbered 14 Black players. The 1968 Tigers (8-3) were ranked No. 16 when they routed all-white No. 12 Alabama 35-10 in the Gator Bowl on Dec. 28 in Jacksonville, Florida.

Although 14 Black players don't sound like much by today's standards of predominantly Black rosters, Missouri was ahead of most schools, and a decade ahead of its nearby neighbors in the South. A year later Colorado, another Big Eight team, numbered only seven Black players when the Buffaloes defeated Alabama 47-33 in the 1969 Liberty Bowl. Similarly, USC won the 1967 national title with only seven Black players.

Missouri broke its color line in Devine's first season when Stevenson and West were promoted to the varsity as sophomores, in 1958. They had arrived in 1957 on the freshman team in the era when the NCAA prohibited freshmen eligibility.

FRANK BROYLES AND THE MISSOURI COLOR LINE

In one of those vagaries that make integration contradictions difficult to decipher, Frank Broyles recruited the pair in 1957, but Broyles left Missouri after one year to take the Arkansas job. Broyles was an unlikely figure for such a groundbreaking move. At Arkansas, he led all-white teams from 1958 to 1970, failing to recruit a Black player until Jon Richardson on the freshmen team in 1969.

In those days, Arkansas competed in the Southwest Conference against segregated Texas schools. Broyles, if he recruited Black players, had the entire state of Texas' Black athletes as a rich talent pool open to him.

"Dan accelerated the progress recruiting Black athletes, but Frank broke the ground," said Russ Sloan, a Missouri Hall of Famer who lettered for Broyles in 1957 and Devine the next two years. "You'd wouldn't have expected Frank to take the initiative considering his background, but that's what he did."

Broyles had spent his life in segregation. He grew up in Decatur, Georgia, and he played for Bobby Dodd at all-white Georgia Tech in the 1940s. He entered coaching as an assistant at two all-white schools, Baylor and

Florida, until Dodd brought him home to Georgia Tech, 1951-57. He was seeking a head coaching opportunity by the time the Northwestern job opened in 1955, but the position went to Lou Saban for a year and then Ara Parseghian.

By 1957, Missouri's legendary coach, Don Fauret, decided to retire following a third-straight losing season in a career dating back to 1935. At the end of Fauret's tenure, he implemented the ill-fated "Missouri Plan." His hope was to build a program with talent from within the state, but his idealistic plan backfired. Missouri high-school football wasn't strong enough to provide a full roster of Division I talent.

Fauret, serving in the dual role of football coach and athletic director, had previously tried to hire Broyles as his backfield coach in 1956, but Broyles remained at Georgia Tech. When Fauret retired, he pushed for Broyles as his 1957 successor. Broyles, in his 1979 book *Hog Wild: The Autobiography of Frank Broyles*, written with Jim Bailey, explained why he took the job despite his reservations about the "Missouri Plan."

"I wanted the job," Broyles wrote. "I took the approach I could coach and win on that Missouri Plan."

Broyles noted in *Hog Wild* that 13 players he recruited as freshmen in the 1957 class played as seniors on Devine's 1960 team, flirting with a national title before suffering the upset loss to Kansas.

However, Broyles doesn't reference two that stood out among the baker's dozen of 1957 recruits—Stevenson and West. Stevenson was from Vashon High, the Black school in St. Louis. West was from Jefferson City High, an integrated Missouri school. Stevenson was a mid-year enrollee in January 1957. His early enrollment accounts for why he was considered the first Black scholarship player over West, a traditional fall 1957 arrival.

Broyles goes on in the book to describe how Missouri's promising 1957 season unfolded with its 5-4-1 record. Just two years earlier the Tigers finished 1-9. Despite the promising 1957 season, Broyles explains he had had his eye on the Arkansas job since his days as a Georgia Tech assistant coach. Broyles and Arkansas athletic director John Barnhill first struck up a relationship when Georgia Tech and Arkansas met in the 1955 Cotton Bowl, won by the Yellow Jackets, 14-6.

However, Broyles, who died in 2017, didn't explain in his book his recruitment of Stevenson and West. At Arkansas—where he held the dual leadership role of athletic director and football coach—he didn't explain why he failed to recruit Black athletes on a campus with Black graduate students dating to 1948. Arkansas dressed Jon Richardson of Little Rock, its first Black varsity player, in 1970.

Broyles' dismal record on segregation was included in Richard Pennington's 1987 book, *Breaking the Ice: The Racial Integration of Southwest Conference Football*.

Upon Broyles' death in 2017, Pennington posted an article on August 16, 2017, on his website, *RichardPennington.com*, stating Broyles was the only coach who wouldn't agree to an interview for his book on desegregation. He did speak with Texas's Darrell Royal, SMU's Hayden Fry, Baylor's John Bridges, TCU's Fred Taylor, Texas Tech's J.T. King and Houston's Bill Yeoman.

Pennington says he lumps Broyles with Royal as "cowards" for failing to act. Alabama's Bear Bryant in the Southeastern Conference and Clemson's Frank Howard in the Atlantic Coast Conference dragged their feet over a similar time period. However, Bryant, decades later, benefitted from revisionist history surrounding the 1970 USC-Alabama game as a pivotal moment, shifting the narrative to him as a crusader. The success of spinning the myths pushed the true pioneers of the 1960s into the shadows, although they deserve credit for clearing the road for USC to play a 1970 game in Alabama without incident.

Adding to the mystery behind Stevenson and West breaking the color line in Missouri was the lack of media coverage. In fact, Stevenson said he accepted the scholarship unaware he was Missouri's first Black athlete. Broyles had assigned assistant coach John Kadlec to recruit Stevenson. Kadlec recalled the recruitment in a story posted in *SB Nation* on May 1, 2013.

"I guess I inadvertently never mentioned to him that he was going to be the first Black player," Kadlec said. "Norris, years later he brought that up to me. He said, 'You know, Coach, you never mentioned that to me.' And I go, 'Well, you know, Norris, I guess I recruited you as a football player—not as the first Black player. I considered you a football player.'"

Snowden and Sloan both said they don't remember Broyles discussing why he desegregated Missouri's program or expressing a need among the returning white players to welcome the newcomers. They added the same was true of Devine when Stevenson and West moved up to the varsity to take starting jobs from white players. But coaches set a tone—overtly or not—with their leadership. How the players respond to that leadership is a measure of a coach.

Stevenson's younger brother, Gerald Stevenson, wrote a guest story published in the *Columbia Missourian* on Feb. 12, 2013, that sheds some light his brother's attitude about blazing a trail.

"Apparently, Norris saw a bright light in MU," Gerald Stevenson wrote. "Oh, he was well aware of the university's racist past. But Norris was hardly ever preoccupied with just negative and ugly aspects of a situation. His modus was to evaluate a situation, weigh the advantages as best he could and make his decision accordingly. He was annoyed by any unnecessary distractions, including some Black critics and cynics fueled by misplaced envy. He dismissed their dissent as quickly as if swatting flies. Still, he was not waylaid into believing that MU had miraculously drunk from the Holy Grail and emerged singing, 'We Shall Overcome.'"

Snowden viewed Devine transitioning Missouri into the 20th century first as a player and later as a coach. Upon graduation, Snowden worked as an assistant coach with the freshmen team while attending law school. He later practiced law in Kansas City, his hometown. He was an agent for Missouri athletes along with launching his political career.

"I think one reason the transition went well without problems was Norris and Mel were such terrific guys and great players," said Snowden. "When I got to Missouri, I didn't know any Black players. You're just a kid happy to be a part of everything. We didn't think about race, but we all learned a lot from having Nelson and Mel as teammates."

Sloan, an All-Big Eight end and Missouri Hall of Fame inductee in 2011, echoed Snowden. Sloan went on to a successful coaching career at Northeast Missouri State, a Division II program now known as Truman State. He also served as athletic director at Southeast Missouri State and Fresno State.

"The beautiful thing about Mel and Norris was people gravitated to them," Sloan said. "Mel was more outgoing. He was cut up and loved to sing. Norris was more reserved and more serious. Both guys were well respected. I didn't sense ill feelings toward them on the team at any time."

Gerald Stevenson's article also credited his brother's 1957 freshman classmate, Jim Miles, a halfback. At the time, no doubt there were racist players with stereotypical Southern beliefs, but their attitudes didn't surface in ugly incidents. That's particularly significant considering it was still a time when Missouri's band played "Dixie" at games and campus fraternity houses flew the Confederate flag.

Miles has passed away, but his widow, Mary Lou Miles, shared stories he told her about the team. In the 1958 season, the year Miles, Stevenson

THE RIGHT THING TO DO 71

and West joined the varsity as sophomores, Missouri traveled to Texas A&M for the third game of the season.

The team arrived in segregated College Station for dinner together in the hotel's ballroom above the restaurant. The next day the Tigers played poorly in a night game and lost, 12-0. The players had the option of attending a team dinner or using the meal money to eat at a restaurant on their own. Miles was among nine players, including Stevenson and West, who opted for a restaurant. The team bus parked near campus hangouts. However, Miles led the party of nine into a restaurant refusing to serve Stevenson and West.

"Jim said he told the manager, 'You're serving all of us or none of us,'" Mary Lou recalled. "They all got up and left."

Curiously, Devine mentions learning about the Texas A&M incident in his autobiography:

"I prided myself on preparation, every detail, and even though we had lost the game, having our players in problems like this was far worse than a losing a football game. I should have known this was a possibility and been prepared for it. I vowed to never let something like this happen to my team."

But he did, in Miami a year later.

"I don't know why," Snowden said. "It's hard to explain."

Mary Lou Miles told another story about Jim picking her up for a date when they were in college. Mary Lou didn't recognize the car Jim was driving.

"Jim had loaned his car to Mel because Mel didn't want his car to be recognized picking up his white girlfriend for a date," Mary Lou said.

Miles' leadership, it should be noted, transcended egos involving playing time. In the three years they were on the varsity together as running backs, West and Stevenson had more carries and yards each year than Miles.

Stevenson's career was topped by his best game as a senior in 1960. He led the Tigers to their first win over Oklahoma in Norman in 24 years, Nov. 12, 1960. He ran for 169 yards, with touchdown gallops of 77 and 60, to help rout the Sooners 41-19. Missouri climbed from No. 2 to No. 1 with a 9-0 record, replacing Minnesota.

The final three weeks reshuffled the top ranking.

On Nov. 5, No. 3 Minnesota upset No. 1 Iowa and jumped to No. 1 in place of the Hawkeyes.

On Nov. 12, Minnesota was upset by unranked Purdue, 23-14. That was the same week No. 2 Missouri routed Oklahoma to assume the top ranking.

On Nov. 19, Missouri's 23-7 upset loss at Kansas cost the Tigers a national title. In those days, the final poll votes were taken at the end of the regular season. The same day Missouri lost its game, Minnesota upset No. 4 Wisconsin.

In the final poll to end the regular season, Minnesota was No. 1 and Missouri No. 5. Minnesota was declared national champion.

Missouri finished No. 5, but the Tigers beat No. 4 Navy and Heisman Trophy winner Joe Bellino in the Orange Bowl, 21-14. President-elect John F. Kennedy, a Navy fan as a World War II Navy hero, was in attendance.

Missouri officially finished 10-1 overall and 6-1 in the Big Eight, although with Kansas later forfeiting its win over Missouri, the Tigers have been sometimes listed as 11-0 and 7-0 in league play. The Tigers' No. 5 ranking remained the school's highest end-of-season football rating until head coach Gary Pinkel guided Missouri to No. 4 in 2007 and No. 5 in 2013.

AN EARLIER MILESTONE

The upsets late in the regular season left behind some intriguing considerations of Black historiography—how history was or wasn't recorded.

If Missouri had avoided the upset against Kansas and won the national title, Devine's 1960 team would have earned a place in history as the first Southern school with Black athletes to win a national championship. Stevenson and West would be the South's first Black players to win a national title.

Oklahoma won the 1956 national title with its last all-white team. Prentice Gautt was on the 1956 freshmen team before he joined the varsity in 1957 as Oklahoma's first Black player. He was a two-time All-Big Eight running back in 1958 and 1959 and played eight years in the National Football League.

Another 14 seasons passed until Alabama shared the 1973 national title with Notre Dame. When Alabama won the UPI national title in 1973 (Notre Dame took the AP, NFF and FWAA crowns), it marked the first time a Southern school with multiple Black players won a national title.

If Missouri had won the 1960 national title and the media had done its job of noting Stevenson and West were the first Black players from a Southern school to win a national championship ring, the milestone could have advanced the pace of schools recruiting Black athletes. But whether the media would have properly covered the moment is a big "if."

As an example, Minnesota quarterback Sandy Stephens was the first Black quarterback to earn All-American honors and lead his team to a national title in the same 1960 season, but the accomplishments weren't trumpeted until years later. Similarly, Michigan State's Jimmy Raye's accomplishment as the first Southern Black quarterback to lead his team to a national championship was ignored at the time.

Devine's final Missouri team in 1970 totaled 13 Black players and was paced by two NFL-bound offensive stars. Running back Jim Harrison led the team in rushing with 702 yards and 12 touchdowns. Wide receiver Mel Gray caught 26 balls for 705 yards and nine touchdowns as a junior in 1969 and 27 passes for 449 yards and two TDs in 1970.

Harrison, from San Antonio, Texas, went on to play four years with the Chicago Bears. Gray, from Santa Rosa, California, played 12 seasons with the St. Louis Cardinals.

Gray had spent a year in junior college before arriving in Columbia as a sophomore in 1968. He said one reason he committed to Missouri was Devine allowed him to both play football and run track. Gray won the California high-school state title in the 100-yard dash in a record time of 9.4 seconds, a mark that stood until the state switched to metric distances in 1979.

Stevenson, who died at age 72 in 2012, finished his college days as a three-year football letterman as well as a track and field star. He was inducted into the Missouri Hall of Fame in 2001. Stevenson went on to play one season in the Canadian Football League with the B.C. Lions. He was a track and field coach for 30 years at two Missouri community colleges, Forest Park and Florissant Valley.

West, who died in 2003 at age 64, was a three-year letterman who led the team in rushing all three seasons. He was enshrined in the Missouri Hall of Fame in 1993. He played two seasons in the American Football League with the Boston Patriots and New York Titans. He returned campus to earn his master's in education degree and served as a principal for 23 years with the Minneapolis Public Schools.

In 2001, Missouri invited Stevenson and West back to campus to serve as grand marshals for the homecoming parade. The school also inaugurated a $25,000 scholarship in Stevenson's name and built the Norris Stevenson Plaza of Champions outside of Fauret Field at Memorial Stadium.

Eventually, Devine's increased opportunities for Black athletes in the 1960s added to significance to the pioneering roles Stevenson and West played.

"Norris and Mel were a year behind me at Missouri, but Dan recruited a lot of Black athletes in the 1960s," said Snowden, a senior in 1959. "Johnny Roland, George Seals, Monroe Phelps…Russ Washington. It's a long list."

By the 1966 season another Missouri milestone was set. Missouri halfback Charlie Brown, an African American from Jefferson City, Missouri, was pictured on the cover of the team media guide with three white teammates.

Interestingly, the photo might have included Willie Lanier under different circumstances. Devine recruited Lanier, but Lanier opted to attend Morgan State, an Historically Black College and University closer to his Virginia home.

Lanier went on to earn enshrinement in both the College Football Hall of Fame and the Pro Football Hall of Fame. He was a 1967 NFL first-round draft pick by the Kansas City Chiefs, playing 11 seasons with a Super Bowl IV title and eight All-Pro selections.

Roland was a running back from Corpus Christi, Texas. He earned All-Big Eight honors in 1964 and 1965. As a senior in 1965, Roland was Missouri's first Black team captain in any sport and was named an All-American choice. The 1965 Tigers (8-2-1) defeated segregated Florida in the Sugar Bowl, 20-18, with Roland throwing an option touchdown pass.

Roland played eight NFL seasons before entering the coaching ranks under Devine with the Packers, in 1974. Roland moved with Devine to Notre Dame for a year in 1975 before he returned to the NFL. By the mid-1980s, Roland and Jimmy Raye were among the NFL assistant coaches mentioned in the media as prime candidates to become the first Black NFL head coach. That milestone, of course, was crossed by Art Shell, in 1989 with the Los Angeles Raiders.

Neither Roland nor Raye received their chance as a head coach, but if they had, their pioneering trails both traced to Michigan State coach Duffy Daugherty. Raye was hired by Daugherty with the Spartans in 1972 before his move to the NFL with the San Francisco 49ers in 1977; Devine coached with Daugherty as an assistant.

Missouri's Francis Peay was another Devine recruit who broke ground both as a Black athlete and Black college coach. He was recruited out of Pittsburgh, earned All-Big Eight honors as a senior offensive tackle in 1965 and was a New York Giants first-round draft pick in 1966. He played nine NFL seasons before entering coaching through Devine, who hired Peay as a Notre Dame assistant in 1977.

Nine years later Northwestern named Peay as the second Black head coach in the Big Ten. Peay had coached at Cal before he joined Dennis Green's Northwestern staff. When Green returned to the NFL, Peay was promoted from defensive coordinator and coached the Wildcats for six seasons.

DEVINE'S MISSOURI LEGACY

Missouri's progress continued, but after a disappointing 5-6 season in 1970, Devine listened when the Green Bay Packers made a pitch to hire him. Devine accepted the job in 1971 as head coach and general manager.

Devine's Missouri legacy established leadership among Southern schools integrating their rosters in the 1960s. But by the turn of the century, old-world racial animus grew between the Black community in St. Louis and the Columbia campus 125 miles to the west. As President Barack Obama said while in office 2009-2017, race in America often takes a step or two forward followed by backlash and a step backward.

Gary Pinkel, hired as Missouri's new head coach in 2001 after 10 successful seasons at Toledo, realized the backlash upon taking the job.

"We realized shortly after I took the job that there was some friction between the African-American community and the Mizzou program, particularly in the St. Louis area," said Pinkel in his 2017 autobiography, *The 100-Yard Journey*. "That was something we had to address. In March 2001, not long after the national signing day, Demetrious Johnson, a former Mizzou player who had influence in the St. Louis area, reached out to me to talk about the problems that had lingered for years."

Among other former players supporting efforts to mend fences was Norris Stevenson.

"Norris would become a close friend and a great asset in the St. Louis community," Pinkel wrote. "It was important that our program recognized Norris' legacy and his significant place in Mizzou history. We established a scholarship fund on his behalf and made his name a more prominent fixture around the program, including the Norris Stevenson Plaza of Champions."

The healing helped Pinkel rebuild the program, compiling a 191-110-3 record in 15 seasons. Missouri shared two Big 12 North titles in 2007 and

2008 and won two Southeastern Conference East crowns in 2013 and 2014.

By the 2015 season, with racial conflicts on Missouri's campus seemingly taking the school backward in time, Pinkel supported his players threatening a protest over racial issues on campus. The players had joined a student-led protest demanding the school's administration address racial issues on campus. One Black student, Jonathan Butler, staged a hunger strike.

The players targeted a boycott of an upcoming game on November 14 against Brigham Young at Arrowhead Stadium in Kansas City. Missouri had a bye week on Nov. 7 as they began to discuss boycotting the next game. Pinkel backed his players with a Twitter post on Sunday, November 8, stating, "The Mizzou family stands as one. We are united. We are behind our players." The school also announced practice on Nov. 8 was canceled.

After a week-long buildup, by Monday, Nov. 9 the school backed down. Chancellor R. Bowen Loftin and President Tim Wolfe resigned over their handling of the controversy and protests. A campus environment that was seemingly regressing to attitudes of the 1950s began to return to the enlightenment Frank Broyles and Dan Devine brought the football program by recruiting Black athletes.

One reason for the threatened boycott success: the story gained heavy national attention. It was the kind of coverage lacking in the 1950s and 1960s when milestones were recorded.

Pinkel retired following the 2015 season. His support of Missouri's players meant he left behind a program that followed the legacy of Devine's Missouri teams.

CHAPTER 6
COLORADO, SONNY GRANDELIUS AND THE ORANGE BOWL

FACT: Colorado's 1961 Big Eight champions, led by team captains Joe Romig and Chuck McBride, declined their invitation to the Orange Bowl. They wanted assurances their five Black teammates received hotel, dining and transportation accommodations due any American citizen.

"We didn't care if we stayed in Miami Beach, but wherever we stayed, we were staying together and eating together as a team. Or we weren't going at all."—Colorado's Joe Romig, College Football Hall of Famer, Rhodes Scholar and astrophysicist.

———

Colorado's 1961 football team gathered in 2011 for a 50th anniversary celebration of their Big Eight championship and Orange Bowl trip. As with any such reunion, backslaps and hugs abounded. Their tales of big plays on the field and off-the-field escapades grew grander with decades of retelling.

Some members had passed away, of course, including Sonny Grandelius, who in 1961 was the Buffaloes' third-year, 32-year-old head coach from Michigan State coach Duffy Daugherty's staff. He died at age 79 in 2008.

Colorado captain Joe Romig. *Courtesy University of Colorado.*

Ted Woods, the team's leading rusher as a 1961 senior and a Canadian Football League veteran, died young in 1988. Woods had returned to campus in the offseason to earn a master's degree in business and then a law degree. He served on many boards as well as Colorado's Minority Advisory Committee. Upon Woods' sudden death by heart attack, Colorado established a law-school scholarship in his name.

But the missing team members deepened the friendship bond. They can eternally take comfort in having lived through turbulent times in America's race relations on the right side of history. The civil rights saga experience by the 69 white players and five Black teammates was worthy of a Martin Luther King sermon.

They stood up to segregation in Miami.

Bill Harris in action. *Courtesy University of Colorado.*

Bill Harris, one of five Black players on the 1961 roster and the team's third-leading rusher, took the microphone during the reunion. Harris was a former Colorado Alumni C-Club Director after playing five years in the CFL and three seasons in the National Football League. Harris called up the other three surviving Black teammates as he reminded the audience the Buffaloes had initially turned down the Orange Bowl invitation.

"The four of us thank you for what you did," Harris said.

What they did was tell the City of Miami and the Orange Bowl they wanted assurances their five Black teammates would receive the same hotel, restaurant and travel accommodations due any American citizen.

"Bill delivered a beautiful speech about how thankful the four of them were," said John Meadows, a sophomore end on the 1961 team. "You talk about not a dry eye in the house. I'm starting to tear up telling you about it now."

The moment epitomized a verse from the school's fight song, "shoulder to shoulder."

The Buffaloes' steadfast posture grew from their acrid experience traveling to Miami for their third game of the season. Colorado played the University of Miami in a nonconference date on October 13 at the Orange Bowl. Upon the team's arrival at the airport, Colorado's Black players were transported on a different bus and stayed at a different hotel. Road trips come and go quickly, so soon enough the Buffaloes were back home after defeating the Hurricanes 9-7 before 40,393 fans.

"Quite frankly, many guys were unaware of what happened," Meadows said. "When you're that age you get on the bus where you're told and what time you're told."

Another reason for the lack of awareness was the Black players didn't draw attention to their second-class treatment. Despite growing up in northern states, they were accustomed to double standards in the nation's various forms of systemic racism.

But once the Buffaloes were back on campus, Colorado team captains Joe Romig and Chuck McBride called a meeting in the locker room. Romig, a lineman, is a College Football Hall of Famer, Rhodes Scholar and astrophysicist. McBride, a linebacker, went on to a long coaching career as an assistant best known for his time as Nebraska's defensive coordinator directing the renowned Blackshirts defense under head coach Tom Osborne.

"It was more of a here's what-happened-type meeting," Meadows said. "We were already back home, so we couldn't do anything about it. And with the rest of the schedule, we weren't going anywhere we'd expected to have that problem again."

SHOULDER TO SHOULDER

But as midseason arrived, the Buffaloes continued to defy preseason projections. The 1961 Buffaloes were coming off 5-5 and 6-4 seasons in Grandelius' initial two years as a first-time head coach, but 1961 turned out to be his breakout year. The Buffaloes opened with back-to-back Big Eight wins at Folsom Field, defeating Oklahoma State 24-0 and Kansas 20-19. The Kansas victory was a sign the Buffaloes could be a surprise contender. The Jayhawks had won the league title in 1960 until they were forced to forfeit two games and the title for using ineligible players.

The season's fifth week, October 28, Colorado traveled to Oklahoma and defeated the Sooners, 22-14. It was Grandelius' second straight win over Oklahoma and legendary coach Bud Wilkinson. Colorado had never beaten the perennial power since joining the Big Eight in 1950. Grandelius' predecessor, Dallas Ward, had posted a winning overall record of 63-41-6 in 11 seasons, but he was fired for an 0-8-1 record against Oklahoma.

Then came the pivotal sixth week. The No. 8-ranked Buffaloes were 5-0 overall and 4-0 in the Big Eight as defending conference champion Missouri's No. 10-ranked Tigers (5-0-1, 3-0-0) arrived for a showdown in Boulder.

Missouri head coach Dan Devine and Grandelius were old Michigan State friends. Grandelius was an All-American halfback at Michigan State in 1950, the same year Devine joined Daugherty's staff. Devine's final year under Daugherty, 1954, was Grandelius' first of five seasons as a Daugherty assistant. They were two of four future head coaches on Daugherty's famed 1954 staff, along with Bob Devaney (Wyoming and Nebraska) and Bill Yeoman (Houston).

On gameday, Colorado beat Missouri 7-6 before the largest home crowd of the year, 43,000. The Buffaloes had a one-game lead on Kansas and Missouri with two conference games to play. Since the Big Eight champ had an automatic invitation to the Orange Bowl, that meant Miami's segregated hotels and restaurants—not the sunshine and beaches—were back on the players' minds.

A week later, the Buffaloes stumbled with a loss at home to Utah, 21-12, but the nonconference result didn't change the Big Eight standings. Colorado clinched the league title the next game, November 18 at Nebraska, with a 7-0 victory. The Buffaloes owned a one-game lead and the tiebreaker with one to play over Kansas, while Missouri fell two games back with a loss the same weekend to Oklahoma.

PASSING ON AN ORANGE BOWL TRIP

But the Orange Bowl officials didn't travel to Nebraska. They saved extending their formal invitation for the following week. The Buffaloes' final league game was November 25 against underdog Iowa State. With the title in hand, Romig and McBride called another team locker-room meeting. The Buffaloes decided they weren't returning to Miami. That is, not unless the team was assured there would be no repeat of the indignities their Black teammates experienced in October.

"We didn't need a vote," Meadows said. "It was an easy decision. Those were our guys. They were our teammates."

Ironically—and it's a prime example of how frustrating life can be for African Americans navigating a society riddled with daily prejudices—the only objections raised were from the five Black players. Harris, known as "Buffalo Bill Harris," explained why in an interview for this book a month before his death on April 5, 2022 at age 76.

"We didn't want to be the reason the team didn't go to the Orange Bowl," Harris said. "But Joe and Chuck said that's the way it was going to be."

Because of the informality of the meeting, the players overlooked the need to inform Grandelius—not to mention the school's athletic director or president. And word never leaked to the media, although that likely didn't matter. The 1960s sports media avoided race, and the Denver and Colorado media members were true to times with their brethren.

"No, there was never anything in the newspapers about it," Meadows said.

On gameday, the Buffaloes manhandled Iowa State 34-0 to wrap up an unbeaten 7-0 conference record and a 9-1 overall mark. The fans threw oranges onto the field. The players reveled in the celebration before they retreated to the locker room. After a few more minutes of backslapping, Grandelius called for the players' attention at the center of the locker room. He introduced three Orange Bowl officials. The trio dressed in orange jackets joyfully extended the invitation.

Then, Romig and McBride stepped forward.

"We're not going," Romig said.

The room fell silent. Grandelius and Orange Bowl officials stood with slack-jawed expressions.

"Sonny just about crapped his pants," said Meadows, laughing at the six-decade-old memory.

Eventually, the players explained their stance to Grandelius and the Orange Bowl officials.

"We didn't care if we stayed in Miami Beach, but wherever we stayed, we were staying together and eating together as a team," said Romig, recalling events for this book. "Or we weren't going at all."

Once Grandelius understood the situation, Meadows and Romig added, he supported the decision. Grandelius, in addition to his Michigan State background playing with Black teammates and coaching Black athletes, spent his first two years out of college as a lieutenant in the newly integrated U.S. Army. Grandelius served in Korea and was decorated with a Bronze Medal for bravery.

"Sonny supported us," Meadows said. "Sonny was great. He was from Michigan State. Two of our assistant coaches were from Michigan State."

He referred to Buck Nystrom, an All-American lineman for the Spartans in 1955, and John Polonchek, a three-year letterman and Grandelius's college roommate.

"We didn't think anything of having Black teammates," Romig said. "It wasn't a big deal to us. Sonny had recruited and coached Black athletes at Michigan State. He supported us."

Harris added, "We didn't have problems on the team."

Details are fuzzy in memories on how exactly the players explained their point to Grandelius, school officials and the Orange Bowl. That's another failure of the 1960s media to record the first draft of history.

But if the players had thought of it, a profound method would have been pointing out the irony of Woods representing the United States in the 1960 Rome Olympics. Woods, who won the 1960 NCAA 400-meter title in a meet-record 45.7 seconds, was named to the U.S. track and field team's 1,600-meter relay team that won the gold medal, although Woods was an alternate for the gold medal race.

Romig and coach Sonny Grandelius.

In other words, Woods could represent his country in a U.S. uniform in Italy, but he wasn't welcome to stay in a Miami hotel.

No matter the method delivering their point, the City of Miami and Orange Bowl officials got the 20th-century message. They agreed to the U.S. Constitution-protected conditions. The return trip went off without a hitch—other than No. 7 Colorado's 25-7 loss to No. 4 LSU. And since polls were voted upon at the end of the regular season rather than after bowl games in those days, the final No. 7 ranking was the highest in program history.

The one-sided loss was a disappointment, but no one blamed the result on distractions over the Orange Bowl saga. If anything, Grandelius was overly zealous in preparing his team.

"Before we left for Miami, Sonny had us out there practicing two-a-days in the cold," Romig said. "He had us scrimmaging on Christmas Day."

For anyone wondering why NCAA rules are strict about practice time in modern football, those are two good examples.

There was another factor contributing to Colorado's players arriving for the Miami regular-season game unaware of the indignities awaiting their Black teammates. The Buffaloes historically didn't have Black players. Colorado's Black population in 1960 was only 2 percent. In 2020, it's only 4 percent.

Franklin Clarke—named for President Franklin D. Roosevelt—was the school's first Black football player as recently as 1955. Clarke was from Beloit, Wisconsin, but he attended Trinidad State, a community college in Colorado, before transferring to Boulder. He was honorable mention All-Big Eight in 1955 and went on to play 11 NFL seasons, three with the Cleveland Browns and eight with the Dallas Cowboys.

John Wooten of Carlsbad, New Mexico, arrived in 1955 and played on the freshmen team. He earned All-American honors as a senior offensive lineman in 1958 and enshrined in the College Football Hall of Fame in 2012. Wooten played 10 NFL seasons, including blocking for Pro Football Hall of Famer Jim Brown with the Cleveland Browns. Wooten, though, established a bigger name in football history as an NFL executive with three franchises and serving as the director of the Fritz Pollard Alliance, which promotes opportunities for Black coaches.

Despite Clarke and Wooten not arriving until the mid-1950s, the first two Black players left footprints.

Romig, who was on the 1958 freshman team, recalled being brought up to practice with the varsity or play on the scout team. He often faced Wooten, then a senior, and another of the Buffaloes' top linemen, Mel Semenko, then a junior. Semenko eventually played three seasons in the Canadian Football League.

"Wooten and Semenko used to throw me around," Romig said.

Bobby Anderson, a Colorado All-American running back in 1969, was born in Midland, Michigan, but after his family moved to Boulder, has often said he was drawn to Colorado football as a fan early in his grade-school years because of Clarke and Wooten.

When Grandelius arrived in 1959, there were two Black players on Colorado's roster: Woods from Pittsburgh and Oliver Martin from Denver's Manuel High. Woods was entering his first varsity season as a sophomore and Marvin his junior year. Romig, who attended Lakewood High in suburban Denver, and Marvin were old friends. As two of the state's top high-school wrestlers, their coaches got them together as workout partners.

Grandelius recruited Harris in his 1959 class out of Hackensack, New Jersey.

"Sonny heard about me from some friends in New York," Harris said. "I had a game in high school when I ran for a touchdown, and I ran out of my shoes. The next thing I knew that was all over the sports pages, and I was hearing from Sonny."

Apparently, other schools' coaches didn't have friends like Sonny's, who read the newspapers. Harris, a high-school senior in the 1958 football season, drew interest only from Iowa and Ohio State among major schools.

"It was frustrating to only hear from Iowa and Ohio State," Harris said. "In those days, you thought about attending Black schools. I was hearing from Grambling."

Colorado was off Harris' radar, but Grandelius, with a helping hand from Harris' mother Christine, soon convinced him to take a recruiting trip to Boulder.

"He recruited my mom first," Harris said. "He came to our home, sat down with my family and sold them on Colorado. I liked he was straightforward—not behind the scenes stuff."

Harris, it turned out, was ready to commit before he arrived on campus. He flew into Denver, followed by a 28-mile drive to Boulder. The contrast from grey urban grittiness of New Jersey to the clear blue skies of the Rocky Mountains as the backdrop to CU's campus in a valley was striking.

"I came over Highway 36 into Boulder. I said, 'Oh, my goodness!' We stopped to take in the scenic view. That was it."

In Colorado's 1960 recruiting class, Grandelius signed three more Black players: Ed Coleman, a receiver, Carnegie, Pennsylvania; Noble Milton, a halfback, Herminie, Pennsylvania; and Al Hollingsworth, offensive tackle, Omaha, Nebraska.

Harris added Grandelius was conscious of the obstacles a Black recruit faced far from home while attending a nearly all-white school next to a whiter community.

"Sonny took good care of the Black players and led us in good directions," Harris said. "He made connections for us with Black mentors in Denver. He looked out for us."

Grandelius appeared to be on his way to building a Big Eight power, but only a month after the Orange Bowl, rumors surfaced of a football slush fund used in recruiting. The NCAA investigated and released inconclusive findings on April 27, 1962, but in a power struggle played out among university regents. Grandelius was fired on March 17.

Both Romig and Meadows said there were violations, but other coaches at other schools survived such controversies when supported by the administration. Meadows said some players were reimbursed for travel expenses to return home. He explained some older players who were recruited by the previous coach were angered Grandelius's younger recruits were getting money.

"I liked Sonny a lot," Romig said. "When he came here, they recruited people like they did in the Big Ten. There was rule breaking. But if the administration had stuck with Sonny, Colorado would have been a powerhouse in the mid-1960s."

More importantly, though, was Grandelius's presence as Colorado's head coach in 1961. The college landscape, especially in the 1960s, was ruled by iron-fisted, intolerant coaches.

With the media's cooperation, Colorado's bold stance went unknown and unappreciated by the public. How many minds might have been opened up by the Colorado story?

"It would have been good for the country," Romig said. "It would have drawn attention to the inequities and motivated people to correct them. The USA is very keen on football. To have football players speaking out, that's different than left-wing people speaking out."

Grandelius's dismissal sent Colorado's program into reverse. Bud Davis coached one year with a 2-8 record. Eddie Crowder succeeded Davis, but his 1963 and 1964 teams also posted 2-8 records until he turned around the program. The Buffaloes posted three straight winning seasons followed by a 4-6 record and a bounce back in 1969 with an 8-3 mark. The 1969 season included beating Alabama coach Bear Bryant's all-white team in the Liberty Bowl. But Colorado's 1969 roster only had seven Black players. The Black athlete opportunities had only grown by two in the previous eight years.

The program continued its up-and-down history until Bill McCartney arrived in 1982 and eventually guided Colorado to a 1990 national title. McCartney had emphasized recruiting Black talent, but the school was still dealing with the issue of minorities on a white campus in a white community. *Sports Illustrated's* Rick Reilly wrote a scathing article in the February

27, 1989, issue detailing the number of McCartney minority players that had been arrested. Some of the cases involved responding to racial taunts.

In the same article, Colorado academic advisor Theo Gregory was quoted: "If you're a Black football player here, you're ethnically a minority because you're Black, socially a minority because you're an athlete, culturally a minority because you might come from the projects, economically a minority because you can't afford to drive a BMW and physically a minority because you're bigger than everybody else. Somebody racially slurs you, and you might have a tendency to overreact."

What if Colorado had established a culture of racial understanding on campus and in the Boulder community dating to the 1961 season? All that goodwill from an unknown story went unused.

But that's not the fault of the 1961 players. They remained proud of their time representing the 1961 Buffaloes and their legacy. The pride oozes from Meadows' voice while retelling events.

He has remained in Boulder since his college days, including 35 years as an executive with the Coors Brewing Company. He also served a stint as Colorado associate athletic director. He has turned 80, but continues to work as an agent for several women's basketball coaches.

But Meadows' life story in Colorado includes an ironic twist. Grandelius had recruited him out of Royal Oak, Michigan. After the 1960 fall season on the freshmen team, Meadows, feeling homesick, he hoped to leave Colorado and transfer to Michigan State. Meadows grew up a Michigan State fan. The Spartans' 1957 Final Four basketball particularly captured his heart while he was a sophomore in high school. That season, Johnny Green led the Big Ten champions to their first Final Four.

The 1957 Final Four in Kansas City, Missouri, remains one of the dramatic in college basketball history. North Carolina, led by national Player of the Year Lennie Rosenbluth, beat the Spartans in triple-overtime in the semifinal. The Tar Heels survived another triple-overtime game in the final with a win over Kansas and Wilt Chamberlain.

"I remember listening on the radio to that Final Four with Johnny Green and Lennie Rosenbluth," said Meadows, referring to a time before the NCAA basketball finals were on TV. "I can recite the play-by-play verbatim."

Meadows, upon returning home for Christmas, contacted Daugherty, who had recruited him in high school. He asked if he could drive up to East Lansing and while there asked Daugherty to take him as a transfer.

Daugherty agreed but with conditions.

"Duffy said, 'We'll take you because you're a Michigan boy. But you have to promise me you will go back to Colorado, go through spring ball and not flunk any classes.'"

Meadows agreed. To his surprise, by the end of spring football and spring classes, he felt a deeper bond with his Colorado teammates. He decided to stay with the Buffaloes. Upon returning home for the summer, he drove back to East Lansing to tell Daugherty he decided not to transfer.

"Duffy told me, 'That's the best decision you could make. Good luck to you.' I realized later Duffy knew what he was doing telling me to go back to Colorado for spring ball and keep my grades up. He gave me the best advice I could ever receive. I don't think you'd see that from college coaches today. I'm a huge fan of Duffy Daugherty. I always root for Michigan State when they play Michigan.

"Duffy used to send me Christmas cards to me and my wife up until a year or two before he died, and I never played for him."

The 1961 Colorado football team deserves a proper place in the pantheon of sports breaking down narrow-minded prejudices. It's one of college football's best stories rarely told.

The courage the Colorado players showed was missing from too many Americans who looked the other way as the civil rights movement progressed. Such silence—Martin Luther King Jr. called it the "appalling silence of good people"—allowed for segregation in the form of Jim Crow laws in the segregated South and systematic racism elsewhere to continue a century after the Civil War.

Coincidentally, there was another 1961 case—one that escaped history—of a football team bound for a major bowl threatening a protest over segregation. UCLA's eight Black players said they would not take the field in the Rose Bowl upon learning Alabama could be their opponent. They had learned Alabama coach Bear Bryant was seeking a backdoor entry to the Rose Bowl in place of the traditional Big Ten entry. The story is elsewhere in this book, Chapter 25, "UCLA and Jim Murray Battle 'Bama, Bryant."

In both cases, the sports media of the 1960s failed to properly report on the reactions of college football players standing up to segregation. *Los Angeles Times* columnist Jim Murray wrote a column that confronted Bryant, but otherwise the Los Angeles and national media tip-toed around the issue.

Imagine if such stories were covered by today's media standards. Reporters and outlets would have blanketed the story like around-the-clock coverage of Missouri's 2015 team protesting racism on campus. Or San Francisco 49ers quarterback Colin Kaepernick taking a knee at the expense of his career to protest police brutality.

Or imagine if the producers that green light sports documentaries dug a little deeper in research to tell the full story of Colorado and the Orange Bowl, UCLA and the Rose Bowl or Duffy Daugherty's impact on the college football integration through his own teams and his assistant coaches as head coaches.

Instead, the college-football desegregation story that HBO, Showtime and ESPN have fallen all over each other to produce have been based on the false premise the 1970 USC-Alabama game led the way. Events from the 1960s paved the way for USC to travel to Alabama in 1970 without incident.

Those steps include Colorado's 1961 football team taking a bold stance in Boulder.

CHAPTER 7
OKLAHOMA, CHUCK FAIRBANKS AND BARRY SWITZER

FACT: Oklahoma, like many schools in the 1960s, followed an unwritten quota limiting Black players on rosters to single digits. That changed in the late 1960s and 1970s under Chuck Fairbanks and Barry Switzer.

"Chuck and I felt the same way. We wanted the best athletes. Recruiting Black athletes was the right thing to do." —Barry Switzer, Oklahoma's offensive coordinator under Chuck Fairbanks prior to 16 years as head coach.

Chuck Fairbanks and Barry Switzer seemed an odd couple to push Oklahoma's slumping mid-1960s football program into the 20th century of equal opportunity. They were from opposite backgrounds and worked together only one season as assistants, 1966.

Fairbanks, a native of Charlevoix, Michigan, played three seasons at Michigan State, 1952-54, on integrated teams.

Switzer was from the segregated South, playing at all-white Arkansas from 1958-60 and coaching at his alma mater from 1961-65. The Razorbacks remained all-white until 1970.

However, it turned out Fairbanks as head coach (1967-72) and Switzer as offensive coordinator fit like a glove. They were like-minded coaches in both football schemes—innovative option offenses—and progressive attitudes—recruiting Black athletes. They followed Daugherty's practice of ignoring the long-standing college custom of limiting rosters to a half-dozen or so African Americans.

"Chuck and I felt the same way," Switzer said. "We wanted the best athletes. Recruiting Black athletes was the right thing to do."

Oklahoma numbered only six Black players on its 1966 varsity roster under head coach Jim Mackenzie. Fairbanks took over in 1967 and pushed the needle toward double digits. By the 1971 Game of the Century, when No. 1-ranked Nebraska beat No. 2 Oklahoma 35-31, the Sooners numbered 16 Black players and seven Black starters, including running back Greg Pruitt, a two-time All-American pick in 1971 and 1972 recruited out of segregated Houston.

Under Fairbanks, Oklahoma won or shared three Big Eight titles in 1967, 1968 and 1972. He was *The Sporting News* Coach of the Year in 1971. When Fairbanks left for the New England Patriots as their head coach in 1973, Switzer was promoted. Switzer (1973-88) continued pushing the numbers into the 20s and 30s until the roster was predominantly Black in the 1980s.

In Switzer's 16 seasons as head coach, he won or shared 12 conference crowns and three national titles. He was *The Sporting News* Coach of the Year in 1973 and the Walter Camp Coach of the Year in 1974. The College Football Hall of Fame enshrined him in 2001.

Fairbanks died in 2013 at age 79, but his son, Chuck Fairbanks Jr., spoke for him when he and Switzer were interviewed for this book.

Chuck Jr. combined his father's football instincts on and off the field. He had the talent to play quarterback at Norman High and at the University of Houston under Bill Yeoman, a former Daugherty assistant who desegregated the Cougars' program in 1964. After Chuck Jr.'s playing days, he practiced his father's recruiting savviness as a salesman in the car business. Chuck Jr. owns and operates Chuck Fairbanks Chevrolet in DeSoto, Texas, near Dallas.

"My dad was a good salesman with all colors," said Chuck Jr. "He was able to recruit well in Black communities. He knew the coaches, and he always said, 'You have to get to know the momma.'

"He was always comfortable coaching and recruiting Black athletes. A lot of Black athletes who played for my dad were at his funeral. They said they felt he was a fair- and open-minded man."

An irony of Fairbanks/Switzer sharing social attitudes: Fairbanks grew up Charlevoix, Michigan, a community that was whiter than Switzer's hometown of segregated Crossett, Arkansas.

Charlevoix is a small postcard resort town on Lake Michigan near the northern tip of the state's Lower Peninsula. Fairbanks graduated from Charlevoix High in 1951. Charlevoix's 1950 census population of 2,700 was whiter than a winter snowfall, but his teammates the next four seasons included Black All-American stars from Michigan factory towns.

"My dad always talked about how he didn't know anything about Black athletes until he got to Michigan State," Fairbanks Jr. said. "He had grown up in northern Michigan, but when he got to Michigan State, he was around all these great Black athletes."

Biggie Munn was Michigan State's head coach from 1947-53 with Daugherty his top assistant until he was promoted to head coach, 1954-72.

"My father, from listening to him over the years, thought the world of Biggie Munn and Duffy Daugherty," Chuck Jr. said. "He had journals and notes he took from them in his playing day. He studied their coaching styles. Michigan State was foundation of his football roots."

The Michigan State assistant coach who recruited Fairbanks was Dan Devine, a Spartans assistant (1950-54) under both Munn and Daugherty. Devine, prior to his five seasons at Michigan State, was the head coach at East Jordan High, a one-school town near Charlevoix.

East Jordan had been dominated by Charlevoix, a powerhouse in the area, until Devine arrived and managed "upsets" with tie games in 1948 and 1949. Fairbanks was a sophomore and junior on those teams, and Devine returned in 1950 to recruit Fairbanks to play for the Spartans.

But there is more to the small-world story. Fairbanks' girlfriend and future bride—Virgeleen Thomson, affectionately known as "Puddy"—was an East Jordan cheerleader and babysitter for Devine. As Chuck Jr. tells the story, his father was at a dance when he asked Charlevoix's Tuck Thomson about the pretty girl across the room. Tuck told him it was his sister, one of 12 Thomson siblings on the family's dairy farm. Chuck and Puddy were married 63 years until he died in in 2013.

In 1952, Fairbanks' sophomore year, the Spartans won the national title behind All-American quarterback Tom Yewcic. But Fairbanks also regaled his son with stories about Willie Thrower, Michigan State's backup quarterback. Thrower was the first Black quarterback in the modern era of the NFL with the Chicago Bears in 1953 as a rookie undrafted free agent.

Thrower was popular with the players and fans despite his backup role. The legend was he could throw the football 100 yards, but he admitted when asked it was actually "only" 80. In the Spartans' one-sided wins that brought on the backups, Michigan State's fans were known to chant, "We want Willie! We want Willie!"

"I remember my dad telling me about Willie Thrower and how talented he was throwing the ball," Chuck Jr. said.

Fairbanks was a junior on the 1953 Big Ten title team that defeated UCLA in the 1954 Rose Bowl, 28-20. Two of the Spartans' four touchdowns were scored by Black athletes from Flint, a Michigan factory town known as Buick City.

Fairbanks Sr., who played end for the Spartans, cut his coaching teeth as a high-school head coach at Ishpeming (1955-57), a mining town in Michigan's Upper Peninsula near Marquette. But he climbed the college coaching ladder in warm-weather states through his Michigan State connections.

His first college job at Arizona State (1958-61) was through Devine and Frank Kush, the Sun Devils' head coach, 1958-79. Devine had brought Kush, an All-American lineman, with him when he landed the ASU job (1955-57). When Kush was promoted to head coach in 1958, he contacted Fairbanks, his teammate at Michigan State. Fairbanks was an ASU assistant from 1958 to 1961.

Next, Bill Yeoman, Houston's head coach from 1962-86, offered Fairbanks a bump in pay and responsibility as a Cougars assistant (1962-65). Fairbanks' next move to Oklahoma didn't include a Michigan State connection, but the offer from Mackenzie was another step toward his goal of becoming a head coach.

A COACHING FRATERNITY

Switzer, living in Norman in his retirement years, became close to Daugherty through Fairbanks. Switzer thus has a perch on the Fairbanks branch of the Daugherty coaching tree without having coached under him. Another Daugherty/Switzer link was Daugherty's long friendship with Bud Wilkinson, the Sooners' College Football Hall of Fame coach, 1947-63, with three national titles.

"Duffy was one of my favorites," Switzer said. "I got to know him first through the Kodak All-American Coaches Clinics he put on every year with Bud Wilkinson. As coaches with integrated teams, we were in our own bubble. Black kids knew they could turn to us as their coaches. Sometimes you also had to be their dad."

Switzer grew up in the "swamp bottoms" of Crossett, a segregated town of 5,000.

In Switzer's 1990 book, *Bootlegger's Boy* with Bud Shrake, he candidly tells the story of his father Frank as a bootlegger and womanizer. Swamp bottoms of Arkansas sounds like something out of a Mark Twain book, but Frank Switzer wasn't your typical son of the South. The Switzers were more Neil Young and "Southern Man" than Lynryd Skynyrd and "Sweet Home Alabama."

Barry explained his father employed African Americans, and he gained respect that a typical Southerner lacked for Blacks. He also routinely competed in playground sports with Black youths he met while walking through their neighborhood to his all-white school.

"That's the way I grew up," Switzer said. "My Daddy was a bootlegger, and all the people that worked for him were Black gentlemen. They were always around us kids.

"Back then, a bank wouldn't loan a Black man $200. I saw this happening. I saw my dad take care of the Black community. He would loan them money. He was a bootlegger, but at the same time he took care of people. It was important I learned that from him. I knew I was doing the right thing when I was recruiting Black athletes. I never thought about it."

Switzer left home to play at Arkansas for legendary coach Frank Broyles as a lineman and a linebacker, 1958-60. His first year out of school Broyles hired him as an assistant, 1961. He coached running backs on the 1964 national championship team, which included two linemen that went on to greater football fame—Jerry Jones and Jimmy Johnson. Jones, owner of the Dallas Cowboys, hired Johnson as his head coach, and the Cowboys won Super Bowl titles in the 1992 and 1993 seasons. When Jones and Johnson had a falling out, Jones hired Switzer, and the Cowboys won Super Bowl XXX after the 1995 season.

That 1964 Arkansas team beat Nebraska in the Cotton Bowl 10-7 to finish 11-0. Alabama was voted the national champion by the Associated Press (writers) and United Press International (coaches), but in the poll era, the Razorbacks were named No. 1 by the Football Writers Association of America, and Notre Dame was the National Football Foundation's choice as national champion.

The 1965 season was Switzer's final one at Arkansas before he followed Mackenzie to Oklahoma as offensive-line coach. Having spent his playing and coaching career at one school under one coach, Switzer believed the move to Oklahoma enhanced his resume to someday becoming a head coach.

Mackenzie's task was rebuilding Oklahoma football. After Bud Wilkinson, who won national titles in 1950, 1955 and 1956, retired following the 1963 season, the program dropped off. Gomer Jones, Wilkinson's assistant for 17 years, was promoted to head coach. His Sooners were 6-4-1 in 1964 and 3-7-1 in 1965. Jones' loyalty to the program as an assistant didn't buy a third year.

Mackenzie's Sooners opened 1966 with a 4-0 record, but three losses by a combined seven points down the stretch resulted in a 6-4 finish. Mackenzie, though, was named the Big Eight Coach of the Year with wins over Texas in the Red River Rivalry and No. 4-ranked Nebraska. There were reasons for optimism over the program's direction.

AN UNEXPECTED PROMOTION

In the offseason, Devine, then Missouri's head coach, asked Fairbanks if he wanted to rejoin him as the Tigers' offensive coordinator. But since Fairbanks had only been at Oklahoma for one season under Mackenzie, he turned down the offer.

As it turned out, fate intervened. Mackenzie dropped dead of a heart attack on April 28, 1967, at age 37. Oklahoma president George Cross, recognizing the start of 1967 fall camp was only a little more than three months off, stayed in-house. But he bypassed Mackenzie's top assistant, Pat James.

Fairbanks, who was 33 years old, was promoted to head coach. Fairbanks named Switzer, who was 32, his offensive coordinator.

"My dad wasn't a popular choice in 1967," Fairbanks Jr. said. "He had never been a head coach, and a lot of people wanted a higher-profile name. But the President of the university took a liking to my dad. President Cross believed in him."

Fairbanks and Switzer had only worked together a year, but Oklahoma clicked under their partnership. The Sooners won the 1967 Big Eight title and finished with a 10-1 record, including a win over Tennessee in the Orange Bowl. Tennessee was ranked No. 2 and Oklahoma No. 3 entering the game in the era when the final polls were voted upon at the end of the regular season.

Oklahoma ran the Power-I offense suited for sophomore fullback Steve Owens' bruising style. The 6-foot-2, 215-pounder led the team with 869 yards rushing and 13 touchdowns in 1967. He was on his way to posting back-to-back, 1,500-yard seasons in 1968 and 1969. Setting an NCAA career rushing record of 3,867 yards propelled him to winning the 1969 Heisman Trophy despite playing on a 6-4 team.

But the Sooners' drop-off to 7-4 in 1968 and 6-4 in 1969 turned the Sooners' fans to grumbling. Fairbanks began to hear calls of "Chuck Chuck." He decided to switch to the explosive Houston Veer option offense from his days with the Cougars under Yeoman.

The Sooners opened the season 2-0, but the victories were uninspiring over SMU and Wisconsin, teams on their way to losing records. The third game was a 23-14 loss at home to Oregon State, another mediocre team that finished 6-5. The hot seat turned hotter.

Switzer had lobbied for Fairbanks to switch to the wishbone to start the 1970 season, but Fairbanks opted for the Houston Veer. With the slow start and the Sooners enjoying a bye week between the Oregon State loss and the Texas game, Switzer pitched the wishbone again. He felt Oklahoma quarterback Jack Mildren was better suited to the wishbone than the Houston Veer, which required more passing ability from the quarterback than the wishbone.

Fairbanks gave Switzer the green light, but a bye week wasn't enough preparation to spring the wishbone successfully on Texas, the innovators of the scheme. The Longhorns introduced the wishbone to college football in 1968 and won the 1969 national title with an 11-0 record. Texas was still rolling as the 1970 edition of the Red River Rivalry at the Cotton Bowl loomed.

The Longhorns were 3-0 and ranked No. 2 after routs of Cal (56-14) and Texas Tech (35-13) and a win over No. 13 UCLA (20-17). Next up was unranked Oklahoma (2-1). Texas rolled to a 41-9 victory.

But Fairbanks and Switzer saw enough from Mildren to stick with the switch to the wishbone. In Oklahoma's Big Eight opener the following week, the Sooners traveled to Boulder and upset No. 13 Colorado, 23-14. By season's end the Sooners returned to the national rankings at No. 20 with a 7-4-1 record. They were second in the Big Eight to national champion Nebraska.

The 1970 turnaround with improving talent launched Oklahoma to back-to-back 11-1 seasons in 1971 and 1972. By the 1971 season, Fairbanks and Switzer had assembled a fully integrated roster with 16 Black players, seven Black starters and a Black team captain, Glenn King.

The 1971 Sooners were 11-1, but they settled for second in the Big Eight and No. 2 in the nation after losing to Nebraska 35-31 in the next iteration of the Game of the Century. The final polls were a 1-2-3 sweep for the Big Eight: No. 1 Nebraska, 13-0 with an Orange Bowl win; No. 2 Oklahoma with a Sugar Bowl win, and No. 3 Colorado (10-2) with an Astro-Bluebonnet Bowl win. Colorado's only losses were to Nebraska and Oklahoma.

The 1972 Sooners finished 11-1 again and No. 2 in the nation, but this time to USC (12-0). However, they won the Big Eight with conference victories the last two weeks of 17-14 win over then-No. 5 Nebraska in Lincoln and then-No. 20 Oklahoma State 38-15.

AHEAD OF THE CURVE IN OKLAHOMA

Fairbanks and Switzer were able to evolve Oklahoma into a fully integrated program ahead of other schools thanks to good timing. Oklahoma institutions complied sooner than other segregated states with the 1954 *Brown v. Board of Education* ruling outlawing segregated schools. The process was well underway in Oklahoma by the 1960s rather than dragged out to the 1970s elsewhere in the South.

The evolution began in the fall of 1955 when four Black players attempted to make the freshmen team as walk-on candidates: George Farmer Jr., Sylvester Norwood, Frank Wilson Jr. and Charles Parker. The foursome endured the practices and racial abuse until one by one they either suffered injuries that ended the season or quit the team over the abuse. None of them played in one of the three freshmen games that weren't played until November.

In the NCAA era of freshmen ineligibility on the varsity, Wilkinson had left coaching the freshmen team to the freshmen coaches. But in 1956 he took an active interest in seeing Oklahoma follow through on integrating its football program.

Prentice Gautt of Oklahoma City's Douglass High had been the first Black athlete permitted to play in the Oklahoma high-school all-star game in 1956. Wilkinson offered him a scholarship to join the freshmen team, but then he met resistance from alumni not to follow through with the free education. The problem was solved when a group of Tulsa doctors and pharmacists combined funds to pay for Gautt's college expenses. Wilkinson subsequently awarded Gautt a scholarship entering his sophomore year. The remaining funds raised were used for other Black students.

Gautt was named an All-Big Eight running back as a junior and senior. His junior season, 1958, Oklahoma defeated Syracuse 21-6 in the Orange

Bowl played on January 1, 1959. Gautt was an Academic All-American pick in 1959 and went on to an eight-year NFL career. He coached at Missouri and earned a Ph.D in psychology.

"Prentice Gautt was Oklahoma's first Black player in 1956, but after that there were only two or three Black players on the team," said Mike Brooks, an Oklahoma football historian. "Then there were four or five. It wasn't until later in the 1970s the team began to get to 40 or 50 percent Black players."

Fairbanks and Switzer began reshaping Oklahoma's rosters by targeting the state of Texas. The 1968 class was Fairbanks' first full year of recruiting as the head coach. The seven Black players formed the largest class of African Americans in program history. The 1968 class included defensive back Glenn King of Jacksboro, Texas. As a senior in 1971, King became Oklahoma's first Black team captain.

Fairbanks and Switzer were both well positioned to dip into the Lone Star State. Fairbanks had recruited Texas as an assistant at both Arizona State and Houston. Switzer also recruited Texas while at Arkansas.

Targeting Texas in the late 1960s also meant no competition from Texas and Arkansas, the two all-white programs dominating the Southwest Conference in the 1960s. The 1968 Texas and Arkansas recruiting classes were all-white. When they did sign their first Black recruits in 1969, they only signed one each.

Oklahoma's 1969 recruiting class included running back Greg Pruitt from Houston's B.C. Elmore High. Pruitt went on to the College Football Hall of Fame and played 12 NFL seasons. Two other 1969 Black recruits on their way to NFL were tight end Al Chandler (seven years) and defensive lineman Raymond "Sugar Bear" Hamilton (nine years). Both were from Gautt's alma mater, Frederick Douglass High in Oklahoma City.

There were seven African-American freshmen in the 1970 recruiting class along with an eighth Black player, Willie Franklin, recruited as a junior-college transfer out of San Diego's Mesa College. Franklin played on the 1970 and 1971 teams and one NFL season with the Baltimore Colts.

By the 1971 season, Oklahoma had "out-wishboned" Texas. The Longhorns' wishbone was based on big backs running inside. The Sooners' scheme focused on blocking mismatches and speed to the perimeter. Oklahoma beat Texas five straight from 1971 to 1975, outscoring the Longhorns 167-60. The scores included 48-27 in 1971, 27-0 in 1972 and 52-13 in 1973.

"We had track meets every week," Switzer said of Oklahoma's 1970s teams.

The 1971 Sooners averaged 44.5 points a game, outscoring opponents 534-217. In 1972, Oklahoma averaged 33.2 points per game, outscoring teams 399-74. Oklahoma's 1971 team set a still-standing NCAA record of 472.4 yards per game. Pruitt set a still-standing national record of 9.0 yards per carry.

"I'll tell you what," Switzer said. "They say records are made to be broken, but our national rushing record will never be broken. Nobody runs the ball anymore. Greg Pruitt averaged nearly a first down every time he touched it."

Pruitt earned All-American honors as a junior and senior, but he introduced himself to college football his sophomore season in the 1970 Astro-Bluebonnet Bowl when the Sooners played all-white Alabama to a 24-24 tie. Joe Wylie was Oklahoma's all-conference back in 1970, but against Alabama Pruitt broke off touchdown runs of 58 and 25 yards to finish with eight carries for 97 yards. Oklahoma finished with 415 total yards and 349 rushing.

Pruitt and the wishbone, Switzer believes, had more to do with Alabama's football revival in the 1970s than the myths surrounding the 1970 USC-Alabama game and USC fullback Sam Cunningham.

"Bear Bryant was smart enough to recognize using the wishbone after we played them," Switzer said. "He saw us with Greg Pruitt put 300 yards on their ass and they went to the wishbone."

The premise of the 1970 USC-Alabama myths was Alabama's loss to USC's Black athletes allowed Bryant to recruit convince his bigoted fans to allow him to Black athletes. Alabama's fans finally accepted an all-white team was too small and too slow to be competitive.

Bryant didn't deliver his new playbook to his team until 1971 fall camp opened, after secretly meeting in the offseason with Royal and his Texas coaches to learn the wishbone.

He closed his practices leading up to the season opener, a USC rematch at the Coliseum. Prior to kickoff, Bryant had his offense warm up on the Coliseum turf in Alabama's 1970 pro-set offense. He sprung the wishbone on the unsuspecting Trojans, winning 17-10.

In the 1970s, there were only two programs with 100 victories, and they both ran the wishbone: Oklahoma (101-13-2) and Alabama (103-16-1).

Fairbanks' last class was in 1972 prior to moving on to the NFL as the New England Patriots' head coach in 1973, but Switzer continued the equal-opportunity recruiting.

BUILDING ON INTEGRATION SUCCESS

"My philosophy was I was going to recruit the best players at all the positions," Switzer said. "I thought that was the right thing to do. I didn't give a damn what they were. I was recruiting to my playbook. All of our coaches felt the same way."

Oklahoma's first Black quarterback was Thomas Lott of John Jay High in San Antonio, Texas. He was a freshman backup in 1975 and three-year starter, 1976-78.

"We started recruiting Black players and Black quarterbacks before Alabama's Bear Bryant and Southeastern Conference schools," Switzer said. "Texas and other Southwest Conference schools didn't start doing it until after we were kicking the s--- out of them."

Lott arrived at Oklahoma five years before Bryant recruited his first Black quarterback, Walter Lewis (1980-83). In 1970, Bryant had told Condredge Holloway, a highly recruited high-school quarterback in Huntsville, Alabama, he would only take him as a defensive back. Holloway instead went to Tennessee as the SEC's first Black quarterback and three-year starter, 1972-74. There is now a statue of Holloway outside Neyland Stadium along with three other Tennessee Black pioneers: Lester McClain, Jackie Walker and Tee Martin.

"I made a comment later in life—people said it was a racist statement—I'd rather recruit a Black quarterback to play for me," Switzer said. "I got my ass chewed out for what I said. I know what I want in my playbook. I know what I want in a quarterback. Every white quarterback I recruited got beat out by a Black quarterback because of the offense we ran. How many white tailbacks are there in college and the NFL? Don't tell me what I need to do. I know what to do to win, and it was the *right* thing to do."

Switzer's recruiting tentacles soon began to stretch beyond Texas. He pursued Tony Dungy of Jackson, Michigan, a star quarterback on his way to a Pro Football Hall of Fame coaching career.

"I thought we could get Tony Dungy," Switzer said. "I visited with him in his home."

Dungy considered Michigan State and other Big Ten schools before he picked Minnesota under Cal Stoll, another former Daugherty assistant. Stoll was a Daugherty assistant from 1959 to 1968, but by the time he arrived at Wake Forest (1969-71) and Minnesota (1972-78), his schools had a track record of recruiting Black athletes rather than implementing a trend as Daugherty's other assistants had done.

Dungy was a three-year starter for Stoll, 1974-76. Black quarterbacks in college football grew increasingly common in the 1970s, although they were recruited for their ability to run an option offense and converted to defensive backs in the NFL.

Switzer landed plenty of other talented players, though. His next national title in 1985 was led by Jamelle Holieway, a Black quarterback recruited from Banning High in Wilmington, Los Angeles, California.

"We became predominantly Black in the 1970s and all of the 1980s," Switzer said. "I still recruited white players. It was never a factor with me. We were never on a quota system like some schools. They only recruited Black skill players."

Oklahoma's 1970s wishbone success led to Switzer as a candidate to succeed Daugherty as Michigan State's head coach. Daugherty and Switzer knew each other from coaching conventions, but they grew closer during in the offseason preceding the 1972 season. Daugherty contacted Fairbanks about learning more about the Sooners' offense.

"Chuck said, 'I want you to spend some time with Duffy,'" Switzer said. "I want you to help him with the wishbone."

During the season, Daugherty called Switzer on Sunday nights with an upcoming opponent's defensive alignment and how he expected the opponent to defend the Spartans' wishbone. Switzer drew up suggested plays. In the pre-Internet age, they exchanged information through the U.S. mail. Switzer had copies run off on a mimeograph machine, stuffed them in an envelope and sent them to East Lansing.

"We didn't even have fax machines back then," Switzer said.

However, the Spartans didn't have Jack Mildren, Oklahoma's 1971 All-American QB, to execute the offense. Nor a Steve Davis, Thomas Lott, J.C. Watts or Jamelle Holieway. Davis led the 1974 and 1975 national championship teams, Holieway the 1985 national title club. Lott led the No. 2-ranked team in 1978 and No. 4 team in 1979.

Switzer's wishbone wasn't a magic formula for the Spartans. Daugherty didn't have a quarterback in 1972—Black, white or plaid—to effectively run the wishbone. After a 0-2 start, Daugherty switched defensive back Mark Niesen to quarterback.

The Spartans' struggles reached 0-4, but they finished 5-5-1. The second-half run included a 19-12 upset of No. 5 Ohio State at Spartan Stadium. The Spartans won with defense and four field goals to go with the one touchdown. Niesen scored the lone touchdown after the Spartans were set up at the Ohio State 6-yard line on defensive back Bill Simpson's fumble recovery. Niesen kept the ball on the option around the left end and tossed the ball in the air in celebration.

"I was tripped up as I was going into the end zone," Niesen said. "I remember I threw the ball in the air. The ref came up to me and said, 'Son, next time you hand that ball to me.' I started laughing and said, 'If there is a next time, I will.' We weren't scoring a lot of touchdowns."

Daugherty had announced his retirement at midseason, sparking the 4-1-1 finish. Once the season concluded, Daugherty encouraged Switzer to seek the job.

"Duffy knew I knew what I was talking about with the wishbone and the difference I could make," Switzer said, "He was trying to get me the job."

Switzer was one of the finalists along with Louisville's Lee Corso (later Indiana's head coach and an ESPN college football personality), Iowa State's Johnny Majors (later a national champion as Pitt's head coach and head coach at his alma mater, Tennessee) and Denny Stolz, the Spartans' defensive coordinator. Stolz, who was Alma College's head coach (1965-70), was pushed on to Daugherty in 1971 with the backing of a prominent booster from Alma, a small town in central Michigan.

During the interview process, Switzer realized neither Daugherty nor athletic director Burt Smith had a voice in choosing the next head coach. The decision-makers were President Clifton Wharton, who was in his third year on the job, and three long-time MSU administration executives: vice-president Jack Breslin, faculty representative John Fuzak and assistant athletic director Clarence Underwood. Daugherty had been feuding with Breslin and Fuzak over cutbacks to the program. Smith was a Daugherty disciple as a former assistant coach.

"Lee and I interviewed on the same day, and Burt gave us a ride back to the airport," Switzer said. "When we got to the airport, Lee asked, 'What do you think?' I said, 'I'll tell you what I think. They'll keep the guy that is there. Burt has no clout in this thing.'"

Stolz was hired, coaching from 1973 to 1975 until he was forced to resign in the wake of an NCAA scandal. Daugherty's son Dan said in interviews years later his father never wanted Stolz to get the job.

Stolz's appointment was announced Dec. 12, 1972. A month and a half later, Fairbanks surprised Oklahoma, announcing on January 26, 1973, he was taking the job as the Patriots' head coach.

"It all worked out," Switzer said. "Chuck recommended me to replace him. If I had been at Michigan State when Chuck took the New England job, I would have committed suicide. I would have jumped off the f------ Kellogg Center. I knew the talent we had coming back and was excited. We didn't lose two games the next three years (32-1-1)."

By 1974, the Sooners had evolved from a 1960s program with as few as four Black athletes to having four Black *All-American* players: running back Joe Washington, linebacker Rod Shoate and the Selmon brothers on the defensive line, Lee Roy and Dewey. In 1975, Washington and the Selmon brothers repeated as consensus All-American picks; Lee Roy also won the Lombardi Award.

A DEFIANT SWITZER

But Switzer did more than continue to buck Oklahoma history: He ignored complaints. They ranged from behind-the-scenes comments from university regents and boosters to hate mail from fans. Such Oklahoma hate mail dated back to Gautt playing for Wilkinson. As Gautt completed his eligibility and prepared for the 1960 NFL draft, Wilkinson showed Gautt a stack of hate mail he kept from him.

They weren't congratulations for his awards earned on the field while playing a pioneering role. And they certainly weren't apologies for attempting to deny him his right to play for his home state university.

Wilkinson's protective manner wasn't unusual for the times.

In the mid-1960s, Southern Methodist coach Hayden Fry had his secretary screen hate mail sent to Jerry LeVias, the Southwest Conference's first Black scholarship player with the Mustangs, 1966-68. He also gave LeVias an unlisted phone number.

Switzer, though, befitting his breezy personality, responded more brashly. He frequently mocked the mail while he shared it with his players.

"Winning takes care of everything," Switzer said. "When I got negative letters from people—especially when I was playing a Black quarterback—I'd read them to our squad, and they'd all laugh at them before we went out to practice. We'd get a kick out of those dumb f----."

Switzer reading the letters served a purpose other than generating some laughs. For the white players slow to accept integration, hearing the ignorance of how bigots sounded in the letters Switzer read was enlightening.

Daugherty also had ignored such hate mail, including when Jimmy Raye was on track to become the starter. In 1965, he was a sophomore backup to All-American QB Steve Juday. At a 1965 post-game party, a booster told Daugherty some Black athletes were OK, but he added they would no longer be friends if he started a Black quarterback.

Daugherty told the booster he didn't have to wait until next year. He and his wife grabbed their coats and left the party. On the way out, Daugherty told the booster they were "no longer friends now."

"That's what Duffy should have done," said Switzer, laughing upon hearing the story. "That was the difference between coaches with Black athletes and a lot of other men. Our world changed a long time before the rest of the world."

SPARTY FOREVER

Although Fairbanks handed off Oklahoma's program to Switzer on his way to the NFL, he remained a proud Michigan State alumnus and returned home to the Charlevoix-East Jordan area throughout his life. He bought a patch of farmland from his old friend turned brother-in-law, Tuck Thomson, and built a cabin.

He invited his Oklahoma coaching staffs for retreats in the winter wonderland. They'd ride snowmobiles through woods.

"I spent a lot of time up there," Switzer said. "It was beautiful."

Fairbanks continued the practice when he was the Patriots' coach, sometimes including players. Same with his days with the Patriots when players, Black and white, would join the trips. Tuck was responsible for assembling an army of snowmobiles. The Charlevoix area had never seen so many Black snowmobile riders racing through the woods, rivers and lakes.

Chuck Jr. was born in Lansing when his father was still playing for the Spartans, although he spent most of his life in Arizona, Texas and Oklahoma. But he says Michigan State runs in his blood. In fact, he feels it has been stamped on him.

In a funny story he told on himself from an era when accepted family discipline included parents and teachers taking a paddle to rear ends, Chuck Sr. kept a green-and-white paddle with the names of his teammates above the refrigerator.

"I've got all those names imprinted on my rear end," Chuck Jr. said. "I don't know what happened to that paddle. I wish we still had it."

There were important names on that paddle, including African-American athletes who helped shape Fairbanks' future.

CHAPTER 8
SUCCESS IN NEBRASKA, ENGINEERED BY BOB DEVANEY

FACT: Bob Devaney followed Duffy Daugherty's blueprint to build Nebraska's back-to-back national championship teams, 1970 and 1971. He tapped fertile western Pennsylvania talent and ignored quotas limiting Black athletes.

"Bob was a character. He would come to my little mining town. He'd be at the Slovenian Club drinking beer and telling stories with mill workers and miners. The next day he was at a black-tie event with top executives and people in Pittsburgh."—Former University of Wisconsin coach/athletic director and Nebraska alumnus Barry Alvarez of Burgettstown, Pennsylvania.

Nebraska linebacker Barry Alvarez squeezed into Tony Jeter's used Chevrolet convertible, taking a seat among a carload of hefty 1965 Nebraska football teammates. They embarked eastward upon a 900-mile trip from campus to their hometowns, mostly steel cities and mining towns around western Pennsylvania and the Ohio River regions.

"There would be six of us that would drive home together," recalled Alvarez, who, of course, went on to greater fame as the University of Wisconsin's College Football Hall of Fame coach, 1990-2005. "Jeter was older than us and he had a car. Most of us lived about 20 miles from each other."

Jeter and Alvarez were part of Nebraska head coach Bob Devaney's early recruiting classes, setting the foundation for the Cornhuskers' rise to a national power. Devaney was 101-20-2 in 12 seasons, 1961-72, with national titles in 1970 and 1971. He was enshrined in the College Football Hall of Fame, in 1981.

Devaney targeting the richly talented region dated to his time as a Michigan State assistant coach, 1953-56. The Spartans enjoyed success in the 1950s under Duffy Daugherty, who was from Pennsylvania. Daugherty successfully recruited his home state as both an assistant coach to Biggie Munn and as head coach.

Michigan State's 1952 national championship team featured three All-American players from the Keystone State: quarterback Tom Yewcic, Conemaugh; guard Frank Kush, Windber; and center Dick Tamburo, New Kensington. There were many other Pennsylvania players over the years, including two more All-American picks, fullback Gerald Panutis of West Hazleton (1955) and guard Ron Saul of Butler (1969).

Devaney also duplicated Daugherty with a color-blind recruiting eye. Daugherty broke the mold of limiting Black scholarship opportunities to an unwritten quota of a half-dozen or so players during his career. The Daugherty blueprint connected Devaney from Michigan State to western Pennsylvania and to a colorblind eye to his jobs as a head coach at Wyoming, 1957-61, and Nebraska, 1962-71.

At Wyoming, he posted five straight winning seasons and a Sun Bowl victory in 1958. Winning in Laramie helped him land the Nebraska job. If he could convince western Pennsylvania high-school kids to travel 1,400 miles from home to play in the isolated cowboy town of Laramie, well, Lincoln was somewhat easier of a sell.

"Bob was a character," said Alvarez, who was from Burgettstown, Pennsylvania, 26 miles from Pittsburgh. "He would come to my little mining town. He'd be at the Slovenian Club drinking beer and telling stories with mill workers and miners. The next day he was at a black-tie event with top executives and people in Pittsburgh. He could tell a great story, but he was a hard-nosed coach. There was no nonsense when it was time to coach. He got after it."

PREJUDICED TOWARD GOOD PLAYERS

Devaney, born in the automobile parts factory town of Saginaw, Michigan, had been a high-school coach in three small Michigan towns that were nearly all-white—Big Beaver, Keego Harbor and Alpena—as well as Saginaw High.

Jeter's passenger manifest reflects both western Pennsylvania and Black talent. Four of the six passengers were African-Americans: Jeter, halfback Charlie Winters, halfback Harry Wilson and halfback Bennett Gregory. Alvarez, grandson of immigrants from Spain, was in the minority.

"Quite frankly, I never paid attention to how many Black players were on other team's rosters or how many Black athletes Bob was recruiting," Alvarez said. "Bob definitely wasn't prejudiced…or he was prejudiced toward *good* players."

In the mid-1960s, Jeter's Chevy transported as many Black players as there were on the rosters of some Cornhuskers foes. Oklahoma, a Big Eight rival border state to the South, was a segregated program until 1957. The Sooners limited their rosters to two or three Black players until the late 1960s. Colorado, another Big Eight rival, had similar 1960s numbers.

Fortunately for those Cornhuskers far from home, the U.S. automobile industry still rolled off hulking models from assembly lines. Every inch of comfort in Jeter's Chevy was needed for a half-dozen big guys seated three across on bench-style seats, front and back.

Size, though, was about the only luxury available in Jeter's high-mileage car. A hole in the right side's floorboard was stuffed with a pillow to obscure a perilous look at the road passing by beneath them. Stretching your legs was at your own risk.

Jeter imposed a rule: no one was to drive over 55 miles per hour, although it was ignored when he dozed off. That would have been fine a decade later when the Arab oil embargo forced everyone to slow down to conserve oil, as the federal government imposed a national speed limit of 55 miles per hour. But this was 1965, and America enjoyed the expanded roads President Dwight Eisenhower's 1956 Federal Highway Act opened to drivers.

The first stop, after 497 miles, delivered Winters at his home in Joliet, Illinois. That was essentially a side trip.

They continued driving another 470 miles to the heart of the region, with hometowns connected through the grandeur, commercial and recreational, of the Ohio River. The second player dropped off was Wilson in Steubenville, Ohio, a steel town. The remaining destinations were just across the mighty waterway that the 1700s French settlers called "la belle riviere"—the beautiful river.

From Steubenville, Jeter's home was six miles across the bridge to Weirton, West Virginia.

Alvarez's final leg from Steubenville was another 18 miles to Burgettstown.

Gregory's destination was 75 miles to Uniontown, Pennsylvania, the hometown of Minnesota's Sandy Stephens, the first Black quarterback to earn All-American honors and win a national title with the Gophers in 1960.

Jeter was a member of Devaney's first recruiting class in 1962. He developed into an All-Big Eight tight end by as a junior in 1964 and a 1965 All-American selection as a senior. The Green Bay Packers, where his older brother Bob was a Pro Bowl defensive back, chose Tony in the third round of the 1966 National Football League draft, although he played his two NFL seasons with the Pittsburgh Steelers.

"When Jeet was drafted, he bought a new car," Alvarez said. "I drove his old car back home and gave it to his father."

Wilson arrived in the 1963 recruiting class. He led the Cornhuskers in both rushing and total yards as a junior and senior in 1965 and 1966. As a third-round 1967 draft pick, he played a year for the Philadelphia Eagles.

Alvarez and Gregory were in the 1964 class.

Gregory was a versatile halfback who caught passes out of the backfield and threw them on option plays. He finished second on the team in rushing and total yards as a junior and senior, earning All-Big Eight recognition both seasons. The Buffalo Bills drafted him in the fifth round, but a midseason knee injury in 1968 ended his pro career after six games.

Alvarez, a three-year letterman as a linebacker (1965-67), entered coaching at the high-school level down the street from campus as an assistant at Lincoln High. He was a head coach at both Lexington High in Nebraska and Mason City in Iowa. Then, he entered college coaching on the University of Iowa's staff (1979-86) under Hayden Fry. Notre Dame coach Lou Holtz hired him as his linebackers coach in 1987 and promoted him to defensive coordinator in the 1988 national championship season.

Wisconsin's job was open in 1990 after Don Morton's disastrous three-year run of 6-29, and Alvarez was hired by then school president Donna Shalala at age 44. Alvarez's rebuilding plan struggled to a 1-10 start, but by his fourth season, the Badgers (10-1-1) won the Big Ten title and Rose Bowl. Alvarez was 120-73-4 with three Big Ten titles and three Rose Bowl victories before retiring as a coach and remaining campus as athletic director another 15 years.

A life-comes-full-circle moment came about when Alvarez was enshrined in the College Football Hall of Fame in 2010 alongside his mentor, Devaney, and Devaney's mentor, Daugherty. In 2014, Alvarez was the recipient of the Duffy Daugherty Memorial Award.

"I know Bob admired Duffy," Alvarez recalled for the audience upon accepting the award. "Those guys were a lot alike, and they were close. Bob had Duffy speak at our banquet my senior year. Duffy had a lot to do with Bob getting into college coaching."

Devaney's balance between work and play was reflected in his *New York Times* obituary upon his death at age 82 in 1997. Longtime sportswriter Frank Litsky's first sentence characterized Devaney as a "raconteur and humorist." Then, the *Times'* story continued by mentioning Nebraska's back-to-back national championships.

The *Times'* article didn't mention Devaney's contributions to college football integration, although the real culprit was the 1960s media that failed to recognize Devaney was a product of Duffy Daugherty's coaching tree—a group that changed the college football into a game of equal opportunity.

WINNING FROM THE START

Devaney's first job as a head coach was at the University of Wyoming (1957-61). He posted winning records seasons all five years, with two outright conference titles and a second shared conference crown in 1961. His 1958 team won the Sun Bowl over Hardin-Simmons.

The downtrodden Nebraska's program's job opened up in 1962 after coach Bill Jennings' 3-6-1 season gave him a five-year record of 15-34-1. It was the Cornhuskers' sixth straight losing season and 18th non-winning season in the last 21. Nebraska officials first sought out Daugherty. He turned them down and recommended Devaney. Daugherty was a voice to listen to in college football through his position running the Kodak All-American Coaches Clinics with another College Football Hall of Fame coach, Bud Wilkinson.

Devaney was 47 years old upon moving to Lincoln. Nebraska, like Wyoming, was a sparsely populated state for Division I college talent. Wyoming's 1960 population was only 330,000. Nebraska's 1960 population was 1.4 million, but there was talent to be mined in its lone urban city, Omaha.

Devaney was fortunate to have on his coaching staff John Melton, another key to successfully duplicating the Daugherty blueprint in both Wyoming and Nebraska. Melton was his top Wyoming assistant, and Devaney brought him to Lincoln. Although Melton was a former Wyoming player and successful high-school coach in the Rocky Mountain state, his roots were in western Pennsylvania. His hometown was Burgettstown. Devaney and Melton returned to Burgettstown in 1964 to sign Alvarez in their second Nebraska class with a full year of recruiting.

Melton died at age 86 in 2013, but he wrote a chapter among collection of coaches and players in a book on Nebraska football, *An Era of Greatness*, published in 2006 by 1972 Heisman Trophy winner Johnny Rodgers.

"Devaney was a great recruiter," Melton wrote prior to his death at age 86 in 2013. "The thing that used to get me was when Bob and I would go to a home on a recruiting trip. They would always have cookies or something like that, and he would say to the mother, 'Would you mind taking a minute and writing down the recipe for these cookies. They are the best cookies I have ever tasted.'

"I used to think, 'God damn liar.' I bet I heard him say that at least five or six times. The mothers would giggle. Bob always said, 'You get the mothers on your side, you will get the kid.'"

Devaney and Melton cashed in on western Pennsylvania talent in their first recruiting class of 1962 with Jeter and Ted Vactor, a running back from the town of Washington, 40 miles outside of Pittsburgh. The 1962 class also included Freeman White, a running back from Detroit. All three were African Americans, and all three went on to play in the National Football League.

Jeter and White were three-year lettermen and NFL draft picks. Jeter played two seasons with the Pittsburgh Steelers after being a third-round pick of the Green Bay Packers, and White four years with the New York Giants as a ninth-round selection.

Vactor only lettered one season, in 1963, but he eventually made it to the NFL. He even managed to carve out a memorable place in Super Bowl history despite a six-year career as a backup defensive back, five with Washington.

In the 1972 season, the Miami Dolphins pursued the NFL's first unbeaten season when they met Washington in Super Bowl VII at the Los Angeles Coliseum. Miami was leading 14-0 in the fourth quarter when the Dolphins lined up for a field goal by Garo Yepremian. Vactor blocked the kick, and the cartoonish Yepremian attempted to pick up the ball to throw a pass. The ball rolled off his hand, Washington's Mike Bass returned the loose ball for his team's only touchdown. Miami held on to win, 14-7.

Jeter, Vactor and White weren't eligible for the varsity until they were sophomores in 1963 due to the NCAA rules of the era, but Devaney nevertheless managed an overnight 1962 turnaround with the roster he inherited. The 1962 Cornhuskers were 9-2 with a bowl game. They beat all-white Miami, 36-34, in the Gotham Bowl played at Yankee Stadium in New York City.

Among the returning 1962 varsity players was Bob Brown, a junior offensive tackle. A year later Brown developed into Nebraska's first Black All-American player. The Philadelphia Eagles took Brown as the second pick of the 1964 NFL draft, and he played 10 NFL seasons. He was inducted into the College Football Hall of Fame in 1993 and Pro Football Hall of Fame in 2004.

Brown arrived from Cleveland, Ohio, as a member of Nebraska's 1960 recruiting class along with his high-school teammate, Gene Young. They represented a notable for a shift in the school's recruiting practices. With the door open, Devaney ushered through more Black recruits, ignoring unwritten quotas limiting rosters around the nation to a half-dozen or so Black players.

Nebraska's first Black player was George Flippin of Henderson, Nebraska, 1891-94. But the Cornhuskers, like many schools throughout out the nation, went decades with few if any Black athletes in the first half of the 20th century, particularly in the 1930s. There was backlash throughout the country resulting from nascent civil rights issues. African Americans who returned home from fighting for democracy in World War II spurred the movement.

Nebraska's 1950 team finished 6-2-1 with a No. 17 national ranking and an all-white roster. The 1950 national ranking was the first and only one compiled by the Cornhuskers between 1940 and Devaney's first ranked team, in 1963.

TURNING THINGS AROUND IN LINCOLN

The 1963 Cornhuskers maintained the 1962 momentum. The Cornhuskers won the Big Eight title with a 10-1 overall record (7-0 in the Big Eight) and beat all-white Auburn in the Orange Bowl, 13-7. Nebraska's final No. 6 ranking was at the time the highest in school history. The league title was the first since 1940, and the Orange the first major bowl since the 1954 season.

The 1963 Nebraska roster numbered nine Black players. The four seniors and one junior were recruited by Jennings in the 1960 and 1961 classes. Four sophomores in 1963 playing their first varsity season were among Devaney's 1962 recruiting class.

By the time Nebraska and Auburn, located on the plains of eastern Alabama, met in the Orange Bowl on January 1, 1964, a curious aberration in Southern media attitudes—at least at one Alabama newspaper—developed in the days prior to the game.

The *Montgomery Advertiser* posted a story that featured Nebraska running back Freeman White as a homegrown kid from Montgomery, the capital of the segregated Alabama. The story, which including a head shot of White wearing his Nebraska team coat and tie, noted White had attended Daisy Lawrence Elementary School—there was no need to mention the obvious, it was a segregated Black school—prior to the family moving to Detroit in 1953. White's family was part of the Great Migration (1910-70) to northern, midwestern and western factory jobs.

As recently as the late 1950s, Southern schools were still protesting Orange Bowl matchups against integrated rosters. The Southern media took editorial slants that Martin Luther King Jr. and the 1960s civil rights movement were threats to the South's way of life.

For the *Advertiser*, highlighting an African-American Alabama native playing major college football also oddly belied Alabama coach Paul "Bear" Bryant's claims he couldn't find Black athletes qualified academically to play for him. Bryant's apologists have used that excuse into the 21st century to claim Bryant conducted a "search" to find a Black athlete.

Nebraska's 1963 Big Eight title began a streak of four in a row, although postseason success escaped Devaney. The 1964 Huskers finished 9-2 with a Cotton Bowl loss to Arkansas; the 1965 champs were 10-1 with an Orange Bowl loss to Alabama; and the 1966 team was 9-2 with a Sugar Bowl loss to Alabama. The bowl losses exposed the Cornhuskers, who ran a double tight-end offense with three backs, as big and slow. The trend continued with 6-4 records in 1967 and 1968.

By 1969, Devaney instructed Tom Osborne, his offensive coordinator, to switch their scheme to an I-formation offense. In *An Era of Greatness*, Osborne wrote about the need to improve speed on both sides of the ball, so Devaney sent him to the West Coast to tap California's deep junior-college talent pool. The college football world took note of USC recruiting

O.J. Simpson out of San Francisco City College. Simpson led the Trojans to the 1967 national title and won the 1968 Heisman Trophy. USC's Clarence Davis, who was one of only five Black starters on USC's 1970 team, was from East Los Angeles Community College.

Nebraska opened the 1969 season 2-2 with losses to No. 5 USC in the opener and No. 7 Missouri in the fourth game, before finishing 9-2. The seven-game winning streak included routing Oklahoma 44-14 in the regular-season finale and romping past Georgia in the Sun Bowl, 45-6. The stage was set for back-to-back national titles, in 1970 and 1971.

Devaney's rosters were fully integrated as Nebraska's unbeaten streak grew to 32 games until a 1972 season-opening loss at UCLA. The 1969 varsity numbered 13 Black athletes, the 1970 varsity 18 and the 1971 Huskers—the last year freshmen weren't eligible for the varsity—included 15. Attrition through graduation and injuries account for the fluctuation and yes, the numbers are small by today's standards, but the Cornhuskers were still ahead of most schools.

Devaney's 1969 recruiting reach stretched to New Jersey, landing two African Americans bound for stardom—defensive lineman Rich Glover of Snyder High in Jersey City and offensive lineman Daryl White of East Orange High. White was Nebraska's original target until learning about Glover. Both were invited the same weekend to visit the campus in Lincoln.

"We met on the plane when we took our recruiting trip," Glover said. "We met the Black players on the team, and they told us Coach Devaney was a good man and there were no racial problems. There weren't many of us, but we were a tight group. Daryl and I decided we'd be roommates."

Glover's All-Big Eight selection in 1971 was a prelude to sweeping a dominant 1972 senior All-American season, earning the Outland Trophy and Lombardi Award honors. His roommate White was All-Big Eight in 1972 and an All-American pick as a fifth-year senior in 1973.

Glover praised Devaney as a father figure. He understood his Black recruits were far from home, literally and figuratively. He helped them adapt to college life on a predominantly white campus in a largely white city. Lincoln's population, despite its rapid growth the past 50 years, has historically remained less than 5 percent Black.

One manner of Devaney's concern was as simple as haircuts.

When Devaney learned his Black recruits in the early 1960s had trouble finding a barber in a white community that understood how to cut their Afro-textured hair, he arranged for Black barbers in Omaha to travel to campus for haircut day. Omaha was a city with an urban population 55 miles northeast of Lincoln.

"He was always watching out for us and what was best for us," Glover said. "For a Black person, the city of Lincoln had some problem areas to stay away from. The coaches made sure we understood that. When Devaney realized we needed a place to hang out on campus, he set up the first Afro-American center on campus. We had study tables and game rooms. The two things he emphasized were always education and then football. He was always making sure we were earning our degrees."

Devaney also was conscious of the distance family members had to travel to see the Cornhuskers play. They were from places as far-flung as the East Coast to Detroit and Chicago in the Midwest and to the West Coast.

"He made sure once they got in town, things were easy for them," Glover explained. "He wanted them enjoy their short time in town."

KEEPING THE TALENT HOME

Nebraska's 1970 national champs were 11-0-1 with an Orange Bowl win over No. 5 LSU, 17-12.

The 1971 Cornhusker national champions were 13-0 with a 38-6 rout of unbeaten and No. 2 Alabama in the Orange Bowl. In the regular-season finale for the Big Eight title and Orange Bowl berth, Nebraska came from behind to beat No. 2 Oklahoma 35-31 in what was called the 1971 Game of the Century.

The improved talent and speed on the 1970 and 1971 teams included two finds in the Cornhuskers' backyard, running back Joe Orduna from Omaha Central and wingback/return man Johnny Rodgers from Omaha Tech. They were significant recruits, as Nebraska had missed out on Black athletes from Omaha in the past, Gale Sayers most painfully.

Sayers, a College Football Hall of Famer at Kansas and a Pro Football Hall of Fame with the Chicago Bears, originally committed to Iowa in the 1961 recruiting class. He later changed his oral commitment to Nebraska, but Sayers flipped again to Kansas. Sayers was a three-time All-Big Eight pick and two-time All-American choice in 1963 and 1964 known as the "Kansas Comet."

Orduna and Rodgers represented two future NFL players for Devaney, with Orduna in his 1966 class and Rodgers in 1969.

Orduna lettered in 1967 and 1968, missed 1969 with a knee injury and led the team in rushing in 1970 with 897 yards and 11 touchdowns. He also caught four TD passes in the 1970 season.

Rodgers was on the 1969 freshmen team and joined the varsity in 1970 as a sophomore. He had 919 total offense yards, with 710 receiving for seven touchdowns and 219 rushing with two TDs.

Jerry Tagge, who grew up in Omaha but played his high-school years in Green Bay, Wisconsin, was the starting quarterback from 1969 through 1971. In 1970, Tagge threw for 1,536 yards and 12 touchdowns with eight interceptions and ran for 153 with five more TDs.

In the 1971 national title season, Tagge and Rodgers returned to their positions, while Bill Olds of Kansas City took over at fullback and Jeff Kinney of McCook, Nebraska, at running back.

Tagge threw for 2,178 yards and 17 touchdowns. Kinney ran for 1,136 yards and 17 touchdowns. Rodgers compiled 1,225 yards of total offense— 956 receiving with 11 touchdowns and 269 rushing with two TDs. Rodgers' all-purpose totals were 2,213 yards with 18 touchdowns. He returned punts 684 yards with four touchdowns and kickoffs 304 with one TD. Olds ran for 527 and a TD and caught 12 balls for 79 yards and another touchdown.

Rodgers went on to win the 1972 Heisman Trophy, but his place in college football lore was secured in 1971 with his epic, 72-yard punt return for a touchdown in a 1971 Nebraska-Oklahoma game.

Nebraska fell short of a third straight national title in 1972 when the Huskers lost their opener at UCLA and were unable to climb back to the top. Nebraska finished 9-2-1 and No. 4 nationally after beating Notre Dame in the Orange Bowl, 40-6. But Nebraska's 1972 season also has a place in history for setting new standards for Black athletes and major college awards.

Rodgers and Glover accounted for the first time that two Black players swept two of college football's most prestigious awards, the Heisman Trophy and Outland Trophy. Rodgers was only the fourth Black player to win the Heisman behind Syracuse's Ernie Davis, 1961; USC's Mike Garrett, 1965; and USC's O.J. Simpson, 1968. Glover was only the second Black athlete to take home the Outland; Minnesota's Bobby Bell was the first in the 1962 season. Glover also won the Lombardi Award, but the 1972 season was only the third year of the honor.

Glover also followed Bell with a rare top-three finish in the Heisman voting. Bell had been second in 1962 Heisman voting to Oregon State's

Terry Baker, but Glover's 1972 finish was the highest for a defensive player since Illinois linebacker Dick Butkus was third in 1964.

Rodgers was a 1973 NFL first-round pick by the San Diego Chargers and Glover a third-round choice by the New York Giants, although both had short pro careers.

Rodgers balked at the Chargers' contract offer and played three seasons in the Canadian Football League with the Montreal Alouettes. He was a three-time All-CFL star with two CFL titles, but when he returned to the NFL with the Chargers, his pro career ended with two unproductive seasons, 1977 and 1978.

Glover played two NFL seasons and one in the upstart World Football League in 1975. After his second NFL season with San Francisco, he entered teaching in the San Jose public school system. He taught physical education and was a coach. Later, he was a *Welcome Back, Kotter* figure as a teacher and head coach at two Jersey City high schools, Dickinson and Ferris.

"Bob Devaney always emphasized education," Glover said. "That was important to my mom (Anne) when I committed to Nebraska. He was a father figure to us. We knew if we had problems, we could come talk to him. He was truly a great man."

CHAPTER 9
HOUSTON'S BILL YEOMAN PIONEERS TEXAS INTEGRATION

FACT: By 1970, 33 of 37 major football programs in the South had recruited their first Black player. Three stragglers who failed to dress a Black player in a varsity game until the 1970s were Texas's Darrell Royal, 1970; Arkansas' Frank Broyles, 1970; and Alabama's Bear Bryant, 1971.

"It's one thing to integrate a team in the South in the 1970s. But how about during civil rights? A lot of stuff was going on. Martin Luther King was assassinated. For Bill Yeoman to come down to Houston and integrate the team in 1964, that's impressive. I remember when I was playing, he was hung in effigy. It wasn't for losing. He was a winning coach. He may not have thought anything about it coming from Michigan State—I never heard him talk about it—but it was more impressive to have done it during the civil rights years."—Houston's Elmo Wright, College Football Hall of Fame wide receiver.

Houston football coach Bill Yeoman wanted to win games, but not so badly it was a life-and-death struggle. Such a single-minded focus was put to the test at a midseason 1966 game.

Two years earlier, Yeoman pulled off more than just a recruiting coup when he signed "Wonderous Warren" McVea out of Brackenridge High in San Antonio. The electric halfback had over 73 scholarship offers with plenty of opportunities to escape his segregated home state. But the athlete gifted with his ability to elude tackles while gaining ground decided to break new ground—the first Black player to sign with a major Texas college.

Yeoman, a Michigan State assistant coach under Duffy Daugherty, arrived in 1962 with ambitious plans to build a program founded in 1946 into a national power. He viewed a tough schedule as an avenue to credibility, even if it meant hostile road games. On the fifth week of the 1966 season, Yeoman took his 4-0 Cougars into the belly of the beast, a last vestige of the antebellum South, Memphis. The neutral site opponent was all-white Mississippi (3-2), a traditional Southern power, on October 22 at Liberty Bowl Memorial Stadium.

As the kickoff approached, McVea and his teammates exited the locker room and approached the field. Bill Yeoman Jr., who often traveled with his father's team, recalled the scene.

"A guard told Warren, 'If they start shooting at you, we're not protecting you.'"

Maybe the guard meant it as a sick joke, but this was the segregated South. Events then and now can suddenly turn into life and death for African Americans. Martin Luther King Jr. was assassinated 16 months later in Memphis.

"My dad told Warren, 'You don't have to go out there if you don't want to.' Warren said, 'Let's go.'"

In an otherwise cleanly played game, Mississippi's players proceeded to administer a beating, defeating Houston 27-6. But the play on the field was nothing compared to the abuse from the fans.

"When we came out on the field, they let me have it," McVea said in a 2015 Houston *Chronicle* interview. "The N-word this, the N-word that—the whole thing. 'Get out of here, you don't belong here.' After it started, I forgot all about it."

McVea was the target, although by 1966 Houston's varsity roster included sophomore halfback Paul Gipson. He signed in 1965 out of Booker T. Washington High, the Black high school in Conroe, Texas. But McVea, a junior, was the first one crashing through the door, and they always draw the most attention. Bigots saw McVea as the face of college football integration, a threat to their 19th-century way of life.

McVea retold the story from that long ago afternoon with a chuckle in that same *Chronicle* story to mark the 50th anniversary of his first varsity game officially breaking the Texas color line. McVea was a sophomore in 1965 in his first year of eligibility.

The 1965 Cougars had traveled to four segregated cities for games: Texas A&M in College Station; Miami; Tennessee in Knoxville; and Florida State in Tallahassee. By the end of McVea's senior season in 1967, he had played in two more games in Deep South segregated cities—Mississippi State in Starkville and Mississippi in Oxford. The Oxford trip was only five years after Mississippi students rioted over the admission of African-American Air Force veteran James Meredith. President John F. Kennedy called in the National Guard and U.S. Army to quell the riot.

But the trip to Memphis was the first for McVea.

SURPRISING ROAD EXPERIENCES

"I had to go to Oxford, I went to Starkville, I went to Tennessee," he said. "I went to the real bad places, and they treated me with total respect. I was the first Black player to play in their stadiums. It's something I'll never forget. But they gave me hell in Memphis. They made up for it in Memphis."

Although North Texas State College has been credited as the first Texas school to sign Black football players with Abner Haynes and Leon King in 1956, that was before the school upgraded from the College Division to larger University Division—essentially today's version of the Football Bowl Subdivision. Yes, North Texas established a milestone, but the haughty schools in the Southwest Conference didn't react to the Eagles' groundbreaking.

McVea's commitment, by contrast, shook up the SWC. The news was an earthquake rippling across the eight SWC campuses—seven in Texas, one in Arkansas. The dominos began to fall. Southern Methodist signed Jerry LeVias in 1965, and he made his varsity debut in 1966, leading the Mustangs to the SWC title. Baylor played John Westbrook as a sophomore in a 1966 varsity game after he made the freshmen team as a walk-on.

By 1968, four more SWC schools—Texas A&M, Texas Tech, Texas Christian and Rice—desegregated with their first Black players appearing in a varsity game. Texas and Arkansas were the last holdouts, when Texas' Julius Whittier and Arkansas' Jon Richardson signed in 1969 and made their varsity debuts in 1970.

Yeoman's crisscrossing the South soon enough caught the attention of

Southeastern Conference schools. Although Houston lost its 1966 game to Mississippi in Memphis, a year earlier the Cougars had gone 2-2 against SEC schools. In 19 games over six seasons, 1965-70, Houston boasted a 11-7-1 against the SEC. Four of the victories were at the expense of ranked SEC teams and a fifth result was a tie with a ranked SEC foe:

- 1965, 2-2: lost to Mississippi State, 36-0; lost to Tennessee, 17-8; beat Mississippi, 17-3; beat No. 10 Kentucky, 38-21.
- 1966, 2-1: beat Mississippi State, 28-0; lost to Mississippi, 27-6; defeated Kentucky, 56-18.
- 1967, 2-1: beat Mississippi State, 43-6; lost to Mississippi, 14-13; and beat No. 5 Georgia, 15-14.
- 1968, 1-0-1: beat Mississippi, 29-7; tied No. 7 Georgia, 10-10.
- 1969, 3-1: lost to Florida, 59-34; beat Mississippi State, 74-0; beat No. 17 Mississippi, 25-11; beat No. 12 Auburn 36-7 in the Astro-Bluebonnet Bowl.
- 1970, 1-2: beat Mississippi State, 31-14; lost to Alabama, 30-21; and lost to No. 13 Mississippi, 24-13.

Houston wide receiver Elmo Wright, the Cougars' first Black consensus All-American player, first Black College Football Hall of Famer and the school's initial NFL first-round draft pick, said he saw indications during his career, 1968-70, Southern fans were accepting integration. He cited a game against Mississippi at Hemingway Stadium in Oxford when he fell to the turf with a knee injury and couldn't get up.

"They wheeled me off the field all the way around the goal posts to the opposite side of the field," Wright said. "The fans in the stands applauded me. I'll never forget it."

Yeoman, in a 2015 *Chronicle* interview before his death in 2020 at age 92, was proud of exposing Southern fan bases to the future.

"That's when integration in the South took place," Yeoman said of his 1960s teams. "Football was so meaningful to those people they couldn't stand to be in a thing where they didn't have a chance. I don't care what they said. They have no idea what our football team did for integration."

In the same interview, McVea said, "Everybody for some reason—and I thank God—everybody was pulling for me, because I think they wanted to get most places integrated."

The comments from Wright, Yeoman and McVea were their way of dismissing the 1970 USC-Alabama game as a tipping point, says Bill Yeoman Jr. Their experiences joined a list elsewhere in the country that debunked myths crafted in Los Angeles and Alabama in the 1990s that the 1970 USC-Alabama game spurred integration. It was fait accompli by the time USC arrived at Legion Field in Birmingham.

"It's one thing to integrate a team in the South in the 1970s," Wright said. "But how about during civil rights? A lot of stuff was going on. Martin Luther King was assassinated. For Bill Yeoman to come down to Houston and integrate the team in 1964, that's impressive. I remember when I was playing, he was hung in effigy. It wasn't for losing. He was a winning coach. He may not have thought anything about it coming from Michigan State—I never heard him talk about it—but it was more impressive to have done it during the civil rights years."

When all-white Alabama's unranked 1970 team upset No. 15 Houston 30-21 on October 24 at the Astrodome, the Crimson Tide beat a Cougars' roster with 11 Black players. Eight of the 11 started a game during the season depending on game plans and formations: wide receiver Elmo Wright, tight end Riley Odoms, running back Robert Newhouse, wide receiver Robert Ford, wide receiver Willie Roberts, wide receiver Earl Thomas, linebacker Charlie Hall and defensive back Charles Ford.

Alabama's win over Houston was one of six over integrated opponents in the 1970 season, although the shallow myth of the 1970 USC-Alabama game was Bryant was tired of losing to Black players when he decided to desegregate.

The march of college football integration may have hastened the retirement of two College Football Hall of Famers, Clemson's Frank Howard (1969) and Mississippi's Johnny Vaught (1970). Both retired without signing a Black player. The Howard and Vaught successors both signed a Black player in their first season.

After McVea, Yeoman, like Daugherty and other Daugherty assistants who became head coaches, added Black athletes each year. He disregarded the unwritten quota limitations of a half-dozen Black players on a roster that integrated northern and western schools had followed into the 1960s. Paul Gipson committed to Houston in 1965 and Jerry Drones signed in 1966. Houston's 1967 recruiting class included four players taken in the 1971 National Football League draft—Wright, first round; Hall, third; Carlos Bell, fourth; and Thomas, sixth.

Yeoman's Black recruits began gaining attention on All-American teams. McVea was second team in 1966 and 1967; Gipson second team in 1967 and 1968; and Wright was honorable mention in 1968 and second team in 1969.

In 1970, Wright stood out in the 1970 *Playboy Magazine* preseason All-American team. Wright and Missouri running back Joe Moore were the only two Black players among the 12 offensive picks. Florida kicker Carlos Alvarez was a third minority. Only two Black All-American picks among the 12 was reflection of schools limiting their Black athletes to single digits.

Among the *Playboy's* 12 choices, six were especially prescient. They were eventually enshrined in the College Football Hall of Fame: Wright, Alvarez, Mississippi quarterback Archie Manning, Arkansas wide receiver Chuck Dicus, Michigan offensive tackle Dan Dierdorf and Tennessee offensive lineman Chip Kell.

Houston's rise eventually gained the school admission to the Southwest Conference in 1976—with the Cougars winning the league title and Cotton Bowl their first season. The rise was sudden but not overnight. The integration doesn't happen with one game.

FROM MILITARY TO MICHIGAN STATE

Yeoman's coaching and recruiting Michigan State's Black athletes followed his experiences as a U.S. Army officer. Yeoman was a West Point graduate who played center on the Black Knights' 1946 national championship team. The Black Knights were coached by the legendary Red Blaik and led by two Heisman Trophy winners, 1945 winner Doc Blanchard and 1946 winner Glenn Davis. As an Army artillery officer, he served in West Germany during the Cold War. His base commander added duties of coaching the base football team.

When his tour was up, Daugherty hired him for his staff. As the 1960s arrived, Yeoman began drawing interest as a head coach material.

"I know he had an offer from somebody in 1961," Bill Jr. said. "Duffy said, 'Stay with me another year, and I'll get you a better head coach job.' Duffy was connected everywhere."

Yeoman remained with the 1961 Spartans, who finished the year 7-2. They were ranked No. 8 in the nation and flirted with a Rose Bowl bid.

"Duffy was a great guy," Bill Jr. said. "I knew him well. Dad always said Duffy could handle people better than anyone. He wasn't the greatest X's and O's coach, but he was the best people person. I think my dad was a combination—he was a great people person and great with the X's and O's. He was the right person for UH."

Yeoman's interview process for the Houston job included him telling athletic director Harry Fouke he wanted to recruit Black athletes. Yeoman's timing couldn't have been better. Fouke had been Houston's AD since 1949 and remained on the job until 1975, but he agreed it was time for Houston to lead Texas college athletics into the 20th century.

In addition to McVea enrolling in the fall of 1964, Houston basketball coach Guy Lewis had the green light to sign his first two Black basketball players, Basketball Hall of Famer Elvin Hayes and Cougars legend Don Chaney. They also lifted Houston to national prominence. Their Final Four trips in 1967 and 1968 both ended in losses to UCLA, but in 1968 the No. 1 Bruins traveled to No. 2 Houston to meet the Cougars.

They played before 53,693 fans at the Astrodome in the first prime-time regular-season college basketball game. Hayes scored 39 points with 15 rebounds as Houston ended UCLA's 47-game win streak, 71-69. TV exposure expanded and eventually the NCAA staged tournament games in domes.

Yeoman, upon landing the job, hit the ground running. He traveled around the area, including sending an early message by visiting African-American communities.

"He went to Antioch Baptist Church, the oldest Black church in Houston," said Bill Jr., who was starting sixth grade in 1962. "One of the members asked, 'Are you prejudiced?' My dad said, 'Absolutely—I'm prejudiced against bad football players.'"

Yeoman's first season finished a promising 7-4, including a Tangerine Bowl win over Miami, Ohio, 49-21, played in Orlando. But the Cougars dipped to 2-8 in 1963 and 2-6-1 in 1964. Yeoman began tinkering with his offense before coming up with the Veer option. The Cougars were 4-5-1 in 1965, McVea's first varsity season where he was hindered by nagging injuries. McVea had trouble throughout his career remaining healthy, and his work ethic and maturity were questioned as far back as his high-school days.

But the Veer was a good fit for McVea and another future NFL running back on the roster, Dickie Post. In 1966, Houston posted an 8-2 record. Post ran for 1,061 yards and McVea 648.

Post was off to a five-year NFL career in 1967. Paul Gipson, Houston's second Black recruit in 1965, was McVea's next running mate. Gipson ran for 1,100 yards and 11 touchdowns, McVea 699 with four touchdowns. But McVea had his moments—much to the dismay of Yeoman's mentor, Duffy Daugherty.

College games are scheduled years in advance, and Daugherty agreed in 1963 to schedule Houston in 1967. At that time it appeared to be a mismatch between the Spartans and Cougars, with Houston 2-8 in 1963 and Michigan State 7-2. Michigan State had played for the Big Ten title down to the final weekend.

Yeoman felt it would help raise his program's profile to play a Big Ten school.

"Duffy was loyal to people and people were loyal to him," Bill Jr. said. "Duffy was very magnanimous to schedule the game. He had everything to lose and nothing to gain by playing that game. My dad was so appreciative."

Scheduling an old friend backfired on Daugherty, even though the Spartans were coming off back-to-back shared national titles with an overall record of 19-1-1. The mercurial McVea was a maturing senior, and the Veer was developing as a befuddling offensive scheme. McVea shredded the Spartans' defense, leading Houston to a 37-7 rout of No. 3-ranked Michigan State before 75,533 stunned fans at Spartan Stadium. The Cougars carried Yeoman off the field.

"My dad felt bad about the score," said Bill Jr. "He was excited for his team, but at the same time heartbroken for Duffy. My dad had two mentors—Duffy and Red Blaik. There wasn't anything he wouldn't do for them."

Sports Illustrated featured the game in an October 2 issue with a story by the legendary Dan Jenkins, his era's godfather of college football sportswriters. Houston's 30-point win was so shocking—the Spartans gave up 8.9 points a game in 1966 and never more than 20—Jenkins wrote, "where are you *Roget's Thesaurus*, now that a man really needs you?"

McVea finished with 14 carries for 155 yards and one touchdown on a 50-yard scamper that Jenkins wrote was "more like 80 with all the cuts and feints. A run by Wondrous Warren seems to last six or seven minutes." McVea also had runs of 48 and 33 yards.

In postgame quotes attached to the official box score, Daugherty said of McVea, "It's been a long time since I've seen someone as quick and skillful."

Among Yeoman's listed quotes, he said, "I'll tell you one thing—if we did anything well today, it was the result of what I learned from Duffy Daugherty. MSU is a great school."

On Houston's return home, they were treated like conquering heroes. A throng of thousands of fans at Houston Hobby Airport blocked the plane from pulling up to the terminal. Houston jumped from unranked to No. 3 in the nation. It was the program's highest ranking until the Cougars defeated Wake Forest 50-6 the next week and climbed to No. 2.

Houston later lost to North Carolina State (16-6), Mississippi (14-13) and Tulsa (22-13) to fall out of the final rankings, but otherwise the Veer sent defensive coordinators to the drawing board to decipher it.

FROM VEER TO WISHBONE

In the offseason, Yeoman began to hear from offensive coordinators about his scheme. Texas offensive coordinator Emory Ballard visited with Yeoman. He devised a modified version he called the wishbone. Texas rode the wishbone to a 1969 national title. Bryant revived his Alabama program by visiting with Texas' coaches in the 1971 preseason to learn the wishbone. Oklahoma also switched to a wishbone, and Barry Switzer won national titles in 1974 and 1975.

Yeoman gained a reputation in football circles as "the father of the triple option," although attention that comes with winning a national title often was directed to Ballard and Texas head coach Darrell Royal. *Sports Illustrated*, in an article September 27, 2018, wrote Yeoman "discovered what many consider the first true triple option."

Wright's first varsity season in 1968 added another dimension to the Veer with a deep passing threat. Houston led the nation with 42.5 points a game and a then-NCAA record of 562 yards per game. Although McVea was the game-changing, landmark recruit for Houston, Wright's arrival on the freshmen team in 1967 bridged Houston's rise as a fledgling program in the 1960s to a Top 20 program in the 1970s.

McVea's teams, 1965-67, were never ranked at the end of the season. In Wright's three seasons, Houston finished No. 18, 1968 (6-2-2); No. 12, 1969 (9-2); and No. 19, 1970 (8-3). The 1968 ranking marked the first time in program history the Cougars finished the year in the Top 20.

As a sophomore Wright caught 43 balls for 1,198 yards (27.9 per catch) and 11 touchdowns and as a junior 63 for 1,275 (20.2) and 14 touchdowns. His senior year, hindered by the late-season knee injury, totaled "only" 47 balls for 874 yards (18.6) and nine TDs.

Wright's school record of 34 career touchdown receptions stood 41 years despite the proliferation of passing games benefitting from relaxed defensive rules favoring the receiver. But two of Wrights' NCAA records from his 1968 season still stand—most 50-yard touchdown catches (eight) in a season and highest average touchdown reception (56.1) in a season.

Wright brought the crowd to its feet with his high-stepping plays and kept the fans watching in the end zone. He has been called the father of the touchdown dance, a reputation he carried into the NFL with the Chiefs.

The dancing, he insists, developed by accident. He said it stemmed from growing up in rural Brazoria County, south of Houston, and from playing in a marching band. He attended a 1-12 Black school and was in the band from third grade until 10th grade.

"I grew up in a rural area and had to jog everywhere," he said. "I developed some legs. My school had a band director that liked to start out his members young to get experience by high school."

As Wright tells it, he enjoyed spiking the ball after touchdowns his sophomore season, but the NCAA put in rules banning spike celebrations. He said he had no plans to come up with something new. He first dance in the 1969 season opener at Florida was a spontaneous reaction to trash-talking with Gators defensive back Steve Tannen.

"He told me I wasn't catching any passes," Wright said. "I told him I catch touchdowns."

Houston had the ball in Florida's end of the field when Wright caught a pass as Tannen hit him. Wright high-stepped his way out of the tackle and continued high-stepping the final 15 yards. Then, he explained, he had so much energy he was unaware he kept his feet dancing in the end zone.

"People were booing me, but I wasn't doing it to showboat," Wright said. "When I got to the sideline, my teammates said I was dancing. I said, 'What?' I didn't even realize it."

Yeoman, as a West Point grad and retired Army officer, wouldn't seem to be the type of coach to tolerate such celebrating. In fact, after a touchdown dance later in the season, Wright said he came to the sideline and Yeoman said, "I'm not sure that's a good idea. You need to think about it."

Wright, laughing as he retold the story decades later, responded, "I'll tell you what, Coach. Next time I'll kneel down at the 1-yard line, and you can let the team get it in the end zone. I was just kidding, but he looked at me like I was crazy. He said, 'Just get it in the end zone.'"

Wright's explosive career surprises him more than anybody. He never would have played high-school football if not for a falling out with his band director his sophomore year. He played football for the first time as a junior, helping his Black high school win a state title. He didn't do much more than run fast and far.

The next year, his Black high school, George Washington Carver, was closed. He was sent to attend newly integrated Sweeney High in the Brazoria County town of Sweeney. He said he still didn't know much about football other than he could outrun his opponents.

"The next thing I know I'm getting a letter from Notre Dame," Wright said. "I thought, 'How do they know about me? I barely know how to play football. I'm a saxophone player.'"

Another school that saw Wright as more than a saxophone player was mighty Texas. Wright took a recruiting trip to Austin and met with Royal in his office. Wright said he liked the idea of becoming Texas' first Black player.

"Royal said he wanted me, and he had another Black player to bring in with me," Wright said. "He said he didn't want to bring me in alone."

Wright may have been referring to Mike Williams of El Paso. In Richard Pennington's 1987 book, *Breaking the Ice: The Racial Integration of Southwest Conference Football*, he mentions that Royal planned to sign Williams, but his low SAT score disqualified him from admission. Pennington's book doesn't mention Wright, but a Houston *Chronicle* story on September 19, 2018, stated Royal pursued Wright.

However, Wright's interest in Texas as its first Black player was soon a moot point.

"I was the first one in my family to go to college," Wright said. "My family didn't know anything about football scholarships and going to college, so we went to my uncle for advice."

Thomas Wright was a principal at a Black high school in Angleton, Texas, near Houston.

"He told me to go to Houston," Elmo recalled. "He said, 'Bill Yeoman has taken a chance on Black kids and helped them out. You need to help him out.'"

Wright laughed telling the story, adding, "Help him out? I didn't know if I could make the team! I still thought of myself as a saxophone player."

In 1968, Royal did sign his first Black player, according to Pennington. Leon O'Neal Jr. of Killeen, Texas, played on the freshmen team, but he flunked out of school before the 1969 season. In 1969, Julius Whittier was the second Black player on Texas' freshmen team. Whittier broke the Texas color line on the varsity as a 1970 sophomore. Whittier went on to a career as a lawyer.

RISING TO THE SOUTHWEST CONFERENCE

Houston continued building on the success of the late 1960s. The Cougars finished in the Top 10 for the first time in 1973 at No. 9 with an 11-1 record. They defeated Tulane in the Astro-Bluebonnet Bowl, 47-7.

The success helped Houston complete its quest to gain Southwest Conference membership, in 1976. The Cougars celebrated by winning the SWC the first year, finishing the season with a 10-2 record and a 21-10 win over Maryland in the Cotton Bowl. Houston was No. 4 in the final poll. The 1979 Cougars (11-1) also won the SWC and Cotton Bowl to finish No. 5.

Yeoman was Houston's head coach 25 years through 1986, compiling a career record of 160-108-8. His last recruiting class included a quarterback named Andre Ware, who redshirted in what turned out to be Yeoman's final season. Ware, in 1989, was the first Black quarterback to win the Heisman Trophy.

Yeoman was enshrined in the College Football Hall of Fame in 2001, joining three coaches from his Michigan State days, Daugherty, 1984; Bob Devaney, 1981; and Dan Devine, 1985. In 2015, Houston unveiled a statue of Yeoman outside of Gate 1 at TDECU Stadium.

Bill Jr. finds it sadly ironic Houston put up a statue of his father before Michigan State planned one of Daugherty. Michigan State athletic director Alan Haller, not long after his promotion from assistant athletic director, announced in January 2022 the school plans to include a statue of Daugherty in the upgraded renovation of its football complex.

"Duffy made Michigan State who they are," Bill Jr. said. "My dad made Houston who they are. Not to have a stadium named after Duffy or a statue of him on campus is criminal. He's not only a Michigan State icon, he is a Big Ten icon. If the Internet existed when Duffy was coaching, he would have been one of the most famous persons around."

Bill Jr. spent enough time with his father in to have his own Daugherty anecdotes from his dad's time at Michigan State or later in life.

"My dad would take me and my brother (Gary) everywhere," Bill Jr. said. "I don't know why. We must have been a pain in the butt. One time we were with Duffy in Detroit when he wanted to stop by the Chrysler House downtown to say hi to some people. He told the guard he was there to see so and so, the chairman. Duffy was told he was in a board meeting and couldn't be bothered. Duffy said, 'Just let him know I'm here.' The next thing we knew the elevator was opening to take us up. They stopped the board meeting for Duffy."

Another time Bill Jr. and his father played golf in Scotland with Duffy. Daugherty was enjoying one of the bonuses for putting on the Kodak All-American Coaches Clinic. His wife Francie was on the trip.

"Kodak sent the coaches and wives for three weeks to England and Scotland," Bill Jr. said. "I got to go one year when Duffy went to Scotland to play St. Andrews. We're on the first tee, and Duffy says, 'Billy, do you think Francie can still see me?'

"I know she can," Bill Jr. replied.

"OK, I'll wait until the second hole."

"We're on the green and Duffy pulls a Scotch bottle out of his golf bag. Francie was a wonderful lady, but she worried about Duffy's health. Duffy enjoyed a nip or two."

Daugherty died in 1987 at age 72 in Santa Barbara, California, where he had retired after his coaching career.

As for Yeoman's legacy, Elmo Wright said as he grew older, he gained greater appreciation for the challenges Yeoman faced desegregating his football team in a conservative, segregated Texas city. After Wright's NFL playing days, he returned to Houston and earned a Master of Business Administration (MBA) degree. He worked 25 years for Harris County in Houston.

"When I worked for the county, I'd have to go out and spend some time in conservative communities," Wright said. "I got a feel for who had your back. It made me realize when I played at Houston, my white teammates had my back. They were leaders. I give those guys a lot of credit, because they were always supportive of the Black players.

"Coach Yeoman brought in players who were open-minded. That had to be part of his mindset when he was recruiting. I don't remember him bringing in any prejudiced guys. That's significant. He didn't bring players that wouldn't accept integration. That was Bill Yeoman. That's what I recognized later in life."

Change is usually faster in sports, but society eventually begins to catch up.

The arc of the Yeoman family experience in Houston can be told in another way. Bill Jr. graduated in 1969 from Robert E. Lee High in Houston, Texas. In 2016, the Houston Interscholastic School District changed the name to Margaret Long Wisdom High. The district decided it was time to honor a long-time beloved teacher over a Rebel traitor who fought to preserve slavery.

CHAPTER 10
EARLE EDWARDS REBUILDS N.C. STATE

FACT: Earle Edwards' first two Black players at N.C. State were walk-ons, Marcus Martin in 1967 and Clyde Chesney in 1969. Chesney earned a scholarship and was N.C. State's first Black player to earn postseason honors as a 1971 Academic All-ACC choice.

"Clyde was an upstanding guy. He wasn't outspoken, but he showed us the way by how he carried himself. He was a respected player on the team, a good player. We learned from him how he navigated situations when he was the only Black player on the team and one of the few Black students on the campus."—Charley Young, one of N.C. State's first two Black scholarship recruits along with Willie Burden.

Earle Edwards badly wanted to be a football head coach. He confirmed how badly when he sought the vacant job at North Carolina State in 1954. At the time the Wolfpack program was one of the worst in the nation.

His background was anything but N.C. State-like. He had been an assistant coach for 13 years at his alma mater, Penn State, but when Joe Bedenk was named the new coach in 1949 over him, he moved on. He landed at Michigan State on Biggie Munn's staff the next five years. But when Duffy Daugherty was promoted after the 1953 season, Edwards was on the move again.

If ever there was a time to wait for a better job opportunity, this was it.

N.C. State was a major rebuilding project, while Michigan State was consistently winning. The two schools were also as the opposite ends of the civil rights spectrum. N.C. State's football team was all-white. Michigan State's history of leading college football integrated was established.

During Edwards' five seasons in East Lansing, the Spartans were 41-5. N.C. State's 1953 team—the one Edwards was about to inherit—had lost nearly double that total with a 1-9 record and winless mark in the Atlantic Coast Conference.

Earle Edwards and star quarterback Roman Gabriel. *Courtesy N.C. State.*

Compounding N.C. State's lack of a football tradition was the considerable shadow of the Wolfpack's basketball program built by Everett Case (1946-64). Case, from Anderson, Indiana, infused the Raleigh school with Hoosier passion for basketball on his way to enshrinement in the Basketball Hall of Fame and Naismith Basketball Hall of Fame.

Soon enough, the state caught basketball fever. Football rules the Southeastern Conference, but to this day the Atlantic Coast Conference is a basketball league.

To keep up with N.C. State, the University of North Carolina hired noted St. John's University coach Frank McGuire. He maintained his recruiting base in New York boroughs, and Tobacco Road was born. Lennie Rosenbluth of the Bronx was the 1957 national Player of the Year as he led the Tar Heels to the NCAA title with an unbeaten 32-0 record.

Part of the ACC's reputation grew from the drama of the ACC Tournament champion gaining the NCAA automatic bid—the only ACC bid until the tournament expanded—over the regular-season champion. Case had pushed for that format when the ACC was founded in 1953 with N.C. State, North Carolina, Wake Forest, Duke, Maryland, Clemson and South Carolina (Virginia joined in 1954). With time, all conferences adopted the money-making postseason conference tournament.

The growth of basketball at N.C. State magnified the drastic disparity in facilities for Edwards to consider.

The basketball team played in Reynolds Coliseum, an edifice that was for many years was the South's largest arena. Reynolds, when it was renovated in 2016, added statues outside of basketball coaches Case, Norm Sloan (1974 national title), Jim Valvano (1983 national title) and women's coach Kay Yow, one of the women's game's early giants whose teams dominated the ACC, advancing to the postseason 29 times.

Meanwhile, the football program played in dilapidated 19,000-seat Riddick Stadium, now a campus parking lot. The facility was so inadequate the football players dressed in the Reynolds basement and walked to the football field. The Wolfpack's budget allowed for fewer scholarships and assistant coaches than its rivals in the ACC.

The only thing football and basketball shared were all-white rosters until the late 1960s.

If all of that wasn't enough to give Edwards pause, there was another red flag for him to consider. He couldn't count on support from N.C. State's chancellor, Carey Bastian.

"N.C. State's chancellor was considering cutting football," said Tim Peeler, a Case biographer widely recognized in ACC circles as an expert on N.C. State athletics history. "But the football program was so far in debt, he was told about the lawsuits the school would face. And when the ACC was formed in 1953, the new league wouldn't take N.C. State without a football team."

N.C. State would have otherwise been embarrassingly left out of a league that included three in-state neighbors—North Carolina, Duke and Wake Forest.

Off the field, a Confederate soldier statue stood on the state capitol's grounds, just a short jaunt from Raleigh's downtown and the N.C. State campus. The monument to pro-slavery rebels wasn't taken down until 2020 in the wake of Black Lives Matters protests following the death of George Floyd while in police custody.

This climate wasn't Edwards' background. He was a northerner from Pennsylvania. He was an assistant coach at Penn State in the late 1940s when Wallace Triplett and Dennis Hoggard were the football team's first two Black players.

But despite the monumental challenges facing Edwards, he took the job. And he succeeded, with time, both on and off the field.

Clyde Chesney, a walk-on who was N.C. State football's first Black starter. *Courtesy N.C. State.*

On the field he won five ACC titles—three outright (1957, 1964, 1968) and two shared (1963, 1965). In 1967, the Wolfpack won its first bowl game in school history, defeating Mississippi State 14-7 in the Liberty Bowl played in Memphis. Despite a career record of 77-88-8 in his 17 seasons at N.C. State, he was the four-time ACC Coach of the Year.

Off the field, Edwards integrated the program in the late 1960s, although at first it was only with two walk-on players. Marcus Martin made the team during spring football as a freshman. Clyde Chesney made the team when he came out for the team in 1968 spring drills. Still, Edwards' roster accepted integration without the type of incidents that plagued other Southern schools and fan bases.

Such shameful episodes began with Maryland as the first ACC school to integrate. The Terrapins signed Darryl Hill as a transfer from the Naval Academy, where he had been Navy's first Black football player in 1961, the same class as 1963 Heisman Trophy winner Roger Staubach.

Hill sat out 1962 until he was eligible in 1963, but in his one season of remaining eligibility (he also had been at Xavier in 1960), he led Maryland in receiving with 43 catches for 516 yards and seven touchdowns. He also ran 21 times for 108 yards and eight TDs. But his productive season wasn't easy.

Throughout a season that saw Maryland finish with a 3-7 record, Hill endured cheap shots from opponents and at road games racial taunts from bigoted fans. The season opener at home against N.C. State was played without incident—other than the Wolfpack, on its way to sharing the ACC title, whipping Maryland, 36-14.

The problems awaiting Maryland were road trips to South Carolina (second game), Wake Forest (sixth game) and Clemson (ninth game). Upon Hill signing with Maryland, South Carolina and Clemson threatened boycotting the 1963 games. They didn't carry through on the threat, but the fans weren't so apologetic.

For the South Carolina game, safety concerns were so grave the National Guard was posted outside Carolina Stadium (now Brice-Williams) in Columbia.

The sixth game was at Wake Forest in Winston-Salem, North Carolina. The Demon Deacons' fans taunted Hill during warmups. The abuse continued until Wake Forest star Brian Piccolo silenced the crowd. Piccolo put his arm around Hill and walked with him around the field. Piccolo's life, while playing for the Chicago Bears, inspired the TV movie *Brian's Song*. It was based on his friendship with Gale Sayers, a Black teammate, and Sayers' support as Piccolo turned ill with cancer and died in 1970.

The ninth game was at Clemson, a South Carolina campus. Hill's mother was denied entry to Memorial Stadium. Clemson president Robert C. Edwards came down from the press box and escorted Hill's mother to watch the game with him. Edwards had been pushing Clemson coaches to integrate their programs since 1963. Clemson coach Frank Howard, enshrined in the College Football Hall of Fame in 1989, retired after the 1969 season without ever recruiting a Black player. His successor, Cecil

"Hootie" Ingram, in his first season signed Marion Reeves as the program's first Black player.

These were the battles fought in the 1960s to clear the way for games in the 1970s to be played without incident.

Martin and Chesney cleared the N.C. State path for Charley Young and Willie Burden, teammates at Raleigh's Enloe High. They were Edwards' first two Black scholarship recruits in the 1970 class.

"Those things didn't happen to us," said Young, referring to the 1960s incidents at other ACC schools.

N.C. State's campus had desegregated in 1951. In 1956, Irwin Holmes enrolled and began to break sports barriers. Holmes and Manuel Crockett were the first Black athletes to participate in an ACC competition at an indoor freshmen track meet in February 1957.

But Holmes' better sport was tennis. He was named team co-captain in 1960, making him the first Black ACC team captain in any sport. Holmes was featured in *Sports Illustrated's* Faces in the Crowd.

He was N.C. State's first Black graduate that same spring with a degree in electrical engineering. He worked 19 years at IBM, including as a senior manager for computer development, responsible for two patents in the growing industry.

N.C. State's basketball program's first Black player also was a walk-on. Martin went out for football as a freshman during 1967 spring drills, while Al Heartley arrived in the fall of the 1967-68 school year to make the basketball team as a walk-on.

But racial progress in American often takes a step backward after a step or two forward. About a month before Martin's 1966 fall enrollment at N.C. State, the Ku Klux Klan attempted to overshadow Martin Luther King's appearance on July 10, 1966, at N.C. State's Reynolds Coliseum. The KKK's response was to announce plans for its own parade through downtown Raleigh streets, concluding with a rally at Municipal Auditorium.

When King's N.C. State speech had to be postponed until July 31 due to his commitments to aid protests of housing conditions in Chicago, the KKK also rescheduled to the same date. According to reports in the *Raleigh News & Observer*, King spoke to an integrated audience of 5,000 people on July 31 at Reynolds Coliseum, while the KKK drew 1,800 bigots at the downtown Auditorium.

The 1966 football season also marked the opening of Carter Stadium (now Carter-Finley). Ironically, Martin performed on the Carter turf as a member of the marching band before he was a football player. He arrived at N.C. State on an academic scholarship out of Watson High in Covington, Virginia, in addition to a spot with the marching band.

As spring 1967 rolled around, Martin decided to try out for the team as walk-on candidate. He made the cut and returned with a roster spot in the fall 1967 roster. He traveled with the team to some games, but he didn't play in a game. He was on the team but not the travel roster for N.C. State's 1967 Liberty Bowl win over Georgia, 14-0.

In 1968, he was N.C. State's first Black player to see the field when he came off the bench against South Carolina, a midseason game the Wolfpack won 38-12 on Oct. 12 at Carter Stadium. It turned out to be the only appearance of his career, but he was part of N.C. State's 1968 outright ACC title.

Martin quit the team in the 1969 fall camp. Peeler wrote in a story on the N.C. State athletic website that, although Martin made the second team in 1969 spring drills, he quit after he was demoted to the third team in fall camp. Peeler cited a quote in the N.C. State student newspaper, the *Technician*. The quote from Martin said he quit "quietly and without a fuss."

Chesney, similarly, arrived on his academic scholarship in the fall of 1968 out of E.E. Smith High in Fayetteville, North Carolina. Chesney was from the same high school as Jimmy Raye. Raye's success as an E.E. Smith legend motivated Chesney to try out for the N.C. State team in 1969 spring drills.

He made his varsity debut in the fall and cracked the starting lineup on Nov. 15, 1969, against No. 18-ranked Houston. It turned out to be a long day as the Wolfpack suffered a 34-13 loss. Houston was coached by Bill Yeoman, who was hired by Daugherty in 1954 after Edwards left. (He was profiled in the previous chapter.)

Chesney's first start has been remembered in N.C. State annals, but it was overlooked—like so many Black sports milestones throughout the nation, North and South—in real time. In a typical oversight of the 1960s mainstream media, Chesney's start was reported without historical context.

Peeler, in a 2012 obituary on Chesney written for the N.C. State website, noted an Associated Press pregame report printed in newspapers before the 1969 Houston game "was brief and missed the point completely." The AP story read, "Clyde Chesney will move into a starting role at defensive end for North Carolina State Saturday against Houston replacing Jerry Miller, who has withdrawn from the school for personal reasons."

Chesney maintained his starting job the next two years, and Edwards rewarded him as the school's first Black scholarship football player. Chesney established another milestone as N.C. State's first Black player to earn postseason honors on the 1971 Academic All-ACC team.

Another Peeler website story featured Chesney explaining his motivation to try out for the football team in 1969 spring drills.

"I was always competing with myself to see if could excel in the classroom. I personally disliked the stigma of the dumb athlete and tried to be a good student as well. I had decided against competing at the intercollegiate level but being Black at a predominately white university offered me a challenge that quickly dispelled my idea of not playing. I wanted to prove that I could be a decent student as well as an athlete at North Carolina State."

Although Martin and Chesney had different college athletic experiences, they both proved more than worthy of the academic scholarships they were granted. That leaves an open-ended question of how many African Americans—athletes or just students—would have benefitted from financial support if not for prejudices of the era.

Martin returned to his home state and became a doctor as the first African-American graduate of Eastern Virginia Medical School, in 1976. He went on to a career with titles at the University of Virginia as Professor of Emergency Surgery, Assistant Dean of the School of Medicine, and a Vice-President and Chief Officer of Diversity and Equity.

Chesney went on to earn an N.C. State master's degree and a Ph.D from Michigan State. He was an administrator at Tennessee State when he died in 2012 at age 63.

Young and Burden arrived at N.C. State on the freshman team as Chesney entered his junior season, in 1970. However, with NCAA rules of the time limiting Young and Burden to the freshmen team, they weren't full teammates with Chesney until they were sophomores on the varsity while Chesney was a senior, in 1971.

"Clyde was an upstanding guy," Young said. "He wasn't outspoken, but he showed us the way by how he carried himself. He was a respected player on the team, a good player. We learned from him how he navigated situations when he was the only Black player on the team and one of the few Black students on the campus."

By 1968, N.C. State's *Technician* wrote an editorial encouraging the athletic department to actively recruit Black athletes rather than just accepting walk-on candidates. This was common in the South. Student newspapers and student groups at Alabama and Texas urged their football programs to integrate.

Edwards, like other coaches in the South, could have acted to integrate his program sooner than accepting a walk-on player in 1967, but adding Martin and Chesney to the roster was more than Bear Bryant, who carried a big stick as the preeminent coach in the South, did. At Alabama's 1967 spring drills, Bryant cut five Black players who attempted to make the Crimson Tide as walk-on candidates.

The fair chance Martin and Chesney received from Edwards to make the team also was more supportive than what Arkansas coach Frank Broyles provided a 1965 walk-on, according to Richard Pennington in *Breaking the Ice: The Racial Integration of Southwest Conference Football.*

Pennington, in an August 16, 2017 article he on wrote on his website, *RichardPennington.com*, noted that after African-American Darrell Brown made the freshman team in 1965 as a walk-on, there was an effort by freshmen team coaches Jack Davis and Lon Farrell to "run off" Brown.

Pennington noted a quote from Brown in a *BleacherReport.com* story written October 7, 2011, by Rus Bradburd: "Let me sum up my history with Arkansas football," Brown said. "As a running back, I was simply a tackling dummy."

At N.C. State, football progress was marked by Martin playing in a 1968 game. In basketball, Heartley was awarded a scholarship his sophomore season, 1968-69. Heartley was named a team captain as a junior in 1969-70.

By the fall of 1969, Edwards officially began to recruit Young and Burden as Enloe High seniors, but the informal recruitment began Young's junior season in 1968. Young said when his growth spurts led to injuries, Enloe's coaches arranged for him to receive treatment at N.C. State from the school's trainers.

One of the trainers was Chester Grant, who for three decades was the athletic department's only African-American employee. He worked from 1948 to until his retirement in 1970. He was presented with a new car and other gifts at halftime of the 1970 homecoming game against Virginia.

"I got to know them, and they got to know me," said Young of Grant's influence having him meet the coaches. "Willie was my teammate and a good player, so they learned about him. We ended up both deciding to go to N.C. State, but they were individual decisions."

Young said they took trips to North Carolina and Duke and visited the state's Black colleges. He added he heard from Wake Forest but didn't make a trip. Out-of-state schools also contacted Young, but he said he didn't make any trips.

Young added his integration experience prior to college also was largely without incidents. He grew up attending a Black school, Mary E. Phillips, through sixth grade. Charles B. Aycock Junior High opened as an integrated campus his seventh-grade year, in 1964. He and Burden were football teammates at Aycock.

The Aycock's campus was built adjoining Enloe, which had opened in 1962 as Raleigh's first integrated high school. Young and Burden entered Enloe as tenth graders, in 1967.

"It seemed like a natural progression going from Aycock to Enloe to N.C. State," Young said.

Once Young enrolled at N.C. State and lived in the dormitory, he said he didn't experience racial slurs and prejudice beyond the racism that still can rear its ugly head in America in the 21st century. He recalled only one potentially volatile incident when some white students harassed some Black female students at their dormitory.

"We made our opinions known, but there wasn't a fight," Young said. "It was more of a standoff and expressing opinions."

He also had some uncomfortable moments in a French class and crossing through the tunnel under the train tracks connecting the campus.

"In the French class, there were times when I think some of the students that spoke better French said things and laughed among each other," he said. "It felt like they were making racial comments, but I didn't know for sure.

"The only other thing was you'd see slurs among the political comments painted on the tunnel walls connecting the campus. But they were always covered up pretty quickly."

"The Free Expression Tunnel" runs under train tracks that split the campus. They have a long history of social commentary expressed by students.

But as it turned out, Young and Burden never played for Edwards. They played for freshmen coach Jim Donnan, a former N.C. State quarterback for Edwards who went on to become a head coach at Marshall (1990-95) and Georgia (1996-2000).

"Jim Donnan ran us to death," Young said. "We were the best conditioned freshmen team in the country. We slaughtered teams. The only time we were around Earle was when we were brought up to the scout team to practice against the varsity."

Edwards decided to retire after the 1970 season before Young and Burden joined the varsity, in 1971. Edwards' teams slipped to 3-6-1 in 1969 and 3-7-1 in 1970. Al Michaels, Edwards' long-time assistant, coached the team one season, finishing 1971 with a 3-8 record.

"Earle was a good guy," Young said. "Al was a good guy, too."

LOU HOLTZ AND THE STALLIONS

Lou Holtz was hired in 1972 as the new coach, and he harnessed the talent he inherited. The former Ohio State assistant, a head coach for the first time in his career at William & Mary from 1969 to 1971, was on his way to the College Football Hall of Fame with a 1988 national title at Notre Dame.

Holtz's N.C. State record was 33-12-3 in four seasons with two bowl victories and three teams that finished the season ranked in the Top 20. He left in 1976 for one ill-fated season with the New York Jets before returning to the college ranks.

"Lou Holtz was both funny and crazy," Young said. "He'd throw that clipboard half the football field. If we didn't start out practice with enough energy, he'd make us start over even if we were 30 minutes into it. But he was a great coach. Willie and I both went to a tribute for him they had in Atlanta after he retired."

Although Young didn't have complaints with the N.C. State football program, he considered transferring after his sophomore year due to the lack of a Black social life on campus. By then Holtz had taken over the program.

"I guess he had heard about what I was feeling and wanted to know what I was planning to do," Young said. "Holtz told me everything was going to be different. I never really had a plan. I didn't know how to go about transferring. I didn't even know if I'd have a scholarship at a new school."

The Stallions, L-R: Stan Fritts (33), Charley Young (30), Roland Hooks (42) and Willie Burden (10). This was Lou Holtz's backfield just four years after Chesney was N.C. State's first Black starter. *Courtesy N.C. State.*

By 1972 and 1973, Holtz rotated Young, Burden, Stan Fritts and Roland Hooks—all future pro players—in a versatile backfield that came to be known as "The Stallions." Fritts and Hooks arrived in the 1971 recruiting class. Fritts was white and from Tennessee; Hooks was Black from West Craven High in Vanceboro, North Carolina.

The 1973 team won the ACC title as the Wolfpack rushed for 2,995 yards, a 273.2 per-game average that set a school record. Fritts posted the school's first 1,000-yard rushing season, while Burden was the ACC Player of the Year.

Burden finished his career with 491 carries, 2,529 yards, 22 rushing TDs, 55 receptions, 646 receiving yards and one TD.

Fritts, who played with the Cincinnati Bengals, finished with 534 carries, 2,542 yards rushing, 41 touchdowns, 25 receptions, 367 receiving yards and one TD.

Young's numbers were 317 carries, 1,657 rushing yards, 16 TDs, 10 receptions, 150 receiving yards and one TD.

Hooks, who played with the Buffalo Bills, finished his career with 246 carries, 1,368 yards rushing, 12 TDs, 32 receptions, 417 yards receiving and four TDs.

"Those were four of the best years of my life playing on the team, although there was loneliness because there weren't many Black students on campus," Young said. "On the weekends, I'd pay a quarter to ride the bus back home. The campus was only 20 minutes away, but it was like living in an all-white town on the West Coast. It was another world.

"I think for the early '70s, it was a good experience. We didn't have the problems I heard Black athletes at other schools in the South went through, even though they played just a few years earlier than us in the '60s. If we did have any problems, we knew we could always go to Earle. There were probably some guys on the team that thought differently about things—like there are anywhere—but Willie and I didn't experience problems."

Young was a first-round draft pick of the Dallas Cowboys in 1974, playing four years until injuries cut short his NFL career. He returned home to a career in the Wake County Sheriff's Department until his retirement. He served 28 years in juvenile investigations.

Burden, the ACC Player of the Year in 1973, played eight years in the Canadian Football League with the Calgary Stampeders, entering the Canadian Football Hall of Fame in 2001. Burden earned a master's degree from Ohio University and a Ph.D from Tennessee Tech. He was an associate professor of sports management at Georgia Southern when he died in 2015 while awaiting a heart transplant.

Burden's oldest son, Willie Burden Jr., who played football at Georgia Southern and is a lawyer for the International Brotherhood of Teamsters in Washington, D.C., said based on conversations he had with his father about his N.C. State experience, his father's sentiments matched Young's feelings.

"My dad certainly felt the culture of the program was invested in him as more than just an athlete," Burden Jr. said. "He talked about study hall and the academic expectations for them as N.C. State athletes. He felt the standards shaped the foundation of his future. The discipline he was exposed to helped him to get his doctoral degree. And definitely he harped on education in our family.

"I also remember my dad saying he never had issues with teammates. He never felt any over racial hostility on campus. He felt very highly of the football coaches."

Ironically, as Young reflected on his time at N.C. State, he added he heard more overt racial slurs directed at him during his pro career with the Cowboys when he traveled through small Texas towns.

"The Cowboys had a basketball team that went around to towns to play charity games," Young said. "Roger Staubach and Drew Pearson were on our team. It was terrible what you'd hear from people in those towns. They didn't want to let us eat in their restaurants. And this was the mid-1970s."

Young and center John Fitzgerald, a white player, once drove for treatment at a team doctor's office in a town outside of Dallas.

"You could hear people talking about us, saying racial things like, 'What's the big white guy doing with me.' Oh, my God, it was bad."

Although Holtz raised the Wolfpack's profile once the school welcomed the talent that comes with a fully integrated roster, Edwards remained close to the program and a popular figure in town. He was known to visit practices. He was inducted into the N.C. State Hall of Fame and the North Carolina Sports Hall of Fame. Amedeo's Restaurant, a popular haunt among N.C. State fans since 1963, located across from campus, features the "Earle Edwards Booth."

When Edwards died in 1997 at age 88, his ashes were sprinkled over Carter-Finley Stadium.

That same year, the City of Raleigh presented Young and Burden with the key to the city on "Charley Young and Willie Burden Day." The ceremony was held at Enloe High.

Although Edwards and Daugherty have differing legacies in college football's integration history, they remained close on many levels. Both publicly advocated as early as 1966 for a college football playoff.

They also didn't mind scheduling a game against each other, a practice rarely seen among coaching friends these days. N.C. State opened its 1966 season at Michigan State. The Spartans were the defending national champion from the 1965 season.

The 1966 N.C. State-Michigan State game also was the first career start for Jimmy Raye, who joined the Spartans in Daugherty' 1964 recruiting class of Fayetteville, a U.S. Army base town an hour south of Raleigh. On August 26 the *Raleigh News & Observer*, breaking from the custom of avoiding race in sports stories, noted the irony of Raye starting against N.C. State despite not being recruited by the Wolfpack, North Carolina or Wake Forest.

"Anyone of those three schools would have been alright with me," Raye said in the article. "But I didn't get the chance to go."

The Spartans beat N.C. State 28-10 on their way to a 9-0-1 record. Raye still has the N.C. State game ball from his first career start. It's proudly on display at his home in Pinehurst.

Raye recalled years later, "I had heard people tell me later that after that game, Edwards decided it was time to start recruiting Black athletes."

CHAPTER 11
WYOMING: CHALLENGES FOR BOB DEVANEY AND LLOYD EATON

FACT: Lloyd Eaton was not from Duffy Daugherty's coaching tree, even though Daugherty protégée Bob Devaney brought Eaton from Northern Michigan to Wyoming. Eaton imploded his unbeaten 1969 season with his iron-fisted response to the Black 14.

"The University of Wyoming might have been a welcoming, positive experience for some Black football recruits in the late 1950s and early 1960s. By 1969, however, Lloyd Eaton assured it was not. For Black intercollegiate athletes across the country, the racial ideas and attitudes of individual coaches, athletic directors, or boosters were sometimes more important than state laws, community integration, or legal decisions." —Lane Demas, Central Michigan University history professor and author of Integrating the Gridiron: Black Civil Rights and American College Football.

Bob Devaney and Lloyd Eaton, a couple of Michiganders, built Wyoming football from a program with no Black athletes in the 1950s to boasting one of the more progressive rosters by the late 1960s. Wyoming's 1969 team numbered 14 Black athletes in the cowboy town of Laramie—double the seven that led USC in heavily populated and diverse Los Angeles to the 1967 national title.

Wyoming was Devaney's first job as a head coach in 1957 after four seasons as a Duffy Daugherty assistant at Michigan State. Devaney's plan was to follow Daugherty's blueprint of tapping fertile western Pennsylvania talent and to ignore unwritten quotas limited Black scholarship opportunities.

Eaton and John Melton, a Wyoming alumnus and western Pennsylvania native, helped Devaney duplicate Daugherty's success. Wyoming posted five straight winning seasons by the time Devaney landed the Nebraska job in 1962. He brought Melton with him to Lincoln, and Eaton was named his successor.

Melton's Wyoming presence was to Devaney's uncanny benefit. Devaney arrived as an outsider, but Melton was a local favorite to head off those pratfalls. Melton found talent willing to leave Pennsylvania for the Rocky Mountains. At Nebraska, he recruited Barry Alvarez out of their shared hometown, Burgettstown.

"John Melton was a great recruiter and coach," Alvarez said. "He had a lot to do with helping Bob build his programs."

Melton's path from Burgettstown to Wyoming was serving in the military. He used the G.I. Bill to enroll at Wyoming and play football. Melton was a senior fullback on Wyoming's undefeated 1950 team (10-0) that won the Gator Bowl. The Cowboys began 1950 unranked and climbed to No. 18 and then No. 14. They beat Denver 42-14 in the regular-season finale to finish No. 12 in the era when final polls were conducted voted upon at the end of the regular season.

In the Gator Bowl, then in its sixth year, the No. 12 Cowboys made the 1,800-mile journey to Jacksonville, Florida. They won 20-7 over No. 18 Washington and Lee, a former Division I program from Lexington, Virginia.

Melton, upon college graduation, remained in his adopted state, accepting his first job as a high-school coach in Thermopolis. Devaney, noting Melton's success as a high-school coach as well as his Pennsylvania roots, brought him back to Laramie on his inaugural 1957 staff.

Melton's playing days were Devaney's link to Wyoming's success under Bowden Wyatt in the post-World War II years, 1947-52. Wyatt was 39-17-1 in six seasons. When Wyatt left for Arkansas in 1953, Phil Dickens, the head coach at Wofford University in South Carolina, was hired. Dickens was 29-11-1 with a 10-0 season in 1956. But Dickens, like Wyatt, soon left for a higher profile school, taking the Indiana job in the Big Ten.

Devaney's first season in 1957 started 3-0-1 until the Cowboys slumped in the second half. However, one win and two ties in the final six games accounted for a record above .500 at 4-3-3. Wyoming improved in 1958 to an 8-3 mark, earning a Sun Bowl bid in El Paso, Texas. The Cowboys won 14-6 over Hardin-Simmons, coached by College and Pro Football Hall of Famer Sammy Baugh.

Devaney's Wyoming recruits from Pennsylvania began to influence the program his next three seasons. Wyoming quarterback Andy Melosky of Allentown, Pennsylvania, led the 1961 Cowboys to the Skyline Conference title. Center Stan Popeck of Washington, Pennsylvania, also earned All-Skyline recognition.

Wyoming was 6-1-2 in 1961, beating North Carolina State 15-14 in Laramie and tying Kansas 6-6 on the road. The only loss was to Arizona, then an independent but later a Western Athletic Conference rival with Wyoming.

Devaney's ability to recruit talent to a sparsely populated state relied on a continued connection with Michigan high schools as well as national recruiting. Mike Walker of Detroit led the 1961 Cowboys in receiving and total offense and was named All-Skyline. Other Michiganders earning All-Skyline honors were tackle Dan Grego, Grand Rapids; end Bob Knight, Adrian; and offensive lineman Dick Williams, Ann Arbor.

Other 1961 All-Skyline picks were Chuck Lamson (Ames, Iowa) and Chuck Schmitt (Chicago). Massachusetts has been never known as a high-school football hotbed, but three Massachusetts recruits who earned All-Skyline honors were Bob Bisacre, Lawrence; Kevin Ward, Wakefield; and Bill Levine, Winthrop.

Trust and connections are vital to a coach convincing talent to leave for a school far from home. That was another foundation Alvarez learned from Devaney and Milton and utilized as Wisconsin's head coach.

"A lot of it starts with building relationships in an area where coaches trust you and can identify players that they think will fit in your program," Alvarez said. "They know if they sent you players before and you treated them well. They know you're going make sure their kids go to school, get a chance to graduate and treat them right on the football field. They showed you really cared about their kids. Then, the high-school coach sells you to the kid. They say these guys are good guys, they're legitimate guys and you're going to get treated right there."

Devaney also began to gain commitments from Black players. Wyoming's first Black football letterman was Taft Harris in 1933, but the Cowboys' roster was all-white when Devaney arrived in Laramie. By the time Devaney left for Nebraska with a 35-10-5 five-year mark, there were three Black players on Wyoming's roster, including Mike Walker.

Eaton took over the Cowboys in 1962. He continued expanding the number of Black athletes on his roster, and there some big seasons on the horizon, even though the competition was stiffer in the newly formed Western Athletic Conference. The league formed in 1962 with Arizona, Arizona State, Brigham Young, Utah, New Mexico and Wyoming.

Eaton's 1966 and 1967 Cowboys posted back-to-back 10-1 seasons with 5-0 WAC titles. The 1966 Cowboys beat Florida State 28-20 in the Sun Bowl. The 1967 team ranked No. 6 but lost to unranked LSU 20-13 in the Sugar Bowl. The 1966 team finished the year ranked No. 15 in the Associated Press poll and the 1967 Cowboys No. 5 by AP (writers) and No. 6 by United Press International (coaches).

Wyoming's record in 1968 slipped to 7-3, but the 6-1 league mark was good for a third straight WAC title. But the 1969 season imploded with Eaton's self-inflicted wounds.

VEERING OFF COURSE IN WYOMING

Eaton and Devaney were long-time friends and colleagues, but Eaton's 1969 actions revealed he wasn't from the Daugherty coaching tree. Daugherty and Devaney recruited Black athletes to help them win football games and provide them a free education. Eaton recruited Black athletes to win football games.

Wyoming was off to a 4-0 start with a No. 18 national ranking, including a 3-0 record in Western Athletic Conference play. They appeared on their way to a fourth straight WAC title, but trouble was on the horizon.

Wyoming's fifth game was October 11 at home against Brigham Young University, a school sponsored by The Church of Jesus Christ of Latter-day Saints. The players asked Eaton if they could protest the church's discriminatory practices against Blacks. (Pre-1978, Blacks were barred from entering the priesthood and were segregated from the white members of the LDS.) They also said they were subjected to racial epithets from BYU's players in their 1968 game at Provo, Utah. One form of protest they suggested was Black armbands.

They presented their case, but there was no discussion: Eaton dismissed them from the team. The case drew national attention and the players became known as the Black 14. The national media that avoided race in sports stories throughout the 1960s adopted new attitudes following the 1968 Mexico City Olympics. There was no avoiding the story of Tommie Smith and John Carlos standing on the Olympic medal stand with heads bowed and black-gloved fists raised to protest America's treatment of African Americans.

Eaton, though, was behind the times. His iron-fisted dismissals without debate equates to the modern-day, right-wing political commentators like Fox News's Laura Ingraham telling pro LeBron James, a socially conscious pro basketball player, to "shut up and dribble." At the time, Eaton had the support of the Wyoming administration and fan base, although some faculty members protested the players were denied their academic freedom of expression.

Among Wyoming's Black 14 were two future NFL players: Joe Williams, who played at a segregated Black high school in Lufkin, Texas, and Tony McGee, from Battle Creek, Michigan. Williams played four NFL seasons and McGee 14.

Wyoming, despite facing BYU with a short-handed lineup, defeated the Cougars 40-7 to improve to 5-0 overall and 4-0 in the WAC. The Cowboys won again the next week, beating San Jose State in a nonconference game, 16-7, to improve to 6-0 with a No. 15 ranking. Next up was a road trip to WAC rival Arizona State—a school led by Frank Kush, another Daugherty protégé who provided Black athletes opportunities.

Arizona State defeated Wyoming 30-14, setting off a streak of four straight double-digit road losses. The Cowboys lost at Utah, 34-10; at New Mexico, 24-12; and a nonconference game at No. 19 Houston in the Astrodome, 41-14.

The promising 1969 season ended with a 6-4 thud. Eaton returned to coach in 1970, but the damage was done. The program's downward spiral continued with a 1-9 record. Eaton was fired at the end of the 1970 season.

How do we explain Eaton, parting from Devaney's example, while undermining his own team and coaching career? Eaton left coaching and was considered a recluse until his death at age 88 in 2007.

Lane Demas offered an explanation based on his years of research on race in sports. The Central Michigan University history professor with a Ph.D wrote extensively about the Black 14 in his 2011 book, *Integrating the Gridiron: Black Civil Rights and American College Football*. He also is the author of a 2017 book, *Game of Privilege: An African-American History of Golf*.

"Contrary to the idea that institutions embraced integration at a single moment—decreed by governors, regents, or university presidents—the acceptance of Black athletes ebbed and flowed, often dependent on the whims of a specific athletic director, a new head coach, or fan sentiment during a particular season," Demas said. "The University of Wyoming might have been a welcoming, positive experience for some Black football recruits in the late 1950s and early 1960s. By 1969, however, Lloyd Eaton assured it was not. For Black intercollegiate athletes across the country, the racial ideas and attitudes of individual coaches, athletic directors, or boosters were sometimes more important than state laws, community integration, or legal decisions."

Wyoming suffered a Black 14 aftermath through five more losing seasons. But the fifth, a 2-9 record in 1975, was a turning point with Fred Akers as the new coach. He had been Texas' offensive coordinator on the Longhorns' national championship teams. Texas began fielding integrated rosters with Julius Whittier signing in 1969 and joining the varsity as s sophomore, in 1970.

Akers' 1976 squad posted an 8-4 record. His 1976 offensive coordinator was Jimmy Raye, Michigan State's pioneering Black quarterback. Raye was out of a job entering 1976 after four years as a Michigan State assistant. The Spartans forced Denny Stolz to resign in the wake of an NCAA scandal. Raye had planned to take a job at San Jose State, but Duffy Daugherty steered him to Akers and Wyoming.

"I told Duffy I was thinking of taking a job at San Jose State," said Raye, "but he told me, 'No, you're not. You're going to Wyoming.' I said, 'Why would I want to go to Wyoming?' He told me, 'Because Fred Akers is the head coach there. Frank Broyles and Darrell Royal will retire soon, and Fred Akers will be the new head coach at Arkansas or Texas in a year or two.'"

Daugherty was in the loop with the coaching fraternity and proved prescient.

"I talked with Duffy a lot in my career," Akers said in a 2014 interview prior to his death at age 82 in 2020. "Whether he knew it or not, I considered him a mentor. We exchanged a lot of ideas we thought would make our teams better. Duffy always put on a good clinic. It was a strong point for him. He was a unique individual."

Wyoming's 1976 season included, by coincidence, a trip to Spartan Stadium the second week of the season to face Michigan State and new coach Darryl Rogers. The Spartans struggled in the first half until pulling out a 21-10 victory. Wyoming ran off five straight wins on the way to an 8-3 regular season. The Cowboys earned their first bowl bid since 1967, although they lost to No. 8-ranked Oklahoma in the Fiesta Bowl.

"Wyoming turned out to be one of my greatest experiences in coaching," Raye said. "I was concerned about taking my family to a city with only one other Black family, but we really enjoyed Laramie. My wife was involved in civic activities. I used to drop my kids off at school and wonder what I done to them with my selfish coaching desires sending them to a school with no students like them. But my kids enjoyed the school. They didn't want to leave for Texas."

Wyoming's 1976 turnaround led to Texas bringing Akers back home.

In the offseason preceding the 1977 season, Raye helped with the finishing touches of the 1977 recruiting class and began to lay the groundwork for the 1978 recruiting class. That included mending fences with Black high-school coaches, many of them still bitter that former Texas coach Darrell Royal failed to recruit Black athletes until 1969.

"I'll bet you people in Houston still remember Jimmy Raye and how he recruited for the University of Texas," said Akers in 2014.

But Raye was gone before the kickoff of the 1977 season, which included Earl Campbell winning the Heisman Trophy. Raye's appearance speaking at a coaching clinic in San Antonio unexpectedly led his first job in the National Football League with the San Francisco 49ers, in 1977. Meanwhile, Wyoming's program continued to recover from the shameful 1969 season. The Cowboys won back-to-back WAC titles in 1987 and 1988 under head coach Paul Roach, who, ironically, had been an assistant coach under Eaton.

Eaton was soon enough a forgotten man in college football, but Wyoming recognized the need for a reckoning. In 2002, the school dedicated the Black 14 sculpture, placing it on display in the Wyoming Union. The sculpture was funded by the Associated Students of the University of Wyoming.

In 2019, on the 50th anniversary of the Black 14, Wyoming president Laurie Nichols and athletic director Tom Burman invited the surviving members back to campus. The players were presented with jerseys, lettermen jackets and the opportunity to speak about diversity and their experience before groups on campus.

Nichols and Burman signed a letter that the university posted as an apology on its website (*uwyo.edu*), dated May 21, 2019.

To Members of the Black 14:

"As president, and athletics director at the University of Wyoming, we have had the pleasure of getting to know many of you as members of the Black 14 while discussing the 50th anniversary. It has been an honor and privilege to reconnect with you and hear your story. That story is heart-wrenching, and we feel it is extremely important for this institution to reflect on that difficult time here at UW and across the country. As an institution, we believe we have learned and grown from what you had to endure. The college experience should be a rich one, and one of the best times of a young person's life. You were deprived of that experience for reasons that were not of your doing. Not to be heard, to be shunned, and to have your collegiate careers derailed as both students and athletes is a tragedy. Unfortunately, it continued beyond your time here.

"We embrace the University's mission of nurturing, 'an environment that values and manifests diversity, internationalization, free expression, academic freedom, personal integrity and mutual respect.' We believe that mission rose in part from your courage and sacrifice.

"We applaud you, but most importantly, respect you for rising above that difficult time to build productive lives. You remained faithful to your convictions as you moved forward, all the while continuing to tell the compelling story of the Black 14. As you told that story, it would have been easy to attack the university that turned its back on you. But you demonstrated immense character and integrity in avoiding that path. Your actions then, and throughout these 50 years have definitely made a difference, not only on this campus, but throughout our country.

"Please accept this sincere apology from the University of Wyoming for the unfair way you were treated, and for the hardships that treatment created for you. We want to welcome you home as valued members of this institution, and hope you accept our old Wyoming saying, "once a Cowboy, always a Cowboy."

With Warmest Regards,
Laurie S. Nicholas, President
Tom Burman, Athletics Director

CHAPTER 12
DAN DEVINE AT NOTRE DAME: IMAGE IS EVERYTHING

FACT: Dan Devine and Bear Bryant both arrived as head coaches in 1958 at their Southern state's flagship school. Devine coached integrated teams throughout his final season, 1970, increasing the number of scholarship athletes each year. Bryant didn't recruit a Black athlete until 1970, even though Alabama's campus desegregated in 1963, and President Lyndon B. Johnson signed the Civil Rights Acts of 1964 and 1965.

"It did not take a genius at that time to know something was wrong with this picture, and to know that his failure to stand apart from the worst of his region's culture diminished him as a man on something as profoundly important as this."
—Pulitzer Prize winner David Halberstam in a 2002 ESPN article on Alabama coach Bear Bryant dragging his feet on integration and the civil rights movement.

Dan Devine's 2000 book, *Simply Devine: Memoirs of a Hall of Fame Coach*, featured a cover photo of him engulfed in Notre Dame regalia. Trophies and memorabilia decorated his home office. He wore a blue Notre Dame shirt with an interlocked gold ND crest. He's clutching an Irish trademark gold helmet.

The Irishman and devout Catholic is smiling, proud of his six Notre Dame seasons and a 1977 national title. He should be. Devine was enshrined in the College Football Hall of Fame in 1985 with a career record of 173-56-9, a .755 winning percentage. His Notre Dame record was 53-16-1 (.768) from 1975 through 1980. But even without his Notre Dame years, his career was worthy of the Hall of Fame. Devine was 27-3-1 (.900) in three seasons at Arizona State, 1955 to 1957, and 92-38-7 (.707) in 13 at Missouri, 1958-70.

But there is a problem with the book cover. His smile appears forced, coaxed by the photographer and book's marketing personnel. He looks as uncomfortable as Notre Dame fans were with him. They never embraced him. His crime? He wasn't Ara Parseghian, the popular coach he succeeded.

A more comfortable setting for Devine would have him posed in the Arizona State maroon and gold or Missouri's old gold and black. Those fan bases loved him as their coach and their former coach.

Devine, in retirement, was welcomed home to the Valley of the Sun. He served as a fundraiser for the Arizona State's Sun Angel Foundation, 1985-92. He left only because Missouri asked for his help. The athletic department was in financial distress, and Devine agreed to return to Columbia as the Tigers' athletic director, 1992-94.

Such affection was missing then and now at Notre Dame. When his five-year contract wasn't renewed, he announced on August 15 the upcoming 1980 season would be his final one. Notre Dame proceeded to contend for another national title, but the fans were unmoved.

John Feinstein, who covered college sports for the *Washington Post* before he launched his bestselling book-writing career, visited with Devine on campus prior to Notre Dame traveling to face Alabama late in the 1980 season. At the time, a fifth bowl was a matter of which bid to accept. And a second national title was in reach. Feinstein's *Post* piece, published on November 12, appropriately summed up Devine's swan song.

"Consider the record: Four bowl bids in six years, one national championship achieved, a second being worked on. A record of 7-0-1 this year and a six-season mark of 51-14-1. A winning percentage of almost .800.

In return, the coach is being run out of town.

The coach is Dan Devine and the school is Notre Dame, and that should at least partly explain the situation. Since the day he arrived in 1974 to succeed Ara Parseghian, Devine has not been able to escape the shadow.

Parseghian was emotional and easy to identify with; Devine is low key and distant. Parseghian was colorful and glib; Devine is colorless and often fumbles for words. Parseghian took a 2-7 loser and won immediately; Devine took a winner and won slightly less.

The alumni have never accepted him, many of the players have made fun of him and the press, at times, have ravaged him."

Feinstein's summary was accurate. The unfair part was the public perception.

The Notre Dame-Alabama matchup paired the college game's two active winningest coaches for their showdown on November 15 at Legion Field in Birmingham. In those days, Alabama moved its big games from campus to Legion Field. ABC featured the broadcast back in the days when it was a treat to be on national television. Both teams were still in the running for a national title. Fewer people, though, understood or appreciated that Devine enjoyed a 3-0 record against Bryant.

His first win over Bryant was in the 1968 Gator Bowl. Devine's integrated Missouri team, ranked No. 16, beat Bryant's all-white Alabama roster, ranked No. 12, 35-10.

The next two times they met were regular-season contests. By then, Bryant had read the Declaration of Independence, having integrated his rosters in the 1970s.

In 1976, Alabama's No. 10-ranked team traveled to South Bend and lost to Devine and the No. 18 Irish, 21-18.

In the 1980 game, Notre Dame was ranked No. 6 and Alabama No. 5. Notre Dame won at Legion Field before 78,873 fans, 7-0. Devine was an underdog in all three wins over Bryant without a loss. Bryant's career record was 323-85-7. Is there another coach who faced him multiple times and never lost?

But, in the true test of a leader, Devine was the one who cast a shadow over Bryant. The social issue of their time and surrounding college football was integration and the civil rights movement. Devine had a long track record of leadership from the 1950s through his final season. Bryant dragged his feet until he was one of the shirkers to get on the bus with Georgia, LSU and Mississippi. Alabama's campus was desegregated in 1963, but Bryant didn't recruit a Black player until 1970. The 1964 and 1965 Civil Rights Acts President Lyndon B. Johnson signed didn't move Bryant either.

Pulitzer Prize winner David Halberstam and a *New York Times* best-selling author, wrote a 2002 ESPN article about Bryant's legacy. The headline: "**Just a coach, not a leader.**"

Halberstam: *"...the Bear was very late to the dance, especially because people are always talking about football coaches as leaders. In this case, he did not lead very well. We know that he was a divided man on this, and we know that he was* slow, much too slow to act, and so here we have the real test of a man in conflict with himself, and the complexity that takes us inside even the honored and most successful of men."

Bryant has many apologists in the media, which led to not one but three premium networks—HBO, Showtime and ESPN—falling over themselves to falsely portray Bryant as a crusader on integration. The films don't include Halberstam's view.

"It did not take a genius at that time to know something was wrong with this picture, and to know that his failure to stand apart from the worst of his region's culture diminished him as a man on something as profoundly important as this."

Devine is at the opposite end of the spectrum but unjustly ignored. He had been passing the college coach test of leadership since his years as a Michigan State assistant, 1950-54. He learned from his mentor, Duffy Daugherty. Devine followed Daugherty's blueprint, increasing the number of Black scholarship players at each job he took.

"Image is everything," as tennis legend Andre Agassi's Canon cameras commercials declared in a successful advertising campaign.

Another ironic failure of the media has been how the film industry treated Bryant and Devine.

The networks embellishing the impact of the 1970 USC-Alabama game and their films were HBO's *Breaking the Huddle*, 2008; Showtime's *Against the Tide*, 2013; and two ESPN films in 2019 and 2020. One was for the 150th anniversary of college football in 2019 and the other for the 50th anniversary celebrating the 1970 game. Bryant's star power green-lights films.

Not so for Devine. Movies on a colorless coach don't get funded, even though his story includes legitimate drama. He pushed for progress against the tide of the 1950s and 1960s.

The only film involving Devine relied on fiction to portray him as the bad guy in the 1993 movie, *Rudy*. Hollywood embellished the ending of Notre Dame walk-on player Rudy Ruettiger's career as a scout team player. In the script, Ruettiger is counting on dressing for the team's final 1975 home game of his career, but Devine again leaves his name from the list. Notre Dame's players object, filing into his to turn in their jerseys as a message to Devine that Rudy can dress in place of them.

Notre Dame legend Joe Montana, a freshman quarterback in 1975, was among players, along with Devine, saying it never happened. Devine explains in his autobiography the scene's development. He says screenwriter Angelo Pizzo, who also wrote the 1986 blockbuster film *Hoosiers*, told Devine the *Rudy* movie would only be successful with

Devine as the heavy. That's how writers add drama to stories lacking a denouement.

"I told Angelo I would do everything to help Rudy, including being the heavy," Devine wrote.

Devine, who never read the script before the film was released, then added, "I didn't realize I would be such a heavy."

Here again is a contrast between Devine and Bear Bryant in the realm of film and image casting. Screenwriters don't ask Bear Bryant or John Wayne to play the heavy.

The timing of Halberstam's 2002 ESPN article was to critique the upcoming ESPN movie, *Junction Boys*. The film was about Bryant's first preseason camp in 1954 as Texas A&M's new coach. Bryant staged the camp in an isolated setting in brutal conditions. He imposed inhumane practices while denying water breaks.

Bryant comes off as the tough drill-sergeant coach willing the most out of his athletes while molding them into men. Halberstam was critical, writing, "Rarely have I seen a movie so well-promoted by a network—if anything, it struck me as I watched, that more time and energy and perhaps money had gone into promoting it than making it."

That's not all. Halberstam apparently couldn't resist digressing from critiquing *Junction Boys* to bringing up Bryant's poor integration record. That speaks volumes and reflects Halberstam's journalism career. He covered the civil rights movement early in his career for two Southern newspapers, the *Daily Times Leader* in West Point, Mississippi, and *The Tennessean* in Nashville.

Martin Luther King Jr. spoke about "the appalling silence of and indifference of the good people who sit around and say wait on time."

Halberstam expressed his contempt for Bryant's silence later in his *Junction Boys* critique.

"The great test of him as a man was not whether he gave or did not give water to his players that first summer. The great test of him was how he handled the subject of race as Alabama's football coach—as the South's signature coach on a subject of great importance, whether or not to go after black players despite regional prejudice—during a terrible time, when the entire nation, but most importantly the deep South was being torn apart on the issues of race, prejudice and traditional culture. I happened to be working as a reporter in the South in those years, and I remember what he did not do, as well as what he did do. The Supreme Court in 1954 had mandated integration, but the deep South states, most especially Mississippi, Alabama and Georgia were complete in their resistance to change. And Bear Bryant had arrived in Alabama, his old school, in 1958, in time to be there through much of the most bitter and painful part of that struggle."

At Arizona State, Devine grew the numbers from three on the 1955 team he inherited to seven on his final team, in 1957. At Missouri, the Tigers' numbers grew from two Black players on his first team in 1958 to 13 on his final team, 1970.

Although college football integration was fait accompli by 1975, Notre Dame was one of the schools that still had low numbers of Black players, but Devine's recruits noticed the difference under him. Devine's first full year on campus of recruiting was the 1976 class. There were 10 Black recruits, the largest class in the program's history, including All-American running back Vagas Ferguson of Richmond, Indiana.

"Being a kid, you don't realize things like that other than you know you're in the minority," Ferguson said. "We knew the football players and all the other Black students on campus we were in the minority. We talked about it in groups, but basically it was just about trying get your education. We knew it was an opportunity."

Notre Dame, with its national recruiting base, had a history of avoiding recruiting Black athletes for fear of alienating prospects from the South. There were a few exceptions, though. The school's first Black players didn't arrive on campus until the 1950s. Wayne Edmonds was a lineman, 1953-55; Richard Washington a halfback, 1953; and Aubrey Lewis a halfback, 1955-57.

In the 1966 Game of the Century matching Notre Dame and Michigan State, Notre Dame had one Black player, Alan Page. Daugherty's Spartans lined up 20 Black players.

Although Parseghian only had one Black player on his team, it had more to do with Notre Dame than him. Parseghian had coached Black athletes at Northwestern (1956-63). At Notre Dame (1964-74), he began to recruit more Black players in the late 1960s, with his 1973 national title team featuring 13 Black players. Graduation, injuries, academics and other reasons for attrition account for fluctuating final roster numbers, but Devine's 1977 national title grew the number to 17.

Devine's struggles to gain favor with Notre Dame fans may have been doomed from the start. Not only was the popular Parseghian retired, Devine arrived in the wake of a highly publicized and ugly departure from the Green Bay Packers. Despite an NFC Central title in 1972 with a 10-4 record, the fans ran him out of town after back-to-back seasons of 5-7-2 and 6-8.

Packers fans had previously turned on Phil Bengsten, defensive coordinator on Vince Lombardi's two Super Bowl championship teams. Bengsten's three seasons after taking over an aging roster resulted in three losing records. Bengsten's record was 21-25-1. His crime was the same as Devine's—they weren't Vince Lombardi.

Devine's final season grew uglier. He accused some fans of shooting and killing his dog, although years later it was revealed a farmer near the Devine property had shot the dog for raiding his chickens. *Time* Magazine wrote a story on Devine with the headline, "**Haunted in Green Bay.**"

Devine, with such recent history, failed to excite the Notre Dame fans. His first Notre Dame season saw a winning record of 8-3 and national ranking of No. 17, but no bowl trip. The 1976 season was a little better, 9-3 and ranked No. 12 with a Gator Bowl win. But neither season satisfied a fan base that expects national titles. Parseghian had won three in 11 seasons: 1964, 1966 and 1973.

"The sad thing about Dan was Green Bay ran him out," Ferguson said. "When he got to us, he was shell-shocked. He didn't talk a lot. He was withdrawn. But what I admired about him is he let his coaches coach. That's why we played so well. He wasn't the type to inspire us. We were prepared for every game."

Playing "well" for Devine finally developed in 1977, although the season opened with him on the hot seat and the temperature rising until a 1-1 start had fans posting "Dump Devine" signs.

Notre Dame opened 1977 ranked No. 3 and defeating defending national champion Pitt, the No. 7-ranked team, 19-9. In the second game the Irish, still ranked No. 3, lost at unranked Mississippi 20-13. The Irish wilted in the 90-degree heat at Memorial Stadium in Jackson, Mississippi. The third game, Notre Dame dropped to No. 11, traveled to Purdue and won an uninspiring game, 31-24.

By the time Michigan State arrived for the fourth game on October 1, Notre Dame dropped to No. 14. Outside the football offices, Devine's parking spot was marked on the curb with block black letters was crossed out with a sweeping red X.

The Friday night before the game, the students gathered in the old fieldhouse for their traditional home-game pep rally. The band played. Streamers flew back and forth. On stage was All-American senior defensive end Ross Browner. Browner, microphone in hand, rallied the students.

"We know we've got the best fans!" Browner said, the fans roaring in response.

"We know we've got the best players!" he said with another cascading roar.

"And we know we've got the best coaches!" Silence.

They didn't boo, but they went silent as effectively as flicking a light switch to darkness.

Notre Dame beat Michigan State, with junior Joe Montana coming off the bench to rally the Irish to a 16-6 win and 4-0 record. But the season's turning point with the fans wasn't for another two weeks. Fifth-ranked USC arrived to play No. 11 Notre Dame in South Bend in the "Green Jersey Game."

Devine, the dull coach, came up with a masterful motivational ploy. A few weeks earlier he had ordered green jerseys for the Irish to wear. Notre Dame warmed up in its traditional blue tops and then retreated to the locker room to find green jerseys at their lockers. The players donned them in excitement. The crowd roared as they emerged from the stadium tunnel onto the field. Notre Dame routed USC, 49-19.

The Irish continued rolling to nine straight wins and a 10-1 record. They climbed to No. 5 entering the Cotton Bowl against No. 1 Texas and fullback Earl Campbell. Notre Dame routed the Longhorns, 38-10, jumping to No. 1 in the final poll votes. They vaulted past No. 2 Oklahoma, which lost to No. 6 Arkansas, 31-6; No. 3 Alabama, which beat No. 9 Ohio State, 35-6; and No. 4 Michigan, which lost to No. 13 Washington, 27-20.

Three months after Notre Dame's students were unable to muster a cheer for Devine at the urging of their All-American leader, they were celebrating a national championship.

The national title brought down the "Dump Devine" signs, but Devine still wasn't Ara Parsgehian. He wasn't embraced. He also hasn't been properly remembered for the diversity milestones he brought to the football program. The 1977 team included two Black players as All-American choices, defensive end Ross Browner and cornerback Luther Bradley. Notre Dame's third All-American pick was Ken MacAfee, a white tight end. More Black All-American picks than white was a first at Notre Dame.

Although Browner and Bradley were recruited by Parseghian, three of Browner's four seasons developed under Devine. Browner was Notre Dame's first Black player to win prestigious postseason awards—three of them in all. He won the 1976 Outland Trophy, 1977 Maxwell Award and 1977 Lombardi Award.

The 10 Black freshmen in Devine's 1976 class boosted the roster number to a program high of 23. Although Ferguson was among the 10, Notre Dame originally wasn't on his radar.

"I really didn't think about Notre Dame," he said.

He thought of himself as a Big Ten player. He noted his hometown of Richmond on Indiana's southeastern border of Ohio was closer to the Ohio State campus in Columbus, 107 miles, than Notre Dame in South Bend, 202 miles. Both Ohio State coach Woody Hayes and Michigan coach Bo Schembechler, who ruled the Big Ten in the 1970s, made recruiting trips to Richmond.

Michigan had an edge following his recruiting trip to Ann Arbor for the 1975 Ohio State-Michigan game. Although No. 1 Ohio State defeated No. 4 Michigan, 21-14, Ferguson was enthralled by the crowd of 105,464 fans greeting the team as he ran behind it onto the field.

But in those days, recruits typically didn't make their commitment announcement until after Christmas or as late as the February signing day. By then, Ferguson's mindset toward Notre Dame changed based on how Irish assistant coach Brian Boulac pursued him.

Boulac, Devine's offensive-line coach and recruiting coordinator, was a holdover from Parsehgian's staff. He was a Irish letterman, 1960 to 1962. Boulac was a senior when Dick Arrington, a rare Black recruit in those days, arrived on Notre Dame's 1962 freshmen team. Arrington was an All-American lineman as a senior in 1965. As a heavyweight wrestler, he placed third in the 1965 NCAA meet.

"Coach Boo recruited just about all the Black athletes," Ferguson said. "He had played there and graduated there and came back there to coach. When he talked to you, there was no color. He made you feel not so much you're going to be a star player, but we're going to make sure you get an education.

"For me, coming my background raised by my grandparents, that was always preached to me. Education, education, education. He talked to my grandparents, and they fell in love with him. They felt he cared more about education than football."

Ferguson added "what sealed the deal" to his Notre Dame commitment was touring campus separately with Browner and Bradley.

"They both said the same thing, but at different times," Ferguson said. "Browner said, 'I'll tell you what, if you come to Notre Dame, you better come as a student first.' Then I was with Luther later and first thing out of his mouth was, 'If you don't plan on being a student first, don't come here. You come here to graduate.'

"I didn't need to hear anything else. I didn't hear that anywhere else. Ohio State and Michigan just talked about playing football."

Whatever restrictions on Black recruits in the past, they were erased by Devine. Boulac had a free rein to target the best players.

"He recruited Black players from Texas, Washington, East St. Louis…he was everywhere. I think that was a key to Devine having him. Coach Boo understood how to recruit Black athletes."

Ferguson added another irony to his success at Notre Dame was both Ohio State and Michigan had recruited him as a defensive back, but he preferred offense. He felt Notre Dame recruited him as a running back.

"I think coach Boo knew that, so he only talked about offense," Ferguson said, chuckling.

However, when Ferguson arrived on campus for preseason practices, he found himself splitting time between offense and defense. He didn't have to worry about it for long, though. After a few days, running backs coach Hank Kuhlman quietly told Ferguson, "Just stay over here. Don't go over to defense." Ferguson said that was an example of Devine letting his "coaches coach."

Devine certainly noticed Ferguson on offense from his place in a tower above the practice field, but he didn't shout over his bullhorn to get Ferguson back on defense. Instead, he did single out Ferguson, expressing anger over his stutter-steps faking directions as he hit the line of scrimmage. Ferguson, laughing, recalling how Devine shifted into a high-pitched voice.

"He'd yell from the tower, '*FERGUSON! Run north-south!*'"

Ferguson, as a sophomore backup on the 1977 title team, shared the team lead with six touchdowns while rushing for 493 yards on 6.2 yards per carry. As a junior he ran for 1,192 yards and seven touchdowns. He was a senior All-American pick in 1979 with 1,437 yards and 17 touchdowns. He was fifth in the Heisman Trophy voting.

After he played five NFL seasons, he worked a stint as a salesman for Belden, a Richmond, Indiana, company. When he wanted to work with kids, he changed careers. The Richmond school district hired him first as an interim high-school athletic director, and with time he transitioned to administration. He has been the district's Equity Officer the past 20 years.

His new career brought back thoughts about the lack of Black recruits and students at Notre Dame, and the increasing overall number under Devine. He broke down a chart of the Black players his four seasons, 1976-79. The numbers changed with graduation, injuries, academics and other forms of attrition. With the 10 freshmen in 1976, the roster grew to 23 Black players. It dropped to 17 in 1977. It was back up to 18 by his senior season, 1979.

"It shows you how racism had continued," Ferguson said. "It was unbeknown to the players then, but I can see it clearly now. It's mind-boggling. We had 10 Black players in my freshman class and one the next year with only Jim Stone. It's satisfying that we're making progress in race relations, but it's something we still deal with."

Devine arguably could have recruited more Black athletes in his six seasons, considering how his numbers pale compared to the modern game. But the measuring stick that matters was he didn't continue the status quo, the pattern of most of his peers until quotas broke down in the 1970s.

He pushed the needle forward at Notre Dame just as he had done at Arizona State and Missouri. Those open-minded attitudes were part of his Michigan State experience.

In fact, an innocent question that angered Devine following the 1977 Michigan State-Notre Dame game indicated his passion for the Spartans and Duffy Daugherty's legacy. In those days, postgame interviews weren't the orchestrated events they are now with the coach and players at a table. Reporters could interview their subject in the locker room.

In 1977, the sports editor for *The State News*, Michigan State's student newspaper, wanted to ask Devine what he thought about the Michigan State-Notre Dame rivalry now that he was on the other side of it. It would make for a good state-of-the-rivalry story.

Notre Dame, of course, was still a national brand. But since the 1966 Game of the Century, Michigan State had only finished the year ranked once, No. 12 in 1974. A year later the NCAA announced an investigation into head coach Denny Stolz and his staff for recruiting violations. In 1976, the NCAA brought down the hammer with three years of probation. The recruiting fallout set the program back into the 1980s.

The State News sports editor found Devine in the back of the locker room with about four other Notre Dame writers standing around him. The kid joined the semi-circle. Devine, who had been nursing an ulcer, sipped milk from a coffee cup, grinning, clearly happy with the result as he answered questions about the game.

Then the kid asked Devine for his opinion about Michigan State holding up its end of the rivalry. Devine went Jekyll and Hyde. He launched into a tirade. He blamed the Michigan State administration for cutting Daugherty's football budget at the end of his tenure. He eviscerated Stolz getting the program on probation.

"There's nothing wrong with Michigan State except the people that got them on NCAA probation!" Devine bellowed "They created this mess. Michigan State is a great school. They didn't deserve this!"

Here was a spontaneous story handed on a silver platter. Devine answered the question without answering the question.

However, the stunned young reporter, mistakenly feeling as if Devine was yelling at him, retreated, confused, from the scene. He didn't realize until he was a more mature writer how he should have handled the story. His thoughts summoned his journalism classes and trusted journalism advisor, Dr. Mary Gardner, and theory learned in the classroom.

Didn't he need to give an MSU administrator and Stolz for their chance to respond to Devine's tirade? This story required follow-up phone calls—a task never taken up. Nor, it should be added, was it covered by the veteran reporters that witnessed Devine's tirade defending Daugherty and Michigan State.

Here was another moment of Dan Devine standing up for principles evaporated into the air. So much of his career remained unappreciated.

"Image is everything"—fortunately for Bear Bryant, unfortunately for Dan Devine.

CHAPTER 13
THE 1967 NFL DRAFT THAT CHANGED THE FACE OF THE LEAGUE

FACT: Four of the first eight picks in the 1967 NFL draft were Michigan State players, a record no school has come close to matching.

"I said, 'Who are you?' The guy says, 'My name is Sid Hartman from the Minneapolis Tribune.' I told him, 'That's great news and I'm glad you shared it with me.' After a while I hung up, and about a week later I got my first call from someone at the Vikings. That's all the fanfare we got back in those days." —Gene Washington.

A half-century ago the NFL Draft was so simple NFL commissioner Pete Rozelle stood at a chalkboard in a New York hotel ballroom, scrawling names in chalk as they were called out.

The anticipation hovering over the draft was not about who would go where. It was a relief—to the owners, not the players—that the athletes were taken by only one team. The 1967 draft was the first since the NFL-AFL merger, ending bidding wars for talent between 16 NFL franchises and nine AFL teams. (A tenth AFL team, the Cincinnati Bengals, launched after this draft and was part of the 1970 merger.)

The 21st-century draft inundates all of us with wall-to-wall coverage. We have live coverage on two networks, ESPN and NFL Network. Mock drafts have been drawn and redrawn since the day the previous draft ended. There is a TV green room for the top picks, their families and agents. Instant analysis is offered on the live coverage.

That's far from the way it was in 1967: no television coverage, no in-depth media analysis.

Four African-American Spartans were taken among the first eight draft picks: 1, Bubba Smith, Baltimore Colts; 2. Clint Jones, Minnesota Vikings; 5. George Webster, Houston Oilers; and 8. Gene Washington, Minnesota Vikings. Six of the top eight choices were African-American players, with Syracuse's Floyd Little (Denver Broncos) and UCLA's Mel Farr (Detroit Lions) the sixth and seventh picks.

Compare that to the 1966 NFL draft: among 16 first-round picks there were 14 white players and only two Black athletes (Dick Leftridge of West Virginia and Francis Peay of Missouri). There was only four Black athlete first-round picks overall among 24 teams (15 NFL, nine AFL). In the AFL, there were three white players in the first round also chosen in the NFL draft. Of the remaining seven picks, five were white and two Black (Karl Singer of Purdue and Aaron Brown of Minnesota).

In the 1965 NFL draft, Gale Sayers of Kansas and Clancy Williams of Washington State were the only two Black athletes chosen among 14 first-round picks. In the eight-team AFL, there were only two Black players selected in the first round: Sayers and Jerry Rush of Michigan State.

In today's electronic world, TV seeks "feel good" stories, but in the 1960s the media avoided race in sports. As a consequence, many stories about African-American pioneers were overlooked, including how the 1967 draft changed the face of professional football.

Virtually every year is now an extreme contrast. Among the 32 first-round picks of the 2020 NFL Draft, 29 were Black players. There were two white quarterbacks (Joe Burrow and Justin Herbert) and one Samoan quarterback (Tua Tagovailoa).

As for media coverage, forget about a 1967 green room for players to huddle with family and agents and hangers-on before a player was chosen.

Listen to how Washington, who unlike today's prospects leave school to train for the NFL combine and workouts, learned the Vikings took him. He was still on campus completing work toward his degree.

"The draft was going on, and I just happened to be in the football office," Washington recalled. "One of the assistants called out to me, 'Gene, you've got a phone call.'"

Keep in mind in those days the phone was wired to the wall.

"The guy says, 'Congratulations, Gene. You've been drafted by the Minnesota Vikings in the first round. And Gene, you will be playing for Bud Grant. Bud is coming down from Winnipeg in the Canadian Football League to coach the Vikings.'"

But the guy on the other end didn't identify himself.

"I said, 'Who are you?' The guy says, 'My name is Sid Hartman from the *Minneapolis Tribune*.' I told him, 'That's great news and I'm glad you shared it with me.' After a while I hung up, and about a week later I got my first call from someone at the Vikings. That's all the fanfare we got back in those days."

The 1967 NFL Draft seems quaint by today's standards, but Bubba Smith would have been perfect for the modern TV show. After Smith's playing career was cut short from a path to the Pro Football Hall of Fame by a knee injury, he gained further fame as a pitchman with Dick Butkus for Miller Lite commercials. He also played Moses Hightower on the Police Academy movies.

"Oh, that would have been something else," said Jones. "Bubba would have loved the media festival. Bubba was a character, and he would have loved coming out on that stage."

CHAPTER 14
POLYNESIAN PIONEERS: CHARLIE WEDEMEYER AND BOB APISA

FACT: The San Francisco 49ers keep alive Charlie Wedemeyer's story with the Charlie Wedemeyer Prep Coach of the Week and Prep Coach of the Year awards. Steve Mariucci began the awards while he was the 49ers' head coach, 1997-2002.

"What better way to honor high-school coaches and to honor Charlie for his contributions to the Bay Area? Every one of our players in the NFL had a person who influenced them and mentored them as they were coming up. Hopefully parents provide influence, but sometimes it's a particular coach or two. I know how important my high-school coaches were to my development and maturity in my upbringing. My coaches, in football, basketball and track, were, outside of my dad, the most influential people I knew."—Steve Mariucci

---

Pioneers come in all shapes and sizes, and college football integration in the 1960s also came in all shapes and sizes—including Hawaii and Samoa. In 2022, Michigan State all-purpose player Charlie Wedemeyer joined teammate Bob Apisa—both were from Hawaii—in the Polynesian Football Hall of Fame.

The common thread connecting college football from the segregated South to the middle of Pacific Ocean for noteworthy careers was Michigan State coach Duffy Daugherty. He broke ground recruiting far and wide to find players on his 1965 and 1966 national championship teams. We've discussed Daugherty's Underground Railroad in previous chapters, but here we'll look at his pioneering efforts in another area: a Hawaiian Pipeline.

Hawaii wasn't seen as a recruiting hotbed in the 1960s, and the connection to Michigan State wasn't about escaping discrimination, but it was about opportunity, with Hawaiian and Samoan players eventually impacting the college football world.

The University of Hawaii didn't field a Division I program until 1974. Daugherty, with the help of Hawaii legend Tommy Kaulukukui, recruited 10 Hawaiian players from 1954, his first season succeeding Biggie Munn, to his final year upon retirement, 1972. Kaulukukui earned honorable mention All America as a halfback for the Rainbows in 1935 and was Hawaii's head coach in 1941 and 1946-50, compiling a career record of 42-19-3.

Daugherty and Kaulukukui struck up a friendship when Michigan State played at Hawaii, in 1947. Once Daugherty was named head coach, he told Kaulukukui anytime there was a player in Hawaii with Big Ten talent, he'd save a scholarship for him. The first recruit in Daugherty's initial class came in 1954: William Kaae, out of Honolulu Farrington.

Daugherty's 1965 and 1966 title teams featured three players from Honolulu high schools: Dick Kenney, Iolani, kicker, Hawaiian/Irish ancestry; Apisa, Farrington, fullback, Samoan; and Wedemeyer, Punahou, quarterback and flanker, Hawaiian/German.

Apisa was college football's the first Samoan All-American player in 1965 and 1966. He is considered the godfather of Polynesian football, launching the wave that now permeates all levels of football from the middle of the Pacific Ocean to the mainland, coast to coast.

Wedemeyer established himself as a national inspiration on and off the football field with his life told in two films. He courageously fought a lengthy struggle against an insidious disease with no cure, amyotrophic lateral sclerosis (ALS), commonly known as Lou Gehrig's Disease.

The two films portrayed him continuing to coach his Los Gatos High School football team in the San Francisco Bay Area from a golf cart following his diagnosis. When he lost his voice to the disease, his wife, Lucy, his high-school sweetheart at Punahou, read his lips to relay play calls.

The first film was the 1988 CBS-made-for-TV movie *Quiet Victory: The Charlie Wedemeyer Story*. Michael Nouri played Wedemeyer and Pam

Dawber played Lucy. The other film was the 1990 Public Broadcasting Service documentary, *One More Season*.

Wedemeyer's story could have faded into history with contemporary stories of others fighting ALS picking up the torch. Those battles continue the awareness for families to find support systems and others to donate to fund research for a cure.

But Wedemeyer's courageous life continues to come back to life every year for a new football season. The San Francisco 49ers began sponsoring the Charlie Wedemeyer Prep Coach of the Week and Prep Coach of the Year during Steve Mariucci's tenure as head coach, 1997-2002, a program that continues to this day.

"What better way to honor high-school coaches and to honor Charlie for his contributions to the Bay Area," said Mariucci, now an NFL Network analyst. "Every one of our players in the NFL had a person who influenced them and mentored them as they were coming up.

"Hopefully parents provide influence, but sometimes it's a particular coach or two. I know how important my high-school coaches were to my development and maturity in my upbringing. My coaches, in football, basketball and track, were, outside of my dad, the most influential people I knew."

Many NFL programs are often marketing tools overstating the team's involvement with the community, but Mariucci launching the awards and the time he committed to presenting the weekly awards underscores both the value he placed on a high-school coach and his respect for Wedemeyer.

Mariucci later coached the Detroit Lions, but he still lives in the Bay Area while working for the NFL Network as an analyst.

"It is quite a statement by the 49ers to continue the program," he said. "It's a very cool thing."

Wedemeyer's "shaka spirit" returned to his home state in 2021 for his posthumous induction into the Polynesian Football Hall of Fame in Hawaii. He was honored as a contributor for his coaching career, but he also was a legendary high-school career at Punahou School and as a quarterback and flanker at Michigan State, including the Spartans' 1966 national championship team.

"This is pure joy for our family," Lucy said. "More people can know about someone that faced adversity and never gave up. He's being honored beyond his success for his athletic ability. His legacy has lived on for how he carried himself and for the love he had for his players and other coaches. He had such great respect."

Wedemeyer was named in the Polynesian Hall's Class of 2021 with Al Noga and Niko Noga. The Samoan Noga brothers both played at Hawaii and in the NFL. The 2022 class included Tommy Kaulukukui, providing another Michigan State connection to Wedemeyer's induction. Kaulukukui was the one connecting Wedemeyer with Daugherty.

At Michigan State, Charlie was a backup quarterback and holder in the 1966 and 1967 seasons and flanker as a senior in 1968. He received his master's degree from Central Michigan University before he started his teaching and coaching career at Los Gatos.

In the 1984 NFL season, with Super Bowl XIX scheduled for Jan. 20, 1985 at Stanford Stadium, a dinner at a San Jose hotel ballroom was organized in Wedemeyer's honor to raise money for medical expenses. Super Bowl XIX coincidentally turned out to be a Bay Area festival, with the 49ers defeating the Miami Dolphins.

The NFL Alumni Association, spurred by 49ers legend R.C. Owens, sponsored the $100-a-plate dinner. 49ers coach Bill Walsh took time from Super Bowl gameday preparations to attend, presenting Wedemeyer with a signed football:

"To Charlie: From one coach to another, with lasting respect, Bill Walsh."

Wedemeyer could only flash a broad smile, by then having lost his ability to speak. Lucy rose from her seat next to Charlie and draped a Hawaiian lei around Walsh's neck.

"Charlie was so very humbled," Lucy said, looking back on the extraordinary night. "These were people he admired, and he was overwhelmed they took time to be with him. He was struggling to stay alive at that point. He almost didn't make it to the dinner. It was a pure joy for him to be in the company of those football icons."

Wedemeyer had been diagnosed with ALS in 1977 and given one to three years to live. He overcame several brushes with death, managing to survive 33 years, his will fighting for what turned out to be more than half his life. His body finally gave out at age 64, June 3, 2010.

Mariucci was one of the speakers at a June 11 memorial held at the San Jose Sharks' hockey arena to accommodate the people wishing to attend.

"I didn't know Charlie when he was playing at Michigan State," Mariucci said. "But I knew the team he played on and that Duffy had Hawaiian players."

Mariucci learned about Wedemeyer when he first moved to the Bay Area as an assistant coach at Cal in 1987. Cal recruited Wedemeyer's son,

Kale Wedemeyer, a 1989 letterman for the Bears. Kale, motivated by his father's fight against ALS, became a doctor. Dr. Kale Wedemeyer is a pain management specialist at Stanford Health Care.

"I didn't get to know him until I was the 49ers coach," Mariucci said. "It was hard for him to communicate when he came to our coach-of-the-week ceremonies, but you could always read his smile."

Each week, Mariucci invited Charlie, Lucy and the coach to be honored to watch practice at the 49ers' facility before the ceremony. Some weeks the visit was covered by a local TV station. One week Mariucci took Charlie into his office and invited him to sit behind his big desk, a command position tracing back to Walsh, the Pro Football Hall of Famer.

"I really appreciated who Charlie and Lucy were as a team and family," Mariucci said. "They did their speaking engagements together on living with ALS. I think that had a huge impact on him defying the odds. He lived with that disease a lot longer than normal.

"I think God kept him alive so he could enhance the lives of others while he and Lucy spread the word about the disease. It was miraculous to watch them live the way they did and the attitude they had about it. It was unbelievable."

As Wedemeyer's story of coaching with ALS spread beyond a local story and later nationally, Charlie and Lucy also were invited to share his inspirational story and his faith from the Bay Area to Honolulu to England, France, Switzerland and Italy. A third documentary, *Courage to Live*, was produced.

Wedemeyer's Los Gatos record in nine seasons was 78-18-1. The Wildcats won seven league titles and the school's first California Interscholastic Federation Central Coast Section title (essentially a regional state title in the enormous state).

At Punahou, a private school dating to 1841 and the alma mater of President Barack Obama, Charlie starred in football, basketball, and baseball. He also was a karate Black Belt. Charles in Hawaiian translates to Kalekauwila, which means "God of Lightning."

Lucy said Charlie was such a high-school legend when she and Charlie went to a local restaurant the owners were honored to have him as a customer. High-school sports ruled in a state without pro sports or a Division I college program.

"Charlie never had to pay," Lucy said.

Another restaurant set aside a double crust banana pie on Friday nights to be sure they didn't run out by the time Charlie arrived after games.

Charlie joined more than just his teammate Apisa with his Polynesian Football Hall enshrinement. Other previous inductees included his older brother, Herman Wedemeyer, and his high-school coach, Charles Ane II.

Herman Wedemeyer was an All-American halfback at St. Mary University's in Moraga, California, who was fourth in the 1945 Heisman Trophy voting. He played Det. Duke Lukela in the original *Hawaii Five-O* TV series. Herman was in the Polynesian Hall's inaugural class in 2014, which also included Junior Seau, a Samoan who was the first Polynesian named to the Pro Football Hall of Fame, and Navy coach Ken Niumatalolo, the first Samoan Division I head coach.

Ane played seven years in the NFL with the Detroit Lions before returning home to coach at Punahou. His son Charles "Kale" Ane III also took the Hawaiian Pipeline to Michigan State, 1972-74. He put together his own seven-year NFL career. Father and son were later coaches together at Punahou.

Although the Super Bowl XIX week fundraising dinner in January 1985 was an NFL-driven event, Wedemeyer was never far from Michigan State. Daugherty traveled from his Santa Barbara retirement home and made sure those in attendance knew of Wedemeyer's Michigan State background. The affable Daugherty grabbed the microphone at one point, taking on an impromptu Master of Ceremonies role.

"Everything he did was with great determination," Daugherty says in the PBS film. "He was the finest blocker on our team. At 5-8, 175 pounds, he would knock those big 6-4, 258-pound ends flat on their backs. He had that explosiveness. No one was too big for him to attack."

Daugherty also marveled at Wedemeyer's uniquely instinctive talent.

"He had great intuitions as an athlete," Daugherty said. "He just did things you couldn't coach."

A story he didn't tell, though, was one that foreshadowed Wedemeyer's coaching instincts. They were revealed defiantly in the 1966 game at Ohio State, played in a torrential rain storm.

"ALWAYS GO FOR IT"

Michigan State trailed 8-3 in the fourth quarter and needed a comeback to preserve its march to facing Notre Dame in the Game of the Century, a battle of unbeaten teams at the end of the season. The Spartans overcame the muddy field and dropped balls in the rain when Jimmy Raye completed 4-of-7 passes to gain a first-and-goal at Ohio State's 2-yard line.

From there, though, it took four plays on a sloppy field to get the footing to find the end zone. Apisa managed to score on fourth-and-one dive when he extended the ball over the goal line with 7:09 to play. Ohio State coach Woody Hayes ran down the sideline, complaining to officials so vociferously he nearly started a riot. Fans booed the refs and threw bottles at Michigan State's players.

The TD gave the Spartans a 9-8 lead, but in the muddy conditions Daugherty called for an extra-point kick. Kenney had earlier connected on a 27-yard field goal, essentially an extra point.

Wedemeyer, though, changed the play in the huddle to a two-point conversion pass. As Wedemeyer changed the play call and broke the huddle, he took a knee awaiting the snap, flipped the ball to Kenney, curled uncovered into the end zone and caught a two-point pass from Kenney.

Michigan State held on for an 11-8 victory.

Hawaii fans had adopted the Spartans as a team to watch in the era before UH was a Division I program. The headline in the *Honolulu Star-Bulletin*: "**Hawaiians 11, Ohio State 8.**"

The Ohio State game predated Wedemeyer's Los Gatos days, so it naturally wasn't part of the scripts for *Quiet Victory* or *One More Season*. But imagine if such a scene was written for a movie.

It could have portrayed Daugherty initially waving his arms, yelling "No! No! No!" Then as the play worked, pumping his fists and shouting, "Yes! Yes! Yes!"

Apisa, assigned to block the left defensive end, initially was surprised Wedemeyer changed the play. But then his mind flashed to practice that week.

"Charlie and Dick worked on that that play all week," Apisa said. "At one point I said, 'Come on you guys, we're playing Ohio State. Get serious."

Lucy, enduring the rain storm in the stands, was less surprised than anyone. It fit with Wedemeyer's mindset "to always go for it," a mindset he always showed as a coach.

"Charlie always loved a trick play," she said.

The impish Daugherty didn't finish his time with the microphone until he sang the Michigan State fight song for Charlie, a locker-room tradition after every Michigan State victory.

"Duffy had the ability to make kids from Hawaii think snow was fun,"

Lucy said. "His teams had players from all over the country, but they were like a family. Duffy always stayed in touch with Charlie."

Lucy and Charlie Wedemeyer at a Punahou School event. *Photo courtesy Lucy Wedemeyer.*

ONCE A SPARTAN....

Lucy's support roles included two of Charlie's last interactions with Michigan State.

His final trip to campus was 1987 when he was presented with the Breslin Life Achievement Award. He was the second recipient for an award presented to varsity athlete alumnus whose post-college career brought great honor to the school. Breslin was a former football player who served decades at the top of Michigan State's administration.

Lucy's most recent trip to campus came in 2018 when the Lansing All-Stars semi-pro football team was inducted into the Greater Lansing Area Sports Hall of Fame. Charlie played quarterback and called the plays for a team primarily made up of former Michigan State players; they went 28-0 in 1969 and 1970.

In Michigan State's 2001 trip to the Bay Area for a bowl game, the Silicon Valley Football Classic at San Jose State's Spartan Stadium, then-

MSU head coach Bobby Williams invited Wedemeyer to speak—through Lucy—to the team.

True to Wedemeyer's love for Michigan State, Lucy says Charlie never lost his distaste for anything about the University of Michigan. As a junior in 1967, Wedemeyer scored at Michigan on a reverse touchdown run as a flanker and also completed a two-point conversion pass. The Spartans won 34-0.

"Anytime we saw someone with a Michigan shirt, he'd want to say something to them about their ugly helmets," Lucy said. "I'd tell him, 'I'm not going to say that,' but he'd make me. Those were amazing times for us at Michigan State."

Lucy said Charlie struggled with his identity when his body betrayed him, but he began to learn his Los Gatos players viewed him as a coach and mentor rather than a former all-around athlete. Wedemeyer never dwelled on his illness with the players. His players appreciated him for his humor and ability to tease them.

"Kids would come over to our house to visit with him," Lucy said. "Their parents would call our house; they knew where their kids were if they hadn't come home yet. It meant so much to Charlie to be their coach."

Wedemeyer was a Los Gatos teacher and assistant coach when he was promoted to head coach in 1977, not long before his ALS diagnosis, but he continued teach another four years. Even when he was no longer in the classroom after the 1980-81 school year, he remained the head coach through the 1985 season.

He was named Coach Emeritus following the 1985 season and remained with the program on the sidelines through what was his final fall season, in 2009.

The final years he coached from a golf cart with a respirator to breathe. At the time of the fundraiser, the upcoming 1985 fall season was announced to be his ninth and final year as the Los Gatos head coach.

ALS is such a cruel disease for the victim and challenging for the family, 80 percent of ALS victims helplessly have their partner leave them. Lucy has remained an ALS advocate in the decade since Charlie's death.

Although Charlie's illness shattered his life, his love for teaching and coaching was evident to all. His mantra to his players: "Football is the one classroom where kids learn to live. They learn to live with victory and defeat and life."

Lucy's role helping Charlie continue to coach was a full-time commitment. She relayed practice instructions during the week and game-night play calls from the golf cart. It worked fine until one game Charlie called "max" on a play—meaning maximum pass protection. Football players and coaches understand the vernacular. Lucy didn't.

She wondered if there was a new player on the team. She reminded Charlie there was no one on the team named Max. She looked at Charlie, and his lips said, "Yell, max! Right now!"

Too late. Los Gatos had to call a timeout.

"That's when I was fired as a coach," said Lucy, although she was immediately hired back with no one else able to read his lips.

Wedemeyer's Los Gatos assistant coaches never heard the Ohio State story, so they didn't fully understood Charlie "always wanted to go for it." And that turned out to be a good thing.

Otherwise, his assistant coaches could have spoiled what turned out to be a true-to-life, tear-jerker ending to *Quiet Victory*. No embellishment, no rewrite, was needed. The script wrote itself.

The movie, sticking to reality, builds up to Wedemeyer coaching his final game, Dec. 13, 1985, in the CIF-CCS championship. Los Gatos faced Mountain View St. Francis, a traditional power that eliminated Los Gatos a year earlier in the CIF-CCS semifinals.

The 1985 title game was tied 6-6 until Los Gatos scored a go-ahead touchdown. Wedemeyer, *always going for it*, ordered a two-point conversion pass play that worked for a 14-6 lead. Those two points stood up as the difference after St. Francis scored a touchdown but failed on its own two-point play.

Los Gatos was still leading 14-12 when it had a chance to put the game away late in the fourth quarter. The Wildcats had recovered a fumble and were positioned to score until the possession stalled. Los Gatos faced a fourth-and-goal from the 2-yard line. Lucy read Charlie's lips and said to the assistant coaches, "Go for it."

A touchdown and extra-point kick would have provided a nine-point lead with less than a minute to play. But the assistant coaches misunderstood Lucy. They sent in the field-goal team. The kick was wide. The score remained a precarious 14-12 as St. Francis took possession.

Then, with the drama building, St. Francis completed a desperation pass in the final seconds to set up a game-winning field-goal attempt. The drama, in real life and with the film sticking to the facts, intensified until it burst into relief.

Los Gatos blocked the field-goal try to clinch the victory.

The players swarmed Wedemeyer's golf cart, reaching out with hugs.

They got down on a knee and listened as Lucy read Charlie's lips. His message: "You guys played like champions. I'm so proud of each and every one of you. You have accomplished something no other Los Gatos team has done and you're going to remember it the rest of your lives."

Looking back, imagine if the coaches had understood Charlie wanted to go for a touchdown and Los Gatos did indeed score for a 21-12 lead. That two-score lead provided a happy ending, but it lacked last-second drama to bring on the movie tears. The movie's producers and director would have sent that ending to rewrite for some embellishment.

No need with The Charlie Wedemeyer Story. Truth is stranger than fiction.

The dramatic finish aside, there was some incongruity between Wedemeyer's playing days and his own coaching career.

As a coach, Wedemeyer was a task master. No profanity was permitted from his Los Gatos players or assistant coaches. In the movie, the team rule comes across when a wise-guy quarterback scoffs at Wedemeyer, "Bullshit!" Wedemeyer calmly tells him to take a lap, a standing team rule.

"Actually, it was, 'Take a mile,'" said Lucy, revealing a rewrite the director or writers must have felt necessary. "They had to run four laps around the track."

Nevertheless, "Take a lap" got the movie message across to the audience. And as it turned out, also to the film crew.

Apisa was a Hollywood stunt man who also had many parts over the years in the Hawaii-based TV shows *Hawaii Five-O* and *Magnum, P.I.*, and in movies played a role in *Quiet Victory*. He was the Kahuna that blessed Charlie in Hawaiian Pacific Ocean ceremony after Charlie's ALS diagnosis.

Apisa offered an explanation for squaring Wedemeyer's image as the demanding coach with the sophomore backup quarterback that changed Daugherty's play call. Apisa said Daugherty wasn't one of the era's tyrannical coaches, a stereotype that Hayes, Michigan's Bo Schembechler and Indiana basketball coach Bobby Knight aptly fulfilled.

"The old man gave us some space," said Apisa, now older than Daugherty was when he died in 1987 at age 72. "We were an unbeaten team."

Lucy added, "I think it also says Duffy had confidence in Charlie."

The Polynesian Football Hall of Fame enshrinement brought it all together—Punahou, Hawaii, Michigan State, Los Gatos and a courageous fight against a disease with no cure.

CHAPTER 15
GIDEON SMITH, FERRIS STATE, MICHIGAN STATE AND STATUES

FACT: Gideon Smith, born the son of former slaves in 1889 in Virginia, was the first Black football player at both Ferris State and Michigan State and a Black national championship coach at Hampton.

"These are great opportunities for schools to wrestle with the past. We can celebrate the guys and look internally at what happened, but then I think the worry is it dissipates. Everybody pats themselves on the back, but we move on." — Dr. Louis Moore, Grand Valley State University professor and author of two Black sports books, on the importance of honoring Black pioneers.

The Vanderbilt University Sports and Society Initiative assembled a panel discussion in 2021 that included Dr. Louis Moore, a Ph.D professor at Grand Valley State University in Allendale, Michigan. The subject matter was Black athletes, an open-ended topic considering today's Black athletes dominate rosters compared to the early days of limiting or excluding Black players.

Moore is the author of two books, *I Fight for a Living* and *We Will Win the Day: The Civil Rights Movement, the Black Athletes and the Quest for Equality*. He and Dr. Derrick White, a Ph.D professor at Kentucky, host a podcast, *The Black Athlete*.

One of the opinions Moore offered during the panel discussion was his belief all schools with football programs should have a statue dedicated to their school's first Black player. The daily campus presence can serve as an educational tool to understand the long arc of the Black athlete's acceptance. As Martin Luther King Jr. said, "The arc of the moral universe is long, but it bends toward justice."

It is important to not forget Black pioneers were needed to pave the way for future Black athletes.

Consider Black athletes on football rosters prior to the 1970s. Syracuse's Jim Brown, a dominant running back who finished fifth in the 1956 Heisman Trophy voting, and Ernie Davis, the first Black Heisman winner in 1961, stand out as dominant Black athletes, but their stardom provides a misleading picture of the overall rosters. There weren't many other opportunities for Black players to join the huddle.

A statue of the Black pioneers can serve as a conversation starter in addition to honoring an individual that overcame the times he endured.

"It's a good place to start for schools to understand what really went on," Moore said. "At some places, why did it take so long for the first Black player? Other schools had a Black player in the 1890s but then not another for a long time. What happened with the gap?"

Until a backlash throughout the nation in the 1930s, Black athletes were stars in college football. There was no better example at the college and pro levels than Fritz Pollard. He was a Walter Camp All-American back at Brown University and played on Brown's 1916 Rose Bowl team.

As a professional, he played for the Akron Pros and served as a head coach in a league that was the forerunner to the NFL. But his career ended in 1926 when the NFL banned Black players, a practice that remained in place two decades until the Los Angeles Rams signed Kenny Washington and Woody Strode in 1946.

Another early Black player in the NFL was Gideon Smith, teammate of the immortal Jim Thorpe with the Canton Bulldogs. Smith's name is recognized in the Pro Football Hall of Fame in Canton, Ohio, as one of the league's first Black players.

Smith, though, holds a more unique place in college football history as the first Black player at two Michigan schools—Ferris State University (1910-12) and Michigan State University (1913-15)—and a Black national championship coach at Hampton (1922).

Smith was named to the Ferris Hall of Fame in 2020, although the COVID-19 pandemic delayed enshrinement ceremonies until 2022. Smith had previously been enshrined in the Michigan State Hall of Fame in 1992 and the Hampton University Hall of Fame in 2009.

After his playing days, Smith was a teacher, football coach and assistant athletic director at Hampton, an Historically Black College and University in Virginia founded as Hampton Normal and Agricultural College. His record as head coach from 1921 to 1940 was 102-47-13. His teams won five Central Intercollegiate Athletic Association titles: 1922, 1925, 1926, 1928 and 1931.

Smith was born the son of former slaves in 1889 in segregated Virginia. Ferris State, then known as Big Rapids Industrial School, had formed a working agreement with Hampton. A dozen or so Black Hampton students traveled to Big Rapids to gain an education to transfer to a four-year school, included a young Smith.

He was in the right place in the right time for both his education and tapping an unknown athletic talent.

Ferris State founder Woodbridge N. Ferris, who later served as Michigan's Governor (1913-17) and as a U.S. Senator (1923 until his death in 1928), had been inspired to launch the program upon reading *Up From Slavery*, Booker T. Washington's autobiography. Washington had been a student and later teacher at Hampton before he moved to Tuskegee Institute in Alabama.

The Hampton students made the 877-mile journey to Big Rapids, a small lumber town in the middle of the Great Lake State's lower peninsula. The Hampton students were prepared to transfer to a four-year school, most often Michigan State, then known as Michigan Agricultural College.

Smith joined the Ferris football team as its only Black player. He also was the only Black player upon transferring to Michigan State.

Smith played for the Spartans from 1913-15. He led Michigan State, then an upstart program, to its first two wins over the University of Michigan, a national power, in the 1913 and 1915 seasons. The 1913 team also achieved Michigan State's first unbeaten season. In 1953, Smith traveled from Virginia to be part of Michigan State's halftime celebration honoring the 1913 team.

Smith was a dominant lineman playing alongside Blake Miller, one of Michigan State's first two All-American picks on the 1915 team.

"Oh, boy, there was a football player," said Miller in an interview about Smith recorded by the Michigan State Sports Information Department. "Gideon and I, I don't think we had three yards against us the whole season. I never saw a lineman that could stop players the way he did. He'd just reach with his arm like that and if he'd get hand on them, he'd bring them down....Oh, he was a terrific tackle. No one could get by him."

There was one more way Gideon Smith and Woodbridge Ferris seem connected.

"If I had my way, there would be in every community a life-sized statue of Abraham Lincoln," said Ferris among his quotes listed in a school biography on him.

He believes appreciation for the Great Emancipator's life can never be overdone. Smith was born in 1889. Would his parents still be slaves if not for Lincoln elected as president in 1860 and his 1863 Emancipation Proclamation?

Woodbridge Ferris's time running a college campus was long before Americans appreciated the impact of sports on society and progress. He might not have understood the case for a football player statue on every campus until he learned about the rich life of Gideon Smith had been greatly influenced by Ferris—the founder and the institution.

Smith's storied career also deserves a call from a fourth hall, the College Football Hall of Fame, and a fifth hall, the Black College Football Hall of Fame. He has been on the College Football Hall of Fame ballot since 2017 among the Divisional coaches, a category for schools that aren't in what is now known as the Football Bowl Subdivision.

But attracting votes for a career that played out a century ago during segregation isn't easy. How many 21st-century voters understand the significance of his coaching career?

Ferris, during its run to the 2021 NCAA Division II national championship, and Michigan State on its way to a Top 10 ranking in 2021, could have both spread Smith's story through the simplicity of a statue's presence on campus. TV game broadcasts love such video opportunities.

That goes back to Moore's points—statues educate, generate conversation. Race and sports help transform American society.

PIONEER STATUES

In recent years, some college football programs have honored their true 1960s pioneers.

"These are great opportunities for schools to wrestle with the past," Moore said. "We can celebrate the guys and look internally at what happened, but then I think the worry is it dissipates. Everybody pats themselves on the back, but we move on.

"A school may have integrated, but there are continuous problems on campuses. It's good to recognize what happened, but we have to continue to work on problems."

Michigan State announced plans on Martin Luther King Day, Jan. 17, 2022, to recognize its history established under Daugherty. The decade was highlighted by the 1965 and 1966 national championship teams featuring two-time All-American players George Webster, Bubba Smith, Gene Washington, Clinton Jones and Bob Apisa. Prior to the 1966 season, the five players were posed with Daugherty.

Michigan State athletic director Alan Haller said the statue was part of the renovation of the football facility.

"As we look at the renovation of the football building, one of the things that are included in the plans is we're going to put a statue out front of the new football complex of the iconic picture of Duffy and the five athletes," Haller said. "That will be the first thing you see as you go into the building."

A list of schools with statues and memorials:

- **ALABAMA, 2022:** A plaque honoring John Mitchell and Wilbur Jackson as Alabama's first two Black players was unveiled on April 16 prior to the spring game played at Bryant-Denny Stadium. Mitchell was the first player in a game as a junior-college transfer who started the 1971 season opener against USC. Jackson, who signed as a freshman in 1970, entered the USC contest later as a sophomore backup. Freshmen were ineligible by NCAA rules until 1972.
- **TENNESSEE, 2021:** The school unveiled four statues of Black pioneers prior to the Volunteers opening the 2021 season against Bowling Green. The players were Lester McClain, Tennessee's first Black player and the first Black SEC player to score; Jackie Walker, the Tennessee's first Black All-American player in 1970 and 1971; Condredge Holloway as the first Black quarterback in the SEC, 1972-74; and Tee Martin the first SEC Black quarterback to win a national title, 1998.
- **IOWA, 2021:** It's now Duke Slater Field at Kinnick Stadium, so named to honor the 100th anniversary of the Iowa Black lineman who earned All-American honors on the Hawkeyes' 1921

national championship team. Iowa had previously recognized that 1921 team in 2019 with a bronze relief, which includes Slater, in the stadium's north end-zone wall.
- **TEXAS, 2020:** A statue of Julius Whittier was unveiled on Nov. 21, 2020. Whittier was the Longhorns' first Black football player, who signed in the 1969 recruiting class. The statue was erected in just seven months after a group of Longhorns athletes protested social injustice on campus and a lack of recognition for African-American students.
- **KENTUCKY, 2016**: The Wildcats unveiled statues of the school's first four Black players. Nate Northington and Greg Page were signed as the Southeastern Conference's first two Black players in 1966. Wilbur Hackett and Houston Hogg signed a year later.
- **HOUSTON, 2015:** The Cougars honored Bill Yeoman with a statue outside TDECU Stadium. Ironically, that means Yeoman, a Michigan State assistant coach under Daugherty, was honored with a statue for his pioneering role before his mentor. Yeoman arrived at Houston in 1962 and recruited Warren McVea in 1964 as the Cougars' first Black athlete. The Cougars' success under Yeoman, a College Football Hall of Famer, led to the school's admission to the Southwest Conference. He won four SWC titles.
- **UCLA, 2014:** Jackie Robinson first arrived at UCLA in 1939 as a football star, although history remembers him most for breaking the Major League Baseball color line in 1947 with the Brooklyn Dodgers. UCLA retired Robinson's iconic baseball No. 42 in all sports. Robinson also starred for the Bruins in basketball, baseball and track and field. UCLA, in 1981, named its new campus baseball field Jackie Robinson Stadium.
- **AUBURN, 2012:** The Tigers inaugurated the James Owens Courage Award to honor its first Black football player, signed in 1969. Each year the award is presented to a current or former Auburn player for his courage in the face of adversity. Owens' career launched one year ahead of Wilbur Jackson as Alabama's first Black collegiate athlete.
- **SYRACUSE, 2009:** The school unveiled a statue of Ernie Davis on the University Quad. Davis was the first African-American to win the Heisman Trophy, in the 1961 season. Prior to Davis, the highest finish by a Black athlete in the voting was Syracuse's Jim

Brown, fifth in 1956. After Davis, Minnesota's Bobby Bell was third in 1962 and Michigan State's Sherman Lewis third in 1963.
- **SOUTHERN METHODIST, 2009**: Each year the Mustangs designate a player that best represents Jerry LeVias' groundbreaking career with the honor of wearing his jersey, No. 23. LeVias was the Southwest's Conference first Black scholarship player when SMU coach Hayden Fry brought him to the Dallas campus. The All-American receiver was a six-year NFL veteran and named to the College Football Hall of Fame in 2001.
- **DRAKE, 2006**: Drake Stadium's turf was named Johnny Bright Field for the school's quarterback/halfback, 1949-51. In a 1951 game against segregated Oklahoma A&M, Bright was attacked on the field with dirty hits that broke his jaw and sent him to the hospital. A photographic sequence of the assault published in the Des Moines *Register* won a Pulitzer Prize.
- **SYRACUSE, 2005**: Wilmeth Sidat-Singh's No. 19 jersey as a football and basketball star was retired and hangs in the JMA Wireless Dome (formerly the Carrier Dome). In 1937, Sidat-Singh was forced to sit out a game at Maryland due to the gentleman's agreement requiring northern schools to bench their African-American players. Syracuse lost 13-0, but the next year, with Sidat-Singh playing quarterback, the Orange won 53-0. Sidat-Singh died in 1943 while on a training mission as a Tuskegee Airman. His plane's engine failed and he crashed into Lake Huron's Saginaw Bay. When Maryland honored Sidat-Singh during a 2013 Syracuse-Maryland game, among the awards Sidat-Singh's family members accepted was recognition from the Wounded Warrior Project.
- **WYOMING, 2002**: The school dedicated the Black 14 sculpture, placing it on display in the Wyoming Union. The sculpture was funded by the Associated Students of the University of Wyoming as a step to apologize to the 14 Black players who were unfairly dismissed from the team in the 1969 season. The players wanted to wear Black armbands in the upcoming game against Brigham Young, a school owned by the Mormon Church. The players protested the Mormon Church's prohibition against Blacks serving in the clergy. Wyoming coach Lloyd Eaton dismissed them from the team without discussion.

- **MISSOURI, 2001:** The Tigers dedicated the Norris Stevenson Plaza of Champions in 2001, the same year the school inducted the running back into its Intercollegiate Athletics Hall of Fame. Stevenson was Missouri's first Black scholarship recruit, in 1957. He was a three-year running back (1958-60) for head coach Dan Devine, a former Michigan State assistant. As a senior in 1960, Stevenson ran for 169 yards to lead No. 2-ranked Missouri past Oklahoma, 41-19. The Tigers jumped to No. 1 in the next poll, although they finished the year No. 4.
- **IOWA STATE, 1997:** Ohio State athletic Gene Smith was Iowa State's AD when the Cyclones renamed their stadium Jack Trice Stadium, in 1997. A statue of Trice also was unveiled outside the stadium. In 1923, Trice died from internal injuries suffered in a game against Minnesota. Iowa State canceled future games with Minnesota due to the deadly cheap shots Trice suffered on the field.

CHAPTER 16
WILLIE RAY SMITH SR., THE CHIEF ENGINEER

FACT: In the 1966 Game of the Century, Michigan State started three Black players from the Houston area that Willie Ray Smith steered to Duffy Daugherty's Underground Railroad. That was more than Notre Dame's entire roster with one Black player, Alan Page.

"He could very easily have adopted the attitude of, 'Yeah, well, now you need me. I've been trying to do this for a long time—to heck with you.' But that wasn't his attitude at all. I sought his counsel, and he gave it freely. He told me where the mistakes had been made and what I needed to do to get things right."—Texas coach Darrell Royal.

Willie Ray Smith Sr., an uncommon coach with a common surname, lived most of his dynamic life treated as a second-class citizen in segregated Texas. His stature, though, grew with the times.

So did college football through his bond with Duffy Daugherty.

Smith ultimately established multiple legacies—an influential high-school teacher and coach, Michigan State Underground Railroad's chief engineer and University of Texas coach Darrell Royal's Thurgood Marshall.

Willie Ray Smith Sr. with his three sons. *Courtesy Beaumont Enterprise.*

Smith's foundation, his first identity, was laid while he coached high-school football for 33 years at three Texas Black schools (Dunbar in Lufkin, 1942-46; Wallace in Orange, 1947-56; and Charlton-Pollard in Beaumont, 1957-74), winning 235 career games and two Black state titles.

Over that time he sent 20 of his athletes to play pro football and dozens to college, including his three sons, Willie Ray Jr. (Iowa), Bubba (Michigan State) and Tody (Michigan State/USC). Bubba and Tody also played in the NFL.

Smith coached the final 18 years of his career at Charlton-Pollard High in the Beaumont Independent School District, near Houston. As the community went through the painful process of court-ordered desegregation, Smith was tabbed to serve the district as a liaison officer between schools.

When Smith retired and the district recognized his career, it was decided the typical honor of naming a football field after him wasn't enough to match his legacy. The Beaumont district named Willie Ray Smith Magnet Middle School for him.

A TEXAS COACHING LEGEND

Despite Willie Ray Smith's onfield record, he was an accidental football coach. A severe leg injury suffered as a youth left him with a life-long limp, preventing him from playing sports as a kid. He also was deemed unfit to serve in the military as an adult when World War II broke out.

With the Dunbar football coach drafted into the Army prior to the 1942 season, the school's principal turned to Smith, even though he had never played or coached the sport. Smith prepared for his first season studying football textbooks.

Although that was the extent of his X's and O's background, Smith's peers later said he had greater strengths. He gained a reputation as a disciplinarian with a keen eye for talent. He fit his athletes with their best positions.

One of Smith's rival coaches at Port Arthur Lincoln was Joe Washington Sr., the father of 1970s Oklahoma All-American running back Joe Washington Jr. In Texas, the Beaumont, Port Arthur and Orange area was known as the "Golden Triangle" of high-school football talent.

"Willie Ray Smith is the best judge of talent I have ever seen," Washington Sr. told the *Beaumont Enterprise*. "He puts the best kids in the best spots with no politics and no negotiations."

Smith coached at Dunbar four years, until World War II ended. Dunbar's former coach returned home and reclaimed his job.

However, it wasn't the end of Smith's coaching career.

Emma Wallace, the principal at Orange's Wallace High and the school's namesake (it had been renamed from Moton High to honor her leadership as a leading Texas educator), hired Smith with the task of starting a football program.

In Smith's second season, the Wallace Dragons finished as the 1947 state runner-up while competing in the Prairie View Interscholastic League, the governing body for Texas Black sports.

That was the first of three straight state final trips, capped by a state championship in 1949. Wallace won a second state title in 1954. The Dragons drew crowds of 5,000 fans with Black and white spectators attending.

However, when Emma Wallace retired in 1952, friction developed between Smith and the new principal. Smith resigned after five seasons to take the job at Beaumont's Charlton-Pollard for the next 18 seasons. It turned out to be his highest-profile stop, with pro talent that included his three sons.

To have a middle school named for a football coach is exalted status, but one of Smith's former high-school players later felt a football award was needed. In 1992, Jess Phillips, who had played for Smith at Charlton-Pollard on his way to an All-Big Ten career at Michigan State and 10 seasons in the NFL, launched the first Willie Ray Smith Offensive and Defensive Player of the Year Awards.

The award soon gained prestige and has continued the past 30-plus years.

"The kids call it the Heisman Trophy of southeast Texas," said Jorge Ramos, a sportswriter at the *Beaumont Enterprise*.

The 2019 defensive award recipient was junior linebacker Tyrone Brown of West Orange-Stark. He said the award first captured his imagination as a sixth-grader. That was the 2014 season when future Alabama and Arizona Cardinals defensive back Deionte Thompson won it while playing for Brown's alma mater, West Orange-Stark.

CHIEF ENGINEER

His second identity has a place in Michigan State football lore.

Smith was commonly known as the father of Charles "Bubba" Smith, Michigan State's College Football Hall of Fame defensive end. Bubba was the most popular player among fans on the Spartans' 1965 and 1966 national championship teams. Fans at Spartans Stadium took delight in chanting, "Kill, Bubba, kill!"

So, that's a legacy any father would enjoy.

But Willie Ray's true place in Michigan State lore is his involvement in coach Duffy Daugherty's Underground Railroad teams. Similar to his accidental coaching career, Willie Ray became an accidental engineer on the Underground Railroad. It was through his respect for Daugherty.

When Smith's oldest son, Willie Ray Smith Jr., a running back, had an unhappy career at Iowa, plagued by injuries and isolation on a white campus, Smith asked Daugherty to take his second son, Bubba.

In Daugherty's 1974 book, *Duffy*, he says Smith called him and asked him "to take a chance on my boy Bubba and make a man out of him."

Despite Willie Ray Sr.'s reputation as a strict disciplinarian, Bubba apparently was as rambunctious with his parents in his youth as he turned out to be for Daugherty during Smith's first two unproductive years at

Michigan State (one on the freshmen team in 1963 before NCAA's permitted varsity eligibility).

Bubba ran plenty of disciplinary laps, Daugherty and Smith's Michigan State teammates say. But the light finally flicked on his junior year, the first of back-to-back consensus All-American seasons. Bubba was the first pick of the 1967 NFL draft on a path to the Pro Football Hall of Fame with a Super Bowl title and two Pro Bowl trips before a knee injury in the 1972 preseason sidetracked his career.

Willie Ray had turned to Daugherty for the trust the Spartans coach established with Southern Black high-school coaches, starting in the late 1950s. The reputation was born from speaking at a national coaching clinic in Atlanta.

When Daugherty learned the Black high-school coaches were denied entry, he put on his own free clinic for them, continuing the practice over the years. From that point, the Southern Black high-school coaches began to lay the tracks to Michigan State's Underground Railroad. In those days a high-school coach was the most influential figure in a teenager picking his college future.

In all, Willie Ray Sr. sent nine players from the Houston area to play for the Spartans. Three Houston-area players started in the 1966 Game of the Century matching Michigan State against Notre Dame: Bubba Smith, Gene Washington and Jess Phillips.

Bubba and Phillips played for Willie Ray Sr. at Charlton-Pollard. Both Willie Ray Sr. and Bubba told Daugherty about Washington, a three-sport star at Baytown Carver, a Charlton-Pollard rival.

"I never would have made it to Michigan State without Bubba and his father," Washington said. "Duffy didn't know anything about me. I was running hurdle times in high school that were among the fastest in the nation, but because I was at a segregated school, my times didn't make the national lists. I wasn't a big-time recruit.

"When I got to Michigan State, I discovered right away how nice it was on the campus. I never wanted to go home back to segregation because of the way people treated you and your family. My (assigned) roommates at Wonders Hall were two white swimmers, and we've been lifelong friends."

Gene Washington, Bubba Smith and Jess Phillips kneeling. Phillips, an All-Big Ten and NFL vet, started the Willie Ray Smith award in Texas. *Courtesy Michigan State University.*

THE HARD LESSON

Willie Ray Sr. and Willie Ray Jr. learned the hard way a Black kid from the South faced a challenge of escaping segregation, especially when injuries are added into the mix.

Willie Ray Jr. may have been the best of the nearly two dozen NFL players from Beaumont—before his injuries. That has been and has remained a widely held opinion in Beaumont.

Jerry LeVias, a College Football Hall of Famer and six-year NFL veteran from Beaumont, unequivocally calls Willie Ray Jr. the town's greatest football player. LeVias was in middle school when Willie Ray Jr., a 6-1, 190-pounder, was running up and down the field. He thinks he had Gale Sayers-like talent.

"I was just a little kid, but I didn't think anybody was as good as Willie Ray," LeVias said. "Things happen to you along the way in life. Some guys don't realize how blessed they were to be healthy going through high school and college and on to the pros. They don't have things happen to them like injuries. I said a prayer for him when I heard the news. God can give him rest and peace of mind."

LeVias' opinion didn't change even after seeing Gale Sayers and Willie Ray Jr. pitted against each other in a touch football game.

When Willie Ray Jr. left Iowa for Kansas, he struck up a friendship with Sayers, the Kansas Comet on his way to becoming a College and Pro Football Hall of Famer. In the summer of 1963, Sayers, from Omaha, Nebraska, spent time with Willie Ray Jr. in Beaumont. Sayers was coming off a 1,125-yard sophomore season.

On an otherwise typical Beaumont summer day, LeVias, who was entering his junior year at Hebron High, and friends had gathered at Magnolia Park for some touch football. As their game progressed, Willie Ray Jr. and Sayers showed up unannounced. They joined the game.

"Willie Ray was on one team and Gale on the other—*oh-h-h*, you're talking about a show they put on!" LeVias said. "I had heard of Gale Sayers, but I hadn't seen him play. Willie Ray could have been as good as Gale Sayers if he didn't get hurt. I made that statement to Gale. He said I was entitled to my opinion, but he also respected what I said."

Willie Ray Jr., the oldest of Willie Ray Sr.'s three sons, was a Texas high-school legend playing at Charlton-Pollard. But late in his senior season of high school he suffered a knee injury on a late hit, then suffered another knee injury at Iowa while playing on the freshman team.

By his first Iowa varsity season in 1962 as a sophomore, he was struggling with loneliness and injuries. His playing time was limited to 37 carries in nine games for 136 yards. He left Iowa City.

Willie Ray Jr. had to sit out the 1963 season as a transfer to Kansas. Still, he wasn't ready for action even with the extended time off: sports medicine was primitive in the 1960s compared to today's surgeries, arthroscopic tools and therapies. His knee didn't hold up for his final two seasons of eligibility. In 1964, he carried only seven times for 11 yards and one touchdown, with two receptions for 20 yards. In 1965, he was moved to wide receiver. He caught three balls for 132 yards and one touchdown.

But, like LeVias, those college numbers never changed Bubba's opinion of his big brother. Willie Ray Jr.'s daughter Jamila Smith-Loud said her "Uncle Bubba" often regaled her with stories about her father.

"Bubba always said my dad was the best he had ever seen," said Smith-Loud, a Google researcher in the San Francisco Bay Area. "He said he always tried to be like him."

As Willie Ray Jr.'s career ended, Bubba and Tody were on their way to earning All-American honors and playing in the NFL. Bubba was the No. 1 overall pick of the 1967 draft. Longtime NFL writers say he was on his way to the Pro Football Hall of Fame until a severe knee injury in 1972. Tody was a 1971 first-round draft pick by the Dallas Cowboys.

It would have been merely human for Willie Ray Jr. to have felt a toxic mixture of self-pity and jealousy, but his daughter said she didn't see it in him while she grew up in the 1980s and 1990s.

"I was born in 1978, so a lot of time had passed by then, and he had gone through that process," Smith-Loud said. "From my perspective, he enjoyed watching his brothers playing in the NFL. He took solace in his high-school career. It had been good to him. It just wasn't meant to be."

We'll never know how good he could have been, but we do understand the cruel twists of fate he was forced to live with. They delivered to Michigan State his "little" brother—one of college football's greatest defensive players, contributing mightily to two of the most dominant teams in college football history.

This tale of recruiting's vagaries—not to mention injuries sidetracking a career--explains why Willie Ray Jr.'s unfinished football life was, in a cruel twist of fate, instrumental to Michigan State football history. Willie Ray Sr. was intent on finding a better environment for Bubba.

Up until then, Bubba had planned to attend Iowa to play alongside his big brother, whom he idolized. But Willie Ray Jr. told Bubba on his recruiting trip to Iowa City that he was out. That's when Willie Ray Sr. placed his call to Daugherty.

Willie Ray Jr. had the shortest football career, but the longest life of the siblings. He died at age 77. Bubba died at age 66 on Aug. 3, 2011. Youngest brother Tody Smith, who played at Michigan State before he transferred to USC after a falling out with Daugherty, died at 50 on July 18, 1999.

Patriarch Willie Ray Sr. was 81 when he passed away in 1992, following in death the family matriarch, Georgia, also a long-time teacher.

"Bubba's father was extremely important to Michigan State," Jimmy Raye said. "He was not only an outstanding coach in Texas, he was a leader among the outstanding coaches in the South. He sent Duffy his sons Bubba and Tody, Gene Washington, Jess Phillips and other players. He influenced Texas coaches. He was a pioneer of significant magnitude."

A ROYAL APOLOGY

Darrell Royal, as his surname suggests, coached Texas football dripping with royalty. The College Football Hall of Famer reigned 20 years, winning unbeaten national championships in 1963 and 1969 and posting six double-digit victory seasons.

Royal won while not only ignoring at athletes at Black high schools, he actively alienated the Texas Black high-school coaches. He stated in 1963 he could win national titles without Black athletes. That was substantiated in 1969 when the Longhorns were the last all-white team to win a national title, although by then Royal saw the writing on the wall.

Royal signed Julius Whittier as his first Black recruit in 1969 out of San Antonio. Whittier was Texas' first Black letterman, 1970-72, but Royal otherwise was having trouble gaining commitments from Black athletes.

That's when he turned to Smith.

Royal admitted he had been wrong not to recruit Black athletes prior to the 1970s. Texas *royalty* sought Smith's advice on how to mend fences with Black high-school coaches, particularly those in the talent-rich Golden Triangle. That included Smith at his Beaumont school, Charlton-Pollard High.

Smith's own sons were among those Royal shunned, rationalizing the practice in a dubious claim he made to Bubba Smith. Bubba related the story in a 2008 HBO documentary on the desegregation in college football, *Breaking the Huddle*. Bubba said Royal told him he could give him a scholarship, but the alumni and fan base wouldn't allow him to play.

"He could very easily have adopted the attitude of, 'Yeah, well, now you need me. I've been trying to do this for a long time—to heck with you.'" Royal said in a retirement video tribute to Smith. "But that wasn't his attitude at all. I sought his counsel, and he gave it freely. He told me where the mistakes had been made and what I needed to do to get things right."

The video serves as an annual evocation when shown at a banquet for the Willie Ray Smith Offensive and Defensive Players of the Year. The area's high-school players covet these honors as the "Heisman Trophy of Southeast Texas."

Both men are long gone, Smith having died at age 81 in 1992 and Royal at 88 in 2012. But Smith's role as Royal's Thurgood Marshall deserves more attention, even if Royal was late to seeing the light. An apology was more than Alabama coach Paul "Bear" Bryant offered once he finally recruited his first Black athlete in 1970, a year after Royal.

The uncommon man not holding a grudge was no surprise to Garland Boyette, a nine-year NFL veteran in the 1960s who played for Smith at Wallace High, a Golden Triangle school in Orange.

"He was into helping kids," said Boyette. "Most of the kids he coached were poor. He wanted to help them get to college."

CHAPTER 17
MICHIGAN STATE AS THE NORTH STAR FOR SOUTHERN PIONEERS

FACT: From 1959 to 1972, Duffy Daugherty recruited 44 players escaping segregation spanning 10 of 13 Southern states—all but Alabama, Tennessee and Maryland. Michigan State led college football integration with Daugherty's expansive network unlike any other college coach.

"Michigan State should be proud of what they did. Instead of sitting back and waiting for someone to tell their story, if I was a Michigan State recruiter in a living room with a kid's family, I'd be saying, 'Do you know the history of Michigan State?'" —Jerry LeVias

---

Wilbur Hackett grew up in the West End of Louisville, the Black section of the segregated Kentucky city, aware earlier than most African-American youths that Heisman voters finally had gained enlightenment. Black players in the 1960s began to finish among the finalists.

The transformative moment, of course, came when Syracuse halfback Ernie Davis was named first Black Heisman winner in 1961. The best player in the land wasn't overlooked for the color of his skin by Heisman voters.

President John F. Kennedy, upon learning Davis was in New York to receive the Heisman from the Downtown Athletic Club the same day JFK was in town to deliver a speech, requested a special meeting. Kennedy spoke to the National Association of Manufacturers on December 6 at the Waldorf Astoria. He met and congratulated Davis afterward outside the ballroom. Then he departed for the airport.

Hackett, though, was aware of more progress beyond Davis's milestone. In the fall of 1963, he was a freshman at duPont Manual High. That same season Michigan State All-American halfback Sherman Lewis finished third in the Heisman voting to Navy quarterback Roger Staubach.

"Sherman Lewis was from my high school," said Hackett, boyhood respect palpable in his voice more than a half-century later. "I dreamed about playing at Michigan State."

Until Davis, the Heisman was a club of exclusivity for white players. Just four years earlier, Jim Brown, Syracuse's all-everything fullback, finished fifth in the 1956 Heisman voting.

Fifth!

The voters determined there were four players better than the great Jim Brown. The late Dick Schaap, a National Sports Media Hall of Famer from his print journalism and TV careers, brought up the oversight many times around the time of the annual Heisman presentation. Schaap had played lacrosse for Cornell against Brown, a multisport athlete who also played on Syracuse's basketball team and lettered in four sports, including track.

In the 1956 Heisman voting, Notre Dame's Paul Hornung won with 1,066 points despite playing on a 2-8 team. The next three—all white players—were Tennessee's Johnny Majors, 994; Oklahoma's Tommy McDonald, 973; and Oklahoma's Jerry Tubbs, 724. Brown totaled a distant 561. He had only 121 first-place votes out of 903.

Brown's finish was an indictment of the voters, but at the same time cracking the top five was a breakthrough. Illinois' Bill Burrell, a Black lineman, was fourth in 1959. The 1960 finalists were all-white, but the 1961 runner-up to Davis was Ohio State's Bob Ferguson, a Black fullback. In 1962, Minnesota's Bobby Bell, a Black defensive lineman later converted to linebacker with the Kansas City Chiefs, was third in the voting.

And then came Lewis in 1963 to continue the trend. By 1965, USC running back Mike Garrett was the second Black Heisman winner.

Lewis' ascent came under Daugherty, so it's no surprise Hackett's high-school connection to Lewis inspired him to consider Michigan State. He took two recruiting trips.

"I met Duffy and spent some time with him; he was a great man," Hackett said. "He made me feel like Michigan State was the right place for me. He was open and genuine. I loved my time there. The people were so nice. Duffy was so genuine about recruiting African-American athletes. I spent time with Bubba and Webster and other guys. Bubba was as big as a house."

Hackett's first recruiting trip was to East Lansing and the Michigan State campus. The second was to Michigan State's 37-19 win over Indiana on Nov. 12, 1966, at Bloomington's Memorial Stadium. A week later, Michigan State and Notre Dame played to a 10-10 tie in the Game of the Century at Spartan Stadium, a seminal moment in college football history .

Hackett, a linebacker, was an easy sell.

He was ready to commit to Michigan State, but the world began to change between his freshman year, 1963, and by the time he was a senior in the 1966-67 school year. In the fall of 1966—Hackett's junior season—Kentucky broke the Southeastern Conference color barrier with two Black recruits on the freshman team, Nate Northington and Greg Page. (NCAA rules didn't permit freshmen eligibility until 1972).

Although Hackett's home-state university made history, he remained enraptured with Michigan State's march to 1965 and 1966 unbeaten Big Ten championships and national titles.

"Kentucky wasn't even on my mind," Hackett said.

However, it was on the mind of Hackett's parents, Wilbur Sr. and Ollie, once Kentucky coach Charlie Bradshaw extended their son a scholarship offer. Bradshaw also recruited Houston Hogg, a running back, to join Hackett. This was different than Southern coaches who recruited one Black athlete at a time.

Hackett began to realize his parents wanted him to stay closer to home. Lexington was only 80 miles from Louisville, East Lansing 367. His mindset changed to being the "good son."

"They said it was up to me, but they wanted to me to go to Kentucky," Hackett said. "My parents were big Kentucky fans from when Bear Bryant was coaching and winning at Kentucky and Adolph Rupp was winning NCAA basketball titles.

"I never asked my dad why they were Kentucky fans until about 10 or 15 years ago. I said, 'Why, since you couldn't go to the games?' He said they didn't see color. They listened to the games on the radio. Kentucky won and was their team. They were thrilled I went to Kentucky. They went to every one of my games."

Hackett and Hogg played on the 1967 freshman team and made their varsity debuts as sophomores in 1968. Hackett was the SEC's first Black football starter as a sophomore in 1968, and he was the first SEC Black team captain in any sport as a junior in 1969. (Tennessee's Lester McClain began his sophomore season in 1968 as a backup.)

Hackett wasn't alone in the segregated South viewing Michigan State as the North Star. The land-grant university founded in 1855 as Michigan Agriculture College grew into a world-class university under the direction of John Hannah, who promoted civil rights.

Hannah served as the first chairman of the Civil Rights Commission established by President Dwight Eisenhower in 1957. That same year the "Little Rock Nine" battle erupted over the integration of Central High in Little Rock, Arkansas. Eisenhower sent in U.S. Army troops to protect the nine students chosen to integrate the school.

The first to graduate was Ernest Green, who received an anonymous scholarship to Michigan State. It wasn't until after Hannah's death when family members went through his papers did Green learn Hannah was his benefactor.

"Michigan State was a launching pad for people of color," said Green, who went on to a career promoting opportunities for people of color and serving as an Assistant Secretary of Labor in President Jimmy Carter's administration, 1977-81.

The first Southern Black recruit in 1959 was Clifton Roaf of Pine Bluff, Arkansas. Daugherty learned about him through Michigan State School of Education professor Raymond Hatch, who was researching Pine Bluff's "separate but equal" Black and white schools during segregation. Roaf was a football star and valedictorian at Pine Bluff's Black school, Merrill High.

Merrill Principal M.D. Jordan and football coach Ervin Phillips were aware of Michigan State's reputation and asked Hatch to contact Daugherty on Roaf's behalf about a scholarship opportunity. Roaf took a trip to Michigan State—Phillips drove him —and Daugherty offered what turned out to be the first of 44 Underground Railroad commitments.

"I told my mother I was never coming back to the South," said Roaf before his death in 2017. "I broke her heart. She cried. When I left to get on the train, she couldn't come with us. She told my dad, 'Take his suitcase and put him on the train. I can't watch him leave.'"

A knee injury during 1960 spring football as a freshman, on top of a knee injury Roaf suffered in high school, essentially ended his career prior to the fall of 1960 as a sophomore. He never played a down, but he remained with the team and graduated. He became a dentist and returned to Pine Bluff to treat an underserved community. His Michigan State bride,

Andree Layton Roaf, was a lawyer later and the first Black woman named to the Arkansas State Supreme Court.

Their son Willie Roaf was the brawn of the family, earning induction into both the College Football Hall of Fame (Louisiana Tech) and Pro Football Hall of Fame (New Orleans and Kansas City). Willie had his father introduce him in Canton. Their daughters, Phoebe and Mary, both earned Ph.D degrees.

Jerry LeVias was another Southern pioneer who imagined boarding Daugherty's Underground Railroad. Willie Ray Smith Sr., the Texas high-school legend, tried steering LeVias to Daugherty. LeVias was the quarterback at Hebert High, another Beaumont school that was Charlton-Pollard's rival.

"Duffy got a lot of us from Golden Triangle," said LeVias, referring to the towns of Beaumont, Orange and Port Arthur outside of Houston that produced so many college and NFL players. "Everybody knew about Duffy Daugherty and Michigan State. Duffy was at the right time, and he was way ahead of his time."

LeVias had reservations about Michigan's cold weather, but he unexpectedly gained a chance to stay closer to home. Southern Methodist coach Hayden Fry offered him a scholarship as a freshman in 1965 to play for the Dallas school. LeVias was the first scholarship Black football player in the Southwest Conference.

He earned All-American honors as a receiver on his way to the College Football Hall of Fame and a six-year NFL career, but his life off the field wasn't as enjoyable as it would have been in East Lansing. At SMU, he endured students ostracizing him, cheap shots from opponents and death threats before games.

"It would have made sense to go to Michigan State," he said.

A pivotal moment to his SMU experience was meeting Dr. Martin Luther King Jr., who spoke at SMU in the spring of 1966. MLK helped him understand the need to control his emotions when he faced racism on and off the field.

"I can't really tell you why I went to SMU," LeVias said. "The Lord works in mysterious ways. But the way things turned out, I did the right thing. If I had gone somewhere else, I might not be as strong of a person as I am. I met Dr. King and got his advice."

LeVias added Fry and Daugherty were the two most genuine coaches he encountered.

"College football needed Duffy Daugherty and Hayden Fry to do the right thing," LeVias said. "Michigan State should be proud of what they did. Instead of sitting back and waiting for someone to tell their story, if I was a Michigan State recruiter in a living room with a kid's family, I'd be saying, 'Do you know the history of Michigan State?'"

Rufus Cormier, a retired Houston lawyer, played with LeVias at both Hebert High School and SMU as an offensive lineman. Willie Ray Smith also tried to steer Cormier to Daugherty, and Cormier took a recruiting trip to East Lansing. When he compared Michigan State to other trips, he learned there were more factors for a Black pioneer athlete to consider than the opportunity to play major college football.

"I really enjoyed meeting Bubba and the other Michigan State players," Cormier said. "They liked it at Michigan State. When I went to Colorado, one of their three Black players told me, 'Don't come here. There is no social life.'"

Daugherty, similar to North Carolina basketball coach Dean Smith, was better respected for his civil rights stances in the 1960s in Black communities than white. African Americans understood the racist barriers Daugherty confronted. A difference, though, was Smith's career overlapped into the 1970s, 1980s and 1990s. The media, bolstered by cable and the Internet, began to seek out and celebrate crusaders. A result was President Barack Obama awarded Smith the Presidential Medal of Freedom in 2013.

Dr. Dennis Thomas, a College Football Hall of Famer from his career at Alcorn State and former commissioner of the Mid-Eastern Athletic Conference, a league of Historically Black College Universities, agrees Daugherty has never received his proper credit.

"Obviously, Duffy Daugherty was a very successful coach, but I have more respect for him as a human being," Thomas said. "He didn't see color. He saw performance. He saw character. He was doing it before it was fashionable. I want to commend you for chronicling and bringing those stories into the public light. I want to tell you how much respect I have for Duffy Daugherty and for you telling the stories."

But it was not only Southern Black high-school coaches and athletes who recognized Michigan State as a North Star for Black players. Ernie Pasteur was a star fullback at Queens Street High, a Black school in Beaufort, North Carolina, while Norm Clark was a white coach in nearby Morehead City. Clark felt Pasteur was a Big Ten talent and contacted Michigan State on Pasteur's behalf.

Pasteur, similar to Hackett, was drawn to Michigan State having seen Lewis on TV along with Dewey Lincoln, another Black star. Lincoln, who was from Hamtramck, Michigan, was honorable mention All-Big Ten in both 1961 and 1962.

Injuries slowed Pasteur's career, but he struck up lifelong friendships among players on two of college football's greatest teams. He graduated to a career in education, including serving as a high-school principal. There is more on Pasteur and his family in Chapter 30.

Daugherty's volunteer Southern "scouts" included Bob McLelland, a white sportswriter in Roanoke, Virginia. His background was similar to Clark—he understood Michigan State was a path to opportunity for Southern Black athletes. McLelland contacted Michigan State about Charlie Thornhill, the first Black player in the segregated city to be named to the all-region team.

Vince Carillot took the phone call from McLelland, studied Thornhill's film and convinced Daugherty to offer Thornhill a scholarship despite Daugherty's reservations about Thornhill's 5-foot-9 height. Thornhill, converted to linebacker, led the 1965 and 1966 teams in tackles as an All-Big Ten pick. With opponents avoiding All-Americans Bubba Smith and George Webster, the ball was funneled to Thornhill.

Another North Carolina recruit who was committed to Daugherty but went on to an NFL career without playing for the Spartans was Doug Wilkerson of Fayetteville's E.E. Smith High, the segregated city's Black school. E.E. Smith was also the alma mater to Michigan State quarterback Jimmy Raye. They had been high-school teammates in the fall of 1963, when Wilkerson was a sophomore lineman on the varsity and Raye a senior.

By Wilkerson's senior year he was committed to join Michigan State's freshman team in 1966, which would have reunited him with Raye on the varsity in 1967. He was ready to depart for East Lansing until his scholarship was suddenly revoked in the spring—but not by the NCAA or Daugherty. Smith principal E.E. Miller telephoned Daugherty and informed him that Wilkerson's punishment for an incident on campus included the loss of his Michigan State scholarship.

The principal's decision stemmed from a fight on campus. A teammate had egged on Wilkerson for weeks to a foot race with a wager. Wilkerson ignored him until finally relenting. When he won the race, the antagonist refused to pay up.

"Doug took him out behind the school and dropped him on his head," said Jimmy Harvey, a junior at E.E. Smith who went on to play football and baseball at Winston-Salem State University. "The message was clear to the rest of us: If they could do that to Doug, the best athlete in the school, you better stay out of trouble."

Wilkerson and Daugherty, of course, could have ignored Miller's decision. There were no NCAA violations or legal authorities involved. Wilkerson said Daugherty never tried to intervene. Wilkerson said in an interview before his death in 2021 they accepted Miller's punishment.

"That was Mr. Miller's decision—he was the principal," Wilkerson said. "It would have been nice to have gone up to Michigan State and played with Jimmy, but that's the way it came down. I never looked back and always kept moving forward."

Wilkerson instead attended North Carolina College (now N.C. Central), an Historically Black College and University in Durham. He was a first-round draft pick of the Houston Oilers in 1970 and a three-time Pro Bowler with the San Diego Chargers (1980-82).

In 1967 Lester McClain was Tennessee's first Black scholarship player and the SEC's first Black player to score a touchdown when he caught six TD passes as a sophomore in 1968.

However, McClain wasn't an original target in Tennessee's 1967 recruiting class. The Volunteers pursued two high-school seniors in 1966. One was Albert Davis, a lineman from Alcoa, Tennessee, and the other Tommy Love, a running back from Sylva, North Carolina.

When Love picked Michigan State over Tennessee, McClain received the available scholarship offer along with Davis. However, academic issues prevented Davis from enrolling. He played at Tennessee State, leaving McClain as the Volunteers' lone pioneer.

Tennessee's Chuck Rohe, who served in a dual role as the track and field coach and the football recruiting coordinator, led the school's desegregation. Rohe had been pushing Tennessee to integrate its athletic programs, but he was denied permission. He finally received the green light with Tennessee's 1967 class after Kentucky broke the SEC color barrier a year earlier.

Illinois's recruitment of Bobby Mitchell out of Hot Springs, Arkansas, in 1954 was a happenstance. Hot Springs federal judge Henry Britt, an Illinois alumnus, tipped off his former college roommate, Illinois assistant coach Mel Brewer. Mitchell had planned to play at Grambling State until Illinois offered him an opportunity.

Minnesota's 1960 national championship team was sometimes referred to as launching an Underground Railroad, but there was no comparison to Daugherty's network. Minnesota coach Murray Warmath lacked Daugherty's network but still recruited Bobby Bell of Shelby, North Carolina, among five Black players on the 1960 national title roster. Bell, a College and Pro Football Hall of Famer, was a sophomore in his first varsity season among the 1960 Gophers.

Bell said North Carolina coach Jim Tatum informed Warmath about him. Tatum had seen Bell play in a Black high-school all-star game in the winter of 1959.

Explained Bell, "Coach Tatum told Coach Warmath, 'This guy can play for you. If he doesn't, I'll pay his scholarship.'"

Bell hadn't envisioned escaping segregation until his sudden opportunity.

"My Dad told me if I had a chance to go to a big school, I should take it," Bell said. "That got me out of North Carolina and a chance to do a lot of things. Everything was segregated down there. You had to ride in the back of the bus. I got a good education. I got to see the world. I made a lot of great friends."

Bell played on the Minnesota 1959 freshman team, but he quickly contributed to the future as a recruiter. He told Warmath to recruit his friend Carl Eller, whose was a year behind Bell while attending Atkins High in Winston-Salem. Eller told Warmath he'd accept the scholarship if Warmath also took his high-school teammate, Jay Sharpe. Eller earned stature as a College and Pro Football Hall of Famer, while Sharpe was a productive running back.

Tragically, Tatum contracted a form of typhus fever—a bacterial infection—on July 13, 1959, lapsed into a coma and died 10 days later. North Carolina promoted assistant coach Jim Hickey (1959-66) to succeed him.

The Tar Heels' football program remained segregated until Ricky Lanier was recruited in the 1967 freshmen class by head coach Bill Dooley (1967-77). Lanier played on the freshmen team in the fall of 1967, the same 1967-68 school year Charlie Scott played his first varsity season for the Tar Heels as a sophomore. Scott has been credited with desegregating Atlantic Coast Conference basketball under head coach Dean Smith.

Lanier had been a record-setting quarterback at E.J. Hayes High, a Black school in Williamston, North Carolina. His high-school coach was Herman Boone, who later gained fame in the movie *Remember the Titans* as the Black coach at a desegregated high school, T.C. Williams, in Alexandria, Virginia. As was often the case with Black quarterbacks, Lanier was switched to wide receiver his 1970 senior season.

Two years later, Charlie Baggett, who played quarterback on North

Carolina's 1971 freshman team, transferred to Michigan State when the then-Tar Heels coach Bill Dooley told him at the start of the 1972 season that he was switching him to wide receiver. Baggett contacted then-Michigan State assistant coach Jimmy Raye, who had played quarterback at the same North Carolina high school as Baggett, E.E. Smith in Fayetteville.

Prior to Daugherty's influence on the 1960s, Grambling State's Garland Boyette, an eight-year NFL veteran, said Southern Black players hoped integrated Big Ten programs or schools in the West might have one scholarship available for a Black Southern recruit out of the half-dozen. Boyette had played for Willie Ray Smith Sr. at Wallace High in Orange, Texas, but that was before Smith was recruiting as an engineer for Daugherty's Underground Railroad.

"We knew schools above the Mason-Dixon Line would only take so many Black players," said Boyette, a 1958 high-school graduate. "A lot of guys fell through the cracks before Michigan State came along. We had three guys make the NFL off my high-school team."

All three played at Grambling State, an Historically Black College and University, for coach Eddie Robinson on their way to the NFL, although they were from different Wallace classes. Boyette played nine years with St. Louis Cardinals and Houston Oilers; Ernie Ladd, eight years, mostly San Diego Chargers; and Preston Powell, one year, Cleveland Browns.

Boyette, though, began his college experience as one of those Southern Black players to land a Big Ten scholarship, thanks to Northwestern alumnus John Hardey. Boyette had worked a part-time job at Hardey's hotel, the Jack Tar Orange House.

Boyette said upon arriving at Northwestern, he noticed the lack of Black teammates and students. He left preseason camp after two weeks to launch his career at Grambling State, located in Louisiana across the Texas border.

"A lot of it is an individual thing," explained Boyette. "I saw how few Black people were on campus, and I thought it would be hard socially."

Michigan State halfback Clinton Jones, an African American from Cleveland, said he considered Michigan State's campus "an oasis" from racism. He was voted Mr. MSU in the spring of 1965, while playing football and running the hurdles in the indoor and outdoor track and field teams.

Bubba Smith also felt freely accepted around campus. One time he came across some white students at the Brody Complex in the middle of a water balloon fight. They asked Smith to join in the fun. He did.

Johnette Howard, a long-time sportswriter for national outlets such as *Sports Illustrated*, *ESPN* and the *Washington Post* and a bestselling author of a biography on Billie Jean King, *All In*, earlier in her career wrote a story on Smith for the *Detroit Free Press*.

"He led such a segregated life growing up, that when he first got to Michigan State, he said he joined the first fraternity that approached him," Howard said. "One of his friends said, 'Bubba, don't you know that's a Jewish fraternity?'

"Smith answered, 'They look white to me.'"

Jim Proebstle, Michigan State's starting tight end on the 1965 national title team, felt the Spartans had a good chance to land future College and Pro Football Hall of Famer Alan Page in Daugherty's 1963 recruiting class. Proebstle and Page had been teammates at Canton (Ohio) Central Catholic under John McVay, the Crusaders' head coach until he left for MSU as a Daugherty assistant, 1962-64.

Proebstle, a year older than Page, was a natural choice to serve as Page's host. That Proebstle was a white player and Page was Black didn't matter at Michigan State.

"Alan was a hell of an athlete and at the top of everyone's recruiting list," Proebstle said. "Alan enjoyed his trip to East Lansing and was a great fit with our players. He enjoyed the visit. I think the problem was his mother's strong belief as a Catholic.

"It's important to know that Alan transferred from an underserved public high school in East Canton to Central Catholic in Canton as a sophomore. I'm sure his parents continued to have a big influence on Alan to continue this track record of success. They wanted him to attend one of the top Catholic universities in the country."

At Notre Dame, Page was one of only two Black players on the 1964 and 1965 varsity rosters. He was the Irish's lone Black player in the 1966 Game of the Century against the Spartans. It wasn't until the early 1970s Notre Dame's rosters hit double digits for Black athletes.

Clinton Jones, Page's teammate with the Minnesota Vikings, said Page once told him during their NFL days that Michigan State was his first choice, but his parents wanted him to attend Notre Dame. Page, who attended the University of Minnesota Law School during his NFL career and served as a Minnesota State Supreme Court Justice, has declined to do interviews on his football career.

Notre Dame's Terry Hanratty was a white quarterback, but he also shed light on how athletes gained respect and trust in Daugherty through the recruiting process. Michigan State was Hanratty's second choice while he was recruited out of Butler, Pennsylvania.

"Duffy Daugherty was such a wonderful human being," Hanratty said. "No one can ever turn me against Michigan State. When I told Ara I was coming to Notre Dame, I knew I had to call Duffy. I'm thinking, 'This is going to be horrible,' because you hear all these stories about coaches jumping on kids."

Clinton Jones had such a moment. Ohio State head coach Woody Hayes cussed him out on the phone when Jones told him he was committed to the Spartans.

"I told Duffy," Hanratty said, "and he went on for 20 minutes about what a great school Notre Dame was and what a great guy Ara was. He made that very difficult call for a 17-year-old kid special. I'll always have a fondness for Michigan State because of Duffy."

A quartet of Michigan State quarterbacks joined by Terry Hanratty during a reunion. L-R: Eric Marshall, 1963-67; Steve Juday, 1962-65; Jimmy Raye, 1964-67; John Mullen, 1963-66; and Terry Hanratty, 1965-68.

CHAPTER 18
A MISSISSIPPI KID'S SIXTH-GRADE DREAM, 1963

FACT: Eric Marshall dreamed of escaping segregation to Michigan State since sixth grade. He was one of two Black quarterbacks on the Spartans' mid-1960s rosters at a time other schools avoided recruiting any Black QBs.

"When I was in sixth grade, we had to give a speech about what we wanted to do in life. Mine was about how I was going to Michigan State University to play football and graduate. The other kids laughed at me. It was the impossible dream. No one we knew was able to go to a Big Ten school." — Eric Marshall.

Trucks rumbled outside Eric Marshall's home in the middle of a 1962 Oxford, Mississippi night, awakening the 17-year-old, his mother, grandparents and two younger siblings. The noise and reverberations shook windows and rattled nerves.

What was it? Anybody would be alarmed, but Marshall's hometown embodied the heart of the Jim Crow South—if not its geography. Degradations and the Ku Klux Klan were never too far from a Black neighborhood.

Or maybe the commotion was White supremacists gathered on the nearby University of Mississippi campus. The Ole Miss Riot of 1962 had erupted.

A mob, 3,000 students and outsiders, attempted to block Air Force veteran James Meredith's admission as the school's first African-American student. U.S. Attorney General Robert F. Kennedy had sent 500 federal agents to enforce the court orders.

That night Marshall had gone to bed buoyant. He was on the cusp of fulfilling his childhood dream, escaping segregation aboard Michigan State coach Duffy Daugherty's Underground Railroad.

Marshall had booked passage as a two-time state championship starting quarterback from Oxford Training School (later Central High School), the city's Black high school.

"When I was in sixth grade, we had to give a speech about what we wanted to do in life," Marshall said. "Mine was about how I was going to Michigan State University to play football and graduate. The other kids laughed at me. It was the impossible dream. No one we knew was able to go to a Big Ten school."

Eric Marshall while attending Michigan State. *Courtesy Eric Marshall.*

In Oxford, the ground had shifted beneath Marshall's feet as he witnessed a pivotal civil rights moment. In East Lansing, Michigan, he was in step with college football's new landscape.

Marshall was never more than a backup quarterback, but all that mattered to him was fulfilling his Underground Railroad dream and earning his political-science degree. He had the last laugh on his sixth-grade classmates as a high-school senior.

"I read them my scholarship letter from Duffy."

AMERICAN HISTORY FROM 651 N. SEVENTH STREET

But back to that 1962 Mississippi night.

Young Eric Marshall peeked out a window at 651 N. Seventh Street and felt relief. The hotspot was elsewhere. He stepped onto the front lawn with his mother, Susie Marshall, a venerable educator for the area's Black schools. They saw Army transports rolling toward campus.

The Ole Miss Riot of 1962 lasted Sunday, Sept. 30 through Monday, Oct. 1.

Federal agents, having exhausted their tear gas supply, were under siege at the campus Lyceum Building. The mob threw Molotov cocktails. Cars were set afire. A third of the 500 agents were wounded. Two people were killed—a French journalist, shot in the back, and a curious bystander, shot in the forehead. Dan Rather, then a young CBS reporter, described the campus as a "war zone."

Other Black families joined the marshals outside watching the troops, sent by President John F. Kennedy to quell the riot. The soldiers disembarked, block by block, sealing off intersections.

"I saw the efficiency of the military," Marshall said. "They knew what they were doing and took over the city. I never forgot that."

Those images served him well soon enough. Marshall's 1968 graduate-school plans with his political-science degree were disrupted. An Army draft notice landed with a thud in his 651 N. Seventh Street mailbox. American history found his street address again.

Marshall arrived in Vietnam 50 years ago, serving 13 months from July 1970 to August 1971.

Maybe the local draft board thought he was just another a Black body to send to the front lines—they went in disproportionate numbers—but Marshall was a college graduate. That qualified him for Officer Candidate School.

"I was going to Vietnam anyway. I might as well go as an officer. I signed up for Ranger training, jump training, jungle training. It was a good thing, too. When you first get there, your men think you're some lieutenant that doesn't know what's going on over there. My training gained their confidence."

Only in America can history flip circumstances so soon and dramatically.

In 1962, Marshall was a bystander on racially blood-stained Mississippi soil; he watched the Army protect a descendant of slaves from Confederate progenies. Eight years later he was an Army officer on blood-stained foreign soil; he commanded a melting-pot platoon.

Marshall, 74, eventually retired from two careers. First as an Army lieutenant colonel, having served 24 years around the world, including a diplomatic trip to Moscow while stationed in West Berlin. Next as a high-school principal in the San Francisco Unified School District.

All these years and events later, throughout twists and turns, he is proud of his life's journey. Today's athletes can learn from him—that life can still turn out fulfilled.

CU CHI'S TREACHEROUS TUNNELS

Cu Chi was a Viet Cong stronghold, perilous for its network of tunnels hiding men and supplies. First Lieutenant Marshall and his men had their heads on a swivel, watching for ambushes popping up.

A platoon is 35 to 40 men. Marshall's soldiers were Black and white, including white Southerners who grew up accustomed to Jim Crow laws.

"When you're in the infantry, you've got to fight together to stay alive," Marshall said. "You understand bullets don't discriminate. There is no time for prejudices. I felt responsible for my men's lives, and they trusted me."

Finding tunnels meant confronting claustrophobia, crawling into a hole in the Earth. Tunnels weren't simple passageways; they were multi-level. Marshall's life was defined by tunneling to the other end; he rode the Underground Railroad to a North Star future. So, he didn't leave the job to privates:

"The Army trains you to lead by example; the men watch you. Those tunnels were amazing with what they had down there."

He completed his Vietnam tour and awarded a Bronze Star Medal, but there was no decoration among those filling his uniform chest for the one that brought him the most pride.

"All my men made it home. We had some shot up and sent to the rear, but we didn't lose one. That told me I had made the right decisions under fire."

Two of Marshall's famed Michigan State teammates went to Vietnam, but they traveled in comfort on USO/NFL tours. The Houston Oilers' George Webster was among 15 players in 1970 and the Minnesota Vikings' Clinton Jones with 17 in 1971.

Neither player, though, huddled up with Marshall. Cu Chi wasn't a safe-haven USO Tour stop. Marshall's Michigan State's teammates, who called him Ruben for his middle name, Rubenstein, raised their respect for a man they had already held in high esteem as a quintessential team player.

"Ruben is an American hero," Jones said. "He was our hero at Michigan State. He never wasted any energy. He always did everything 100 percent."

Stories of young Vietnam officers like Marshall don't sell movie scripts to expose America's underbelly, like *Apocalypse Now*, *Platoon* or *Full Metal Jacket*.

Nor was he famous enough for an inspiring story like wounded Vietnam veteran Rocky Bleier's experiences, with his book and 1980 TV movie, *Fighting Back: The Rocky Bleier Story*. Bleier, opposite Marshall on the 1966 Game of the Century sidelines as a Notre Dame halfback, recovered from losing part of his right foot to win four Pittsburgh Steelers Super Bowl rings for the 1974, 1975, 1977 and 1978 seasons.

Bleier never met Marshall, but learning he served in Vietnam was all he needed to know.

"The soldiers serving today are truly heroes, but for those of us who served in Vietnam, that was not the case at the time," Bleier said. "Unfortunately, Vietnam veterans didn't get recognition for their commitment and their service."

Bleier has spent the last half-century trying to understand what happened to his country, the soldiers that served, sharing his observations and helping others come to terms with America's haunting Vietnam history.

"That whole experience—whether staying in, spending two years after being drafted or four years after enlisting—they had to repress their feelings about how the American public viewed them. They didn't get the immediate recognition that could have been so helpful in a lot of ways. Helpful in their perception of themselves, helpful with post-traumatic stress disorder, helpful how they approached the rest of their life thereafter.

"I think whether they had a great experience or a bad experience—whatever it was—they needed someone to say, 'Thank you for your service and for putting your life on the line.' I look at Vietnam veterans and what they faced. In my mind they are heroes for the commitment they made. Right or wrong, drafted or enlisted, they put in their time serving their country."

Maybe the movie character Marshall most resembles, oddly enough, was played by Tom Hanks in *Forrest Gump*. The difference, of course, was Gump fell into everything by dumb luck, Marshall planned and adapted to events. Life imitates art—or is it the other way around?

Both had devoted education-minded mothers; both witnessed a pivotal civil rights moment at a hate-filled Deep South campus; both played for a College Football Hall of Fame coach; both served in Vietnam; both went on a diplomatic mission to a Communist country; and both crossed paths with historic figures and moments. Only Gump was invited to the White

House, but Marshall's story still has a Zelig feel for showing up in so many places in time.

But movies aren't made about anonymous soldiers that did their job, harrowing or not.

"Sometimes the unsung heroes have the greatest impact," said Herman Bulls, a West Point graduate and retired colonel now in a second career as a vice-chairman of a Fortune 500 company, JLL in Washington, D.C.

Bulls related to hearing Marshall's story for more than their shared Army officer careers.

Both were Black high-school quarterbacks from the South. As a senior in the fall of 1973, Bulls was the first Black starting quarterback at Coffee High in Florence, Alabama. West Point head coach Homer Smith recruited him. As a West Point cadet, Bulls viewed with great respect the Vietnam veterans that returned to campus to teach. As a tribute to their dedication, he requested a tour on West Point's faculty before his retirement to the business world.

"Lt. Col. Marshall's peers from those Vietnam years were the same officers that introduced me to the military as my tactical officers and instructors at West Point," he said. "They were a group that fought an unpopular war and, like Lt. Col. Marshall, made a big difference preparing the next generation for success."

ROSEY MICHIGAN STATE

Marshall first dreamed of attending Michigan State through summer visits to his father in Muskegon, a city on Lake Michigan's harbor shore.

Joe Marshall, like other Southern African Americans of the time, had relocated seeking a factory job. Marshall's parents were divorced, but both guided him. His father regaled him with stories of Black stars from Michigan factory towns, Flint and Saginaw, leading the Spartans to 1954 and 1956 Rose Bowl victories.

As a high-school quarterback, Marshall had an arm and inquisitive mind. He took a Saturday morning cafeteria job on the Ole Miss campus, coveting the bonus in exchange for the menial work. African-American employees were permitted to attend Ole Miss games in a roped-off section at Hemingway Stadium (now Vaught-Hemingway Stadium).

"I'd bring a pencil and pad of paper and diagram the plays," he said. "I was interested in how plays worked, especially the passing plays."

The Rebels were a throwing team. Ole Miss quarterback Jake Gibbs was third in the nation in 1960 with 12 touchdown passes, although he became better known for playing parts of 10 seasons with the New York Yankees.

"I'd show those plays to my high-school coach," said Marshall, referring to Al Dowsing. "We'd work on them during the week."

He also picked up that Gibbs called audibles; Dowsing trusted his quarterback to change plays. In Marshall's senior year, a late-game audible preserved the school's fifth straight unbeaten season and a Black state title for Northern Mississippi (Southern Mississippi Black schools had their own tournament).

With the defense overloaded, Marshall changed the play. Halfback Leroy Jenkins broke off a long run to set up the game-winning score.

WORTH THE WAIT

Marshall had three teammates play at an Historically Black College and University, and he gained his own scholarship offers from Jackson State and Tennessee State, HBCU powerhouses.

But even though Daugherty didn't have a scholarship available until the winter quarter of January 1963, Marshall's heart remained with riding the Underground Railroad. Marshall stayed home the fall of 1962 until boarding for the New Year.

He spent 1963 on the freshman team, but as a 5-foot-9, 165-pound passing quarterback, he was a tough fit into Michigan State's ground-oriented offense. On the varsity, ankle injuries and a broken clavicle buried him on the depth chart. He missed one year on the redshirt injury list.

Raye emerged as the 1965 backup to All-American QB Steve Juday, routinely entering games, including key plays in the Rose Bowl.

Marshall also was behind Charlie Wedemeyer and Bill Feraco on the depth chart, playing a valuable role on the scout team. He took more snaps directing the upcoming opponent's offense than the Michigan State game plan.

He expresses no regrets.

"That's the way it was, and I just tried to do what I could to help the team. I enjoyed school and my classes. When other students learned I was from the South, they'd ask me what segregation was like. I told them you learned to live with it. I also told them there were separations in the North, too, but I could deal with it."

That quote was more than a septuagenarian accepting the past. He had said essentially the same thing as a fifth-year senior. After Daugherty gave Marshall snaps in the midseason Notre Dame game, he was featured in the *State News*, the student newspaper, in a Nov. 16, 1967 article under Don Kopriva's byline. He quoted Marshall about his backup role.

"You've got to keep the team up, give them all the support you can," Marshall said. "But for me, as a quarterback, one of the main things I do on the bench is analyze the defense of the other team, to see which back might be weak. I watch the ends very carefully."

That's how Raye remembers Marshall.

"He was a tremendous teammate. He never once complained about his status on the team. He was great on the scout team for our defense running the opponent's offense and had great camaraderie with the defense. All the guys on defense really liked him."

In 2016, Marshall attended a 50th anniversary celebration for the 1966 national championship team that also recognized the 1965 national champs. Washington introduced Marshall to the Friday-night dinner audience, citing his Vietnam service and career in public education. At halftime of Saturday's game, he was introduced on the field with the rest of the players.

In 2017, he attended the 51st anniversary of the Game of the Century, a joint Notre Dame-Michigan State affair when the Irish played at Spartan Stadium. It was the last time he saw defensive coordinator Hank Bullough, who died two years later at age 85. Bullough was as much his coach as any other assistant; together they prepared the defense.

"Hank always told me I was his quarterback," Marshall said. "Hank pushed me."

As the Spartans prepared for the 1966 Game of the Century, Marshall played the role of Notre Dame quarterback Terry Hanratty. The two met for the first time at the joint reunion.

"It was pretty to cool to meet someone that played you," said Hanratty, an All-American, three-time Top 10 Heisman finisher and owner of two Pittsburgh Steelers Super Bowl rings. "You don't read about everybody, but there are no small roles in a big game. You've got to have your scout team give you a really good look for what to expect on Saturday. It's not an easy thing to do.

"For us, how do you have someone emulate Bubba Smith, who is 6-8, 285 pounds, or George Webster, who's 6-5, 230 and can run like a deer? There was a lot of talent on both teams. I still say to this day those are the two best teams ever to play each other."

A MOTHERLY EDUCATION ADVOCATE

Marshall's mother, who lived to age 100, did more than spur her family's academic quests. On Dec. 27, 2013, the *Oxford Eagle* ran a front-page story chronicling her life with this headline:
 "Beloved educator Susie Marshall passes away."

A 1930s graduate of HBCU Rust College in Holly Springs, Mississippi, she served Oxford and Lafayette County schools 41 years (1937-78). From 1952 to 1964, she was Lafayette's Supervisor for 26 Black schools.

In 1955, a year after the *Brown v. Board of Education* Supreme Court case holding that public school segregation was unconstitutional, Marshall convinced the *Oxford Eagle's* young white publisher, Jesse Phillips, to photograph inferior conditions at Black schools. The state resisted *Brown v. Board* until 1970, but at least by then Marshall had the law on her side—if not cold hearts and cruel minds.

"She was a brilliant lady," said Phillips in the 2013 article. "Her life was dedicated to providing the best possible education for the African-American students. I respected her as an outstanding educator all the years that I've known her."

Eric also was quoted: "I watched her and how she undertook difficult choices and it helped me make the decisions I did. She was my inspiration."

His first life-altering decision was at age 22 in June 1968, upon opening his draft notice.

Does he seek a college deferment like so many others? President Bill Clinton avoided Vietnam with college deferments. Vice-president Dick Cheney had five deferments. President Donald Trump also had five. President Joe Biden was granted deferments.

Or does he sign up for OCS?

Marshall didn't see a dilemma. His mother and father taught him to look for open doors.

"I felt blessed I had an opportunity to go Michigan State and graduate. It was a dream come true. When my friends laughed at me in sixth grade, it *really* was the impossible dream. I felt I owed it to my country."

It started out a four-year hitch until he discovered the meritocracy of the Army.

"To be an officer meant something to me. I realized I could make a difference the rest of my life. I liked what being an officer meant as a human being. You could help other people, Black and white."

From 1977 to 1981 he was posted in West Berlin, behind the Iron Curtain, encircled by the Soviet Union-controlled East Germany. There were other foreign posts in Italy and Japan. Stateside he served at the Pentagon, Chicago, Fort Benning in Georgia, Fort Bragg in North Carolina and the Presidio in San Francisco.

Along the way, Marshall earned a Master's in Education Administration from the University of Southern California.

As retirement approached while based in San Francisco, it was suggested he take a job as a junior ROTC instructor at the city's public schools. He rose to principal at Burton High, a school that opened in 1984 through a consent decree between the City of San Francisco and the National Association of Advancement for Colored People. The school sends 75 percent of its diverse and economically disadvantaged students to colleges and universities.

American attitudes and reactions toward racism are in constant flux, sometimes forward, too many times backward. They often have been exploited over the flag and patriotism.

The Army officer in Marshall required his high-school students to stand for the National Anthem. He wasn't shy about grabbing a shoulder with stern words. The Black man in him, especially from the South, understands why today's college and pro athletes take a knee protesting abusive police tactics.

The veteran in him has a clear opinion on Trump politicizing the flag; Trump criticizes athletes for expressing their opinions.

"What does he know about disrespecting the flag?" Marshall said. "He didn't serve a day in the military. How would he know?"

A story in the *The Atlantic* attributed quotes through sources that Trump has said soldiers who served and died in Vietnam and other wars were "losers" and "suckers."

From Aug. 5, 1964 to May 7, 1975, 2.7 million Americans served in Vietnam, out of 9.1 million Americans that did a military tour, according to government records. Marshall and others like him signed up with a purpose. It was true then, and it remains so now, with the uptick of American volunteers following the 9/11 terrorist attacks.

"I don't think any of us felt like they were losers or suckers," Bleier said. "If we did something we didn't want to do, there was still a sense of patriotism—however you wanted to define it. At the core there was a sense of commitment that allowed those people to go."

THE NEW SOUTH'S OPEN DOORS

A week upon Marshall's return home from Vietnam, he and his mother walked in downtown Oxford, not far from campus, when a car backfired.

"I immediately got into the down position by a trash can," said Marshall.

He laughs now, but he remembers getting up, brushing himself off and noticing "people looking at me strangely."

A Black man creating a scene on 1962 downtown Oxford sidewalk was no laughing matter, but in 1971 Marshall went about his day's business, including entering stores that not long ago had banned him because of his skin color.

The segregated world he left behind had changed so much, his mother, at age 59, stepped through the Ole Miss door Meredith had opened. She earned a master's degree in 1972, the same year the football program dressed its first Black player, Robert Williams.

Marshall's daughter, Erica Marshall Lee, is an assistant professor in clinical psychiatry at Emory University and attached as a faculty coordinator at Grady Hospital in Atlanta. She has three Ole Miss degrees: bachelor's, master's and Ph.D.

Her father wanted her to attend Stanford, her grandmother Ole Miss, but she preferred UCLA. When a UCLA campus housing arrangement fell through at the last minute, her default destination was the school that barred her father.

Education as a Marshall was a given, even as an Army brat growing up on bases around the world. But what she observed looming larger than her father's college degree was the respect he commanded. White soldiers addressed her father, "Yes, sir" or "No, sir"—respect he didn't necessarily have off the base. That was especially true in Georgia and North Carolina.

"I think what I gained was the hard work and the regimentation of the military," she said. "I saw the respect he had as an African-American male."

There were other changes. North Seventh Street, the route the Army took to campus in 1962, was renamed Martin Luther King Drive.

In 2006, Ole Miss unveiled a campus statue of Meredith. In the summer of 2020, protests by the state's Black college athletes played a role in the Mississippi state legislature voting to remove the Confederate Battle emblem from the state flag.

The 21st-century athletes made a bold and justified statement. That was more than the 1960s Rebels coaches and players learned from the Ole Miss Riot of 1962.

Retrospective football stories from 1962 focus on an unbeaten all-white Ole Miss believing its shot at a national championship was robbed. Conjecture lingers that the 10-0 Rebels were victims of reverse racism in the poll voting, finishing No. 3 behind No. 1 USC (11-0). That ironic victimization was placated in 2012; the school awarded the players symbolic national championship rings.

Such stories, though, overlook legendary Ole Miss coach Johnny Vaught's reaction to an integrated campus; he maintained the status quo. It was left to his successor, Billy Kinard, to play the Rebels' first Black player in 1972, the same year Ole Miss, Georgia and LSU were the last three SEC holdouts.

PART II: THE TRUE 1960S PIONEERS AT SOUTHERN SCHOOLS

CHAPTER 19
BLAZING A TRAIL THROUGH THE ACC

FACT: Wake Forest was the first school from a major Southern conference to recruit Black football players out of high school.

"It took the courage of three white men to offer us scholarships in 1964. Bill Tate, Harold Tribble and Gene Hooks put themselves in danger. The KKK was around in those days in North Carolina." — Wake Forest's Bob Grant.

Wake Forest's 2021 football season stood out for more than head coach Dave Clawson's team winning the Atlantic Coast Conference's Atlantic Division title, posting a double-digit victory season and breaking into the Top 25 rankings.

The school's administration in Winston-Salem, North Carolina, took its turn setting the record straight on the story of how college football integration evolved and the pivotal role it played. Until then, Wake Forest, like other schools, sat by idly and allowed myths and outright fiction surrounding the 1970 USC-Alabama game to control the narrative how college football integration unfolded.

The truth always has a lot of ground to make up on a false narrative, but Wake Forest is finally telling its story—better late than never.

In 1964, Bob Grant and Kenneth "Butch" Henry were the first Black players to sign scholarship offers out of high school from a program in a major Southern conference. It took decades, but the pair was finally recognized by Wake Forest with the school's inaugural Trailblazer Award in 2021.

Grant proudly returned to campus to represent both players at the Friday and Saturday events since Henry was unable to attend for health reasons. Presenting the Trailblazer Award and the media attention attracted was about more than ceremony—it also about educating the fan base. Only a minuscule number of fans, including Wake Forest partisans, understand the ground broken by the pair.

"Wake Forest University has many pioneers, but Robert Grant and Kenneth 'Butch' Henry are more than pioneers," Wake Forest athletic director John Currie said upon establishing the award on July 21, 2021. "They are trailblazers. Bob and Butch were the first Black football student-athletes to enroll at a Division I institution in the South, joining the Wake Forest family in the fall of 1964.

"Being the first two Black football players at Wake Forest took tremendous courage. It took deep faith to believe that their teammates, the coaching staff, our university's leadership and the Winston-Salem community would offer steady support during uncertain times. They were transformational leaders, displaying their abilities, talents, character and fortitude to persevere and mark trails for future student-athletes of color at Wake Forest."

Like so many of the integration pioneers in college football, Grant and Henry endured cheap shots while playing against all-white opponents, heard racial insults from all-white crowds and felt cold shoulders on their own campus from classmates and some professors opposed to progress.

"They had to be strong to let that roll off their backs," said Bill Tate, Wake Forest's coach from 1964 to 1968. "These are kids who had to put up with that."

Grant, though, says they wouldn't have a place in history without the support from Tate, president Harold Tribble and athletic director Gene Hooks.

"It took the courage of three white men to offer us scholarships in 1964," Grant said. "Bill Tate, Harold Tribble and Gene Hooks put themselves in danger. The KKK was around in those days in North Carolina."

Southern white terrorists bombed and lit up Black homes and churches and intimidated white citizens supporting civil rights.

"You have to remember 1964 was only a year after the KKK killed four little girls in Birmingham when they bombed the 16th Street Baptist Church," Grant said. "It was only a year after (civil rights leader) Medgar Evers was assassinated in Mississippi. It was only a couple months after (James) Chaney, (Andrew) Goodman and (Michael) Schwerner were murdered in Mississippi. It was a dangerous time in 1964."

Goodman and Schwerner were white college students from New York and Chaney an African American from Meridian, Mississippi, who worked together to register voters in the Freedom Summer of 1964. The 1988 movie *Mississippi Burning* was based on their murders.

Tate arrived at Wake Forest in 1964 from integrated Illinois, where he had been a player and assistant coach at the Big Ten Conference member. Tate had played for Illinois from 1950-52 as a fullback. He was the MVP of the 1952 Rose Bowl, running for 150 yards and two touchdowns on 20 carries to lead a 40-7 win over Stanford. He served as an Illinois assistant coach from 1959 to 1963 before landing the Wake Forest job.

When Tate was hired, Tribble and Hooks told him they wanted to integrate the program. Tate, with his background, told them he was ready to join the challenge.

"Dr. Tribble one day in February of 1964 called and said he wanted to talk to me," Tate recalled. "I walked over to his office for a chat. He asked me what I thought about recruiting Black athletes, and I told him I was all for it."

Although it's accurate that former ACC member Maryland broke the conference's color line in 1963 with Darryl Hill, the Terrapins' running back was a transfer from two schools, Xavier in Cincinnati and Navy in Annapolis. He was an isolated example and not part of a future pattern unfolding at Wake Forest. Hill sat out 1962 as a transfer and had only one season of eligibility remaining at Maryland in 1963.

At Wake Forest, Grant and Henry were three-year lettermen (1965-67) in an era prior to the NCAA permitting freshmen eligibility. Wake Forest's pioneering 1964 class included William Smith as a third Black recruit out of high school, although he left the school. He served as a medic in Vietnam on his way to becoming a doctor.

In 1965, Tate added running back Jimmy Johnson and center Howard Stanback; in 1966, lineman Bill Overton; and in 1967, quarterback Freddie Summers. Also in 1967, Wake Forest basketball coach Jack McCloskey signed Gilbert McGregor as that program's first Black player.

Summers was the first Black starting quarterback at a major Southern school as a junior-college transfer in 1967, although that landmark has been often erroneously listed as Georgia Tech's Eddie McAshon, in 1970.

Grant, who founded the Retired NFL Players Congress in 2013, seemed destined to play a pioneering role upon graduating from Georgetown High, a Black high school during segregation in Jacksonville, North Carolina. But first he planned to attend Michigan State.

Daugherty stopped at Georgetown High on his annual sweep through the South. Grant turned out to be an easy sell.

"Duffy told me about all the great players he had returning and how they were going to win a national title," Grant recalled. Included in that assessment: Jimmy Raye, a quarterback at Fayetteville's Black high school, E.E. Smith. Raye was destined to become the South's first Black quarterback to win a national title, but in 1964 he was merely a high-school rival to Grant. E.E. Smith had defeated Georgetown twice in North Carolina's Black high-school athletic association state playoffs.

"Bob and I have been great friends a long time," said Raye, whom Wake Forest invited to attend the weekend ceremonies. "This is a great honor for Bob and long overdue. He competed hard and had an outstanding career. I'm proud to be a part of the event."

Grant explained he signed a scholarship offer with Daugherty before the Spartans' coach left campus, but his future changed when legendary Georgetown coach Gideon T. Johnson called him into his office. Johnson had been contacted by Tate, who offered Grant a Wake Forest scholarship. Johnson tried to impress upon Grant the role in history he would play clearing a path for future Black athletes in the South.

The Demon Deacons, though, were a bottom-level ACC football program. To this day, the school has won only two ACC titles, in 1970 and 2006.

"I told him, 'Why would I want to go to a school that gets beat up all the time,'" Grant recalled. "I'm going to win a national title at Michigan State."

Johnson, though, was a giant in the community in an era when high-school coaches played a large role in their athletes' college destination. Grant accepted his coach's advice to set out on a pioneering trail. Other Southern schools began to follow.

Grant's Wake Forest career also established milestones that went unrecognized and don't appear next to his name in biographical Google searches.

In 1966, as a junior, Grant was the first Black player at a major Southern conference to earn all-league honors. He was a first-team All-ACC defensive lineman.

In 1968, he was the first Black player from a major Southern conference to be taken in the NFL draft, a second-round pick by the Baltimore Colts. Grant played in two Super Bowls, the SBIII loss to the New York Jets and the SBV win over the Dallas Cowboys.

How can such obvious stories of true 1960s pioneers breaking barriers get pushed into the shadows?

The short answer: a perfect storm of the 1960s mainstream media avoiding stories about race, then leaving behind a vacuum of unrecorded Black milestones. The vacuum was duplicitously filled decades later by myths and fiction surrounding the 1970 USC-Alabama game at Legion Field in Birmingham. The myth has Bear Bryant taking USC Black fullback Sam Cunningham into his locker room to show his players what "a football player looks like." Cunningham years later began to admit in interviews the locker room scene never happened, explaining he got caught up in the tale.

However, the USC-Alabama fairytale successfully served its purpose.

An example of how entrenched the Cunningham myth is entrenched in college football lore was repeated in *The New York Times* obituary for Cunningham, published Sept. 9, 2021. The story stated USC was the first integrated team to play in Alabama. The *Times* posted a correction on Sept. 13, 2021, stating other integrated teams had previously played in Alabama.

However, the correction failed to mention that in 1969 Southeastern Conference rival Tennessee's integrated roster routed Alabama's all-white team at Legion Field, 41-14.

"People are written out of history," Grant said. "It's not an accident."

FOLLOWING WAKE FOREST

By 1966, Duke was the third ACC school with Black football players. N.C. State and North Carolina were on board by 1967.

Similar to Grant, McClain's place in history—he scored six touchdowns in 1968—doesn't show up in Google searches about his career. The same is true of Hackett as the first Black team captain in any SEC sport as a junior in 1969.

Grant continues to be involved in the game by leading the Retired NFL Players Congress. The organization serves retired players and their families

"To me it's about helping other people," Grant said. "Color, gender, religion and politics shouldn't matter. The division taking place in this country today is a crying shame. It's a crying shame. Once again, there is a reason for it. It's not happening accidentally."

CHAPTER 20
MLK, SMU'S JERRY LEVIAS AND SWC INTEGRATION

FACT: SMU coach Hayden Fry recruited Jerry LeVias out of Beaumont, Texas, as the first Black scholarship football player in the Southwest Conference, in 1965.

"Jerry took the brunt of it. He was an extraordinary athlete, an exceptional student and an incredibly strong and courageous person. His performance on the field, despite the many challenges he faced, was largely responsible for SMU's football resurgence in 1966. He made it much easier for those of us who followed." — SMU teammate Rufus Cormier.

Martin Luther King Jr. initially hesitated to accept an invitation to speak at Dallas's Southern Methodist University in 1966, a time and place where resistance to integration persisted despite passage of the 1964 and 1965 Civil Rights Acts.

The Nobel Peace Prize winner explained in a letter to SMU Student Senate leader Bert Moore the school had rescinded an invitation a couple years earlier. Moore, who won election as Student Senate vice-president despite opposition campaign posters around campus labeling him an "integrationist," appealed to SMU president Willis M. Tate.

Tate assured King the invitation would be honored. MLK traveled to the SMU campus on March 17, 1966 to speak at McFarlin Memorial Auditorium before a capacity audience of 2,700. He delivered a familiar address, stating "we have come a long, long way in our struggle to make justice a reality for all men, but we have a long, long way to go before the problem is solved."

The great orator's words remain as true today as then.

Perhaps King's most immediate impact that night was fortifying a burgeoning football trailblazer, Jerry LeVias. Tate arranged King's private meeting with LeVias, the first Black scholarship football player in the Southwest Conference after SMU head coach Hayden Fry recruited LeVias out of Beaumont, Texas, in 1965.

"He told me he heard I was, 'a fine, young Christian man,'" recalled LeVias, the reverence for King still palpable in his voice more than a half-century later. "We talked before he went on stage. He told me, 'This is the thing I want you to remember…always keep your emotions under control.'"

King wasn't known as a football fan, but without his words perhaps LeVias doesn't survive the racial abuse he endured. Countless times he leaned on MLK's advice to complete his trailblazing path. His success created avenues for future Black athletes in the bigoted South.

"When I had players spit on me, I wanted to fight back, but I learned to live with no emotions. Nothing could get to me."

Fry provided similar support.

"Coach Fry always told me, 'If you don't want them to get your goat, don't tell 'em where it's hid.'"

LeVias was smaller than his listed height and weight as a 5-foot-9, 175-pound receiver and return man, but he played with a big heart. He endured, leading SMU to the 1966 SWC title, the Mustangs' first conference championship and Cotton Bowl berth since 1948. He was second-team All-America in 1967 and first-team pick along with Academic All-American honors in 1968. He played six years in the National Football League and was enshrined in the College Football Hall of Fame in 2003.

SMU winning with LeVias opened eyes, expanding minds that otherwise might have remained closed to the emerging zeitgeist of the times. Southwest rival Baylor awarded John Westbrook a scholarship in 1967 after he had made the team in 1966 as a walk-on. Texas Tech signed Danny Hardaway in 1967. TCU signed Linzy Cole from the junior-college ranks in 1968. Texas coach Darrell Royal and Arkansas coach Frank Broyles, who led the SWC's dominant programs in the 1960s, also joined the 20th century.

The pioneering steps were needed in a climate clinging to the past. Texas A&M coach Gene Stallings, a Bear Bryant protégé, had said as late as 1965 he didn't think Black and white athletes could co-exist in a locker room. A&M didn't sign a Black football player until 1971, Jerry Honore.

Fry, though, recruited three more Black athletes the year after LeVias arrived. Rufus Cormier, Walter Haynes and Lee McElroy made their SMU varsity debuts in 1968. The road they encountered was not necessarily easy, but one that was smoother.

"Jerry took the brunt of it," said Cormier, who went on to a 40-year law career, including a partnership at the Houston firm of Baker Botts LLP. "He was an extraordinary athlete, an exceptional student and an incredibly strong and courageous person.

"His performance on the field, despite the many challenges he faced, was largely responsible for SMU's football resurgence in 1966. He made it much easier for those of us who followed."

Tate, for whom SMU's lecture series is now named, died in 1989. Fry lived to 90, passing away in 2019, with LeVias remaining in touch with his old coach until the end. Bert Moore was a retired dean of the School of Behavior and Brain Science at UT Dallas when he died in 2015.

But the change LeVias set in motion continues to be seen year after year on the field. Black athletes now represent typically 60 percent or more of the nation's Division I college football rosters.

Each year SMU selects a player representing LeVias' courage to wear his No. 23 for the season.

"A LIVING HELL"

LeVias earned a special place in college football history, but he has described his experience as a "living hell." He said the Serenity Prayer to begin each day. He also felt strength from fulfilling his Grandmother Ella's request that he wear No. 23 for Psalm 23.

"She wanted God to watch over me," LeVias said. "She told me to be her David against Goliath."

But he couldn't avoid loneliness and racist behavior. As the only Black male living on campus, LeVias was without a roommate. Students ostracized him walking across campus and in the classroom.

On the practice field there were cheap shots from teammates; they unintentionally provided previews of tactics from future opponents his first varsity season. He said of his first season in 1966, "They only needed me on Saturdays."

On the road he was taunted. At Texas in Austin, some Longhorns fans waved nooses at him. But in 1966, the reaction was to laugh or look the other way at Texas fans waving a noose as a Black man.

Fry grew concerned enough to assemble an informal security team intended to blend in with the team traveling party. He also gave LeVias an unlisted phone number and had his secretary screen his mail.

But by the 1966 regular-season finale at TCU at Amon Carter Stadium in nearby Fort Worth, the media learned the Fort Worth police and FBI had deemed credible a death threat against LeVias. On gameday, he was escorted to and from the team bus. The police and FBI also were positioned around the stadium scanning for a sniper.

A newspaper headline prior the 1966 SMU-TCU game read—in the vernacular of the times—"**SMU Negro LeVias is Object of Abuse.**"

Jerry LeVias escorted by various FBI and other Fort Worth cops escorting from the locker room to the team bus. *Photo courtesy Jerry LeVias.*

Despite the pressure, LeVias scored on a 68-yard touchdown reception in the 21-0 victory that clinched the SWC title.

"Years later Coach Fry joked to me nobody wanted to stand next to me on the sideline," LeVias said.

For the next two seasons, Fry continued the practice of an informal security team, but he also requested the media not report the safety precautions.

"He asked Blackie Sherrod and others not to write about it," said LeVias, referring to the preeminent sports journalist of the era in Dallas-Fort Worth. "He was afraid if it was always in the news some nut would do something."

BREAKING SEC GROUND AT AUBURN

LeVias was a Southwest Conference pioneer as the first Black scholarship football player, but as a senior in 1968 he performed with equal valor while entering the belly of the beast.

The Deep South. The Southeastern Conference.

College football lore paints a picture of USC's integrated team arriving at Legion Field in Birmingham to play Alabama in 1970 as a tipping point in college football integration. The story the sports media missed in real time involved SMU and LeVias "integrating the end zone" at Auburn. He was the first Black player to score in an SEC stadium.

The senior All-American receiver/return man led the Mustangs to a 38-27 win over the Tigers, catching five passes for 100 yards, scoring a touchdown on a 38-yard reception and finding the end zone a second time on a two-point conversion reception.

Another easy TD was missed, according to a notation on the play-by-play sheet. Early in the third quarter, SMU quarterback Chuck Hixon overthrew LeVias. The sheet reads: "3-7-A32 (third and 7 at the Auburn 32): Hixon-LeVias-incomplete-overthrew LeVias, had plenty of room."

The "had plenty of room" commentary remains rare for a play-by-play account, which adds to the imagination. The fleet-footed LeVias must have been *very* wide, wide open.

The game wasn't as close as the final score—SMU led 30-14 in the fourth quarter—and the comfortable lead was in contrast to the environment. It was an eye-opening experience for a white crowd. LeVias and his two Black teammates, starting defensive lineman Rufus Cormier and backup halfback Walter Haynes, played through jeers as they ran from the stadium tunnel to the field.

Such nonconference games typically were scheduled years in advance. In other words, Auburn's administration and fans weren't expecting the previously all-white Mustangs to show up with three Black players for the game in Auburn, Alabama.

SMU flew from Dallas into Birmingham. Alabama's largest city was known in the 1960s as "Bombingham" for the attacks on Black homes and churches. George Wallace, the state's governor from 1963 to 1967, campaigned on preserving segregation. In the 1968 Presidential election, he ran as an Independent.

Before the team boarded its flight in Dallas, a friend gave LeVias a "Vote for George Wallace" straw hat as a joke. He wore it on the flight in youthful, defiant humor.

"I wanted to make fun of them," LeVias said, chuckling. "They were threatening my life."

There was no laughing when the flight landed. The players felt the climate of hate on the two-hour bus trip to the city of Auburn.

"There were big posters of George Wallace everywhere," Cormier said.

LeVias felt another death-threat scare upon arriving at the hotel.

"I threw my bags down and was lying on the bed," he said. "Then I heard this ticking sound. I jumped out of my bed and ran into the hallway yelling, 'Something is in there ticking!' It turned out somebody staying in the room before me had set an alarm clock."

On game day LeVias, Cormer and Haynes were booed as they took the field, but the Mustangs were ready to play with their dominating performance.

Fans everywhere typically greet the visiting team with boos, of course, but these taunts were guttural. Cormier said by 1968 some of their white teammates had gained empathy for SMU's Black players enduring racism.

He added one white teammate wrote them a letter on the 50th anniversary game, apologizing for not recognizing the hate and providing them more support.

MORE HATE AT TCU

Despite LeVias' Wallace straw-hat levity, when SMU played three weeks later at TCU, he admits the pressure to be the "Jackie Robinson of the Southwest Conference" finally broke him.

LeVias' habit throughout his career outrunning racism had been to get off the ground quickly from a tackle to avoid late hits (football's dark ages were a long way from today's safety rules). But on one tackle, he was pinned at the bottom of a pile. A TCU player spit into his face.

Enraged, LeVias retreated to the bench, threw his helmet, sulked and said he was done playing. Fry came to the bench, consoled him and offered his Southern Fried humor about "hiding his goat" and not letting down the team.

Late in the game with the score 14-14, TCU was forced to punt. LeVias took the field, telling Fry he was taking the punt to the end zone. His electric 89-yard touchdown sealed a 21-14 victory.

"That was the only time I hated," LeVias said. "That was one of my best touchdowns, but I can't take pleasure in it because I hated."

FRY'S RECRUITING PITCH

If not for Fry, LeVias would have missed his destiny that has established him as a Texas football icon.

He grew up a high-school star at Hebert High in segregated Beaumont, a refinery town near Houston. He played at SMU in Dallas. He spent two of his six NFL seasons with Houston's original AFL/NFL franchise, the Oilers.

He now serves as an ambassador for Houston's second NFL franchise, the Texans, and has a seat on the Board of Directors for the Texas Bowl, played in Houston.

UCLA had been LeVias' first choice as a college destination, wanting to follow his cousin Mel Farr, a UCLA All-American halfback. Farr, a 1967 first-round draft pick of the Detroit Lions who played seven NFL seasons, was two years older than LeVias, but they had been teammates at Hebert.

"He was like a big brother to me," LeVias said. "I followed him everywhere."

At the same time, Willie Ray Smith Sr. tried to recruit LeVias on behalf of Michigan State coach Duffy Daugherty's Underground Railroad teams. (We cover Smith's role in Chapter 16.)

LeVias' high-school coach, Clifton Ozen, knew his star player wanted to follow Farr to UCLA, but when Fry called Ozen asking him to set up a home visit, Ozen encouraged LeVias to meet with Fry.

"My high-school coach told me, 'Jerry, I know you're kind of committed (to UCLA), but I want you to talk to these people,'" recalled LeVias.

He waited at home with his parents, Charlie and Leura, when two cars arrived with Fry, assistant coach Chuck Curtis, Beaumont school district superintendent Sparky Adams and Ozen.

"It was about 5 o'clock, and they got out of their cars. Coach Curtis was a tall guy wearing a big cowboy hat; he looked like a Texas Ranger. All the neighbors were standing on their porches wondering what the police were doing at our house. Coach Fry went straight to my grandmother's house next door, but the rest of them came to my house. It looked like a raid.

"We talked in the living room until Coach Fry came over. He comes in, says hello and walks straight to the kitchen to my mom. My Dad didn't like that—a white man coming into his house and walking past him to the kitchen. He had a temper; a frown was on his forehead.

"Coach Fry asked my mom about the pinto beans she was cooking. He said, 'You've got to tell me how to cook 'em, because they give me gas.' They talked about cooking pinto beans for 10 minutes, and then he and my mom came into the living room."

Fry finally got down to business.

"He talked about education, saying, 'You're 17, 18 years old right now. You'll have a college degree when you're 22. What are you going to do with it the rest of your life? What if you don't make it on my team? What if you don't make it in pro ball?'"

The education emphasis hit home, but there were other questions.

"SMU was a white school. We didn't know anything about white schools in the Southwest Conference because we knew we couldn't go there. My dad asked, 'Where is that school?'"

Fry's answer alarmed Charlie LeVias.

"Dallas! That's where they shot President Kennedy!"

But Fry, starting with winning over Grandma Ella next door, continuing making the right pitch. On LeVias's campus visit, Fry had him observe classrooms, including one with a seminar in progress, "The Nature of Man."

But it wasn't until LeVias was closer to signing his scholarship that he understood the enormity of his impending trailblazer role. It was a realization arrived at on his own time and own terms.

"Hayden Fry never talked about me being the first Black player in the Southwest Conference," he said.

Although LeVias and Westbrook were the first two Black players in the SWC in 1966, LeVias drew headlines as a highly recruited high-school senior. Westbrook was a Baylor walk-on whose presence wasn't recognized until his sophomore year on the varsity.

"I still didn't know much about it until they had this press conference for me to sign," LeVias said. "I said, 'Oh, man. I can't do this.' But everybody said I had to. My dad said, 'You gave this man your word. Your word is your bond.'"

GRANDMA ELLA

Grandma Ella wasn't a famous leader, but she was plenty influential with her celebrated grandson.

"She was a strong woman," LeVias said. "She was a missionary at the church. When she said something, we listened. She told Coach Fry, 'If my grandson goes to your college, you have to make a promise. Before every game he has to call me for a prayer.'"

That practice already had been routine since high school.

"Before every game four or five of my teammates would be over to my grandmother's place with me for a prayer. It was never to win. It was to step out in the name of the Lord."

At SMU, Fry always double-checked that LeVias had made his call. LeVias chuckled as he recalled the Mustangs' 1966 game at the University of Texas.

"Coach Fry asked me if I had made my call, and I told him the line was busy. He took me outside under the stands looking for a pay phone. When we found one, here came an SMU band kid. Coach Fry asked him if he had any change. The guy said he wanted to buy some popcorn, but Coach Fry said, 'You don't need popcorn. I need the money.' He took his money, and we called my grandmother. I never did miss a prayer."

LeVias and Fry—as improbable as it sounds these days, considering TV cameras are constantly monitoring coaches and star players—were missing from the sideline until just before kickoff. SMU defeated Texas 13-12 en route to the SWC title.

MENTAL HEALTH ADVOCATE

Now add mental health advocate to LeVias' many hats worn.

His time overcoming racism came with a price of ghosts. The vicissitudes of life caught up with the practical advice for the moment he had followed. They haunted him in frightening nightmares.

"My wife (Janice) and dog had to sleep in different rooms," he said. "I had such pent-up anger."

His wife urged him to seek therapy. The nightmares diminished, but episodes reawaken, usually around return visits to SMU.

"My wife will say, 'You were really blasting somebody last night.'"

The therapy process has spurred LeVias to yet another identity: mental health advocate, particularly for African Americans.

"In the Black community, people think if you need therapy you're crazy," LeVias said. "We need to dispel that notion. We need more Black therapists. A lot of Black people won't go because they think a white person can't understand their pain."

He and his wife sponsor two scholarships for minority therapist interns through the Dallas psychology office of Dr. Andy McGarrahan.

LeVias, more than a half-century later, is still paying forward MLK's advice about enduring.

CHAPTER 21
GARY STEELE BLAZES WEST POINT PATH

FACT: West Point didn't record a Black football letterman until Gary Steele took the field in 1966.

"I had a squad leader that will go unnamed that did his best to razz me badly about things. My solution was always to work harder. I had some company mates say, 'Hey, that guy is all over you. Do you think it's prejudice?' I always said, 'I don't know, I've got to work harder.' That was my mentality." —Gary Steele.

Gary Steele grew up around the world on Army bases in Germany, Japan and America where his father was stationed. The base soldiers' sons and daughters of various ethnicities grew up with little racial tension.

Steele later graduated from integrated Woodrow Wilson High (now Harry S Truman High School) in Levittown, Pennsylvania. He was a football and track star talented enough to attract college recruiters.

But when it was time to pick a school, he chose a school that required breaking a racial barrier, even though he wasn't headed for a pioneering role in the Jim Crow South.

He was the first Black football letterman at West Point. Not in 1946 or 1956–1966. The South wasn't the only location for segregation in America.

The late Howard Cosell, who transformed sports broadcasting in the

1960s with his outspoken style, including defending 1960s Black athletes, decided in 1964 to confront the U.S. Military Academy.

Cosell's track record dated back to supporting Jackie Robinson in his retirement years as a civil rights activist. He defended Muhammad Ali's right to change his name in 1964 while many others in the sports media continued to refer to him as Cassius Clay.

Cosell later passionately defended U.S. sprinters Tommie Smith and John Carlos when they raised their black-gloved fists on the medal stand at the 1968 Mexico City Olympics, protesting racial inequality. Other writers criticized Smith and Carlos. A young Brent Musburger, then writing for the *Chicago American*, portrayed Smith and Carlos in a fashion that was especially narrow-minded, referring to them in print as "black-skinned storm troopers."

So, in December 1964, Cosell thought he had a "gotcha" question for Army football coach Paul Dietzel. They both attended the National Football Foundation and College Football Hall of Fame dinner in New York.

When does West Point plan to recruit its first Black football player?

"Well, Howard, I'm glad you asked me," Dietzel replied. "We've got a fine young man from a fine Black family arriving in the fall, Gary Steele."

At least that's the story Steele was told years later about how his commitment spared Dietzel from squirming under a Cosell interrogation.

Steele, though, didn't arrive at West Point intent on breaking barriers. He was following his father and godfather into a military career, with the chance to play Division I college football.

"My whole time at West Point the Army coaching staff and my teammates always treated me as just another football player," Steele said. "I never saw my role as the only Black guy. It was the coaches saying, 'OK, you're third team now. How are you going to move up?'

"'OK, you're second team now. How are you going to move up?'

"'OK, you're first team now. What are you going to do to hold onto it?'"

ARMY HALL-OF-FAMER

As Army's first Black letterman (1966-68), Steele fought to keep the starting job he grabbed as a sophomore with the grip of a bulldog.

As a senior in 1968, he earned second-team All-American honors with 27 catches for 496 yards and three touchdowns on a 7-3 team. He set an

Army single-game record with eight catches for 156 yards against Penn State.

The Detroit Lions drafted him in the 17th round—his selection no doubt tempered by his military commitment. But Steele passed on the NFL opportunity, serving 23 years until he retired as a Colonel.

His college performances earned him induction into the Army Sports Hall of Fame in 2013 both for football and track and field. He was a 6-foot-9 high jumper, having learned the Western roll style in high school. The Fosbury Flop that Dick Fosbury popularized when winning the 1968 Olympics gold medal would have likely made him a 7-footer.

In retrospect, Steele's legacy was worthy of a Cosell follow-up interview, but his career lacked the controversy to intrigue Cosell's inquiring style. Steele said there was no overt racism at West Point, although there were racially tinged moments. An upperclassman harassed him under the guise of acting as a stickler for discipline.

"I had a squad leader that will go unnamed that did his best to razz me badly about things," Steele said. "My solution was always to work harder. I had some company mates say, 'Hey, that guy is all over you. Do you think it's prejudice?' I always said, 'I don't know, I've got to work harder.' That was my mentality."

The lack of racial strife, though, doesn't diminish Steele's place among 1960s college football integration pioneers. Their presence on the field collectively pushed the ball toward an end zone of broader acceptance. They created awareness that often translates from sports to society.

And, remember, Cosell's question for Dietzel wasn't unfair.

Army not having a Black letterman prior to 1966 was a condemning fact, but, in reality, West Point wasn't that much different from schools with a long history of segregation. Well into the 1960s, programs limited their rosters to an unwritten quota of six or fewer Black players.

Steele, admitting he was "a bit naïve," says now he didn't appreciate his role until later in life. He explains his West Point experience was similar to having grown up an Army brat. Race didn't matter among friends living in Army housing.

GOING TO SEE THE JUDGE AND JIM CROW

Steele's first pioneering season included two special moments that opened his eyes to his place in life blazing a trail. One was a road game in segregated Tennessee, and the other at Notre Dame meeting its one Black player, Alan Page.

Army was the Notre Dame's third victim of the 1966 season. The Irish won 35-0 en route to a 9-0-1 record and national title. Army was 3-0 when the Black Knights arrived in South Bend, finishing 8-2.

"I remember lining up against Alan Page," said Steele, who was a sophomore and Page a senior. "*Oh*, he was good."

Page, of course, went on to both the College and Pro Football Hall of Fame. He was the first of two defensive players to win NFL MVP honors (1971; the other was Lawrence Taylor).

After the game Page approached Steele. Page didn't specifically mention they were the only two Black players on the field, but Steele said he felt a pioneering kinship.

"He came up and put his arm around my shoulders," Steele said. "It was like one of those TV commercials of a dad and his kid. He said, 'You played a good game. Keep up the good work.'"

Steele's first and only taste of racial football threats came two weeks later when Army traveled to the segregated South to play Tennessee of the Southeastern Conference. The game was played at Liberty Bowl in Memphis rather than on campus in Knoxville.

On Monday of game week, senior team captain Townsend Clarke told Steele he wanted to talk after practice. A jolt shot through the kid only halfway through his first varsity season, as if the school principal had called him to the office over the public address system.

Clarke was a 1966 All-American linebacker who also played on the Army basketball team.

"Towny said, 'You know, we're playing at Tennessee this week.' I said, 'Yeah, I'm looking forward to it.' It had not registered with me what it meant to play in the South."

Steele continued relating the conversation, with Clarke using Steele's nickname.

"Gummy, look, this is your first game in the South," Clarke said. "It's different down there. We don't know what's going to happen, but as team captain I want you to know we've got your back. We are one with you and you are one with us."

More than a half-century later, Steele recounts the story with respect still dripping from his voice:

"That's leadership," he said.

Clarke was wise to caution his young teammate. An integrated team traveling to Tennessee had a precedent for trouble.

Just one year earlier, Houston, with Warren McVea as its first African-American player, traveled for a midseason game at Tennessee's Neyland Stadium in Knoxville. McVea endured an endless onslaught of racial taunts and slurs from the fans.

"We get to Tennessee and I'm nervous," Steele said. "There was a pass play on the side of the field where the concrete wall and fans were close to the field. The defender and I went up for the ball and we rolled into the wall. I got up and looked up in the stands, but nothing was said. There were no issues the whole game."

Maybe the lack of ugliness had to do with the game played off campus at the Liberty Bowl, although Memphis was hardly a bastion of progressive thought.

Or maybe it was another sign times were changing. Two years later, Tennessee's football program and fans demonstrated they were actually more progressive than some of their Southeastern Conference rivals.

In 1968, the Volunteers' Lester McClain made history as Tennessee's first Black player. As he ran to the huddle as a backup wide receiver for his first play in the season opener, applause rose from Tennessee's Neyland crowd. For the season, McClain caught six touchdown passes, establishing himself as the first SEC Black player to score a touchdown.

As a junior in the 1967 season, Steele had crossed paths with another pioneer, Southern Methodist's Jerry LeVias, the Southwest Conference's first Black scholarship player. Army beat the Mustangs at the Cotton Bowl in Dallas.

All of the games combined as yet another step taken by 1960s pioneering clearing a path, even though they weren't appreciated at the time or as they should be in history.

OH, BROTHER

Although Steele made history playing at Army, his journey wasn't lonesome. Among the dozen or so minority Cadets at West Point was Michael Steele, his younger brother. Michael was recruited as a track and field athlete.

They both were freshmen in the fall of 1965, although Gary was a year older. Gary attended the U.S. Military Academy Prep School to improve his grades, while Michael was a direct admit. As freshmen, they lined up for daily formation outside the Washington Hall dorms.

Michael didn't tell Gary the story until years later, but Michael began to doubt if he wanted to remain at West Point. However, he decided he could stick it out as long as his older brother. Everyday he'd see Gary lined up and realized he had to keep working.

Gary chuckles as he related Michael's admission: "He said he would get up in the morning get in formation, he'd look and say, 'He's still here. I got to stay.'"

Steele also deflects praise for his place in history. During his sophomore season African-American Bobby Whaley was a B-squad player as a senior on his way to graduating with the Class of 1967. Whaley practiced but never played to earn a letter.

But with time Steele began to understand what he contributed to West Point beyond catching passes.

Steele returned to campus later in his career as an officer to serve as an assistant coach on the football team. One of his recruiting targets was Herman Bulls, the first Black quarterback at his high school in Florence, Alabama.

"I do not recall him saying anything specific about his or my race," Bulls said. "His message was that I could get a great education, build upon my leadership skills and have opportunity to continue playing football. He emphasized while playing would be a privilege, it would not be a requirement to keeping my scholarship and getting a great education."

But the face-to-face meeting was enough for Bulls to take a closer look at the opportunity.

"It meant a lot to me as a 17-year-old in high school to see a Black man, who completed the West Point journey and could be a role model," Bulls said. "We need role models for our younger generations, like Gary, in every aspect of society…including government, education and corporate America."

An injury contributed to Bulls leaving the football program after his sophomore year to focus on preparing for his military career upon graduation. He retired a Colonel and then entered corporate world with JLL, a Fortune 500 real-estate management company, serving as vice chairman, Americas. He has been frequently honored as one of the top African-American businessmen in the nation.

In Bulls' 1978 West Point graduating class, he was among 52 African-American newly commissioned officers.

A PLACE IN HISTORY

Steele's realization he was a trailblazer began to fully hit him during a conversation with (Ret.) U.S. Army Lt. Col. H. Minton Francis, who was only the eighth African-American West Point graduate. Francis enrolled in 1940 and was commissioned an officer with his 1944 class. At the time, the military was still segregated until President Harry S. Truman signed his 1948 executive order.

Francis visited an Army spring football practice in the mid-1970s. He and Steele chatted later at the home of a friend.

Francis said, "Gary, there were a lot of folks paying attention to you, hoping you'd make it."

That hit Steele hard like a running a pass pattern over the middle with a headhunting safety waiting to deliver a blow.

"This had been totally lost on me at West Point," Steele said. "I was just trying to stay proficient as a Cadet and a Division I football player.

"As I was preparing to depart West Point in the spring of 1977 for my next military assignment, I looked around at the team assemblage in the auditorium. There were about 25 Black faces in the room. Just nine years ago there was only one. I did indeed feel I had been a part of something bigger than Gary."

Now fast forward a half-century later.

Army, like most Division I football programs, is now 60 percent or more African-Americans. Steele's impact ultimately contributed to the arrival of Darryl Williams as a football recruit graduating in the Class of 1983. He is now better known as General Darryl A. Williams, West Point's first African-American Superintendent.

WEST POINT'S BUFFALO SOLDIERS

As Army brats, Gary and Michael Steele grew up looking forward to watching the latest episode of a late 1950s network TV show, *The West Point Story*.

The show opened with sweeping panoramic views of the scenic West Point campus on the Hudson River. Episodes included unknown actors Clint Eastwood, Steve McQueen, Chuck Connors and Leonard Nimoy on their way to stardom.

The plots were written from actual events, with the names changed. The Department of Defense cooperated, but it's necessary to keep in mind the time period. The stories were vanilla, reflecting only white America.

In the 21st century, there is a West Point Full Circle Story to tell.

A Gary and Michael Steele episode would include their father, Frank, and godfather, Harold "Buck" Robertson, enlisting in 1941 in the segregated U.S. Army. They were assigned as Buffalo Soldiers with the Tenth Cavalry Regiment stationed at West Point, training and maintaining horses for the Corps of Cadets. For two kids that grew up in Harlem, this was culture shock.

"They liked to say the only horses they were familiar with pulled vegetable carts," Gary said.

But they quickly picked up the traditions of the Buffalo Soldiers, the all-Black regiments formed in 1866 following the Civil War. The West Point campus includes a statue of a Buffalo Soldier.

In addition to their routine responsibilities, they were charged with upkeep of West Point fences. That allowed for long rides as if they were cowboys on the romantic Western frontier, riding the length and width of the 16,000-acre installation.

Both made the military their careers; his father retired as a Major and Robertson as a Master Sgt. How could they have imagined returning to West Point to watch their son/godson make history?

But that's how life played out as Gary made his varsity debut his sophomore year. Army hosted Kansas State on Sept. 17, 1966 at Michie Stadium. Gary soon caught a pass.

"They didn't jump and cheer," Steele said. "They knocked knees. To them, history had been made."

But life wasn't done coming full circle.

Another chapter played out in 2010 at the Inaugural Black Service Academy Graduates Super Reunion in Washington, D.C. The event highlighted the oldest living African-American graduate from each of the five academies: Army, Navy, Air Force, Coast Guard and Merchant Marine.

West Point's honoree was Steele's old friend, Lt. Col. Francis, who lived until age 91, passing away in 2014. Gary and Michael made plans to attend. Their father had died in 2003, but they brought with them Robertson. "Buck" proudly wore his traditional cavalry hat with a yellow bandana around his neck.

"I felt it was important these two men meet," Steele said.

Unbeknownst to Buck, Gary had forwarded his bio to the convention, allowing for the Master of Ceremonies to provide a surprise.

"They said, 'Is Master Sergeant Harold Robertson here?'" Steele said. "I elbowed Buck and said, 'Buck, they're talking about you.' And who ended up in the center of the photo with Francis and the others? The Buffalo Soldier."

Steele began to choke up as he relived the moment.

Howard Cosell missed out on revisiting Steele's story. But CBS has a ready-made episode spanning generations if it were to remake *The West Point Story* with scenes from a college football integration pioneer's career.

CHAPTER 22

KENTUCKY'S WILBUR HACKETT AND TENNESSEE'S LESTER MCCLAIN

FACT: Integrated Tennessee routed Alabama 41-14 on Oct. 18, 1969, before 72,443 fans at Legion Field in Birmingham. The Volunteers, Alabama's bitter rival, shocked the Crimson Tide's fans a *year* before USC arrived at Legion Field for a nonconference game.

"I've watched those documentaries and other things on ESPN. Listening to those stories, I'm thinking, 'I guess we didn't play in the same conference as Alabama.' They don't say anything about our game." —Tennessee's Lester McClain, Tennessee's first Black player, 1968-70.

Tennessee's Lester McClain watched *Breaking the Huddle*, HBO's 2008 film, painfully amused. And with good reason.

The documentary suggests segregated football in the South changed through one game, the night USC played Alabama played on Sept. 12, 1970, at Legion Field in Birmingham. The storyline has the crafty Bryant manipulating Alabama's bigoted fans into accepting integration through an embarrassing loss. He wanted USC fullback Sam Cunningham to run roughshod over Alabama's all-white roster to allow him to recruit Black athletes.

"There is more fiction in those 1970 USC-Alabama stories than anything," said McClain, a three-year letterman at the SEC school, 1968-70.

"You'd think that's when the SEC began recruiting Black athletes. I was almost out of school by 1970."

McClain knew from experience Southern fans were already accepting the emergence of Black athletes long before the 1970 USC-Alabama game.

Tennessee's 1969 integrated team traveled to Alabama and routed the Crimson Tide 41-14 on October 18 before 73,433 fans at Legion Field in Birmingham. USC didn't arrive at Legion Field until a year later. The national media fell hook, line and sinker for the unvetted myths of the 1970 USC-Alabama game as an eye-opener for bigoted fans, but at least one prominent national writer, Allen Barra, has raised a question about the 1970 USC-Alabama game's place in history once the myth jumped into books and films.

Barra is a frequent contributor to national publications and author of sports books, including one published in 2005 on Bryant, *The Last Coach*. When the 2013 Showtime film *Against the Tide* was released, *The Atlantic* had Barra write a review in the Nov. 15, 2013, issue.

The headline: **"The Integration of College Football Didn't Happen in One Game."**

"Although no one in the documentary says it, there seems to be a feeling that Southern Cal's rout of Alabama was the shock that the University and a majority of the fans needed to support integration of the football program. But in fact, that same shock probably came the previous year when the Tennessee Volunteers, the team that Bryant always regarded as the Tide's most bitter foe, thrashed the Tide 41-14 at Legion Field in Birmingham. (I know—I was there.) Two of the Vols' best players—receiver Lester McClain and linebacker Jackie Walker—were Black. Why history has chosen to ignore this game and focus exclusively on 1970 Alabama-USC is a mystery."

A good question unanswered by Bryant's apologists.

"I've watched those documentaries and other things on ESPN," McClain said. "Listening to those stories, I'm thinking, 'I guess we didn't play in the same conference as Alabama.' They don't say anything about our game."

The Tennessee-Alabama's rivalry is known as "The third Saturday of October," although the significance has dropped off in recent years. USC, of course, was a nonconference game.

Tennessee routing Alabama 41-14 on Oct. 18, 1969, before 72,443 at Legion Field with Black players was like throwing gas on a fire in a such a bitter rivalry. A century earlier, Alabama's ancestors as Confederate soldiers fought harder when the Union Army enlisted African-American soldiers.

Losing to Tennessee, not USC, cut deeper as the eye-opening moment.

McClain's contribution was limited to one catch for 12 yards, but the dagger was thrust by linebacker Jackie Walker early with a 27-yard TD interception return. Tennessee myth crafters, if they wanted to create fiction, could have beaten USC's myth makers to the punch. They could have had Walker paraded by Bryant through the Alabama locker room and educating Alabama's bigoted fans.

"Jackie Walker was a great player," said McClain of his Tennessee Hall of Fame teammate, who died in 2002. "He still has records."

Walker was the first Black player named to an All-SEC team as a sophomore in 1969. He was SEC's first Black All-American choice in both 1970 and 1971. He was also a team captain in 1971. His resume raises a question as to why he hasn't earned a place in the College Football Hall of Fame. He has the All-American honors, and he shocked Alabama's fans.

Walker's pick was among five career touchdown returns, a total that shares an NCAA record. His five picks are missing from NCAA listings, an oversight venerable Tennessee historian Bud Ford, the school's retired Sports Information Director, has worked to rectify. Similarly, Ford says it was an oversight by the 1968 media not to recognize McClain as the SEC's first Black player to score a touchdown.

Walker's story isn't told in the HBO, Showtime and ESPN films. Additional research beyond the superficial was required to tell more than a simple story.

Only Cunningham has been enshrined in the College Football Hall of Fame, with Walker unjustly overlooked.

As McClain says, Black athletes representing the Southeastern Conference was old news by the time USC arrived in Birmingham. Alabama was the seventh of the 10 SEC schools to recruit Black athletes.

In 1968, McClain took the field for his first varsity game on September 14 against Georgia before 60,603 fans at Neyland. He entered the game as a backup, relaying a play call to the huddle.

"People stood up and applauded," McClain said. "It surprised me. I didn't know what to think. It felt great, but I was just happy to get in the game. I didn't expect that from the fans."

They cheered for him many more times by season's end. He was the SEC's first Black player to score a touchdown with the first of his six TD receptions for the year. But another reason the warm reception pleased

McClain was he had heard the horror stories of Houston's 1966 game against Mississippi down the road in Memphis on October 22 at Liberty Bowl Memorial Stadium.

A security guard told McVea before he took the field that they couldn't protect him if anyone started shooting. Then, fans relentlessly hurled racial epithets at McVea throughout the game. The crowd was only 14,118, but there were enough bigots for McVea to hear them. He said years later it was the only time he was treated that way at the many Southern road games where he played from 1965 to 1967.

Kentucky was the first school to break barriers with two Black recruits in 1966 and two more in 1967. Kentucky's Wilbur Hackett, a linebacker, was a three-year letterman, 1968-70. He was the SEC's first Black team captain in any sport in 1969. He also made the 1968 SEC All-Sophomore team and was named Kentucky's Co-MVP in 1970.

Hackett also was unhappy with *Breaking the Huddle* storyline.

"I was very disappointed with the way they portrayed Bear Bryant," Hackett said. "I have the utmost respect for him as a football coach, but what they showed was totally wrong. They wrote it as if Bear Bryant desegregated the Southeastern Conference."

Hackett added when he saw a similar CBS story a few years ago, he telephoned the network to offer his opinion of its oversights. No one called back, but if an editor or producer willing to listen had called, Hackett's story would have included explaining that Kentucky recruited Black athletes prior to his arrival.

In 1966, Kentucky coach Charlie Bradshaw signed Nate Northington and Greg Page as the SEC's first Black recruits. Then, Bradshaw added two more Black recruits in his 1967 class, Hackett and Houston Hogg, a running back. The HBO film provided cursory mention of Northington, Page, Hackett and Hogg, while sticking to the overall theme of Bryant as a benevolent segregationist.

Northington was the SEC's first Black player in a game in 1967 as a sophomore when Kentucky opened the season at Indiana. Page, though, never played in a game. He tragically suffered a neck injury in 1967 preseason practice. He lapsed into a coma and died 38 days later without emerging.

In Kentucky's second week, an SEC game at Mississippi, Northington was the first Black player in an SEC game. Northington suffered an injury in the first three minutes in what turned out to be the final game of his career. Northington's grief over Page's death was compounded by the emotional tie with the only other Black player on the team. He left the team after five games, eventually transferring to Western Kentucky.

"That was such a devastating thing to happen," McClain said. "He was about to make history and then tragedy happens. There was nobody (at Tennessee) for me to talk to that understood the pain you felt. It was similar to when Martin Luther King was shot. Those were the moments you had as one of the few Black students on campus."

Race, despite progress, was never far away as an obstacle for a Southern pioneer to overcome, clearing a path for future Black athletes and integration progress. Hackett's first Kentucky varsity season in 1968 overlapped with George Wallace campaigning for president as an Independent with an anti-segregationist base. Wallace spoke on Sept. 15, 1968, on Kentucky's campus.

His racism inflamed passions. When a group of Kentucky white male students encountered Black female students at Blanding Tower, a campus dormitory, they shouted the N-word and other racial slurs. When Hackett and Hogg learned from their fellow students what happened, they and a third Black male student went to Blanding to confront the perpetrators.

"They got knocked out; that's all I can tell you," Hackett said. "There were more of them than us, but we beat their asses."

The three African Americans were subsequently called into the office of Jack Hall, the school's Dean of Men.

"It happened at a dorm, so we had to go see the Dean," Hackett said. "He understood what happened, but he said we had to be counseled. When we left, he said, 'Next time you get in a fight, try not to beat them up so bad.' That's a true story."

Six days after the fight Hackett and Hogg made their varsity debuts as sophomores. Kentucky beat Missouri 12-6 on Sept. 21, 1968, at the Wildcats' former stadium, Stoll Field.

Imagine if a dean other than Jack Hall—one not so understanding the abuse African Americans endured—had been in sitting the Dean's chair in 1968 and imposed a suspension or expulsion. Loud voices would have argued integration was a failure. How much longer until Kentucky resumed a commitment to recruiting Black football players?

After all, Kentucky basketball coach Adolph Rupp waited until 1969 to recruit his first Black athlete. The true 1960s pioneers at Southern schools were ostracized on campus, victims of cheap hits in games and endured racial epithets from bigoted fans.

The stories of McClain, Hackett and other pioneers were overlooked in

HBO's *Breaking the Huddle*. A void was left open. The 1970 USC-Alabama game's myths and some outright fiction, crafted in the late 1980s and spread in the 1990s, filled the space. The narrative was captured, pushing aside true 1960s pioneers.

If there was one USC Black player to be celebrated for taking the field Sept. 12, 1970, at Legion Field, it was Trojans' quarterback Jimmy Jones. He was the first Black quarterback to take a snap in an SEC stadium. That's another fact overlooked by a national media rushing to hail Bryant as a hero. Cunningham arrived at Legion Field making his varsity debut as a sophomore, but Jones was an established star.

He had been on the cover of *Sports Illustrated* in the 1969 season. And Jones was the first Black quarterback to appear on the magazine's cover, Sept. 29, 1969, after he led the No. 5-ranked Trojans to a 31-21 win over Nebraska at Memorial Stadium in Lincoln, Nebraska.

But Jones' stature, overlooked by the 1970 USC-Alabama myth makers, has another side to the story, one that shows Bryant was unaware of the progress taking place throughout the country. A top high-school quarterback recruit in the fall of 1970 was Condredge Holloway of Lee High in Huntsville, Alabama. Holloway was not only one of the state's top quarterbacks, he was one of its top athletes as a pro baseball prospect.

He also was Black.

Bryant, ignoring the ground Jones was breaking as USC's second-year starting quarterback, told Holloway he would only recruit him as a defensive back. Holloway signed with Tennessee, where Holloway wrote history as the SEC's first Black starting quarterback. He was a three-year starter, 1972-74. He wrote more history as Tennessee's first Black baseball player.

Holloway says Bryant told him, "Alabama isn't ready for a Black quarterback." The preeminent coach in the South again failed as a leader. He passed on teaching another civics lesson to his bigoted fan base.

Holloway's stature as a pro baseball prospect had nothing to do with Bryant passing on Holloway. Football was his favorite sport. Although the Montreal Expos drafted Holloway with the fourth pick of the first round in 1971, he opted for a two-sport college career.

HBO, Showtime and ESPN may have preferred to focus on a "white hero" like Bryant or USC coach John McKay leading integration to market their films, but McClain says another leader to consider is Tennessee's Chuck Rohe. He served a dual role as Tennessee's football recruiting director and track and field head coach. Tennessee historian

Bud Ford agrees with McClain that Rohe's influence deserves more appreciation.

"Chuck Rohe was so instrumental to integration," McClain said.

Kentucky may have been first, but Tennessee won the 1969 SEC football title and was ranked in the Top 10 at least once every season between 1968 and 1973. The track program was a perennial national power with its first NCAA outdoor title in 1974.

Rohe arrived in Knoxville in 1963 hired with a vision to recruit two-sport football and track athletes and to include African Americans among them. With Rohe's hand in identifying football and track recruits, he saw he could bolster his track roster with football-track athletes. Football, of course, has far more scholarships available than other sports.

Rohe was initially rebuffed by Tennessee athletic director Bob Woodruff about recruiting Black athletes. But in 1965 Rohe hit the football/track jackpot with a white athlete, Richmond Flowers, Jr., a highly recruited prospect from Dothan, Alabama. Flowers earned All-American honors in football and track. He was a 1968 Olympic track team contender in the hurdles until a hamstring injury. In 1969, the Dallas Cowboys drafted him; he played four NFL seasons.

The two-sport star had picked Tennessee once he decided to flee the violent racial climate of Alabama. His father, Richmond Flowers Sr., was the state's Attorney General. Flowers Sr. had opposed George Wallace's segregationist policies and prosecuted Ku Klux Klansmen for killing civil rights workers. Flowers Sr. accused the KKK of burning crosses in his home's lawn and throwing bricks through windows.

Flowers was a success story on multiple levels, but the impetus for Woodruff allowing Rohe to recruit Black athletes came up the SEC road from Kentucky opening its doors.

The turning point at Kentucky was the 1963 arrival of new president John Oswald, who had been the vice-president at the University of California system, Oswald informed all Kentucky coaches he expected them to recruit Black athletes. Three years later football coach Charlie Bradshaw signed Northington and Page.

"By then, a lot of Black athletes were doing well across the country," Rohe said. "It was a natural evolution of the integration process."

Rohe later moved on in his career to his post-coaching days as Executive Director of Florida Citrus Sports and its flagship event, the Citrus Bowl. He understood the significance of what he wrought in the SEC, but he admits to a simpler motivation.

"I wanted to win," he said. "I grew up in Chicago. I went to a typical white suburban high school, but I knew a lot of Black track athletes that I competed against."

His first four Black athletes in the 1967 recruiting class with scholarships were two football players, McClain and Albert Davis, and two track athletes, James Craig and Audrey Hardy. Davis never enrolled, leaving McClain to make history on his own.

Rohe's first football/track recruit was Andy Bennett, arriving in 1968 and joining the varsity in 1969. Rohe said once Tennessee began traveling as an integrated roster, the only problem the team encountered was once in Georgia.

"A restaurant wouldn't take all of us, so we went on down the road to another one," Rohe said.

With the door open for Rohe, Tennessee exploited its expanded recruiting base—racially in football and doubling up in track. Football under head coach Doug Dickey and track under Rohe began to win big.

Dickey's teams beat Alabama three straight years, 1967, 1968 and 1969, with SEC titles in 1967 and 1969. The 1969 conference title, highlighted by thrashing Alabama before the Crimson Tide's fans, prompted Florida to lure Dickey home to his alma mater in 1970.

But the fork in the road he chose was a wrong turn. Dickey was unable to duplicate his Tennessee success in Gainesville.

"After that 1969 Alabama game, Doug Dickey had the SEC by the neck," Rohe said. "Tennessee was talking about him like he was Bear Bryant. We had the world by the tail in football and track."

Dickey didn't appreciate what his 1969 team accomplished, especially Oct. 18, 1969, at Legion Field. He's not alone. Neither does the rest of America. A myth consumed the story of true pioneers. The history will remain lost until there are more schools making corrections, starting with teaching their own fan base.

Kentucky recently joined a list of schools that began to correct history. The school built a statue of its four pioneers outside the football facility in 2016.

Kentucky's Paul Karem and fellow alums believed the time was overdue for their alma mater to recognize their four pioneers, Northington, Page, Hackett and Hogg. Decades of Kentucky alums had cycled through to graduation unaware of their school's history. Same with fans stepping on to campus for games.

By the late 1990s, Karem, who played football at Kentucky in the same era, wanted to shine a light. He proposed a statue honoring the pioneers, but he was met by indifference. Kentucky powers that be also didn't understand their school's history.

The statue project remained on a backburner until one night in 2013 while Karem watched ESPN. The cable network promoted an upcoming *30-for-30* documentary, "The Color Orange." The film featured Tennessee's Condredge Holloway.

Karem eagerly settled into his easy chair to watch the *30-for-30* documentary produced by Kenny Chesney, the country music star who grew up a Tennessee fan.

"I'm thinking to myself, 'OK, Condredge was five years *after* our guys. This is great! Because there is no way they can tell their story without saying the names of our guys and the University of Kentucky.'...they never said a word."

Karem seethed. He had overestimated the media. As historian Ken Burns has often said, telling a full story requires sifting through past media stories that settled for a convenient narrative tied into a bow.

"I was so mad after watching that show. I said, 'What if the families of our guys watched that?'"

Karem went to work, enlisting help from influential Kentucky alums, including two of his UK football teammates, Bob Finnell and Mark Lane. All three men were teammates of the Kentucky trailblazers. Karem is a customer service author and trainer and the Vice President for Business Development at South Central Bank in Kentucky. Finnell is a successful attorney in Rome, Georgia. Lane is an international businessman with over 50 Kentucky athletes hired as employees.

They made another round of pitches.

"I told the people I met with this would be a major public-relations coup for our school," said Karem.

This time the historical context resonated. The statues were approved in 2014 and unveiled in 2016.

"When they were planning it, I thought, 'It's been 50 years without recognition, so if they do it, great; if not, that's fine,'" Hackett said. "But when they unveiled it, I was so excited and proud for all of us. But mostly I was happy for Greg and his family. He was a part of this, too. He gave his life to this. He deserved the recognition."

Kentucky's pioneering football role, though, has been long overshadowed by Kentucky basketball's notorious role in the 1966 NCAA championship game.

Kentucky basketball was infamous for its all-white 1966 team losing to Texas Western (now UTEP) with its five Black starters. The game inspired the 2006 film *Glory Road*. Jon Voight was cast in the role of the racist villain, playing Kentucky coach Adolph Rupp.

"They don't tell you in the film Kentucky had signed Nate Northington and Greg Page to play football before that basketball game was played," Karem said of the 1966 winter football recruiting class. "Our school first recruited them in 1965 when they were in high school. But we're known for that basketball game."

Karem, who lives in Louisville, has noticed a new appreciation for the school's history, particularly in the West End of Louisville, the Black section of town. Muhammad Ali grew up in the neighborhood.

Louisville's Black fans historically resent Kentucky basketball for more than the traditional rivalry reasons. Kentucky fans called the Louisville Cardinals the Blackbirds for signing Black basketball players as early as 1962. Wes Unseld, a two-time All-American pick and NBA legend, signed in 1964.

"You never used to see Kentucky shirts on Black kids in Louisville," Karem said. "Sports heals."

By 2021, Tennessee also unveiled statues of its true 1960s pioneers. There are statues outside of Neyland Stadium of McClain as Tennessee's first Black player in the SEC and first Black SEC player to score, Walker as the SEC's first Black All-American player, Holloway as the SEC's first starting Black quarterback and Tee Martin as the SEC's first Black quarterback to win a national title.

U.S. Army (Ret.) Colonel Jack Jacobs, another type of 1960s American hero as a Vietnam War Medal of Honor recipient, provided an explanation on how some heroic stories become celebrated and others pushed to the corners. In Jacobs' role as an MSNBC military analyst, he commented on air as an Afghanistan War Medal of Honor recipient was honored at the White House. As the segment ended, the show's host asked somewhat rhetorically, how does someone win a Medal of Honor?

Jacobs explained first you have to do something. Then somebody who saw it has to write it up. And, finally, somebody at the top has to salute it.

The true 1960s pioneers continue to wait for their salute dishonorably swiped from them by a myth.

CHAPTER 23
JAMES OWENS' "QUIET COURAGE" BLAZED AUBURN TRAIL

FUN FACT: The running back from Fairfield, Alabama, was Auburn's first Black football player—a year before Wilbur Jackson signed with Alabama.

"Bear Bryant carried a big stick and won a lot of games with a lot of great players. You've got to hand it to him and respect what he did. But then again, you have another school across the state, and we had the first Heisman Trophy winner. We had the first African-American football player. We were way ahead of them in a lot of categories." — Auburn running back Terry Henley.

The old adage, "History is written by the victors," explains why Auburn's James Owens, subject of a 2015 documentary titled *Quiet Courage*, has been overshadowed by Alabama's Wilbur Jackson.

Owens was Auburn's first Black football player (1970-72). He arrived on campus a year prior to Alabama's first Black player, Wilbur Jackson (1971-73). But try explaining that to fans who believe Jackson—through no fault of his own—was first through the door.

Historical memory, too often, is a distorted or erroneous picture. In this case, Alabama legendary coach Paul "Bear" Bryant's wattage brightens the spotlight on the Crimson Tide. The folklore of Bryant as Batman and Jackson as Robin overshadows facts. Bryant made the 1970s his decade with his fourth (1973), fifth (1978) and sixth (1979) national titles, leaving little room for true 1960s pioneers over mythical figures.

History is written by the victors.

Auburn Hall-of-Famer Terry Henley (1970-72) was Owens' backfield mate and his close friend, speaking at the funeral when Owens' heart gave out in 2016 at age 64. Henley said he has grudgingly learned to live with distorted facts embellishing Alabama's role over Auburn's place in history.

"Bear Bryant carried a big stick and won a lot of games with a lot of great players," Henley said. "You've got to hand it to him and respect what he did.

"But then again, you have another school across the state, and we had the first Heisman Trophy winner. We had the first African-American football player. We were way ahead of them in a lot of categories."

Auburn's first Heisman Trophy winner was Pat Sullivan in 1971 and the second Bo Jackson in 1985; Alabama's first was Mark Ingram Jr. in 2009.

Bryant's apologists excuse him for dragging his feet on integration, rationalizing a combination of segregationist Gov. George Wallace—whose influence ran far beyond the governor's office—and Alabama's bigoted fans prevented Bryant from acting sooner. But that disregards an important fact: Alabama's high-school football scene was the true driving force to the state's college football integration.

ALABAMA HIGH SCHOOLS LED THE WAY

Alabama's high schools, under threat of losing federal funding, began gradually integrating their schools in the late 1960s.

By the 1968 football season, the Alabama High School Athletic Association had fully merged with the state's former Black athletics association. High schools that were predominantly white and predominantly Black played each other in regular season games and in the playoffs.

As a result, younger players on Alabama's 1970 football roster had played with and against Black athletes. That fact directly contradicts a linchpin to the 1970 USC-Alabama myths that also contributed to Bryant and Jackson overshadowing Owens and Auburn coach Ralph "Shug" Jordan.

Auburn recruited Owens out of Fairfield High, near Birmingham. Fairfield was closer to Bryant in Tuscaloosa (57 miles) than Jordan and his campus (99 miles). Auburn assistant coach Jim Hilyer first spotted Owens while he scouted a Fairfield game in the fall of 1968. He returned to the Auburn campus and suggested to Jordan they offer Owens a scholarship.

"I came back and said there is a young man at Fairfield High School that fits our needs," says Hilyer. "He's a fine young man with a fine family —and he's Black. Coach Jordan called me into his office and said there will be some kickback." But, Hilyer added, Jordan followed up his cautionary note saying he would back him "100 percent."

It was that easy for Auburn to beat Alabama and Bryant to living up to the U.S. Constitution not long after President Lyndon B. Johnson signed the 1964 and 1965 Civil Rights acts. Jordan never mentioned a fear of George Wallace. And Auburn's fan base never called for Jordan to be fired.

Henley, like Owens, was a senior at Oxford High that same fall 1968 season. His Yellow Jackets played three integrated opponents on their way to a state title for their division with an 11-1 record, defeating Anniston, Gadsden and Talladega. They won the title game against Cobb Avenue High of Anniston, a Black school that gradually added white students.

One of Anniston's Black players was Ken Hutcherson, a future NFL veteran. Hutcherson played at Livingston College, a former Historically Black College and University competing as an NAIA member. The school is now known as West Alabama while competing in NCAA Division II.

The NFL found Hutcherson as a fourth-round draft pick of the Dallas Cowboys in 1974. He also played for the San Diego Chargers and Green Bay Packers in 1975 and the Seattle Seahawks in 1976.

So much for the claim Bryant was scouring the state searching for a Black recruit to integrate his program. Bryant once said in an interview he couldn't find any Black athletes qualified to play at Alabama.

Stories simplifying college football integration to obfuscate Bryant's poor record have been at the expense of the true 1960s pioneers. They also mitigate the price those players paid traveling down the road.

AN APOLOGY

Quiet Courage was produced and written by Thom Gossom Jr., a Black Auburn football player (1972-74) who went into acting and writing.

"If you watch the story on James and the 1972 team, it will bring a tear to your eye," Henley said. "When Bruce Feldman was at ESPN a few years ago writing a story on Auburn, I pleaded with him and others at ESPN to do a *30-for-30* (documentary) on James.

"I don't know why they won't do it. It's a great documentary."

One reason is it requires explaining Wilbur Jackson wasn't the first Black player in the Southeastern Conference and Bear Bryant's role wasn't as a crusader. Bryant was a follower, not a leader. The media and media personalities are heavily invested in a story that casts Bryant as a crusader. Many prominent journalists would have to do some backpedaling to explain having erroneously trumpeting Bryant over others that deserved the credit.

Auburn's story also separates itself from Alabama in another important way: An apology.

Former Auburn athletic director David Housel acknowledged in *Quiet Courage* his school should have done more to support Owens as the only black player.

"In retrospect it was not the way to break the color barrier," Housel said. "There should not have been one person on that island alone."

Of the civil rights movement to end segregation, Housel added, "There were terrible things that happened, but the thing that was most terrible was when good men stood silent. And I think that was true at Auburn and throughout the South…Change should have come quicker, but good men remained silent…."

Bryant, who died in 1983, never apologized for dragging his feet on integration into the 1970s.

Henley also feels regret. He said it wasn't until later in life, upon deeper conversations with Owens, that he recognized he should have done more to support his teammate's difficult transition.

"It was a learning curve for me, the players and the coaches," Henley said. "I was raised in an all-white community."

By contrast, HBO's 2008 *Breaking the Huddle* and Showtime's 2013 *Against the Tide* both celebrate Bryant while focusing on the 1970 USC-Alabama game. The films skip over Bryant's track record of dragging his feet on the social issue of his times.

Although *Quiet Courage* received strong reviews, the HBO and Showtime documentaries gained larger audiences. They left a misleading image of Bryant waving his wand to end segregation on a single night in 1970.

History is written by the victors.

SETTING THE RECORD STRAIGHT

Auburn began setting the record straight in 2012, recognizing Owens for his sacrifices to change the South. The Tigers honored him as the initial recipient of the "James Owens Courage Award" presented annually to a current or former Auburn player.

During a halftime ceremony at the Sept. 15, 2012 game against Louisiana-Monroe, the public address announcer told the Jordan-Hare Stadium crowd of 87,000 that "The James Owens Courage Award will ensure we never forget his legacy at Auburn University."

Another teammate, offensive lineman Mac Lorendo (1970-72), asked Owens if he felt the current Tigers on the field had an awareness of the courage it took to blaze a trail.

"No, no they don't," was Owens' reply, said Lorendo.

Telling Owens' story remains important for a younger generation that doesn't understand segregation was recent history—not ancient. How else are they going to learn the true identity of the first Black college football player in the state of Alabama?

PART III: EXAMINING THE 1970 USC-ALABAMA MYTHS AND FICTION

CHAPTER 24
THE BLACKOUT AND BLANK CANVAS

FACT: Michigan State's Willie Thrower was the first Black quarterback in the modern NFL with the Chicago Bears as an undrafted free agent in 1953. It wasn't until the 1980s the Pro Football Hall of Fame recognized him as a groundbreaker.

"My dad had a big picture of himself on the wall. On the bottom it said, "THE FIRST BLACK QUARTERBACK IN THE NFL, 1953." People told him 'to take it down. You're lying. That ain't you. Take it down.'" —Melvin Thrower on his father's Touchdown Lounge in New Kensington, Pennsylvania.

Name the National Football League's first Black starting middle linebacker.

If you asked that trivia sports question at a watering hole, you'd be met by faces wrinkled in disgust, arms rapidly waving you off dismissively.

"Everybody knows the answer. Willie Lanier, Kansas City Chiefs. Pro Football Hall of Famer. Get out of here!"

Wrong.

Correct answer: "Garland Boyette, St. Louis Cardinals, 1962."

Pay up.

Boyette isn't alone. Willie Thrower was the first Black quarterback in the modern NFL in 1953 as an undrafted free agent out of Michigan State.

Thrower was a backup to Pro Football Hall of Famer George Blanda and played in a single NFL game, but it wasn't until the 1980s that Thrower's place in history was more widely known. The Pro Football Hall of Fame put up a display in 1988 that included him among the league's pioneering Black quarterbacks. His story didn't spread far enough, though. Some folks in Thrower's hometown who stopped by his Touchdown Lounge for a refreshment didn't know his place in history.

"My dad had a big picture of himself on the wall," said Thrower's son, Melvin Thrower. "On the bottom it said, "THE FIRST BLACK QUARTERBACK IN THE NFL, 1953." People told him, 'take it down. You're lying. That ain't you. Take it down.'"

Racism hit Thrower and Boyette with 1-2 prejudice punches, a cross and hook knocking them out of the history pages.

The cross was first was from football coaches and Americans in general. The stereotype was Blacks couldn't play quarterback, center and middle linebacker. Those positions required calling out quick-thinking adjustments and exhibiting leadership.

The knockout punch was from the media. The media was blind to reporting such milestones in real time. It was at best indifferent to the stereotypes and at worst complicit. What the media did and didn't do was significant.

"Those three positions were considered off-limits for a Black athlete," said Boyette in a 2018 interview with WHOU-TV, a Houston station. "I heard so many stories about how you've got to be so smart, you've got to be able to do this, you got to do that. After I played it for a while, gosh, it was tailor made."

Boyette, a nine-year NFL veteran, was an undrafted free agent in 1962 out of Grambling State College (now Grambling State University), an Historically Black College and University (HBCU) in Louisiana, where he played for legendary coach Eddie Robinson. Cardinals coach Wally Lemm started him six of 14 games in 1962 as a rookie middle linebacker.

Lanier didn't play for the Chiefs until the 1967 season as a second-round draft pick from Morgan State University.

A Hall of Fame spokesman said the museum is aware Boyette's story was pushed aside in history books but added similar stories of unrecorded events come up from time to time. The museum is still researching the trail of who might else needs to be considered as the NFL's first Black starting middle linebacker.

Boyette was a victim of the mainstream media of the time—focused on white males—that repeatedly overlooked Black athletic milestones. It has been a befuddling combination of ignorance, negligence and racism. But his omission wasn't alone. Many milestones involving Black athletes in pro and college sports weren't recorded prior to the 1970s.

"I don't think sportswriters felt comfortable writing about it," said Chris Lamb, Chair of Journalism and Public Relations at Indiana University Purdue University Indianapolis, who has written extensively on race and the sports media. "I don't think their editors felt comfortable editing it and the editors probably felt their readers didn't feel comfortable reading it. We won't have progress until you refer to a quarterback and not a Black quarterback. We're kind of there now after 60 years, but we still refer to Black coaches and women coaches. I don't think we've gotten to where we need to be until we no longer use the modifier African American."

Lamb's 2005 book *Blackout* covered Jackie Robinson's first spring training with the Montreal Royals in 1946, a year before he broke the Major League Baseball color line with the Brooklyn Dodgers. The subtitle: "The Untold Story of Jackie Robinson's First Spring Training."

Lamb said he once asked the legendary *Washington Post* sportswriter Shirley Povich, whose career spanned the 1920s to the 1990s, why the media didn't write more about racism in baseball. Povich often wrote about race, including criticism of George Preston Marshall, the owner of Washington's NFL team, for failing to integrate his roster. Povich wrote Cleveland's Jim Brown "integrated" Washington's end zone when he scored against the NFL's last all-white roster.

Povich answered Lamb, saying, "I'm afraid white sportswriters were like the owners. They believed in segregation."

More Black athletes were recruited in the 1960s, but nowhere near the modern game's meritocracy. Race remained the elephant in the room throughout the 1960s despite the mounting unreported Black milestones.

"I thought the point was winning," Lamb said. "Why would you hurt your chances of winning by only recruiting white people?"

Even the greatest sportswriters of the 1960s were guilty of failing to properly document college football's progress toward integration. The late Dan Jenkins, a legendary *Sports Illustrated* writer who wrote the textbook on covering college football, spent time on the Michigan State campus the week of the Game of the Century matching No. 1 Notre Dame and No. 2 Michigan State on Nov. 19, 1966, at Spartan Stadium. The seminal moment in the college football—far more popular than college basketball in those days—drew a record TV audience of 33 million.

As a game story, Jenkins' piece has been considered a classic. When the showdown ended with Notre Dame playing for a controversial 10-10 tie, Jenkins criticized Parseghian, mocking the school fight song in the lead to his story: "Old Notre Dame will tie overall." Notre Dame's students gathered up copies and burned them in a campus bonfire.

But Jenkins' story failed to report on the social significance of Michigan State coach Duffy Daugherty's roster representing the future as fully integrated and Notre Dame as the past with only one Black player. But that's not all. Michigan State quarterback Jimmy Raye was one of only two Black starting quarterbacks in college football. Jenkins only mentioned the fleet-footed Raye as "a flighty junior with a mustache."

As a result of the media's failure to recognize Raye's milestones, it wasn't until 2015 that the National Football Foundation recognized Raye as the South's first Black quarterback to win a national title. That was worth another story the media missed on Black quarterbacks and their lack of opportunities.

As more media members were enlightened, the shift in attitudes helped explain why Willie Lanier was treated with respect never granted Garland Boyette. In the 1969 season, Lanier was a third-year starter for a Kansas City team that won Super Bowl IV in an upset of the Minnesota Vikings. He was among an impressive list of prominent Black stars that included Bobby Bell, Curley Culp, Buck Buchanan, Robert Holmes, Mike Garrett, Warren McVea, Otis Taylor, Emmitt Thomas and Jim Marsalis. Four of them are in the Pro Football Hall of Fame: Lanier, Bell, Buchanan and Thomas.

Whoever first wrote Lanier was the first Black starting middle linebacker mistakenly assumed he was working from a blank canvas. One reference led to another in a different forum. That has been a common fault in the media to this day. The consequence is sometimes a false narrative becomes entrenched at the expense of others.

There is strange irony in Boyette standing out in a crowd as a Black middle linebacker for the predominantly white Cardinals and Oilers rosters, but he wasn't deemed newsworthy. Yet in the late 1960s, Lanier was among a cast of high-profile Black stars, and the media found it easier to single him out as a groundbreaker.

There are other story angles overlooked that separated Boyette from the pack.

As a Grambling State alumnus, Boyette's background should have stood out as an HBCU graduate. By the late 1960s, Grambling enjoyed a reputation for turning out NFL talent, but there had only been a few Grambling/NFL players prior to Boyette: Tank Younger, 1949-58; Willie Davis, 1958-69; Al Richardson, 1960; Jamie Caleb, 1960-65; Preston Powell, 1961; and Ernie Ladd, 1961-68.

Another Boyette story angle was his rise from an undrafted rookie free agent to starting middle linebacker. That remains a story in today's NFL for an HBCU athlete or one from a blue-blood program.

Yet another missed story angle that today's media would cover heavily was Boyette's unique athleticism as a world-class track and field athlete in the decathlon. In the summer of 1960, prior to his junior season at Grambling, he placed fifth in the U.S. Olympic Track and Field trials. The field included the great Rafer Johnson, a UCLA alumnus who added the 1960 Olympic gold medal in the decathlon in Rome to his 1956 Olympic silver medal in Melbourne.

The *St. Louis Post-Dispatch* noted Boyette's top decathlete marks in a story on Dec. 7, 1962. But there was no context explaining he was competing against Rafer Johnson. In the modern media, that's plenty for a cover story. In 1962, Boyette was nothing more than a regional story. The Cardinals' secret was safe.

There was so little was written about the significance of Boyette's groundbreaking rookie season, we don't know from the archives what prompted Cardinals coach Wally Lemm to convert the 6-foot-1, 238-pounder from a college lineman to pro linebacker. Quickness was no doubt one reason. Boyette also played some fullback at Grambling State.

Boyette played one more season in St. Louis before a falling out with Lemm, and Boyette's anger over drafted white players earning more than he was paid as a two-year veteran. He left in 1964 for the Montreal Alouettes in the Canadian Football League. He was named to the All-CFL team in 1965, but they patched up old wounds when Lemm was named the Houston Oilers' head coach in 1966.

For Boyette, Houston was a homecoming. He had played at Wallace High in Orange, near Houston. Willie Ray Smith, the father of College Football Hall of Famer Bubba Smith, was his coach at Wallace.

During Boyette's first year with the Houston Oilers he started three of 14 games and all 14 in 1967, 1968 and 1969. He missed one game in 1970, starting 13 of 13, and started all 14 in 1971. His final season he started eight of 14 in 1972.

Boyette was a reliable player while balancing six years duty in the U.S.

Army reserves. Sometimes he served weekdays, with the Army allowing him free time on the weekend to play in games.

"It is something I have to do," Boyette said in the *Houston Post*, Aug. 11, 1968. "If they had told me I was going overseas, it's not something I would have protested or anything like that. I'd have packed up and gone. It's silly, making a fuss about going into the Army. You have to do it, so you do it."

Boyette never received his due, but his story is far from an isolated example. Many Black athletes were overlooked in the media prior to the 1968 shift in attitudes.

A HIDDEN DEBUT

Although Willie Thrower was overlooked by the media, the fans were aware of him.

When Thrower played against the San Francisco 49ers on Oct. 17, 1953, at Wrigley Field, the *Chicago Tribune* reported it was Thrower's NFL debut. The story lacked important context: he was the NFL's first modern-era Black quarterback.

Thrower entered the game when starter George Blanda had been shaken up on a tackle. The story read, "Willie Thrower, former Michigan State Negro quarterback star making his major league debut, passed 12 yards to (Jim) Dooley, putting the ball on the 4."

At that point, Chicago head coach George Halas sent Blanda back into the game. The Chicago newspaper noted the crowd cheered for Thrower upon his completion and booed when Halas replaced him with Blanda. The Bears scored on a running play in the 35-28 loss to the 49ers.

Thrower moved on to the CFL in 1954, but a shoulder injury ended his career. He worked as a New York social worker before returning home to New Kensington, Pennsylvania, and opening a bar, the Touchdown Lounge, with his picture gracing a wall. Eventually, though, Thrower's hometown accepted his moment in history. The city of New Kensington honored him with a statue outside his high school's football stadium in 2006.

Some credit Fritz Pollard as the first Black NFL quarterback due to his time (1920-21) with the Akron Pros of the American Professional Football Association—the first name used by the NFL. The game of football was much different in Pollard's era, with the modern distinction between quarterbacks and other backs blurred. The Pro Football Hall of Fame enshrined Pollard as a groundbreaking player (one of the first two African Americans in NFL history) and the first African-American head coach in NFL history. If anything, this proves a central point in this book: Black milestones were ignored, and for decades Pollard's considerable achievements in the creation of the NFL were forgotten.

In the late 1960s Marlin Briscoe and James Harris gained attention as pioneering Black quarterbacks. Doug Williams was the first to draw proper attention to his groundbreaking moments. Williams was a first-round draft pick out of Grambling State in 1978 by the Tampa Bay Buccaneers. Later, he was the first Black quarterback to start and win a Super Bowl. In the 1987 season, Washington defeated the Denver Broncos in Super Bowl XXII, 42-10.

The media was guilty of overlooking Black stars in other sports, including Major League Baseball. The National Pastime dominated media coverage until the NFL in the 1970s.

CBS sports reporter James Brown reported a story on Sept. 1, 2021, about an otherwise unknown 50th anniversary. On Sept. 1, 1971, the Pittsburgh Pirates, who were on their way to winning the World Series, started nine minority players, a first in MLB history. The nine starters were African American or African-Latino: Pitcher Doc Ellis; Al Oliver, first base; Rennie Stennett, second base; Jackie Hernandez, shortstop; Dave Cash, third base; Willie Stargell, left field; Gene Clines, center field; Roberto Clemente, right field; and Manny Sanguillén, catcher.

"There are so many people out there that have no clue this day happened," says Oliver in the story.

The local media dubbed them the "all-soul lineup" but otherwise the moment in history wasn't celebrated.

Later in the 1970s the media caught on to the fact there were no Black managers in baseball. But even with that rising awareness, long-time Chicago sportswriter Ron Rapoport explained in his excellent 2021 book on Ernie Banks, *Let's Play Two*, both Banks, in 1973, and Gene Baker, in 1963, had moments as acting managers that were overlooked.

Frank Robinson, of course, was baseball's first Black manager with the Cleveland Indians (1975-77) and his place in history clearly supersedes Baker and Banks as acting managers. But the moments for Baker and Banks were not only overlooked in game stories, in today's media their moment would have sparked follow-up stories with discussion of when baseball would have a Black manager.

Banks, a Baseball Hall of Famer from his playing days (1953-71), was a

Cubs coach following his retirement. When the Cubs played the San Diego Padres on May 8, 1973, at San Diego Stadium, Chicago manager Whitey Lockman was ejected from a tie game in the 11th inning. With Cubs senior coaches Pete Reiser and Larry Jansen away from the team that night, Banks finished the game as the acting manager.

Wrote Rapoport: "He took the job seriously, calling for a bunt that sent Don Kessinger to third in the 12th inning, bringing up Joe Pepitone, who drove in the winning run with a pinch-hit double, and sending relief pitcher Bill Bonham out to earn the save."

Later in life Banks liked to refer to his otherwise unreported place in history, but by doing so he revealed he was unaware his old teammate Gene Baker preceded him by a decade as an acting Black manager.

Baker had played for Cubs (1953-56) and the Pittsburgh Pirates (1957-61). The Pirates made him a coach in the minor leagues before naming him as coach with the Pirates in 1963. He was the second MLB Black coach after Buck O'Neil with the Cubs, in 1962. But whereas O'Neil was initially not an on-field coach, Baker was.

On Sept. 21, 1963, the Pirates played the Los Angeles Dodgers at Dodger Stadium. Pirates manager Danny Murtaugh and coach Frank Oceak were both ejected for protesting an umpire's call, Rapoport wrote. Baker took over as the acting manager, finishing a game that the Dodgers won.

"Social issues and injustice weren't discussed back then in sports," Rapoport said. "If it happened now, it would be a big story. The culture has changed. When it did change, with Tommie Smith and John Carlos, there was hell to pay. There has been more reporting of Black issues in sports since then."

O'Neil's moment as the first Black coach went unappreciated for three decades, but his story was later brought to life by the award-winning historian and filmmaker Ken Burns. His PBS series *Baseball* in 1994 included lengthy segments on and interviews with O'Neil. His engaging personality, captured on film, catapulted him overnight from forgotten figure to baseball icon.

He remained a spry figure into his 90s, becoming a popular figure on the speaking circuit. He appeared at baseball events around the nation, entertainingly speaking of his career in the Negro Leagues with the Kansas City Monarchs and then breaking ground in the MLB with the Cubs.

O'Neil wrote a book in 1997, *I Was Right on Time: My Journey from the Negro Leagues to the Major Leagues*. He reaped the deserved fame for 12 years until his death in 2006 at age 94. He was posthumously awarded the Presidential Medal of Freedom by George W. Bush in 2007 and named to the Baseball Hall of Fame in 2021.

But if not for Burns' passion and commitment to tell baseball's history, O'Neil likely would have died in obscurity.

Burns, while discussing research of his 2021 documentary series on boxer Muhammad Ali, explained historical research requires sifting through myths about figures and moments in time.

"We tend to resort to conventional, superficial understandings, tying things up into a nice bow," he said.

Burns painted in all the blank spots on the pioneering life of Buck O'Neil. The history of Negro Leagues baseball has become far better understood than previously. Facts have replaced myths and filled in blank spots.

The History Channel's 2020 mini-series *Grant* on Ulysses S. Grant showed how revisionist history gained control of the Civil War narrative over facts.

At the turn of the century, President Theodore Roosevelt said America's three great heroes had been Washington, Lincoln and Grant. Military historians in the documentary series detailed how Grant, commanding the Union Army, outmaneuvered Confederate Gen. Robert E. Lee, forcing him to surrender.

But by the 1920s, pro-Southern historians successfully shifted the narrative to "The Lost Cause" against northern aggression. The South fought for states' rights, not to preserve slavery. They cast Lee as the noble general, Grant as a butcher, corrupt and a drunk.

"And so, Confederates lost the Civil War, but they certainly won the war of myth," author and journalist Ta-Nehisi Coates said in the documentary. "And Grant was on the wrong side of that myth."

The Civil War, of course, is an apocalyptic battle. The 1970 USC-Alabama game was just a football game. But just as the Southern historians deceptively posed the Civil War was about states' rights, the USC-Alabama strategy was to aggrandize USC's role and obfuscate Bryant dragging his feet.

They were hugely successful. They reduced to footnotes Duffy Daugherty, his groundbreaking teams, his assistant coaches who followed his blueprint at their new schools and the pioneers at Southern schools like Darryl Hill, Jerry LeVias, Wilbur Hackett, Lester McClain, Bob Grant and James Owens.

The true 1960s pioneers deserve to be written back into history with the respect modern pioneers receive. The media has finally caught up to its responsibility documenting milestones from women athletes in general and specifically Black women athletes.

At the 2022 Winter Olympics in Bejing, Erin Jackson, a U.S. Black woman speedskater, won a gold medal. The lead paragraph written by Tom Hamilton on ESPN's website at 9:53 a.m. on Feb. 13 got to the historic point in the first sentence. The story was among the homepage's "Top Headlines" on Super Bowl Sunday.

"Team USA's Erin Jackson won a brilliant gold in the women's 500-meter speed skating at the Beijing Olympics on Sunday and became the first Black woman to ever medal in the sport."

White male writers failed to write similar milestone stories throughout the 1960s when individual events chipped away at segregation.

CHAPTER 25
UCLA AND JIM MURRAY BATTLE 'BAMA, BRYANT

FACT: Alabama's Bear Bryant admitted in his 1974 autobiography, *Bear*, he attempted to gain a backdoor invitation to the 1962 Rose Bowl for his segregated team to face UCLA in place of the traditional Big Ten entry.

"If we can't play on their field in Alabama, why should they be able to play on our field in Pasadena?" — Kermit Alexander, a star junior halfback on UCLA's 1962 Rose Bowl roster.

The 1962 Rose Bowl established a college football civil rights milestone, but the 60th anniversary of the New Year's Day game came and went without attention or even a fractional accounting. What should be remembered as a tipping point quickly turned into an oxymoron —a "forgotten milestone."

The culprit was a 1960s media custom of avoiding race in sports stories. In this case, the media failed to fully report on the maneuvering of a segregationist coach, Alabama's Paul "Bear" Bryant.

Events began with a small group of UCLA Black students and the Bruins' eight Black players angered upon learning Bryant attempted to gain a backdoor invitation to Pasadena in place of the traditional Big Ten entry. The Black students discussed a gameday protest at the Rose Bowl.

The Black players, led by Kermit Alexander, a future NFL Pro Bowler with the San Francisco 49ers, threatened to not take the field.

The UCLA reaction was largely word-of-mouth—until *Los Angeles Times* sports columnist Jim Murray got wind of it. Murray understood its significance, unlike his peers (including those on his own paper) following media customs. Some looked the other way. Other writers lobbied for Alabama oblivious of social issues.

Despite the *Times'* influential stature in Southern California, the 1961 UCLA protestations weren't reported in the newspaper outside of Murray's two Pulitzer Prize-worthy columns. They were published Nov. 19 and Nov. 20, with Birmingham, Alabama, datelines.

Murray's biting words—his career later included a Pulitzer Prize in 1990 for commentary—derailed Bryant's backdoor maneuvering. A week after Murray's stories appeared, Alabama president Frank Rose announced his school was instead attending the Sugar Bowl in segregated New Orleans.

Not a word was mentioned on the ESPN broadcast of the 2022 Rose Bowl and Ohio State's 48-45 victory. Chris Fowler, the play-by-play broadcaster, made reference to Washington and Jefferson's Charles Fremont West as the first Black quarterback to play in the Rose Bowl in 1922 when Washington and Jefferson played Cal to a 0-0 tie.

That may be technically correct, but it overlooks Brown's Fritz Pollard, a quarterback and halfback in his college career, playing for Brown in the 1916 Rose Bowl. Broadcasters are limited by the research editors and producers present to be aired, but there was no mention of Pollard in the broadcast.

American sports can provide a stage for social change, but telling the stories about race in American sports is often complicated. Major media platforms avoid complicated stories that implicate a legend like Bryant.

Alabama's response, though, demonstrates Bryant clearly got the message when his team wasn't invited. Taking his team north of the Mason-Dixon Line attracted unwanted attention. Bryant retreated into the segregated cocoon for the remainder of the decade. In the South, his antebellum attitudes versus the U.S. Constitution weren't questioned by a fawning media.

For example, Bryant avoided criticism when Alabama's campus desegregated in 1963. He blithely maintained an all-white program another seven years until recruiting his first Black player in 1970, Wilbur Jackson.

He didn't schedule Alabama to play outside the Mason-Dixon until, oddly enough, a 1971 game against USC at the Coliseum. It was likely no coincidence that the 1971 season also was the first year Alabama dressed a Black player in a varsity game.

OHIO STATE ERUPTION OVERTAKES NARRATIVE

In 1961, news cycles moved to the day-to-day beat of newspaper reporting. Today's frenetic minute-to-minute pace fueled by social media, sports cable TV and ubiquitous sports talk radio was decades into the future. Black Historiography—how history was written or ignored—explains how an Ohio State volcanic eruption quickly buried the UCLA/Alabama backstory beneath the lava.

First, Ohio State defeated Michigan 50-20 on Nov. 25 to clinch the Big Ten title. The volcano erupted two days later when the Ohio State Senate Faculty voted to decline a Rose Bowl bid if offered. Ohio State's Senate Faculty had explained it feared coach Woody Hayes, who was in his 11th year with national titles in 1954 and 1957, had turned their school's reputation into a football factory.

Ohio State professor Anthony Menitz of the Philosophy Department was quoted in an AP story published in the Nov. 28 *Times*: "The issue simply is this, we have the opportunity to destroy the image of this being the football capital of the world."

The end result was the Ohio State tale quickly taking over the news cycle. The narrative for posterity formed without UCLA/Alabama in historical memory.

Avoiding race in sports stories traced to the 1930s and the "Conspiracy of Silence," a term used by Black sportswriters. They claimed the mainstream media was complicit in maintaining Major League's Baseball's color line by failing to write about segregation in the national pastime.

In today's media world, UCLA's 1961 players would have gained a place alongside their school's long history of pioneers. The figures include the 1939 UCLA football team with Jackie Robinson, Kenny Washington and Woody Strode. The trio's story was recently retold in the 2021 book *The Forgotten First* by Keyshawn Johnson and Bob Glauber.

All three players, who were from Los Angeles-area high schools, attended UCLA because USC shunned Black athletes in the 1930s. They later wrote more history in pro sports. Robinson, of course, broke Major League Baseball's color line in 1947 with the Brooklyn Dodgers. Washington and Strode broke the same barriers in the NFL in 1946 with the Los Angeles Rams.

Basketball Hall-of-Famer Bill Walton, a socially conscious athlete throughout his UCLA and NBA careers, only recently learned about UCLA's 1961 Black players standing up to Alabama.

"UCLA is full of stories like that," Walton said. "I love that about UCLA. I'm so proud of and grateful for UCLA."

HIDDEN FIGURES

The maneuvering behind the scenes of the 1962 Rose Bowl centers on Bryant and a key ally, Admiral Tom Hamilton. They were old Navy friends from their World War II days.

Hamilton was the commissioner of the Athletic Association of Western Universities (a Pac-12 forerunner founded in 1959), but what stood out in his job title was the unique authority to name the AAWU champion's Rose Bowl opponent. Bryant counted on his old friend for a friendly invite.

The circumstances resulted from controversies seeded in the late 1950s with a West Coast pay-for-play scandal. It broke up the eight-team Pacific Coast Conference, creating a lapse in the exclusive Big Ten/PCC Rose Bowl contract dating back to 1947.

The five-team AAWU was formed: UCLA, USC, Cal, Stanford and University of Washington. The AAWU retained an automatic bid to the Rose Bowl but not the Big Ten. The first two years Hamilton stuck to the New Year's Day traditional matchup. The 1959 season/1960 Rose Bowl paired Wisconsin and the University of Washington and the 1960 season/1961 Rose Bowl featured the University of Washington and Minnesota.

What changed in the 1961 season was Alabama's return to national prominence.

Alabama, Bryant's alma mater, brought him back to the Tuscaloosa campus in 1958 to rebuild the program after successful stints at Maryland (1946), Kentucky (1947-53) and Texas A&M (1954-57). His 1960 Crimson Tide finished ranked No. 9 with an 8-2-1 record.

As the 1961 season unfolded and Alabama climbed toward No. 1, Bryant envisioned an undefeated season and his first national title, both secured on the Pasadena stage of the Granddaddy of Them All. Bryant knew firsthand the prestige of playing in the Rose Bowl—not to mention the financial rewards.

He played 57 minutes for Alabama in the 1935 Rose Bowl when the Crimson Tide beat Stanford. Alabama's fanbase took great pride in participating in six Rose Bowls with a 4-1-1 record. In an era when poll voting declared the national champion at the end of the regular season, the Rose Bowl was the denouement to the college football season.

Alabama's last appearance in the Rose Bowl was in 1946, a year before the Big Nine/PCC contract (the Big Ten was only the Big Nine back then), but times changed by the 1960s. America was coming to terms, slowly, with the civil rights movement. Old-world men like Bryant and Hamilton, who failed to understand progress, were being left behind.

Bryant, who died in 1983 at age 69, was raised in a world of 19th-century Southern attitudes. His career thrived in an antebellum world the Ku Klux Klan violently fought to preserve.

Hamilton was a conservative military officer in addition to old-world man. Decades later, he never forgave Bill Walton for his arrest protesting the Vietnam War as a UCLA student in 1972. When Hamilton, in his retirement years, served on the board of San Diego's Hall of Champions, he told board members that Walton, a San Diego native, would never make the San Diego Hall of Champions as long as he chaired the board.

Walton, an all-time talent honored by the NBA as one of its 75 greatest players, wasn't enshrined in his hometown Hall until 1990—after Hamilton no longer served. Hamilton died in 1994 at age 88.

CRITICAL RACE THEORY

The 1962 Rose Bowl, when studied chronologically in the archives of the *Los Angeles Times*, provided an example of Critical Race Theory through football—without, hopefully, the political football. CRT's purpose is to teach stories that haven't been fully told. Sometimes those stories include exposing painful truths—a revered coach who was a segregationist, in this case.

It's unclear when Alabama was first floated to exploit the Big Ten/PCC contract lapse, but speculation mounted by mid-November. In the Associated Press polls (released on Mondays) Alabama climbed from No. 5 to No. 4 on Oct. 23 at 5-0. The Crimson Tide jumped to No. 2 on Nov. 6 at 7-0.

On the same day the Nov. 6 poll was released, the weekly Southern California Football Writers Luncheon convened at the Sheraton-West on Wilshire Boulevard. The luncheons were routine gatherings to hear from

UCLA coach Billy Barnes, USC coach John McKay, Los Angeles Rams coach Bob Waterfield and other invited speakers.

Ken Hooton, director of public relations for the Southern California Big Ten club, was invited as a Nov. 6 speaker. He foreshadowed impending events, dropping news hefty enough to top Al Wolf's Nov. 7 *Times* story.

The headline: "**Ohio State, Minnesota May Shun Rose Bowl**"

At the time of the luncheon, No. 3-ranked Ohio State and No. 5 Minnesota shared the Big Ten lead with unbeaten conference records.

Hooton, addressing the Big Ten race and Rose Bowl bid, said, "The Academic Senate at Ohio State is opposed to the Rose Bowl game and probably would not let the school accept a bid, were one received."

Although the news was stunning, it wasn't unusual in the 1960s for a college's academic side of campus to wield authority over the athletic department. Notre Dame's administration banned bowl games for academic reasons from 1925 until the 1969 season.

In those days, Notre Dame's bowl ban had no impact on winning national titles, since the final poll votes were tabulated after the regular season and before the holiday bowls. Once the polls shifted the final votes to the conclusion of the bowl season, Notre Dame played Texas in the 1970 Cotton Bowl.

But Hooton's time at the microphone didn't stop with his Ohio State bombshell. He proceeded to inflame the Alabama speculation.

"It is my personal opinion," Hooton added, "that Minnesota wouldn't accept, even though it's an individual matter for the schools now, because a repeat trip would be contrary to Big Ten thinking."

When the 1947 contract was signed, the Big Ten insisted on a no-repeat clause, although it only applied to the Big Ten entry. Minnesota had won the 1960 Big Ten title and played in the 1961 Rose Bowl. Although No. 1-ranked Minnesota lost to No. 6 Washington 17-7 in the 1961 Rose Bowl, the Gophers already had been declared national champion at the end of the regular season.

Wolf's Nov. 7 story, using the Big Five nickname for the AAWU, continued: "So…Alabama may yet be the team which will oppose the Big Five champion next New Year's Day. The Southeastern Conference does not have a tie-up with the Sugar Bowl, or any other bowl. Alabama has expressed a keen desire to play in the Rose, where it last appeared in 1946."

ROSE BOWL SPECULATION

In the Nov. 12 edition of the *Los Angeles Mirror*, the afternoon paper owned by the morning *Times*, sports editor Sid Ziff's column addressed the issue.

The headline: **"One Vote for the South."**

Ziff, noting a new Big Ten/AAWU contract was expected to be announced prior to the 1963 Rose Bowl, suggested taking advantage of the outsider opportunity before the door closed. He nominated Alabama or Georgia Tech, another segregated team from the SEC.

On Monday, Nov. 13, *Times* sports editor Paul Zimmerman wrote in his column similar thoughts favoring the two SEC schools.

In the AP poll released in the same Nov. 13 edition, Alabama (8-0) remained No. 2 with three first-place votes. Texas was No. 1 with 41 first-place votes. Georgia Tech, was No. 9 on Nov. 6, but its upset loss to Tennessee dropped the Yellow Jackets out of the Nov. 13 rankings (the AP poll was only the Top 10 in those days).

Wolf again covered the coaches' luncheon on Nov. 13. His story in the *Times* on Nov. 14 was about an informal poll of writers.

The headline: **"'Bama choice of writers for bowl"**

On Nov. 15, the *Times* published an AP story with a Tuscaloosa, Alabama, dateline.

The headline: **"Rose Bowl Fever falls on 'Bama"**

The story highlighted Alabama's pride in its Rose Bowl history. Curiously, though, the story also noted Bryant declined to answer questions about his Rose Bowl interest. Apparently, no one pressed him.

Two days later, though, Zimmerman's Friday, Nov. 17 *Times* column made it clear Bryant wanted the Rose Bowl bid despite his silence. Zimmerman quoted *Birmingham News* sports editor Zipp Newman:

"The Crimson Tide would walk there if they had to, and that goes for Alabama's president, Dr. Frank Rose, on down, although they can't talk about it yet."

In another story the *Times* published on Nov. 17, this one with a Miami dateline, the AP reported Rose Bowl and Orange Bowl scouts were attending the Nov. 18 Georgia Tech-Alabama game at Legion Field in Birmingham. Hamilton was indirectly quoted through the Orange Bowl's executive director, Van C. Kussrow.

"Hamilton explained to me the Rose Bowl's interest in Southeastern Conference teams," Kussrow said. "He said their position had been made more difficult because Minnesota and Ohio State aren't considered strong possibilities out there."

That was more than Hamilton ever said directly to the *Times* or other Southern California media outlets.

By that same day, Friday, Nov. 17, Murray arrived in Birmingham for Alabama's Saturday, Nov. 18 game. The Crimson Tide (9-0) beat Georgia Tech 10-0 to remain unbeaten.

In the Sunday, Nov. 19 *Times*, Murray's column mocked Alabama's Jim Crow society, fans and media deifying Bryant. They liked to say he could walk on water. Murray's story led with the first reference to UCLA's protestations found in the *Times* archives.

The headline: **"'Bama and Ol' Bear"**

"BIRMINGHAM—The University of Alabama just about wrapped up the all-white championship of the whole cotton-picking world here this weekend in a game quietly relegated to the 18th century before it began by a band of Negro students at UCLA."

Murray, based on his column, seemed assured pressure would prevent Alabama from receiving a Rose Bowl invitation, but it wasn't reflected elsewhere in his own paper. In the same Sunday edition, the *Times*' college football roundup of Saturday game results touted Alabama's hopes.

The headline: **"'Bama scores Rosy win"**

In the Monday, Nov. 20 poll, Alabama had climbed to No. 1 after former No. 1 Texas was upset by Texas Christian.

MURRAY'S MASTERPIECE

Murray saved his best writing—worthy of a 1961 Pulitzer vote recount—for the Monday, Nov. 20 edition.

The headline: **"Bedsheets and 'Bama"**

Murray labeled Birmingham as the "showplace of the South—gateway to the Ku Klux Klan." He continued by writing it was the place where, "when they say evening dress, they mean a bedsheet with eyeholes. And bring a match. We're lighting a cross."

Ouch! But it was fair.

Alabama in 1961 was known for the KKK bombing Black homes and churches. Birmingham, where Alabama played games at Legion Field, was known as "Bombingham." Legion Field was located only blocks from the 16th Street Baptist Church that KKK members bombed two years later, killing "Four Little Girls." The bombing was the KKK's response to Martin

Luther King's "I Have a Dream" speech delivered on August 28, 1963 at the Lincoln Memorial.

"The bombed-out houses aren't the work of the enemy," Murray continued in his column. "White male Americans are the enemies of America here. The Constitution is being torn in half by people whose ancestors helped write it. It doesn't make any sense. It's worse than un-American. It's un-human."

Then Murray got down to Rose Bowl business, explaining he joined Alabama writers on Friday to interview Bryant on the upcoming game at his Bankhead Hotel suite. But Murray's questions weren't about X's and O's.

Courtesy Los Angeles Times.

He wrote, "Coach Bryant," I asked. "What do you think of the announcement out of UCLA that the colored players would not take the field against your team if it got to the Rose Bowl?"

Murray described a silence that fell over the room. Alabama's media wasn't accustomed to hearing reporters press Bryant—and certainly not about segregation. Then Murray quoted Bryant's response:

"Oh," he says. "I would have nothing to say about that. Neither will the university, I am sure."

That Bryant response, especially in retrospect, added new insight to the old joke Bryant didn't have a boss.

Murray's "Bedsheets and 'Bama" story continued, describing the Alabama's sycophantic writers looking at the floor until one with a "beet red" face spoke up: "Tell them West Coast N-lovers to go lick your boots, Bear."

With Murray having brought UCLA's opposition into the open, two Alabama newspapers attempted to discredit the UCLA Black students.

Author Kurt Edward Kemper documents this in his 2009 book, *College Football and American Culture in the Cold War Era.* The *Montgomery Advertiser* reported UCLA's administration was unaware of a Black student organization planning a protest. The *Birmingham News* wrote the protest plans were "greatly exaggerated."

Some context is needed here. These claims were specious with the perspective of time. Black student groups mobilizing and gaining recognition from campus administrators was a product of the late 1960s. African Americans didn't have a voice on campus until examples of UCLA's 1961 students speaking up as activists.

A LONE VOICE

Bryant's lack of comment to Murray suggested he still expected Admiral Hamilton to bring the USS Alabama to the Rose Bowl port.

On the West Coast, Hamilton matched Bryant's silence. He had little to say about the Rose Bowl pairing, even though there was heightened interest over the upcoming Nov. 25 USC-UCLA game at the Coliseum to decide the AAWU title.

It's interesting to note Murray broke a sports media custom in his first year with the *Los Angeles Times* (he wrote from 1961 until his death in 1998 at age 78). He had previously worked for *Time* Magazine as an entertainment writer and on the founding of *Sports Illustrated* in 1954.

A search of the *Los Angeles Times* archives reveals Murray's Nov. 20 column was only the *second* and *last* reference to the UCLA protestations prior to the Rose Bowl. His colleagues failed to pick up on the significance of winning a standoff with a segregationist coach.

"Jim always believed that calling out injustice in the sports world was more important than reporting the results of games," said Linda Murray Hofmans, Murray's wife at the time of his death who now directs the Jim Murray Memorial Foundation. "He wasn't intimidated by other sportswriters, angry readers who demanded he 'stick to sports,' or even legends like Bear Bryant. He was a trailblazer in that regard.

"Most sportswriters of '60s and '70s defended the status quo or looked the other way, but Jim used his column as a bullhorn to fight for civil rights whenever he deemed it necessary."

The Black weekly *Los Angeles Sentinel* and the *Daily Bruin*, UCLA's student paper, were two Southern California newspapers not as likely to follow a 1960s media custom avoiding race, yet they also lacked UCLA protest references.

The *Sentinel* published a story criticizing Alabama as a potential choice but without mentioning a threatened UCLA protest. Brad Pye Jr. wrote the Rose Bowl Committee would avoid "adverse publicity" if it picked Ohio State over Alabama.

The headline: "**Forget Alabama–Bring on Buckeyes**"

Pye wrote, "Alabama hasn't seen fit to put integration in action before now, so there is no reason why it should get an invitation to the Rose Bowl until such a time when it decides to put the American way into action on its own soil."

Melvin Durslag of the *Los Angeles Examiner* also wrote a column criticizing segregated Alabama as a Rose Bowl choice.

The headline: **"Alabama—An Insult to the Bowl."**

But only Murray confronted Bryant about the reaction of UCLA Black students and Black players. Kermit Alexander, a junior halfback in 1961, explained the players' stance in my 2015 interview with him for *FanRagSports.com* (now out of business).

"If we can't play on their field in Alabama, why should they be able to play on our field in Pasadena?" Alexander said.

Alexander added no one in the 1960s media questioned him or his teammates about Alabama. Alexander's subsequent health issues prevented a follow-up interview.

The Alexander interview was framed around the 2015 Missouri protest. By then, an enlightened media thoroughly reported such news and hailed Missouri's football team for threatening a boycott if racial issues on campus weren't addressed. The players were successful, forcing the school's president to resign.

UCLA's 1961 response was fueled by the progress of the civil rights movement. Only six months earlier, May 14, 1961, a white mob in Anniston, Alabama, ambushed and firebombed a busload of 1961 Freedom Riders—including civil rights icon John Lewis—protesting segregation on busses and at terminals.

In the Nov. 2 edition of the *Times*, an AP story with an Atlanta dateline reported a federal judge ordered police in Alabama, Georgia and Mississippi—states where African Americans at bus terminals continued to be arrested—to uphold federal laws outlawing segregated busses.

But there were no follow-up sports stories hailing UCLA like there were for Missouri—only a new narrative that Ohio State turned down the bowl bid. The Ohio State story remained entrenched in time.

PASADENA BIDS

The first Rose Bowl bid was decided on the field when UCLA-USC met Nov. 25 in a winner-take-all game marred by a rain-soaked Coliseum field. The unranked Bruins won the mud bath 10-7 to improve to 7-3.

UCLA's students continued celebrating the Rose Bowl berth at a

Monday, Nov. 27 campus rally. The Tuesday, Nov. 28 *Times* story covering the rally noted Hamilton "would not elaborate" on UCLA's opponent.

Hamilton limited his comments to a list of five schools, two unnamed teams and three Big Ten schools, No. 2 Ohio State (8-0-1), No. 7 Minnesota (7-2) and No. 8 Michigan State (7-2).

Later in the day, Nov. 27, the Ohio State bombshell exploded. Ohio State's Faculty Senate voted 28-25 in a secret ballot to reject the Rose Bowl.

Two days before the vote, the temperamental Hayes added to the professors' perception of him in Ohio State's 50-20 victory over Michigan to clinch the Big Ten title. Ohio State scored its final touchdown with five seconds to play, and Hayes ordered a successful two-point conversion. He repeated the rub-it-in tactic in 1968, scoring a two-point conversion to cap a 50-14 win. In the 1968 rout, Hayes explained to the media he went for two because he couldn't go for three.

Hayes heard news of the faculty Rose Bowl vote upon arriving to speak at his Cleveland hotel. He was reported to have dropped his bags and roam Cleveland's streets without speaking. On the Columbus campus, police estimated student protest crowds of 5,000 on Nov. 27 and 4,000 on Nov. 28. Windows were broken and professors hung in effigy. The *Columbus Dispatch* printed a list of professors that voted.

On the second night of demonstrations, Ohio State team captain Mike Ingram told the students through a loudspeaker the players had accepted the vote and to go home before someone was hurt.

In retrospect, the student protests were another reason for the professors to believe their conclusions football was running amok weren't unreasonable. The examples continued through the march of time. At the 1978 Gator Bowl, Hayes punched a Clemson player on the sideline and was fired, ending his career in disgrace.

Meanwhile, on the West Coast, the *Daily Bruin* reported on Nov. 28 Hamilton had watched the USC-UCLA game and returned to his San Francisco office, commenting only that the selection "might be withheld until after the games of Dec. 2." UCLA athletic director Wilbur Johns said in the Nov. 28 *Times* he deferred all comments to Hamilton.

With Ohio State out, runner-up Minnesota, third-place Michigan State and fourth-place Purdue began lobbying for the Rose Bowl bid. Michigan State and Purdue hoped Minnesota would be skipped over in deference to the no-repeat Big Ten philosophy.

"If we get the bid, we'll call the fastest meeting of our athletic council on record to accept it," said Michigan State athletic director Biggie Munn.

ALABAMA'S AUDIBLE

Hamilton's Dec. 2 games comment referred to Alabama playing its annual Iron Bowl against Auburn and Georgia Tech facing Georgia in their traditional rivalry game.

But Alabama president Frank Rose on Nov. 29 suddenly ended the speculation. Rose said if the Crimson Tide defeated Auburn, the school planned to accept a Sugar Bowl bid. Rose added the Sugar Bowl was the game the players preferred.

Alabama routed Auburn 34-0 and officially accepted the Sugar Bowl bid against Arkansas in New Orleans, but it's difficult to accept Bryant, who coveted a Rose Bowl berth, left the bowl decision in the hands of a players vote.

Either way, unanswered questions remain.

When did Bryant and Hamilton back down? Did President Rose convince Bryant and Hamilton winning a national title in the Rose Bowl wasn't worth the tradeoff? TV scenes would show UCLA's Black students protesting outside the stadium and the Bruins' Black players boycotting out of uniform. A largely world-of-mouth story would result in images leaping onto TV screens.

Alabama would be further portrayed nationally as a backwards state. And this time Bryant's apologists couldn't blame the KKK.

MINNESOTA INVITED

As the Rose Bowl announcement suspense mounted, Murray's Dec. 1 column provided comic relief. He showed he was an equal-opportunity critic of Southern segregationists and Midwestern bullies.

The headline: **"Love That Woody"**

"So Woody Hayes is not coming to the Rose Bowl," he wrote. "Dad rat it! Somebody's always spoiling the fun."

Murray added, "I have seen guys who were ungracious losers. But Woody was the most ungracious winner I have ever seen. He always broke me up. A loud, lovable character who went through life the way his fullbacks go through a line—knocking people down who get in his way. Once it was a couple of sportswriters."

The Rose Bowl selection suspense ended on Dec. 2 with news topping the Sunday, Dec. 3 *Times* sports section.*the*

The headline: **"Minnesota to play UCLA in Rose Bowl"**

In the story, UCLA captain Ron Hull said, "Most of the boys, after Ohio State and Alabama were ruled out, wanted to meet Minnesota. I'm sure we'll give them a game."

There remained no reference to a role played by UCLA's Black students and Black players. Murray deserved a victory lap, but he didn't write about the subject again. If the Alabama story wasn't properly covered in Los Angeles, the deeper story also certainly was brushed aside in the Minneapolis media.

Minnesota All-American pick Bobby Bell, who played in the 1961 and 1962 Rose Bowl games, said in an interview he was unaware of the Alabama backstory.

"We never heard anything about the Alabama and a UCLA protest," said Bell, a College and Pro Football Hall of Famer. "We only knew about Ohio State turning down the bid."

The focus on the Ohio State narrative continued in a Dec. 4 *Times* column written by Braven Dyer. He noted comedian Bob Hope, with his Ohio ties, considered inviting Ohio State's team to attend the Rose Bowl as his guests. Dyer's column included a few jokes from Hope mocking Ohio State's professors.

On New Year's Day, 1962, No. 6-ranked Minnesota dominated the Bruins, 21-3. In the Sugar Bowl, No. 1 Alabama defeated No. 9 Arkansas, 10-3.

Razorback players told reporters Alabama wasn't worthy of its No. 1 ranking, but their opinion didn't matter. Alabama already had been named national champion in the final poll votes released on Dec. 4 at the end of the regular season, although it was a split title.

Among the four organizations the NCAA sanctioned as designating a national champion in the poll era, Alabama (11-0-0) was voted No. 1 by the AP (writers), United Press International (coaches, now USA Today) and National Football Foundation. However, Ohio State (8-0-1) was named national champion by the Football Writers Association of America.

BRYANT'S ADMISSION

The Bear finally came clean 13 years after he sought a Rose Bowl bid upon the release of his 1974 biography, *Bear*, written by John Underwood, an acclaimed *Sports Illustrated* writer.

Bryant not only admitted he both coveted the Rose Bowl berth and blamed Murray for costing him the invitation, he went one step further.

He claimed Murray's two biting columns were motivated by revenge dating to 1955.

Bryant referenced his 1955 Texas A&M team losing to UCLA 21-0 at the Los Angeles Memorial Coliseum.

On Page 174, Underwood wrote Bryant stating: "…I snapped at a writer on the Los Angeles paper after the game. He asked if I had thought we could win, and I said, 'You silly so-and-so, what do you think we came out here for?'

"Those things turn on you. Jim Murray came over and saw us play and made a fuss over our being considered for the Rose Bowl when we won the national championship in 1961. He wrote about segregation and the Alabama Ku Klux Klan and every unrelated scandalous thing he could think of, and we didn't get the invitation."

Murray didn't work for the *Los Angeles Times* or any Los Angeles newspaper in 1955. In the early 1950s, he was with *Time* Magazine and then began working for *Sports Illustrated* in 1953 as it prepared to launch in 1954. Murray's 1961 motives were to offer a civics lesson to Bryant and a Jim Crow state.

Yet, Bryant wanted his readers to believe Murray's motive was petty revenge. Bryant's 1974 criticism of Murray also revealed how detached he was from the real world in 1974, not to mention 1961.

Alabama's campus town of Tuscaloosa housed the Alabama KKK headquarters. Joe Namath, Alabama's legendary quarterback (1962-64), spoke in the 2013 Showtime film of his shock at spotting KKK billboards on his initial bus ride to campus from his home in Beaver Falls, Pennsylvania.

"The first bus ride I took going back into Tuscaloosa, Alabama, scared me a bit," Namath said, in *Against the Tide*. "You know how they have the signs at the side of he road, Lions Club Kiwanis Club. Uh, huh….Ku Klux Klan, home of the Grand Imperial Wizard. What? Because all I ever saw of guys in white capes and burning crosses was in the movies."

BRYANT DRAGS HIS FEET

By 1974, Bryant had plenty of time to reflect on dragging out his resistance to integration, but he never apologized. He never explained why he was apparently oblivious to President Lyndon B. Johnson having signed the Civil Rights Acts of 1964 and 1965.

From 1962 through 1967, Alabama played only all-white Southern teams. The exception was facing integrated Nebraska in the 1966 Sugar Bowl in New Orleans. The 1966 team played eight of its 10 regular-season games at one of three Alabama stadiums, Denny Stadium (now Bryant-Denny) on campus, Legion Field in Birmingham and Ladd-Pebbles Stadium in Mobile. The only road trips were to neighboring states, Mississippi and Tennessee.

Alabama's first integrated regular-season opponent was SEC rival Tennessee in 1968 in Knoxville. In 1969, Tennessee routed Alabama 41-14 at Legion Field. Kentucky led the SEC in desegregation a year ahead of Tennessee, but the Wildcats weren't on Alabama's schedule.

History showed Bryant was a follower, not a leader, in his own conference. Kentucky, Tennessee, Florida, Mississippi State, Vanderbilt and in-state rival Auburn all recruited Black athletes by 1969, prior to Bryant. That was 60 percent of what was then a 10-team league.

The world passed by Bryant while he remained in the cocoon of the segregated South. Alabama's 1970 schedule, planned years in advance, turned out to have seven integrated opponents by the turn of the decade. Oklahoma made it eight for the season in the Astro-Bluebonnet Bowl.

SEC schools also were ahead of Bryant scheduling teams above the Mason-Dixon Line. Kentucky played at Indiana in 1967; Tennessee traveled to UCLA in 1967; and Vanderbilt played at Army in West Point in 1968 and Michigan in 1969.

Florida didn't travel north of the Mason-Dixon Line prior to Alabama in 1971, but the Gators faced integrated opponents in three home games in the 1960s: Northwestern, 1966; Illinois, 1967; and Air Force, 1968. Tennessee played host to two integrated teams in 1965, Houston and UCLA, and one in 1966, Army.

MURRAY CAST AS THE ANTAGONIST

Hyperbole, myths and fiction surrounding the 1970 USC-Alabama game at Legion Field in Birmingham led to another bewildering revisionist history twist gaining a hold in college football lore.

A false narrative crediting Bryant as a crusader and aggrandizing USC's role portrayed the game as an integration tipping point. Bryant as a crusader is like crediting Robert E. Lee for ending slavery. Murray as the bad guy is like blaming Antifa for the Jan. 6, 2021 insurrection at the U.S. Capitol.

Historical memory also has overlooked 30 of the 33 Southern major programs recruiting their first Black player by 1970, including Alabama. Integration in the South was a fait accompli, as the last three holdouts were Georgia, LSU and Mississippi. However, books and films, most of them in the 21st century, regurgitated a rote storyline.

In *Rising Tide: Bear Bryant, Joe Namath, and Dixie's Last Quarter*, a 2013 book written by Randy Roberts and Ed Krzemienski, Murray is taken to task for his Alabama columns.

For instance, Murray is described as "a reporter with thick bookish glasses...."

Of the trip to Birmingham, the book states: "Murray's claims for going to Birmingham were undoubtedly disingenuous. He was a confirmed and accomplished big league pot stirrer, and a minor league social crusader."

What's "disingenuous" about pointing out to a segregationist coach it's 1961, not 1861? What's "minor league" about confronting Bryant face-to-face on social justice on Bryant's own turf?

UCLA's forgotten 1961 role also led to another great irony decades later. The *wrong* Los Angeles school, USC, was cast as a college football integration leader in the sport's lore. UCLA, long before USC, truly played a pioneering role in the 1960s. USC, like Alabama in the SEC, led from behind. USC shunned Black athletes in the 1930s. In the 1960s, the program followed an unwritten quota limiting the roster to a half-dozen or so Black athletes through the 1960s.

The oversights from the sports media avoiding race created a 1960s blank canvas. By the late 1980s and early 1990s, the blank canvas was painted with a false narrative—Bryant secretly scheduled integrated USC in 1970 with the aid of McKay, his old friend, as a game to lose. His grand scheme was to convince his bigoted fans with a loss it was time to let him recruit Black athletes.

However, neither coach mentioned such a grand plan in their books published in 1974. In a fawning 1980 *Time* cover story reflecting on Bryant's career, there was not a single word about the 1970 USC-Alabama game changing history.

It's true USC routed all-white Alabama 42-21, but it's also true a year earlier integrated Tennessee routed Alabama at Legion Field, 41-14.

The regurgitated and unvetted stories also overlook USC was among the schools following an unwritten quota of a half-dozen or so Black players. The Trojans' 1962 national title team had only five Black players and the 1967 national championship roster only seven. UCLA's eight Black players in 1961 grew into double figures later in the decade. Schools like USC were behind the times.

The 1970 Trojans were still shedding the residue of the quota years. USC had only four Black starters that night in Birmingham. Most of the 18 Black players on the roster had been recruited in the previous couple of years,.

Another fact omitted from the myth was Bryant didn't need to lose to USC to convince his fans it was time to recruit Black athletes. He had already signed Wilbur Jackson the previous winter. Jackson watched the 1970 USC-Alabama game from the stands with the freshmen team.

IMAGINARY BLAME

Oddly enough, Alabama authors shaped narratives that also blamed Murray's 1961 stories for costing Bryant a national title five years later when the Crimson Tide finished No. 3 to No. 1 Notre Dame and No. 2 Michigan State.

The Irish and Spartans, after a season-long buildup, played to a 10-10 tie in the Game of the Century on Nov. 19, 1966 at Spartan Stadium. Notre Dame and Michigan State retained their 1-2 rankings in the final poll at the end of the regular season.

One of the Alabama authors claiming reverse racism was Keith Dunnavant, who wrote *The Missing Ring: How Bear Bryant and the 1966 Crimson Tide Were Denied College Football's Most Elusive Prize.*

Bryant author Allen Barra (*The Last Coach*, 2005) reviewed Dunnavant's book on Sept. 2, 2006 for the *Los Angeles Times*. Barra wrote Dunnavant's bias claim "is based far more on emotion than logic and some of that emotion is borderline irrational."

Nevertheless, Dunnavant's stance gained platforms in HBO's 2008 *Breaking the Huddle*, Showtime's 2013 *Against the Tide* and ESPN 2019 and 2020 films portraying Bryant as a crusader.

A segment in *Against the Tide* juxtaposes a quote from Murray's 1961 column as if it was written in the 1966 season. As narrator Tom Selleck read his lines suggesting the 1966 vote was biased, Selleck describes Murray as "the lead voice." The screen then flashes a quote from Murray's 1961 story—"An all-white team has no business being No. 1."

Selleck needed to send the sloppily researched film back to rewrite.

WHAT WOULD MURRAY SAY?

When Murray was awarded the 1990 Pulitzer Prize, he humbly deflected praise with a quip.

He said winning for commentary, "should have to bring down a government or expose major graft or give advice to prime ministers. Correctly quoting Los Angeles Dodgers manager Tommy Lasorda shouldn't merit a Pulitzer Prize."

Murray didn't bring down a government with his 1961 Alabama stories, but he set back a segregationist coach. He exposed Bryant's plot and credited the courage of UCLA students and players to challenge Bryant.

If not for Murray's stories, Hamilton doesn't meet resistance and likely extends Bryant's wish for an Alabama invitation. Another way to put it, though: what if Burt Hooten had not spoken of Ohio State and Minnesota possibly declining a Rose Bowl bid? The prospect spurred the reaction at UCLA and then Murray's attention. That's another reason to think Bryant would have gained his desired bid.

And finally, the unanswered question that no doubt would have generated the most humorous response: What would have been Murray's reaction to Bryant and his apologists years later casting Murray as the bad guy?

We can only imagine his humble quip. There was only one Jim Murray.

Also, imagine what he might have said about the 2022 Rose Bowl broadcast of a game Ohio State won 48-45 over Utah. Not what he would have said about a wild game, although that surely would have been profound. But what about the ESPN crew failing to mention the 1962 Rose Bowl and its 60th anniversary during the pregame shows or game?

American sports can provide a stage for social change, but stories about race in American sports are often too complicated for TV or the average fan. Major media platforms avoid tangled race stories, especially if one implicates a legend such as Bear Bryant.

The 1962 Rose Bowl remained forgotten, even on its 60th anniversary.

CHAPTER 26
MICHIGAN STATE AT SEGREGATED NORTH CAROLINA, 1964

FACT: Michigan State Hall of Famer Clinton Jones scored his first career touchdown at segregated North Carolina. To paraphrase *Washington Post* sportswriter Shirley Povich about Jim Brown scoring in 1961 against Washington, the NFL's last all-white team, "Clinton Jones integrated North Carolina's end zone."

"*I didn't want my parents to be subjected to the kind of humiliation that they might encounter. We knew the only Blacks in the stadium would be the ones working.*" —*Michigan State's Jim Summers of Orangeburg, South Carolina, on how he and teammate George Webster of Anderson, South Carolina, felt about the game at segregated North Carolina.*

We're unable to know a half-century later if Michigan State's Duffy Daugherty or North Carolina's Jim Hickey appreciated Mark Twain's book, *The Innocents Abroad*. But what Twain wrote in 1869 applied to college football integration a century later:

"Travel is fatal to prejudice, bigotry, and narrow-mindedness, and many of our people need it sorely on these accounts. Broad, wholesome, charitable views of men and things cannot be acquired by vegetating in one little corner of the earth all one's lifetime."

Either way, Twain would have appreciated the milestone game the schools played on Sept. 26, 1964 at Kenan Memorial Stadium in Chapel Hill. Twain's down-home wisdom was validated.

The game in Chapel Hill was the back end of a home-and-home series, with the 1962 and 1963 contests played at Spartan Stadium. Michigan State's road game marked the first time a fully integrated college football roster played in a former Confederate state at the height of the civil rights movement.

Prior to World War II, a gentleman's agreement required Northern schools to bench or leave behind their Black athletes when playing Southern schools. The policy largely continued into the 1950s, although there were some exceptions ignoring the agreement following President Harry S. Truman's steps to desegregate the military in 1948. Harvard, with one Black player, played at Virginia in 1947. Notre Dame, with two Black players, visited Chapel Hill in 1953. USC, with three Black players, traveled to Texas in 1956.

North Carolina, though, not only had a track record as one of the few Southern schools that had traveled north and faced Black athletes in pursuit of national exposure, but the Tar Heels took it a step further scheduling Michigan State at Chapel Hill. The 1964 Michigan State-North Carolina game helped open doors in the South the remainder of the decade. The Spartans' makeup surprised no one, with a national reputation for Black stars. North Carolina knew what to expect.

Some 1964 Black athletes on Michigan State's Underground Railroad were recruited from the segregated South, and they initially viewed the road trip to North Carolina with trepidation. They had chilling memories of Jim Crow laws and second-class citizenship. Two Spartans from neighboring South Carolina, Jim Summers and the late George Webster, told their parents to stay home.

"I didn't want my parents to be subjected to the kind of humiliation that they might encounter," said Summers, adding Webster felt the same. "We knew the only Blacks in the stadium would be the ones working."

But Webster and Summers learned along with their teammates some parts of the South accepted change sooner than others. North Carolina won 21-15 on a day without incident on and off the field.

"The only thing I remember from that game was they had a big halfback that went on to play in the NFL, and he ran all over us," said Summers, referring to Ken Willard, who played 10 NFL seasons. "I don't remember their players doing anything dirty or saying anything racial."

Michigan State's Jimmy Raye, who grew up 70 miles down the road from Chapel Hill in segregated Fayetteville, North Carolina, was a freshman in 1964 who didn't travel due to NCAA freshman ineligibility rules of the era.

"I remember the team coming back, and we were together in the Brody Complex," Raye said. "They were disappointed with the loss, but I don't remember anyone talking about incidents."

Jones, making his varsity debut as a sophomore, scored his first career touchdown on his way to the College Football Hall of Fame.

To paraphrase *Washington Post* columnist Shirley Povich about Jim Brown scoring in 1961 against Washington, the NFL's last all-white team, "Clinton Jones integrated North Carolina's end zone." Povich, a giant of the sportswriting industry, had long criticized Washington's openly racist owner, George Preston Marshall.

One of Willard's memories of the game was Smith, a 6-foot-7, 285-pound defensive end ahead of his time, harassing sophomore quarterback Danny Talbott's passing attempts.

"I guess playing those games took the novelty out of it," Willard said. "We heard a lot about how big Bubba Smith was, but I don't remember comments from coaches, players, students or fans about Black players. That's my truthful recollection."

AVOIDING RACE IN THE MEDIA

We must rely on such oral histories to understand this under-appreciated moment in college football. The 1964 media hadn't progressed much from pre-civil rights attitudes of avoiding the subject of race.

The *Raleigh News & Observer* and now-defunct *Raleigh Times* limited their stories to game-day results. Journalists both at the *Detroit Free Press* and *Detroit News* were on strike, but *Lansing State Journal* sports editor Bob Hoerner traveled to Chapel Hill.

Without citing segregation, Hoerner's brief mention was merely that the Spartans were the first Big Ten team to play in Chapel Hill. This was three years before Charlie Scott was North Carolina's first Black basketball player for coach Dean Smith.

The advance game story in the *Daily Tar Heel*—North Carolina's student newspaper—was written by Pete Gammons, who went on to a Hall-of-Fame baseball writing career as Peter Gammons. His Michigan State-North Carolina advance story made no mention of the Spartans'

Black athletes breaking ground in the South. The photo accompanying the story was of Daugherty and Charlie Migyanka, a white player.

The lack of incidents may have contributed to the media avoiding the subject, the norm for the time. But a chance to spread enlightenment was missed.

Willard had grown up in segregated Virginia, and he understood the difference between the Chapel Hill campus and the rest of the South. The University of North Carolina's flagship campus was and still is considered a genteel place and the state's foremost forward-thinking campus.

"It was a different mentality down there," he said. "Chapel Hill was very progressive…and disliked for that reason. We were considered too liberal."

For a perspective on the 1964 climate in former slave states, only a year earlier Maryland's Darryl Hill broke the Atlantic Coast Conference color line as its first Black player.

Hill played Maryland's early-season contest under a death threat at South Carolina (both schools were then ACC members). Fans taunted Hill with racial slurs. On the way to the locker room at halftime, a fan dumped a drink on him. At both South Carolina and later in the season at Clemson, another ACC school located in South Carolina, Hill endured double- and triple-teamed defenses with hard tackles in addition to racial taunts.

North Carolina continued the Daugherty-Hickey blueprint. The Tar Heels played host to Michigan in 1965 and traveled to Michigan in 1966. Indiana was the next Big Ten team to play in the South, with games at Texas in 1965 and 1966.

Willard's theory made sense to Raye, who looked to Michigan State for an opportunity to play big-time college football when ACC schools, including home-state schools North Carolina, N.C. State and Duke declined to recruit him due to race.

"ACC schools had rules against recruiting Black athletes," Raye noted, "but North Carolina had played against Black athletes, and it helped the transition."

CHAPTER 27
DUFFY AND THE BEAR

FACT: In 1966, Alabama's All-American offensive tackle was Cecil Dowdy, a 6-foot-1, 202-pounder taken in the 1967 NFL draft's ninth round. Michigan State's 1966 defense was led by two College Football Hall of Famers: Bubba Smith and George Webster.

"*Bear told Duffy that he thought Michigan State had the best athletes because of all the Black players. Bear said he had some fast and good white players but that Duffy had bigger and faster players. I never forgot his words.*"—Marty Daly, Michigan State equipment manager.

Marty Daly unexpectedly found himself eating breakfast with Michigan State's Duffy Daugherty and Alabama's Bear Bryant, a pair of College Football Hall of Fame coaches, on a February 1967 morning at the Palmer House in Chicago.

Daly was only 22 years old, having recently finished his first football season as Michigan State's assistant equipment manager. Coaches and equipment managers from across the country had assembled in Chicago for the National Sporting Goods Association Convention, Feb. 5-9 at Navy Pier.

At Daly's wide-eyed age, the surprise moment of listening to two coaching giants talk football over breakfast was seared into his memory.

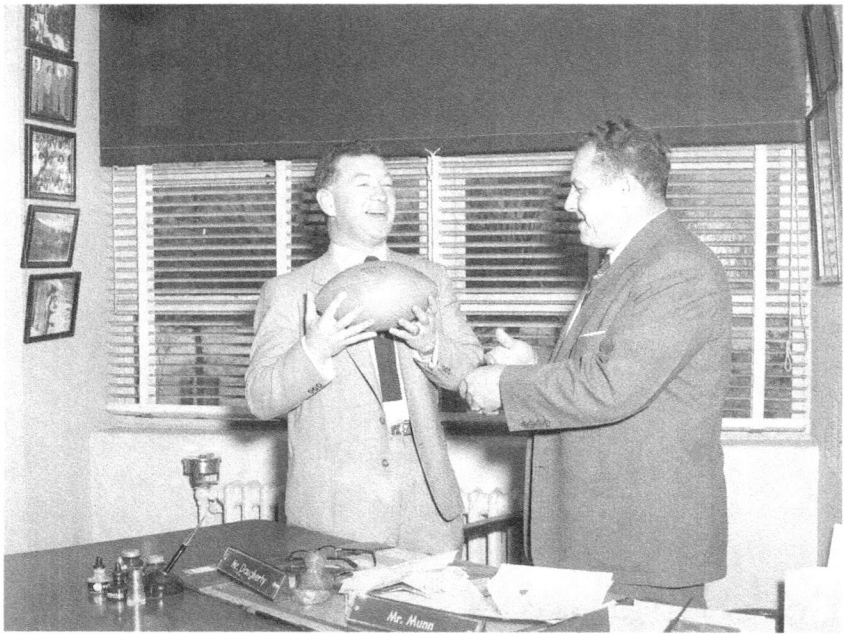

Duffy Daugherty and Biggie Munn. *Courtesy Michigan State University.*

"Duffy and the Bear talked," Daly said. "I just listened to two legends."

The morning began with Daly seated alone when Daugherty entered the hotel breakfast room. He spotted Daly and joined him.

"That's the kind of guy Duffy was," Daly said. "I was just a kid sitting at table, but he knew me from practices. He always talked to the student managers and student trainers. He was a good guy to everybody."

Next, Bryant entered the room alone and spotted Daugherty. He joined his good friend. Naturally, rehashing the controversial 1966 season was a subject of conversation.

Six weeks earlier, Notre Dame and Michigan State entered the Game of the Century, a seminal moment in college football history and quasi-national championship, ranked 1-2. They finished 1-2 in the final polls with identical 9-0-1 records after playing to a 10-10 tie on Nov. 19, 1966 at Spartan Stadium. Meanwhile, Bryant and his fan base claimed all-white Alabama (11-0-0) finishing No. 3 was a case of reverse racism.

But that wasn't Bryant's tone at breakfast in Chicago.

"The Bear was going on about how he needed to get him 'some of those Negro boys,'" said Daly, mimicking Bryant's well-known Southern mumble that pronounced the word as "Nig-ruh."

Daly continued recounting the conversation, substituting "Black" for Bryant's vocabulary.

"Bear told Duffy that he thought Michigan State had the best athletes because of all the Black players," Daly said. "Bear said he had some fast and good white players but that Duffy had bigger and faster players. I never forgot his words."

Daly added Bryant told Daugherty, "I know what you're doing up there. I've got to get me some of those Black players."

Daugherty, Daly said, didn't respond with much more than, "I'm going to continue to recruit down there."

Down there, of course, meant the segregated South. Daugherty's Underground Railroad teams recruited 44 Black players from the South between 1959 and his final recruiting class in 1972. But even before the 1960s, Michigan State had a long history of Midwest-based rosters with Black athletes, including its 1954 and 1956 Rose Bowl teams that gained national attention. *Jet Magazine*, a Black publication, posted a story before the 1956 Rose Bowl citing Michigan State's seven Black players and UCLA's six Black players being the most in Rose Bowl history.

Daly, obviously, was partial to Daugherty. He also wasn't sympathetic to Bryant dragging his feet on integration in a Jim Crow state despite the passage of the 1964 and 1965 Civil Rights Acts. But Daly's respect for Daugherty doesn't negate the veracity of his account of breakfast with Duffy and the Bear.

Jeffrey Marx, a Pulitzer Prize-winning writer and *New York Times*-bestselling author, describes Daly as a man "with a huge heart." They met after Daly had moved on to a job as the Baltimore Colts equipment manager. Marx spent his summers in high school working for Daly at the Colts' training camps.

"Marty is a great guy," Marx said. "I don't know about the Michigan State time period, but I know the person he is and what he did to help out so many other kids. He helped us grow with exposure to people and experiences. Marty was a likable, lovable guy who cares about other people."

Bryant continued to feed his fan base the "poor ol' Bear" charge of reverse racism with the release of his 1974 book, *Bear: The Hard Life & Good Times of Alabama's Coach Bryant*. The complaint in Alabama was the football team paid a price for the TV images of Alabama police commissioner Bull Connor turning fire hoses and police dogs on peaceful civil rights protesters in May 1963.

Bryant explained he thought he could influence the 1966 voters by having a Black man dressed in an "Alabama wardrobe" and having him to stand next to the Bear for scenes to be captured on TV shots:

"I knew they were going to put the camera on me sooner or later, I wanted them to see the Black face over that Alabama shirt. I'm told they had us on about 20 times that day, and he was right here next to me every time. We shut out Auburn 31-0. When the final votes were in the next week, Notre Dame still won the national championship."

The comment, published in 1974, provides insight on how little Bryant understood or cared about the civil rights movement. Did a lesson of civics ever occur to him? Or, if it was about public relations, wouldn't recruiting a Black player be more effective than having a Black man stand next to him for the benefit of TV images?

Apparently not. Alabama's varsity remained all-white until 1971.

The argument rings hollow for other reasons. In 1964, Alabama was voted the No. 1 team in the nation by Associated Press (writers) and United Press International (coaches, now USA Today). In 1965, AP voted Alabama No. 1, although UPI named Michigan State No. 1.

But historical memory is controlled by who captures the narrative.

ENTER THE ECHO CHAMBER

Keith Dunnavant, who we met in a previous chapter, picked up where Bryant left off with the reverse racism charge. Dunnavant successfully floated the conspiracy narrative in his 2006 book, *The Missing Rings: How Bear Bryant and the 1966 Alabama Crimson Tide Were Denied College Football's Most Elusive Prize*.

In addition, Dunnavant also received platforms to spread the narrative in films such as HBO's *Breaking the Huddle*, 2008; Showtime's *Against the Tide*, 2013; and ESPN's film on college football integration, 2019.

In the Showtime film, Dunnavant says, "In 1966, Alabama was the only undefeated, untied team in the country and yet they finished a controversial third. It's the only time in college football history the two-time defending national champion has gone perfect and not been awarded the national title."

Dunnavant's claim making the film's final cut was an example of cavalier editing. The "two-time" claim is overstated, as Alabama split its 1964 and 1965 titles. Here were the champions named by of the four NCAA-sanctioned organizations in the era of poll voting over the three-year stretch of 1964, 1965 and 1966:

- **1964**: Alabama (10-1-0) won the AP and UPI titles. Arkansas (11-0-0), another all-white team, claimed the FWAA title. Notre Dame (9-1-0) won the NFF crown.
- **1965**: Michigan State (10-1-0) claimed the UPI and NFF championships outright and shared the FWAA with Alabama. The Crimson Tide's lone singular title was AP.
- **1966**: Notre Dame (9-0-1) won the AP, UPI, FWAA and shared an NFF co-title with Michigan State (9-0-1).

A simple formula can be used to rank the title teams: one point for each organization title equaling a total of 12. Notre Dame finished with 4.5 points, Alabama 3.5, Michigan State 3.0 and Arkansas 1.0.

When the combined records represented by each school's two championship seasons in the three-year span were added together, the win-loss totals and percentages:

- Michigan State: 10-1-0 plus 9-0-1 = 19-1-1, 90.4 percent.
- Notre Dame: 9-1-0 plus 9-0-1 = 18-1-1, 90.0 percent.
- Alabama: 10-1-0 plus 9-1-1 = 19-2-1, 86.3 percent.

Alabama wasn't the clear-cut "two-time" champions that Bryant's apologists have successfully promulgated. And don't try and tell Oklahoma's Barry Switzer, a College Football Hall of Fame coach who was an Arkansas assistant in 1964, the Razorbacks weren't the best team in the nation.

And here's another way Alabama apologists fail to understand the truth has been shaded.

In the 1964 season, Alabama finished the regular season ranked No. 1 by the AP and UPI polls, but the Crimson Tide lost to No. 5 Texas in the Orange Bowl. However, bowl games were traditionally treated as rewards and national champions were crowned by votes at the end of the regular season.

If there had been a postseason vote in 1964, Alabama (10-1-0) likely would have been knocked from its No. 1 perch in AP and UPI and replaced by either No. 2 Arkansas (11-0-0), which defeated Nebraska in the Cotton Bowl, or Notre Dame (9-1-0).

In 1965, the AP experimented one year with post-bowl vote that delivered Alabama a split title. Otherwise, Alabama finished No. 4 in the regular season.

The regular season ended with No. 1 Michigan State, No. 2 Arkansas, No. 3 Nebraska and No. 4 Alabama. But in the bowl games, Michigan State lost to No. 5 UCLA in the Rose Bowl; Arkansas lost to unranked LSU in the Sugar Bowl; and Nebraska lost to Alabama in the Orange Bowl. With Michigan State, Arkansas and Nebraska losing, Alabama jumped to No. 1.

Without the post-bowl vote experiment, Michigan State sweeps the AP, UPI, FWAA and NFF titles. It's hypocritical of Bryant's apologists to claim the 1964 national title without mentioning its bowl game loss and then turn around and own the 1965 crown as a result of Michigan State's bowl loss.

Dunnvant's claim that Alabama was the team of the decade also has holes in it. He based it on Alabama winning three national titles, but Alabama's 1961 crown was split with Ohio State. The only schools winning undisputed 1960s national title were USC and Texas. And they both did it twice—the Trojans (1962, 1967) and Longhorns (1963, 1969).

Nevertheless, the misleading "two-time champion" narrative spread through an age-old media flaw of following each other. Bryant's apologists captured the narrative. CBS football analyst Charles Davis fell victim when he echoed Dunnavant in a 2019 ESPN film while he was still working for Fox.

"Even with the tie, Notre Dame and Michigan State both finished ahead of undefeated Alabama in the final rankings," Davis said. "Alabama had been No. 1 the last two years, in 1964 and 1965."

Did Davis know those Alabama's titles were both split?

In the ESPN film on recruiting, another Davis quote shows how little he knows about Daugherty's true legacy and how far integration had progressed in the 1960s.

"For Duffy Daugherty," he says, "it wasn't just about being progressive and being Abraham Lincoln, Duffy was about winning football games."

A statement Daugherty only recruited Black players to win games is hypocritical when the same film praises Bear Bryant for recruiting Black athletes only because he had fallen behind the times and needed to win games in the 1970s.

Daugherty ignored unwritten quotas while taking chances on Black athletes. Other schools limited their Black athlete recruits to well-known stars, the equivalent of a 5-star recruit in today's vernacular. Only 10 of Daugherty's 44 Southern recruits were All-American players or All-Big Ten picks. The graduation rate for his 44 Southern recruits was 68 percent.

Skin color was only one difference between the 1966 Alabama and Michigan State rosters.

Bryant had preferred small, quick teams that were necessary in the single-platoon 1950s era of athletes playing 60 minutes, but he was slow to adapt to modern football. In 1964, the NCAA approved two-platoon football. The change opened the door to bigger athletes who didn't have to play 60 minutes on both sides of the ball.

Bryant got away with it in the early 1960s as long as he continued to play only all-white opponents without traveling above the Mason-Dixon Line. But the game and its size of players was quickly passing him by.

In 1966, Alabama's All-American offensive tackle was Cecil Dowdy, a 6-foot-1, 202-pounder taken in the 1967 NFL draft's ninth round by the Cleveland Browns (he lasted only one season with the Browns, and one with the Los Angeles Rams). By contrast, the 1966 Spartans lined up defensive end Bubba Smith (6-7, 285) and rover/linebacker George Webster (6-5, 230).

Who was going to block Smith and Webster? Bryant's concern about Daugherty's Spartans having bigger and faster players apparently was on his mind.

Similarly, Notre Dame featured defensive tackle Alan Page (6-4, 245), and linebacker Jim Lynch (6-1, 235), the Maxwell Award winner.

Again, who was going to block Page and Lynch?

Smith, Webster, Page and Lynch are in the College Football Hall of Fame. Page also is a Pro Football Hall of Famer. Long-time NFL writers say Smith and Webster missed the Pro Football Hall only because of knee injuries.

Michigan State's Jerry West, an All-American offensive tackle in 1966, doesn't see how Alabama's offensive line could have handled the Spartans or the Irish.

"I was a 218-pounder, and I didn't want to block Bubba," West said. "Alabama's 202-pounders wouldn't have wanted to block him, either. Bubba, you had to go low to block; you couldn't keep up with him strength-wise. George was impossible to block. You just hoped you could hit him."

Alabama's three-man defensive line was smaller than Michigan State's offensive backfield. The Crimson Tide's linemen: Johnny Sullivan (6-0, 191), Louis Thompson (6-2, 213) and Richard Cole (6-2, 204). The Spartans' backs: Clinton Jones (6-0, 206), Bob Apisa (6-0, 214) and Dwight Lee (6-2, 202).

Lodewyk Zwarensteyn—Lody to his friends—tells a story of Bryant rejecting an offer from Michigan State athletic director Biggie Munn to play a home-and-home series.

Zwarensteyn is a Michigan State graduate who has remained active in the Michigan State's Alumni Association at the national level and his local club, MSU Club of West Michigan. He is retired from an executive career spanning five decades with Alliance for Health, a nonprofit based in Grand Rapids, Michigan. His tenure included serving as president of the company for two decades.

But in the fall of 1966, Zwarensteyn was a Michigan State sophomore lounging around the living room of the Phi Kappa Sigma House across the street from the East Lansing campus. As usual, on a typical early evening after dinner they put off studying. Naturally, they talked football.

Michigan State, after all, was atop the college football world. At midseason, the defending national champion Spartans were ranked No. 1 and marching toward the Game of the Century against Notre Dame.

Such was the backdrop to Phi Kappa Sigma banter on the 1966 evening when, unexpectedly, a figure loomed large in the doorway.

It was Clarence "Biggie" Munn. His Jenison Field House office wasn't far from the Phi Kappa Sigma house, but Munn didn't arrive as Dean Wormer delivering to Animal House a double-secret probation message.

"He just wanted to shoot the breeze as a fraternity brother," Lody said. "Biggie was a regular guy. We welcomed him anytime."

Munn had been a Phi Kappa Sigma member at Minnesota, where he earned All-American football honors and the 1931 Big Ten MVP award while starring on the track and field team. But in 1966 he was 58 years old. What was he doing at a frat house? Well, they say old football coaches don't know what to do with their time.

"As AD, he liked to talk about all of our teams," Lody said. "We were also winning national titles in hockey (1966), wrestling (1967) and soccer (1967 and 1968)."

On that 1966 evening—in an age long before videotape, social media and sports talk shows igniting rumors into California wildfires—Biggie accused the Bear of ducking Duffy's Spartans.

"He opened up about Bear Bryant," Lody recalled. "Biggie tried to get Alabama on our schedule. Biggie wanted a home-and-home series, making it lucrative. He said he offered Bryant a disproportionate share of the home gate if Alabama would play us in East Lansing.

"Ostensibly, Bryant said he couldn't play us because we had Black players. Biggie was just talking to us matter of fact—from an athletic director's point of view."

Normally, someone from outside Michigan State's athletic office telling a story about Bryant ducking the Spartans isn't enough to make it to print. But at the same time, understand there has been nothing normal about the cottage industry of Bear Bryant mythology profiting the past 30 years at the expense of the true 1960s pioneers. Those men toiled to clear the path that made it possible to play the 1970 USC-Alabama game without incident.

Munn's claim is especially intriguing when juxtaposed with an unsubstantiated claim Keith Dunnavant made in the 2008 HBO film, *Breaking the Huddle*. Dunnavant stated Bryant was unable to find a willing 1960s opponent from above the Mason-Dixon Line. The claim is aired without challenge.

Boston College was the school Dunnavant cited in the HBO film, although there has been no supporting evidence to emerge. Boston College was a curious choice to use considering both the Eagles' lack of a football pedigree and Bryant's wide span of friends to call upon in the coaching fraternity—as the claim also overlooked Bryant and Daugherty were good friends.

A Munn effort to schedule Alabama belies the 1970 USC-Alabama narrative that Bryant was forced to turn to his good friend, USC coach John McKay. The dubious narrative claims Bryant couldn't find a team to travel to the South.

At least in 1966, Bryant was avoiding, not seeking, a game with a fully integrated roster.

CHAPTER 28
THE TIME COVER THAT LAUNCHED A THOUSAND BEAR BRYANT MYTHS

FACT: In a fawning 5,100-word *Time* Magazine cover piece on Bear Bryant published Sept. 29, 1980, there is not a single word about the 1970 USC-Alabama game impacting college football integration. The reason? The myths on the 1970 USC-Alabama game weren't crafted and spread until the 1990s.

"They wouldn't come on the field. It took quite a while before they agreed to play the game." —Ray Uribe, a friend of Michigan State Black player Horace Smith, on Kentucky's Bear Bryant-led team refusing taking the field against Smith in a 1947 game.

The *Time* Magazine photographer, positioned behind a clear glass writing board, snapped frames as Alabama coach Paul "Bear" Bryant drew X's and O's. The Southern football god, deified with the ability to walk on water, was captured on film wearing his iconic houndstooth hat.

Neil Leifer's photo graced the cover of *Time* Magazine's Sept. 29, 1980 issue. The headline with bold type: "**SUPERCOACH**."

The camera saw through the glass board to expose the wrinkles in Bryant's face that added a decade to his then-hard-living age of 67, but the *Time* writer, B.J. Phillips—like so many print and electronic media members before and continuing into the 21st century—never saw through Bryant's cosmeticized past on segregation.

Bryant was profiled as a man who lived life as a 19th-century Jim Crow Southerner, yet magnanimously adapted to the social issue of the 20th century. *Time's* misleading premise perpetuated an age-old media flaw. One story from a national outlet gathers attention. Other writers regurgitate the storyline.

Time's reflective piece on Bryant's storied career appeared two seasons prior to his last game in the Liberty Bowl, Dec. 29, 1982, and his death, Jan. 26, 1983. The story focused on the wins and overlooked a grim record on college football integration. Bryant dragged his feet with all-white teams until 1971—eight years after his campus desegregated and considerably slower than his Southern colleagues.

By 1969, six of the 10 Southeastern Conference members had signed a Black recruit ahead of Bryant, who didn't sign his first Black player, Wilbur Jackson, until 1970. Kentucky (1966), Tennessee (1967), Florida (1967), Auburn (1969), Mississippi State (1969) and Vanderbilt (1969) had signed Black athletes and dressed them in a varsity game ahead of Bryant.

By 1970, when USC arrived at Legion Field in Birmingham, 28 of 31 (90 percent) major schools in the South—including Alabama—had signed a Black athlete. That included all nine Southwest Conference schools, all eight Atlantic Coast Conference schools, Alabama as the seventh of 10 SEC schools, and four schools that were independents at the time: Miami, Florida State, Virginia Tech and Georgia Tech.

Those facts were overlooked decades later as the 1970 USC-Alabama game was embellished and aggrandized into a false narrative as a turning point for college football integration. With Virginia, Clemson and South Carolina joining Alabama by recruiting their first Black player by 1970, college football integration was a fait accompli.

Change was well down the track prior to USC playing Alabama on Sept. 12, 1970 at Legion Field in Birmingham. That explains why there was no overnight reaction to the game in the media. By the 1970, the only three major conference Southern schools without a Black recruit were Georgia, LSU, and Mississippi. They fell in line by 1972.

The myths also overlook an important game in the 1969 season, when integrated Tennessee routed Alabama 41-14 at Legion Field to provide Alabama's bigoted fans their first eye-opener. All-American linebacker Jackie Walker, an African-American, sparked the rout with an early interception return.

The coaches that beat Bryant to joining the 20th century included a progeny, Texas A&M's Gene Stallings, who signed an African-American player two years ahead of his old boss, in 1968. This was the same Gene Stallings who said in 1965 he didn't believe Black and white athletes could get along in a locker room. His comment came in response to Southwest Conference rival Southern Methodist signing its first Black player in 1965, Jerry LeVias.

Bryant remained in his shell while Auburn coach Ralph "Shug" Jordan—his coaching buddy and instate rival—stuck out his neck. Jordan signed James Owens as a Southern pioneer in 1969. Nobody fired Jordan for defying Jim Crow.

The media, particularly in the South, was negligent in not criticizing Bryant recruiting Black players at a time when Jordan and other coaches were ahead of Bryant on the issue of their times.

In the USC-indulgent 2013 Showtime film—narrated by USC alumnus/Hollywood star Tom Selleck for a veneer of credibility—Bryant's negligence was ignored. The film stuck to the rote narrative. Selleck erroneously stated in his narration, "It wasn't as if Bryant and Alabama stood alone. Nearly all of the SEC schools were equally slow to integrate."

No, Bryant *was* almost alone.

His place was glaringly on the opposite side of the 77 percent of coaches on the right side of history.

BEAR BRYANT'S SELF-PROMOTING BRANCH RICKEY CLAIM

Bryant hagiography focuses on his Alabama career (1958-82), but *Time* gave him latitude to reach back to his days coaching at Kentucky in 1946-53. Bryant offered a self-promoting and deceptive quote on his integration attitudes.

"I wanted to be the Branch Rickey of football when I was at Kentucky," says Bryant.

It was a disingenuous comment. Rickey was the Brooklyn Dodgers general manager who defied Major League Baseball, signing Jackie Robinson in 1947 to break the color line. Bryant never defied anyone. Howell Raines, an Alabama alumnus and former executive editor of *The New York Times*, said in the 2013 Showtime's documentary he can't remember Bryant ever speaking up on segregation. Raines faulted him for his reticence.

If Bryant was a victim of having his hands tied at Kentucky, why wasn't he Branch Rickey at Texas A&M (1954-57)? The Supreme Court ruled on *Brown v. Board of Education of Topeka* to end segregated schools in 1954. He had the law of the land on his side by then.

Why wasn't he Branch Rickey at any time his first 13 seasons at Alabama (1958-70)? President Lyndon B. Johnson signed the 1964 and 1965 Civil Rights Acts. An Alabama Black male could look forward to voting but still couldn't play for Bryant.

Bryant's apologists—and they are Roman legions—blame Alabama racist Gov. George Wallace, but Wallace was out of office by Jan. 17, 1967. Bryant's fall 1967, 1968 and 1969 recruiting classes were all-white. And when he did add Wilbur Jackson as his first Black recruit in 1970, Jackson endured his pioneering path as the *only* Black recruit.

Bryant's *Time* quote also ignored the gentleman's agreement requiring northern schools to bench their Black athletes when they played a segregated Southern opponent. Bryant and the gentleman's agreement collided with progress when Kentucky and Michigan State met twice in a home-and-home series, 1946 and 1947.

Michigan State, shamefully, left behind Horace Smith, an African-American backup halfback, when coach Charlie Bachman took the Spartans to Kentucky for a Nov. 2, 1946 game in Lexington. When speculation mounted over Smith's status for Kentucky's return game on Oct. 25, 1947 in East Lansing, Bryant, at best, remained silent.

At worst, Bryant may have staged a small sideline protest over Smith's presence in uniform.

DID BEAR BRYANT PROTEST HORACE SMITH?

Ray Uribe, Smith's long-time friend, claimed Bryant's Wildcats delayed taking the field for the 1947 game with Smith in uniform. Uribe was quoted upon Smith's death in an Oct. 6, 2006 obituary by Mike Pryson in their hometown Michigan newspaper, the *Jackson Citizen-Patriot*. Uribe, who died in 2013, cited Smith's anguish over the 1946 and 1947 games.

Ray Uribe of Jackson remembers a Saturday in October 1947 when the University of Kentucky football team staged a protest on the sidelines at Michigan State University.

That protest was over Spartans' halfback Horace Smith of Jackson, the team's only black player.

"They wouldn't come on the field," said Uribe, a friend of Smith's in high school and college. *"It took quite a while before they agreed to play the game."*

The facts of that afternoon remain unclear for the simple reason the mainstream media avoided race in sports stories. Chris Lamb, as we learned in prior chapters, has extensively covered the phenomenon.

"This was standard operating procedure in the mainstream press," Lamb said. "This was true in both the South and the North. It was worse in the South where newspapers had policies against publishing photographs of Blacks. Northern sportswriters gave their support for segregation by remaining silent on the issue. Baseball or society could not have maintained the color line as long as it did without what one Black sportswriter called, 'The Conspiracy of Silence.'"

The disgraceful custom left the first draft of history of the Kentucky-Michigan State games to be written by the *Michigan Chronicle*, a Black weekly newspaper based in Detroit. To understand the story's moving parts and many names spanning two seasons requires chronologically digging into the *Chronicle* stories on microfilm.

MICHIGAN STATE'S OWN FAILURES

In the 1946 season's third game, Horace Smith was withheld from playing against Mississippi State on Oct. 12, 1946 at Macklin Field (renamed Spartan Stadium in 1957). Michigan State officials explained Smith was out with bruised ribs. The *Chronicle*, seeking further comment on Smith's injury, wrote the university was "unavailable for a statement."

The Spartans' next game was Oct. 19, 1946 at Penn State, a 19-13 victory. The *Chronicle* noted Smith played "brilliantly." The Michigan State box score shows Smith ran three times for a net 20 yards, completed his only pass attempt for 32 yards (halfbacks often threw in the 1940s offenses) and caught two balls for minus-3 yards.

On Oct. 26, Smith again played in an 18-7 loss to Cincinnati at home.

November 2 was the ill-fated trip to Kentucky, a 39-14 Wildcats romp. Horace Smith was left at home.

On Nov. 9, Smith was back in the lineup when the Spartans traveled to No. 11-ranked Michigan. Smith accounted for the Spartans' only score in a 55-7 loss. He threw a touchdown pass to Frank Waters (yes, the same Frank "Muddy" Waters who was Michigan State's head coach, 1980-82).

In the 1946 season's final three games, Smith played in wins over Marquette, Maryland and Washington State. Smith's final numbers in a 5-5 season were 13 carries for 55 yards, 2-of-3 passing for 104 yards and one touchdown and four receptions for 23 yards. He returned five kickoffs for 110 yards.

The season also ended with Bachman resigning, ending his 13-year tenure.

When Michigan State hired Clarence "Biggie" Munn as replacement, *Chronicle* sports editor Bill Matney wrote activists took a wait-and-see approach. Bachman had a reputation for not wanting Black players on his team, but Munn had played with Black athletes at Minnesota (1929-31) and he had coached and faced Black athletes as both a Michigan assistant (1938-45) and Syracuse head coach (1946).

Biggie Munn with HB Horace Smith, No. 18. *Courtesy Michigan State University.*

Additionally, the gentleman's agreement was crumbling. Penn State canceled a Nov. 29, 1946 trip to Miami rather than leave behind its Black players. Nevada did the same for a Nov. 16, 1946 contest scheduled at Mississippi State. All-white Maryland played at Michigan State on Nov. 23, 1946 without holding the Spartans to the racist policy.

But in the 1947 season's second game, Munn disappointed.

Smith did not play in the Spartans' 7-0 win over Mississippi State on Oct. 4, 1947 at Macklin Field. The *Chronicle* asked Michigan Gov. Kim Sigler to investigate Michigan State for discriminatory practices. The Detroit branch of the NAACP also called for an investigation.

The next two weeks, Smith played in wins at Washington State, 21-7, and at home over Iowa State, 20-0.

BEAR BRYANT FUMBLED HIS BRANCH RICKEY MOMENT

As the Oct. 25, 1947 Kentucky-Michigan State game loomed, *Chronicle* sports editor Matney asked Kentucky athletic director Bernie Shively if the Wildcats expected Michigan State to again abide by the gentleman's agreement.

"No comment," Shively said.

Here's where Bryant's silence failed to back up his dubious 1980 *Time* quote. As gameday approached, Bryant had a Branch Rickey opportunity served to him on a silver platter. He could have easily punted the controversy back to the Spartans.

He knew Michigan State was under pressure to play Smith. If Smith didn't play, Bryant could have said he wasn't to blame. Ask Michigan State what happened.

Matney's preview article reflected the scrutiny on the Spartans. Matney quoted former Michigan State halfback Bob McCrary (1933-34), an African American, who had been held out of a 1934 game against Texas A&M played in San Antonio.

But instead of blaming Munn for Smith's 1947 Mississippi State benching, McCrary pointed to Lloyd C. Emmons, a faculty representative and Athletics Board Director for whom Emmons Hall was later named. Into the 1960s, such academic roles on campuses typically carried more weight than the athletic director or coaches.

On gameday, a record crowd of 26,997 turned out to see the Spartans play No. 14-ranked Kentucky at then-26,000-seat Macklin Field. The Wildcats were led by George Blanda, the future Pro Football Hall of Fame quarterback and kicker.

The Horace Smith suspense ended when Munn called his backup halfback over to him to relay a play to the huddle. Smith finished the game with two carries for 11 yards and one incomplete pass, although in a four-back offense he could have been on the field for many more snaps as a blocker.

Kentucky won the contest, 7-6, thanks to Blanda kicking the decisive PAT. Michigan State trailed 7-0 when George Guerre, the team's leading rusher, scored on a 9-yard run, but the extra point was blocked.

Smith was mentioned in the *Chicago Tribune* game story, but only because he was erroneously cited for throwing an interception in the end zone. The Kentucky-Michigan State box score shows quarterback George Smith threw the interception. The *Tribune* story otherwise offered no context to Horace Smith's presence—or race—on the field.

Adding context to Bryant's failed Rickey moment: the 1947 Kentucky-Michigan State game took place shortly after the first integrated World Series concluded with the Dodgers taking the New York Yankees to seven games before falling. You couldn't pick up a sports page without reading about Jackie Robinson transforming history through sports.

Why wasn't Bryant inspired at the very least to speak up on Horace Smith's behalf?

A better Bryant/baseball comparison than Rickey was Tom Yawkey, the Boston Red Sox owner. Boston was the last MLB franchise to integrate, in 1959. Bryant was one of the last coaches to provide to learn civics lessons applied to college football, too.

MICHIGAN CHRONICLE FACED DOWN RACISM

The *Chronicle*'s next issue, Nov. 1, 1947, trumpeted the paper's role with this headline: "**Chronicle Cracks Bias on MSC Football 11**."

Matney added the *Chronicle* stayed on the story despite criticism from Black readers as well as the white public. He expressed dismay with Black readers for not understanding the importance of pressuring Michigan State to abandon the gentleman's agreement.

Matney made no mention of the game starting late due to a Kentucky protest. If it happened and he didn't write it, he may have been focused on patting himself on the back for facing down the Spartans.

Michigan State bounced back from the Kentucky loss to win their final four games, defeating Marquette, Santa Clara, Temple and Hawaii. The Spartans finished 7-2 in Munn's first season.

Smith led the 1947 team in scoring with 30 points on five touchdowns, although he was only fourth in rushing with 39 carries for 172 yards. Smith also completed one of two passes for zero yards, caught two balls for 57 with a TD, returned three punts for 125 and one kickoff for 17.

Smith gained a place in Michigan State football history as the first Black football player to face a segregated Southern opponent, although it must be noted the school has failed to recognize him for his achievement overcoming adversity. He belongs alongside Gideon Smith, Michigan State's first Black football player from 1913 to 1915, and Michigan State's coach Duffy Daugherty's 1960s teams that were college football's first fully integrated rosters.

Oregon State Emeritus Professor Michael Oriard, a college football scholar and former Notre Dame and NFL player, singled out Michigan State in a 2019 ESPN film on "Integration" that was part of a college football 150th anniversary series.

"The fact that Gideon Smith started at Michigan State in 1913," he says, "may be the most significant because as the first Black player at Michigan State, he's in a way the pioneer for the really astonishingly and exceptionally integrated Michigan State teams of in the 1950s and 1960s."

However, Oriard's insight aside, the overall theme of the 2019 ESPN film remained celebrating Bryant as a leader. And there was no mention of Bryant's history involving Horace Smith.

At best, Bryant was silent. At worst he protested, although silence can be considered an equal sin.

SECOND DECEPTION

Bear Bryant, in addition to his Rickey comment, made a second deceptive quote in the *Time* 1980 article about his Kentucky coaching days, 1946-53. He claimed if he couldn't recruit Black players, he'd find a home for them.

"They told me no. So for years, I used to recommend all these great Black players to schools up North."

There are no names to validate Bryant's claim. None. That's considerably fewer than "all these great Black players."

The fiction Bryant steered players to Michigan State has been another example of an age-old media flaw. Print and electronic reporters read what someone else wrote about Bryant sending players and took turns spreading the legend of Bear Bryant as a benevolent segregationist. They didn't check the facts.

A 2013 ESPN article erroneously stated Bryant sent Charlie Thornhill to Daugherty, N.C. State coach Earle Edwards sent Jimmy Raye to Daugherty and Clemson coach Frank Howard sent Webster to Daugherty. Thornhill was committed to Michigan State assistant coach Vince Carillot before Thornhill met Bryant at a Roanoke football awards banquet. Raye was recruited by former Michigan State assistant coach Cal Stoll, but it took Carillot to convince Daugherty to offer Raye a scholarship. Webster's high-school coach, William Roberts, contacted Michigan State.

Bryant may have exploited an old joke told by Daugherty, the late College Football Hall of Fame coach who died in 1987. Daugherty loved telling a good yarn, and he was good friends with Bryant. Daugherty had often joked he "traded" Joe Namath, a white quarterback from Beaver Falls, Pennsylvania, in 1961, for Charlie Thornhill, a Black linebacker from Roanoke, Virginia, in 1963.

The story, though, has been pierced with enough holes to sink the Titanic.

Daugherty wanted Namath, but the school's admission office informed him early in the recruiting process there was no way Namath's poor academic record could gain admission. The storyline, as the myth has been told, continued with Daugherty informing Bryant that Namath was available. In return, Bryant directed Thornhill to Daugherty.

These are the facts from the horses' mouths:

- In Namath's 2012 HBO biography, he says he tried to gain admission to Maryland over the summer but when he failed, Maryland coach Tom Nugent informed Bryant. The Alabama coach, in his 1974 book, *Bear*, with John Underwood, also says Nugent informed him. Neither Namath or Bryant mentioned a role played by Daugherty.
- Thornhill's family and Carillot credited Roanoke white sportswriter Bob McLelland for tipping off the Spartans. Thornhill was the first Black player named the Roanoke area's "Back of the Year," thanks to McLelland's lobbying. The Hotel Roanoke waived its segregation policy to allow Thornhill and his family to attend the Jan. 14, 1963 awards banquet. Carillot said he received an unsolicited phone call from McLelland.

The myth contends Bryant called Daugherty after he met Thornhill at the banquet, but there are four iceberg collisions with that account.

First, Thornhill arrived at the banquet having already committed to Michigan State. It was printed in the Roanoke paper.

Second, Carillot added he had to convince Daugherty to offer Thornhill a scholarship. Daugherty had doubts about Thornhill's 5-foot-9 height, but Carillot had seen Thornhill's film. He also told Daugherty that Thornhill was built like an Olympic weight lifter without lifting weights.

Third, William "Nay" Thornhill, Charlie's younger brother, said Bryant's exchange with Charlie at the awards banquet was limited to Bryant telling Charlie that Daugherty was a good man and he'd enjoy playing for him.

Fourth, Charlie, who died in 2006, never spoke of Bryant influencing his commitment, according to his son, Kaleb Thornhill, a former Michigan State linebacker, co-founder of APEX Academy and former NFL front-office executive.

It seems natural if a man as legendary as Bear Bryant had changed the trajectory of your life, you'd tell a few people about it. Well, Charlie did discuss a man playing such a role—Bob McLelland.

All three Thornhill brothers—Waverly, Charlie and Nay—attended McLelland's funeral.

SPORTS ILLUSTRATED JOINED THE UNATTRIBUTED

Nevertheless, the Bryant "trade" anecdote continues to be regurgitated, including by *Sports Illustrated*. The venerable magazine, without attribution, included the Namath/Thornhill trade fiction in a Dec. 27, 2004 issue. Namath was among several vignettes on athletes under the headline, "**The Road Not Taken**."

The *SI* story included an unattributed quote that Bryant called Thornhill *after* the Jan. 14, 1963 banquet to inform him to expect airplane tickets in the mail to take a recruiting trip to Michigan State. However, Clifton Roaf, Daugherty's first Underground Railroad passenger in 1959 out of Pine Bluff, Arkansas, said he hosted Thornhill on a December 1962 campus recruiting trip.

Years later, there was a claim from Bryant he sent a Black player to Johnny Majors at Iowa State, but Majors coached at Iowa State from 1968 to 1972.

The Namath portion of the "trade" also flies in the face of another Bryant claim.

In a 1967 interview on film that the Showtime documentary included, Bryant said he couldn't find Black athletes academically and athletically qualified to play for him. At the end of the 1967 spring football, he had cut five walk-on African-American players.

Here was another missed moment by a man who claimed he wanted to be the Branch Rickey of football.

Imagine the broader statement of opportunity in a segregated state that Bryant could have made by keeping one of the Black players. Some people might cry affirmative action, but in those days, Bryant had 140-some players on his roster. He exploited NCAA rules with unlimited scholarships by signing players simply so they wouldn't play for Auburn or Mississippi.

With 140-some players on Alabama's rosters, are we to believe there was a clear separation between the worst of those 140 white players and the best of the five Black players? Why couldn't Bryant carry 141 players? That's down to the seventh team. What's the difference?

Bryant's specious academic explanation for his all-white roster also begs an answer on how he could (supposedly) send a qualified Black athlete to Michigan State, the school that rejected Namath's academic record, yet Namath was admitted overnight at Alabama.

Daugherty, always looking to deliver a punch line, has been exploited for another Bryant joke. In 1978, Daugherty was quoted at Bryant's 65th birthday party stating he got out of coaching once Bryant began recruiting Black athletes.

That doesn't add up.

Daugherty's final recruiting class, in 1972, included six Black athletes from Southern high schools.

Daugherty's problem was that among the six, he didn't find another College Football Hall of Famer. However, the 1972 class did include Otto Smith of Columbia, South Carolina, a two-time All-Big Ten player (1974 and 1976). Smith was first team in 1974, the year the Spartans upset No. 1-ranked Ohio State and Heisman Trophy winner Archie Griffin.

Another one of the six was Tyrone Willingham of Jacksonville, North Carolina. He entered coaching as a Michigan State graduate assistant and went on to a pioneering career as a Black head coach at Stanford, Notre Dame and Washington.

THE TIME COVER STORY IRONY

The 1980 *Time* story, when dusted off, ironically presented another instructional lesson on the birth of Bear Bryant mythology. Something was *missing* from the article.

In the 5,100-word *Time* opus, there was not a single word about the 1970 USC-Alabama game. Nothing about Bryant escorting USC fullback Sam Cunningham, an African-American, into the locker room. The myth contends Bryant wanted to show his players what a "football player looked like." The scene proved fictional when Cunningham admitted in 2003 it never happened.

There was no *Time* summary in 1980 of how the crafty Bryant—as the false narrative is told—scheduled USC as a game "to lose." The myth's 1990s narrative was Bryant wanted a loss to convince his bigoted fans it was time to grant the most powerful coach in the South—who essentially had no boss—permission to recruit Black athletes.

Bryant's apologists continue to point to the 1970 USC-Alabama game as the crowning moment of The Bear's career. So, how can there not be a single word in a *Time* story meant to praise him as a leader?

Time Magazine long has been a journalistic icon. Omitting the 1970 game and Cunningham locker-room parade would be akin to telling Martin Luther King's life story without mentioning his "I Have a Dream" speech.

But *Time* didn't commit a journalistic fumble for a simple reason. A 1980 story can't include a narrative that had yet to be manufactured at the time B.J. Phillips wrote the reflective piece.

The Bryant-Cunningham myth was crafted in the late 1980s in a small USC/Los Angeles circle. It began to leak out and spread wider in the 1990s. USC author Steven Travers, who may be the only honest man in the 1970 USC-Alabama myths saga, lays out that timeline to the myth's birth in his 2007 book, *One Night, Two Teams*.

Why so many films and regurgitated print versions of the 1970 USC-Alabama game ignore what Travers wrote has been yet another media failing.

Once the myth spread, the reason it worked was people heard it played to a 1990s sports media soundtrack. They imagined America talking about the game on Sunday morning cable TV shows. And sports talk radio hosts celebrating Bryant daily for his genius.

But that's not what happened.

There was no next-day buzz. The Saturday night game wasn't on TV. Race wasn't mentioned in game stories. There was no cable TV in 1970 to spread a nonexistent buzz. The modern sports talk radio genre of the 1990s wasn't around in 1970.

Cunningham's national profile the remainder of the 1970 season was simply as a promising sophomore fullback. He gained 135 yards at Alabama, but only 353 in the final 10 games. His season total of 488 didn't warrant a treatment to the All-Pac-8 team.

And the 1970 Trojans weren't a juggernaut. They finished 6-4-1 overall, 3-4 in Pac-8 play and without a bowl bid.

Also, understand the 1980 *Time* piece wasn't alone omitting a nonexistent narrative.

In 1991, Leo Ticheli Productions in Birmingham, Alabama, produced a retrospective documentary on Bryant's life, *The Legacy Lives*. The script was written by Al Browning, who covered Bryant's teams for the *Tuscaloosa News*. Browning, who died in 2002, and Bryant were close friends. When Bryant died in 1983, Browning served as the media liaison for the family.

The indulgent film thoroughly covered Bryant's coaching career, including some ballads. The run time was 1 hour, 42 minutes.

There was not *one word* about the 1970 USC-Alabama game. Nor Cunningham. Or the locker room. Nothing.

A close friend of Bryant wouldn't omit a narrative that portrays The Bear as a crusader. He'd highlight it. But Browning, like *Time*, didn't fumble the Sam Cunningham story.

Browning did, however, omit the fact that Bryant was sued on July 2, 1969 by the Alabama's Afro-American student association for failing to recruit Black athletes. The lawsuit provides another gaping hole in Bryant's deceptive 1980 claim he sent Black athletes northward.

In depositions taken by civil rights attorney U.W. Clemon, Bryant repeated what he had said on film in 1967: that he was unaware of Black athletes qualifying academically and athletically to play for him. Clemon added he was prepared to show, through discovery, Alabama's Black high-school coaches said Bryant had no interest in their players.

But the Bryant lawsuit went away when Alabama suddenly found Wilbur Jackson of Ozark, Alabama, in the 1970 recruiting class.

The myth goes Bryant had been searching for the right player—as if he undertook a Branch Rickey-like search for Jackie Robinson. Those claim overlooks the many Black athletes from the South who would have met Bryant's standards. They were playing above the Mason-Dixon Line or they were pioneers signed by one of the 77 percent of Southern coaches who were more progressive than Bryant.

The more likely explanation: As a junior in 1968, Jackson played at segregated D.A. Smith, a school Bryant didn't recruit. As a senior in 1969, Jackson played at integrated Carroll High, a school on Bryant's path.

Auburn found James Owens when Fairfield High desegregated his senior year in 1968.

A major difference, though, has been Auburn officials admit they failed to properly support Owens as the only Black player on a white campus. The school established the James Owens Courage Award, presented annually to a current or former player who displayed courage in the face of adversity.

Alabama makes no apologies. It celebrates a man who dragged his feet on integration.

FRANK DEFORD GAVE SAM CUNNINGHAM ONE SENTENCE

Time's sister publication, *Sports Illustrated*, also published a Bryant opus at the end of his career, a 7,100-word cover story in the Nov. 23, 1981 edition.

The sportswriter giant Frank Deford, a master of long-form stories, was the author. He gave Cunningham's impact on college football *one* sentence. There was nothing about the wily Bryant scheduling USC as a game to lose. Nothing about the locker room.

"Only after Southern Cal and Sam (Bam) Cunningham ran all over the skinny little white boys in a 1970 game, only when it was evident that the Tide couldn't win any longer lily-white, only then did The Bear learn his civics."

Deford's sentence doesn't celebrate a Bryant awakening. Deford's sentence condemned Bryant for waiting until the 1970s.

On Bryant's lack of leadership, Deford added, "It is consistent that the one knock against him as a coach is that he has never had the faith or the daring to be innovative."

CHAPTER 29
DECONSTRUCTING THE 1970 USC-ALABAMA FICTION

FACT: USC fullback Sam Cunningham admitted in a 2003 interview Alabama coach Bear Bryant never took him into the Alabama locker room to stand on a bench so Alabama's players could see "what a football player looks like."

"Gentleman, this ol' boy, I mean, this man, and his Trojan brothers just ran your slow-motion asses right out of your own house. Raise your heads and open your eyes, this is what a football player looks like."—Dialogue attributed to Bear Bryant in a movie treatment by John Papadakis based on Turning of the Tide, *a 2006 book.*

Dismantling the 1970 USC-Alabama game myths requires a guide to follow the ins and outs, but ultimately it is not a difficult task. There are so few facts to holding together the tale's structure.

There is the final score: USC 42, Alabama 21.

There is the performance posted by USC fullback Sam Cunningham, who ran 12 times for 135 yards and two touchdowns.

That's about it. A foundation built of clay should easily crumble.

However, if that same narrative—false or factual—jumped into college football lore without being vetted by media outlets following each other with a rote story, well, then the legend has the half-life of nuclear waste.

Facts aren't needed to support and spread a myth. And that's how the embellished storyline of USC's integrated team routing all-white-Alabama game on Sept. 12, 1970, at Legion Field in Birmingham passed into the intangible world of myths.

The false narrative starts with unsubstantiated claims Bryant scheduled the game as one to lose. He wanted his all-white team embarrassed by Black athletes to manipulate his bigoted fans into allowing the most powerful coach in the South to recruit Black athletes.

To that end, the storyline includes outright fiction claiming Alabama coach Bryant invited Cunningham, stripped to his football pants, into the locker room. Then he asked him to stand on a bench so his players could see "what a football player looks like." The perceived humor was the linchpin to retelling the myth and propelling it into the college-football lore, despite the resemblance of Cunningham standing on a bench to an antebellum slave auction, did nothing to slow the myth.

The myth grew into a cottage industry of books and films at the expense of the true 1960s pioneers. Three cable networks green-lit films: HBO, *Breaking the Huddle,* 2008; Showtime, *Against the Tide,* 2013; ESPN, College Football 150th anniversary series with an integration episode, 2019; and an ESPN E:60 show on the 50th anniversary of the game, 2020.

The myth grew into a cottage industry of books and films at the expense of the true 1960s pioneers. Some basic points contradict the storyline born two decades after the game was played, but they continue to be repeated 30-some years later.

First, the game was not a transformative moment in terms of college football integration. There was no mention of race in game stories.

Second, the myths were originally crafted in Los Angeles two decades after the game was played. The purpose was to aggrandize USC's poor record on integration until the 1970s. Alabama fans, though, quickly embraced a story that obfuscated Bryant dragging his feet on integration into the 1970s. The fan base of an iconic football program and a legendary coach was a broad base for spreading the myth.

Finally, it's important to understand the myths grew at the expense of the true 1960s pioneers. They have been dispossessed of their place in history. The true 1960s pioneers are the ones who endured abuse, physical and emotional, while challenging racism. They are the pioneers who cleared the path that allowed the 1970 USC-Alabama game to be played on a Saturday night in the Deep South without incident.

THE CORNERSTONE

The first imaginary bricks were placed to portray the game as a transformative moment, but the reality was college football integration in the South was a fait accompli by the time USC arrived.

The 1970 season opened with 33 of the 37 major programs in the South already desegregated, including Alabama. Wilbur Jackson watched the 1970 USC-Alabama game with the Crimson Tide freshmen team in the era before the NCAA permitted freshmen varsity eligibility in 1972.

Bryant, at the end of the line, was summed up by legendary sportswriter Frank Deford in his 1981 *Sports Illustrated* article:

"Given the Bear's surpassing popularity, he had it within his power to assume a burden of leadership. Yet he held back on race and let other—and less entrenched—Southern coaches stick their necks out first."

Not just a couple—there were 33 of them.

College football integration in the South was a done deal whether or not Cunningham ran for 135 yards or 35, scored two touchdowns or fumbled twice. There was no Sam Cunningham-inspired awakening in the South on Sept. 13, 1970.

Game stories the next day didn't cite racial progress. Not the next week, the next month or for years. No lengthy magazine pieces were written hailing Bryant for inviting USC coach John McKay and his integrated team to enlighten a Jim Crow state.

The game was played on a Saturday night without a television audience. Cable sports show were years off into the future. Sports talk radio wasn't an omnipresent 24/7 force as it is these days. There was no postgame buzz.

OUT OF DATE SOUNDTRACK

When the myth was crafted in the 1980s and passed around via word-of-mouth as it spread into the 1990s, the listener imagined the soundtrack of USC's national title teams in 1972, 1974 and 1978. Those 1970s USC teams were models of integration.

The 1970 team was not a model of integration. The school was still shedding its poor integration record dating to the 1930s.

USC, like many schools in those days, followed an unwritten quota of a half-dozen or so Black players into the 1960s. USC's 1967 national championship team with O.J. Simpson featured only seven Black players. The

Trojans' 1962 national title roster had only five Black players. Most of USC's 18 Black players on the 1970 roster had been recruited the previous two years, including Cunningham.

BRYANT WINS BY LOSING

The NCAA approving an 11th game in January 1970 opened the door to the myth Bryant scheduled USC as a game to lose. The theory was Alabama was losing games to opponents with Black athletes, forcing Bryant to give in to integration. The myth then dubiously contends Bryant, the most powerful coach in the South, needed a reason to manipulate his bigoted fans into allowing him to recruit Black players.

No evidence has surfaced over the years to support Bryant plotting such a scheme. In addition to Jackson on the 1970 freshmen team, Bryant had gained a verbal commitment from Bo Matthews, a Black fullback from Huntsville, Alabama, for the 1970 recruiting class. Matthews, though, changed his commitment to sign with Colorado.

Clem Gryska, a long-time Bryant assistant coach who later served the Bryant Museum as an ambassador, has said in multiple interviews, including HBO's 2008 film, his boss never scheduled a game to lose it. Gryska died in 2012.

And Bryant wouldn't have known about Cunningham when he scheduled the game. He played on the freshman team in 1969 and wasn't named the starter in his varsity debut until the week of the game.

The myths portray Cunningham as Syracuse's Ernie Davis, the first Black Heisman Trophy winner in 1961, running roughshod over Alabama. However, in the next 10 games, Cunningham gained only 353 yards with two touchdowns. Cunningham's Alabama performance had more to do with facing a weak defense. He didn't earn All-Pac-8 or All-American honors until his 1972 senior season. And USC was not a juggernaut. The 1970 Trojans finished 6-4-1 with no bowl invitation.

Another premise was Bryant couldn't find an integrated team to play in Alabama, so he convinced McKay, his good friend, to play the game. However, neither coach mentioned such an agreement in their 1974 books, *Bear* and *McKay: A Coach's Life*, nor in interviews later in life.

THE FICTIONAL LOCKER-ROOM SCENE

Pulling out the locker-room brick should collapse the myth for the simple reason the principal character said it never happened—and said it as early as two decades ago.

Cunningham, who died in 2021, debunked the myth in a 2003 story by Neal McCready, a *Mobile Press-Register* sportswriter. McCready's purpose for contacting Cunningham was USC's return to the state to face Auburn in the 2003 season opener.

"I made a lot of phone calls, but I finally talked to him," McCready said. "It was a fascinating conversation. He couldn't have been nicer, but he wasn't comfortable talking about it. When I asked about the post-game, he was almost sheepish. He finally admitted it was a myth. He definitively told me it did not happen."

But McCready's award-worthy work was ignored by the national media. The myth continued to spread.

In a 2006 book, *Turning the Tide*, author Steve Yaeger wrote that John Papadakis, a 1970 USC linebacker, loved to tell the locker-room story. The Los Angeles restauranteur's bon vivant personality kept the myth alive. Papadakis attempted to sell a movie script with laughable dialogue from *Turning the Tide*.

The script has Bryant saying, "Gentleman, this ol' boy, I mean, this man, and his Trojan brothers just ran your slow-motion asses right out of your own house. Raise your heads and open your eyes, this is what a football player looks like."

According to Yeager's book, Papadakis' locker-room scene continued with Bryant instructing Alabama's players to "pass below Cunningham, reach up, shake his hand and congratulate him."

Yaeger's book, which also credits Papadakis and Cunningham, makes it clear Cunningham had denied the myth, yet the overall theme of the book remained one that markets the game and Cunningham's performance as a transformative moment.

In the 2008 HBO film, Cunningham dances around the locker-room question. In the 2013 Showtime film, he made it clear the scene never happened.

"It got started I got taken into the locker room, but I didn't go into the locker room," said Cunningham on camera. "I didn't shake any of their guys' hands and didn't get put up on a pedestal. That kind of surfaced and kept rolling for 30-some years."

Those words were straight from the thoroughbred's mouth.

Note Cunningham stated "30-some years." That dates the myth to the 1980s—not the night of the 1970 game. He seemed to understand the myth's origins decades after the game.

Alabama quarterback Scott Hunter, who went on to play in the NFL, also was interviewed in the Showtime film. He scoffed at the locker-room myth.

"Coach Bryant would never have brought in a player and embarrassed us or a team," Hunter said. "He never brought Sam Cunningham into our locker room and said this is what a football player looked like. That didn't happen."

With time, though, Cunningham may have begun to recognize the myth was at the expense of the true 1960s pioneers.

Bob Grant, a former Wake Forest and NFL player, tells a story about Cunningham failing to understand the myth. Grant, who founded the NFL Retired Players Congress and still serves as its chairman, said he and former NFL player Reggie Berry of Long Beach State had a conversation one day with Cunningham about college football integration's history.

They explained to Cunningham that Wake Forest and other Southern schools had integrated long before the 1970 USC-Alabama game.

As Grant recalled, "Reggie told Sam, 'You know, you guys didn't integrate the South.'"

"Yes, yes, we did," Cunningham replied.

Berry proceeded to tell the story about Grant and other true 1960s pioneers breaking barriers throughout the South. Cunningham expressed surprise.

"I didn't know that...." he said quietly.

By 2016, a note of bitterness over being used by the myth's proponents can be detected via a Cunningham quote from an August 31, 2016, story by *Los Angeles Times* sportswriter Zach Helfand. Cunningham said, "It's already a historic story without adding sauce to it, you know what I mean? Everybody wants to make it more than what it is. And what it was was very, very important anyway."

Cunningham, RIP, was innocently caught up in a myth. He later came clean, but he did not earn an honored place above the true 1960s pioneers. Cunningham's only task was taking a handoff and running through massive holes opened by five starting white offensive linemen—five of the 17 white starters on a USC team that was still evolving into a fully integrated program.

The 1970 USC-Alabama game was nothing more than an additional step toward integration with real dues paid by true pioneers.

The myth might have dismissed years ago if the media wasn't so willing to play along with a story celebrating two white heroes, Bryant and McKay.

Lane Demas, the Central Michigan University history professor, says the added storyline of Bryant as a benevolent segregationist allowed Bryant's apologists, in their minds, to equate him with Branch Rickey, the Brooklyn Dodgers general manager who signed Jackie Robinson to break the Major League Baseball color line.

"The USC-Alabama story is in a long line of white myths that serve to deny Black people their *agency* in terms of changing America," Demas said. "Focusing on figures like Branch Rickey or Bear Bryant create narratives in which it is ultimately white people who make cautious, thoughtful, calculating decisions to create change and integrate on their own terms. They become the agents of change, not Martin Luther King, Rosa Parks, or the thousands who struggled in the streets."

THE BIRTH OF A MYTH

USC author Steven Travers, to his credit, not only acknowledges the Bryant/Cunningham locker-room scene was a fictional tale, he broke down the genesis and spread of the myth in his 2007 book, *One Night, Two Teams*.

Although his book cover on the 1970 game includes a misleading subtitle—"Alabama vs. USC and the Game that Changed a Nation"—overall Travers has been the most objective person of the many Trojans backers working to overestimate USC's influence on college football integration.

Travers writes USC coach John McKay was "probably embellishing" when he said he helped Bryant integrate the South. That refers to the unsubstantiated claim Bryant was forced to turn to McKay to schedule an integrated opponent.

Although McKay left for the NFL's Tampa Bay Buccaneers in 1976, that didn't kill the myth. Two former McKay assistant coaches smitten with telling the story were still around the program. Craig Fertig was a Fox analyst for USC games (1992-2003) after his coaching days. Marv Goux, upon retirement, was active in the Trojan Club throughout the 1980s and 1990s. Fertig died in 2008 and Goux in 2002.

Fertig claimed in an old interview included in Showtime's *Against the Tide* McKay received a mysterious phone call from Bryant, asking to meet at a Los Angeles International Airport hospitality room. That's where the scheme was revealed, Fertig dubiously contended.

However, in a *Los Angeles Times* story published Aug. 30, 2000, McKay told reporter David Davis that the 1970 Alabama game was arranged over the phone. McKay, who died in a year later at age 77, doesn't reference a furtive trip to the airport or Bryant plotting a plan to manipulate Alabama's fans. In the same Showtime film McKay's son, J.K., says Bryant and his father spoke frequently on the phone and took long golf vacations to Palm Desert.

Why would they need a secret airport meeting that neither one mentioned in their 1974 books?

Travers also acknowledged USC broadcaster Tom Kelly began to repeat the myth in 1987 as he promoted a USC video, "Trojan Video Gold." Then Travers stated the *Long Beach Press-Telegram's* Loel Schrader was among the sportswriters that first printed the story.

Travers wrote in an email of the locker-room myth: "Very early I knew it was untrue and wrote it, and at least in SC circles debunked a decades-old story and took some heat over it."

Travers' email added Fertig exaggerated the Cunningham story and Papadakis "eventually backed off on the story." However, such admissions are skipped over in subsequent films or print stories.

Travers, though, stands by the overall theme that "USC/McKay was the perfect conduit" despite contradictions as to whether USC was a model of integration.

UCLA SHOWED USC THE WAY

In the 1930s, a national backlash against Black athletes took place. This explains how schools with Black players in the late 1800s and early 1900s didn't have them in the 1930s.

USC's Brice Taylor was USC's first Black player in 1924 and its first All-American player in 1925. These days, that's a convenient story USC likes to promote, but it overlooks the years the school removed Taylor's name from its media guide until the arrival in the mid-1950s of C.R. Roberts, a Black halfback from Oceanside, California, who went on to play in the NFL.

UCLA's 1939 team, meanwhile, featured African-American stars Jackie

Robinson, Kenny Washington and Woody Strode. All three pioneers from Los Angeles-area high schools attended UCLA as a school willing to provide an opportunity.

Robinson, of course, is better known for breaking the Major League Baseball color line in 1947 with the Brooklyn Dodgers. But Washington and Strode also were pioneers as the NFL's first Black players with the Los Angeles Rams in 1946. (Not because the NFL was particularly enlightened: the commission running the Los Angeles Memorial Coliseum required integration in order for the relocating Cleveland Rams to obtain a lease.)

UCLA's rosters long included more Black players than USC. UCLA's numbers remained ahead of USC in the 1960s, including eight Black players in the 1962 Rose Bowl.

USC, despite the Alabama game myths, wasn't even an integration leader in its own city.

MCKAY'S SLOW TRANSITION

In his 1974 book, *McKay: A Coach's Story*, John McKay discussed a time when the father of a Black prospect asked McKay if the lack of Black players on USC's roster indicated prejudice.

McKay wrote, "I admitted USC had a lapse for many years before I got there, but said I could prove that throughout the country there were few or no Blacks playing for major universities...."

McKay's statement was untrue. The 1967 class with only seven Black players was his eighth recruiting class since taking over the program in 1960. He also had been a USC assistant coach, arriving in 1959.

None of USC's 1970 Black starters were recruited out of a Los Angeles-area high school despite USC's location in a highly populated and diverse city.

USC's 1970 team included only four Black starters: junior quarterback Jimmy Jones, junior-college transfer senior tailback Clarence Davis, linebacker Charlie Weaver and transfer senior defensive end Tody Smith. Cunningham began the year as a backup to returning starter Charlie Evans —a white fullback who also scored against Alabama and played in the NFL. Without Smith transferring from Michigan State, it would have been three starters. Of USC's 18 Black players on the 1970 roster, 13 were transfers who arrived in 1969 or 1970 (12 as junior-college transfers).

Davis played at Washington High in Los Angeles, but he was recruited out of East Los Angeles Community College. Weaver was from Richmond in northern California; Jones, Harrisburg, Pennsylvania; Cunningham, Santa Barbara, 107 miles up the coast; and Smith was from Beaumont, Texas.

Davis, born in Birmingham, was portrayed as an example of Bryant recognizing the need to keep Alabama kids at home. That's misleading. Davis' family left Birmingham for Los Angeles when he was age 11.

Smith, who had a falling out with Michigan State coach Duffy Daugherty over injuries in 1967, landed at USC, thanks to Daugherty.

"The story we heard," said Michigan State defensive lineman Pat Gallinagh, an Academic-All-American in 1966, "was Duffy asked Tody where he would have gone if not Michigan State. Tody said USC. Duffy told his secretary to get John McKay at USC on the phone."

McKay's defense in his book also fails to note four 1960s national championship rosters surpassed USC's late 1960s totals of Black players. In the poll era of the 1960s, the NCAA recognized four official national title bodies: Associated Press, United Press International (now USA Today), the National Football Foundation and the Football Writers Association of America.

The four 1960s national champs with double-digit Black athletes: Ohio State, 10, 1961 (FWAA); Michigan State, 23, 1965 (UPI, NFF, co-FWAA); Michigan State, 1966, 20, (co-NFF); and Ohio State, 12, 1968 (AP, UPI, FWAA, NFF).

That doesn't mean McKay was "prejudiced." It does suggest that McKay, like Bryant, was content with the status quo.

ROUTS PRESAGE 1970 USC-ALABAMA

Colorado's 1969 football players celebrated like any team would upon finishing a season with a bowl victory to cap an 8-3 record, earning a No. 16 final ranking in the polls. The Buffaloes, with seven Black players, defeated Alabama in the Liberty Bowl 47-33 at Memphis, Tennessee.

The opponent, city and time in American history provided Colorado coach Eddie Crowder's team an added edge of camaraderie. They were playing a segregated team in a Southern stadium only eight months after Martin Luther King had been assassinated in Memphis.

"We wanted to make a statement we were with our Black brothers," said Bobby Anderson, a senior All-American running back soon drafted in the first round by the Denver Broncos.

Anderson was a team captain along with tight end Mike Pruett and nose tackle Bill Collins. Anderson and Pruett are white, Collins Black. Before the game Anderson suggested Collins represent the team during the coin flip. The three walked to the middle of the field together, but Anderson and Pruett stopped 10 yards short of the coin flip meeting. However, Alabama sent its entire roster out for the coin flip.

"Bill showed great courage," Anderson said. "He had a great game."

The teams traded scores in the first half until Colorado's Steve Engel returned a kickoff 91 yards for a touchdown and a 31-19 halftime lead. As Colorado left the field for the tunnel to their locker room, the Buffaloes said Alabama's fans spit at the Black players and hurled racial epithets.

"We're in the locker room and all of the sudden we heard Bill Brundige screaming," said Anderson, referring to the Buffaloes' defensive end, a white teammate. "He said, 'Did you hear what they were calling our Black brothers?' He was normally a calm guy, but he was emotional. He was livid with the Alabama fans."

Alabama rallied for a 33-31 lead, but Colorado sandwiched two Anderson touchdown runs and a sack for a safety in a 16-0 fourth quarter to close out a 14-point victory.

Anderson finished with 35 carries for 254 yards and three touchdowns —presaging Sam Cunningham in Alabama's next game.

Alabama suffering a one-sided loss was a trend in the second half of the 1969 season, continued with the 1970 opener against USC. The myths posing Alabama's 42-21 loss to USC as a shocking result have been misleading. The USC game was more of the same following a 6-5 season on the way to a 1970 record of 6-5-1.

The 1969 routs:

- Oct. 18, 1969: Tennessee 41, Alabama 14. Tennessee's integrated roster overwhelmed Alabama at Legion Field less than a year before USC arrived. Jackie Walker, a Black linebacker, returned an interception for a touchdown early in the game.
- Nov. 29, 1969: Auburn 49, Alabama 26. Auburn, in its final year as an all-white roster, won the Iron Bowl handily. James Owens, the school's first Black recruit in 1969, was on the freshmen team before joining the varsity in 1970.
- Dec. 13, 1969: Colorado 47, Alabama 33.
- Sept. 12, 1970: USC 42, Alabama 21.

Alabama's fans turned somber in the second half, realizing they were in for another .500 season. Two more 1970 routs followed, with the Tide losing to all-white Mississippi, 48-23, and integrated Tennessee, 24-0.

Another similarity between the 1970 USC-Alabama game and the Liberty Bowl was Bryant graciously visiting the opponent's locker room both times. Bryant's sportsmanship wasn't questioned in the 1960s. Only his civics understanding of the U.S. Constitution and the 1964 and 1965 Civil Rights Acts.

"Bear was a classy guy," Anderson said. "He came into our locker room and congratulated us. At the awards banquet for both teams after the game, he said, 'You big, old Colorado boys ought to be ashamed of yourselves for beating up on my little Alabama boys.'"

Alabama quarterback Scott Hunter said in the Showtime film race had nothing to do with the one-sided USC score.

"The Black players were bigger, stronger and faster and the white players were bigger, stronger and faster," he said. "And if they had any polka-dotted players they were bigger, stronger and faster."

But Showtime's writers, editors and producers chose to gloss over Hunter's comments. The film failed to note USC finished only 6-4-1. USC was not a 1970 juggernaut.

ALABAMA'S GRASS ROOTS

Another historical fact overlooked was Alabama high schools were fully integrated by the 1968-69 school year. Bryant needed to learn what a Black player looked like—not his players.

Until the late 1960s, Alabama's public school system had ignored the 1954 *Brown v. Board of Education* ruling from the Supreme Court to desegregate schools. But when faced with losing federal funding, the high schools desegregated. To paraphrase Ernest Hemingway in *The Sun Also Rises*, it was a little at a time and all at once.

Some schools were ahead of others, but by the 1968 football season the state high-school playoffs included Black and white teammates playing together and against other integrated teams. The Alabama High School Athletic Association had merged with the state's Black schools governing body.

That was a tipping point for Bryant finally joining the right side of history at the college level. The desegregation of University of Alabama football began at the grassroots level. Black athletes were not at schools on

Alabama's recruiting trail—recruiters simply ignored Black high-school campuses.

Wilbur Jackson played his senior year at Carroll High, a desegregated school in Ozark, Alabama. Having played his junior year at D.A. Smith, Ozark's Black school, it's fair to wonder if Bryant would have recruited Jackson if he hadn't moved from a Black school to a predominantly white school. Dunnavant's theory of a search doesn't explain Bryant recruiting Matthews.

There's more to how Bryant was unaware of Black athletes in his own state.

In the fall of 1968, Alabama missed on John Mitchell of Williamson High in Mobile. Mitchell was one of five Williamson High science team members placing third in a state competition. All five were offered Alabama academic scholarships.

Was Bryant's "search" unaware of Mitchell, a student-athlete who had earned a football offer from Grambling in addition to the Alabama academic scholarship?

"We haven't so far found many, if any, who are academically and athletically qualified in both," he said in a 1960s video replayed in the *Showtime* film.

The "search" as defense of Bryant was further contradicted by how Bryant stumbled upon Mitchell to recruit him. Mitchell had committed to USC out of Eastern Arizona Junior College. McKay made the mistake of mentioning to Bryant while they were playing golf he had a commitment from a player from Mobile.

Bryant subsequently asked an Alabama alumnus in Mobile, Judge Ferrill McRae, to call every "Mitchell" in the phone book until the prospect was found. They found him. Mitchell flipped to Alabama. He started the 1971 season opener as a junior, making him officially Alabama's first Black player to see action. Jackson was a sophomore backup in his first varsity season.

So much for a sophisticated "search."

Among the players Bryant overlooked were two future NFL players in his state. Ken Hutcherson of Anniston High was a senior in 1968. He attended Livingston (now West Alabama) on his way to a three-year NFL career. John Stallworth was a senior in 1969 at Druid High, Tuscaloosa's predominantly Black high school in Bryant's backyard. He went to Alabama A&M and on to the Pro Football Hall of Fame.

Bryant apologists might claim grades prevented Bryant from signing

Hutcherson, Stallworth or others, but that excuse ignores Bryant got Joe Namath admitted into school overnight. Namath had been denied admission by Maryland, Michigan State and other schools.

MORE UNFOUNDED CONJECTURE

The 2019 ESPN film included such conjecture from Michigan author John Bacon and others that Bryant gave into desegregation because he was tired of losing to Black players. They cite Alabama's slump from 1966 (11-0) to 1969 (6-5).

Bacon says Bryant "invited Sam Cunningham," although Cunningham was an unknown at the time. He played the 1969 season on the freshmen team. The facts don't back up the conjecture. Bryant's 1967 team was 8-2-1 and ranked No. 8 in the nation. The Crimson Tide did not face an integrated opponent.

The 1968 club was 8-3 and ranked No. 17. It lost to Tennessee with one Black player, Lester McClain, but Alabama beat Miami with its lone Black player, Ray Bellamy. The Crimson Tide lost to integrated Missouri in the Gator Bowl.

The 1969 team was 6-5. Three of Alabama's four regular-season losses were to all-white teams (Vanderbilt, LSU and Auburn). The fourth regular season loss was to SEC champion Tennessee and the fifth to Colorado.

In other words, Bryant's three 1967, 1968 and 1969 teams prior to scheduling USC in 1970 went 2-2 against integrated opponents in the regular season but 2-4 counting integrated bowl opponents. Was Bryant tired of losing to Black players?

Bacon's cavalier summation also overlooks Alabama went 11-1 in 1971 despite only one Black starter and two Black players overall. The Crimson Tide opened the 1971 season with a 17-10 win at USC, turning the tables from a year earlier.

BRYANT WAS TONE DEAF

Revisionist history also fails to explain how Bryant remained tone deaf. Bryant's 1974 book *Bear* includes a disturbing passage that suggests integration meant little to him in 1963 or 11 years later, as he reflected on an infamous day in Alabama history, June 11, 1963.

That was the day Alabama Gov. George Wallace, an avowed racist, stood in the University of Alabama schoolhouse door to block the admission of Vivian Malone and James Hood. Bryant referenced the moment in his book, describing himself having a meal at a Chicago airport prior to a connecting flight. He says in the book he left "a generous" $20 tip, but the waiter chased him down, telling him he didn't want his money.

"He was a white guy, too," Bryant wrote in the book. "I put the money back in my pocket. If he wanted to cut off his nose to spite his face, that was alright with me."

Lane Demas, the Central Michigan professor and author, said excuses for Bryant are intended to discredit the civil rights movement.

"I still believe the Cunningham story is not about celebrating Cunningham or USC, nor is it even really about celebrating Bryant or Alabama," Demas said. "It's one of many white stories that emerge in the South during the 1970s that were meant to denigrate King, the countless marches and protests, the student sit-ins, and even the Civil Rights Act, Voting Rights Act, and U.S. Supreme Court. The ultimate point of the Cunningham-Bryant myth is 'see, we didn't need any of that other stuff.'"

Dr. Harry Edwards, a Professor Emeritus of sociology at Cal and a civil rights activist dating to the late 1960s, points out Southern schools recruited Black athletes to win games, but they continued to fly Confederate flags and symbols.

Threading a ribbon through a Bear Bryant story and tying it into a nice bow has been readily accepted. The myth lives on.

The truth and the true 1960s pioneers be damned.

PART IV: VOICES FROM THE NEXT GENERATION

CHAPTER 30
THE NEXT GENERATION: FAMILIES IMPACTED BY FOOTBALL SCHOLARSHIPS

FACT: A football scholarship is a path far broader than just a lane to pro sports. Education also can change a family trajectory.

"Not in a million years could I have dreamed of all the things that have happened to me. When I came to Michigan State, I was the luckiest person in the world. I'm blessed to have had the opportunities, especially coming from the segregated South with all the things we went through in those days."—Ernie Pasteur, Michigan State player retired from his career in education as a teacher and administrator.

The Next Generation chapter is about family trajectories trending upward from a football scholarship. It spans generations, whether an athlete cashed in on a pro contract or relied on his college education for a career.

This chapter starts with a look back at Michigan State's Willie Roaf, whose parents both graduated from MSU. Roaf cashed in his athletic ability, as his sisters earned Ph.D degrees.

After the Roaf family, there is a feature story I wrote on Michigan State graduate Ernie Pasteur, and the foundation he laid for his family through education.

The chapter concludes with four essays written by those closest to the subject, three by the offspring of a father who set up his family through his educational opportunity. Erica Marshall Lee, a Ph.D professor at Emory University, writes about her father, Michigan State's Eric Marshall; Willie Burden, a lawyer in Washington, D.C., writes about his late father, North Carolina State's Willie Burden Sr.; and Lynnae Pickens, a Wall Street executive, writes about her father, Arizona State's Leon Burton.

Michigan State College Football Hall member Gene Washington and his family tell a similar story. His daughter Maya Washington has written a movie and a film on her father escaping segregation in Texas to change his family trajectory. The book and film are both titled *Through the Banks of the Red Cedar*.

Gary Smith's assignment for *Sports Illustrated* was a profile of Willie Roaf for the issue dated Dec. 27, 1993. The mammoth New Orleans Saints offensive tackle, an overnight millionaire after the 1993 NFL draft, lived up to projections in his rookie year. He was on his way to a 14-year NFL career as well as enshrinement in the Pro Football Hall of Fame and the College Football Hall of Fame.

The sports world loves a story about a Black kid winning the lottery through the draft, but Gary Smith—a National Sports Media Hall of Famer—doesn't write cliché stories. He researched deeper than just Roaf's football family—coaches, trainers, agents, etc.

He met the Roaf family.

At the time the *SI* story was published, Willie's father, Clifton Roaf, was a practicing dentist. He used his Michigan State football scholarship to escape the segregated South's Pine Bluff, Arkansas, aboard coach Duffy Daugherty's Underground Railroad. Cliff never played a varsity down after a knee injury in spring football his freshman year, but Daugherty honored his scholarship. Roaf earned his degree and returned home to Pine Bluff as a "country dentist." Cliff said his parents never could have afforded to send him to college, and he remained "indebted to the people of Michigan State." He died in 2017 at age 76.

Of the 44 Black athletes Daugherty recruited from the segregated South between 1959 and 1972, Roaf was the first.

Willie's mother was Andree Layton Roaf. Andree and Cliff met as Michigan State students on a blind date arranged by Herb Adderley, a

Michigan State All-Big Ten player on his way to the Pro Football Hall of Fame as a Green Bay Packer.

At the time Andree was a practicing lawyer, and within two years she was the first Black woman to sit on the Arkansas State Supreme Court. She was opening doors at the state judicial level that 27 years later led to Ketanji Brown Jackson as the first Black woman named to the U.S. Supreme Court.

Willie's older sisters Phoebe and Mary both hold Ph.D degrees. Phoebe's degrees are from Harvard and Princeton. Mary's are from Georgetown, Northern Arizona and Temple. Mary earned her Ph.D after the *SI* story was published and is now a professor at Cal State Stanislaus.

Yes, Willie won the NFL draft lottery, but his sisters won the education lottery. That's the story Gary Smith blended into a sports magazine takeout piece. You can read the full story here: **https://bit.ly/3YsX0yM**

I asked Smith to reflect on how he shifted his story focus to education over football.

"It didn't require too much brainpower on my part, two minutes into a conversation with Willie Roaf's mother Andree, to know that the Roafs' brainpower was *the* story here, and that the anomaly of her shaking her bookwormy head and ruing her son going 'astray' into college and NFL glory made delightful mincemeat of virtually every sports and racial stereotype out there."

I also asked Smith about Willie's NFL success and other Roaf family achievements in the years after the 1993 *SI* article was published.

Smith: "No Roaf achievement or success can come as any surprise once you learn about all the cultivation that's been poured into that family tree."

Clifton Roaf was the first of 44 Black players Daugherty recruited from the segregated South between 1959 and 1972, but it's unfair to trivialize the Underground Railroad's success to a few star players. Of the 44, only 10 earned All-American and All-Big Ten honors. However, 30 graduated for a rate of 68 percent in an era before colleges instituted academic support systems for athletes.

The difference between Daugherty and other coaches who limited their rosters to six or so African-American players: Daugherty took chances on Black players as well as white prospects and honored their scholarships. Eric Marshall was undersized, Ernie Pasteur injured a shoulder and

Clifton Roaf injured a knee, but they and others graduated and lifted their family's trajectory.

ERNIE PASTEUR'S FAMILY

In the summer of 2021, Ernie Pasteur traveled to Memphis, departing from his home near Michigan State's campus. He was a Michigan State graduate with multiple degrees, involved in alumni activities and retired from a distinguished career as an educator in the classroom and administration.

Ernest Pasteur Sr. traveled as a 76-year-old grandfather. Ernie and his son Ernest Pasteur Jr., known as E.J., both helped settle Ernest Pasteur III, called Tre, as a freshman at the University of Memphis.

Six decades earlier Ernie Sr. escaped the segregated South. Michigan State has been the center of his universe since he arrived on campus in the summer of 1963 as an excited high-school graduate with Division I college football potential. He was fortunate his high-school coaches understood Michigan State coach Duffy Daugherty was willing to recruit players denied opportunity to play major college football in their home state. Daugherty's Underground Railroad was a metaphor, a safe trip northward, rather than Harriet Tubman's guided journeys of peril, but the football and freedom destinations were both symbols of opportunity.

On Pasteur's Memphis trip, the Southern city was the latest stamp in a passport Daugherty presented Pasteur in the form of a scholarship. Pasteur had grown up a University of North Carolina fan in Beaufort, North Carolina, but the Tar Heels' football program remained segregated until 1967.

"Not in a million years could I have dreamed of all the things that have happened to me," Pasteur said. "When I came to Michigan State, I was the luckiest person in the world. I'm blessed to have had the opportunities, especially coming from the segregated South with all the things we went through in those days.

"The highlight of my life was earning three Michigan State degrees. It allowed me to have a successful career in high-school administration and to provide for my family. I was able to retire when I wanted and do what I want to do—not what I have to do."

What he wants to do in retirement includes wintering in Florida or South Carolina, two states that didn't want a younger Ernie Pasteur. And feeling needed for a side trip to Memphis to help his son and grandson.

Although a shoulder injury hindered Pasteur's playing time, his degrees set up his future and his family's foundation with his Michigan State bride, Micki. The legacy of Daugherty's groundbreaking teams extends far beyond its star players.

It was about education and the Next Generation.

Ernest Green, the first member of the Little Rock Nine to graduate from Central High in Arkansas, wasn't a football player, but as a Michigan State graduate, he described the school as a "launching pad for people of color."

With Pasteur's passport, he has crossed paths with many luminaries. He was reminded in 2020 of such a moment upon hearing the news Gen. Lloyd Austin was named the first Black Secretary of Defense. The same then-Maj. Lloyd Austin that Pasteur met through his son, a 1991 West Point graduate.

Austin was E.J.'s West Point tactical officer in a company of 125 cadets. A tactical officer provides direction needed to meet demanding academic and leadership requirements to become an officer upon graduation. E.J. served five years, including duties while stationed in South Korea, upon retiring as a captain.

"We had great respect for Lloyd Austin and how he comported himself," said E.J., who also was a star wrestler on Army's Top 25-ranked teams. "He was a true professional. As a young cadet who looked like me, he was a great leader. I had my share of academic problems. If it weren't for him, I might not have graduated. I wouldn't have had the idea that people who looked like me could go to West Point and be successful."

E.J., understanding his father's history escaping segregation, was motivated through the days of doubt that all West Point cadets experience. On average, a quarter of West Point incoming classes don't reach graduation.

"I wanted to be able to show I could make my own way," E.J. said. "I didn't want to be a financial burden on my parents."

Daugherty's Underground Railroad was an adaptation of what historians call the Great Northward Migration—six million Southern Blacks from 1915 to 1970 seeking factory jobs and freedom from Jim Crow state laws.

By the 1950s and 1960s, Michigan State's reputation for providing opportunity to African Americans was well known throughout the South. Pasteur's high-school coach, Earl Tootle, contacted Daugherty with the help of a white coach, Norm Clark, in neighboring Morehead City. Daugherty's 44 Black recruits from the South represented 10 of 14 Southern states —all but Alabama, Tennessee, Maryland and Missouri.

Pasteur's passport gained an international stamp when he and Micki traveled to watch their son E.J. compete in the 1993 Pan American Greco-Roman wrestling championships in Caracas, Venezuela. E.J. won the gold medal for his weight class, adding his prize to the family sports collection that includes Ernie's national championship rings.

In 2018, E.J. and Ernie were both inducted into the Greater Lansing Sports Hall of Fame: E.J. for his wrestling career that included a University Nationals championship and high-school all-state honors in wrestling and football.

Ernie was a member of the Lansing Stars semi-pro team enshrined for its 28-0 record in 1969 and 1970. Pasteur was among former Spartans, along with quarterback Charlie Wedemeyer, offensive lineman Jerry West and linebacker Charlie Thornhill, on the team.

E.J. is one of three children Ernie and Micki raised along with two daughters, Nicole Dandridge and Traceen Pasteur. They also have three grandchildren.

Clearing paths are at the root of Daugherty's legacy.

Pasteur had embarked upon his post-football journey by the 1970s, first as a high-school teacher at Lansing Sexton. He earned his master's degree and became an assistant principal at age 27 at Grand Rapids Union. He has a picture of himself in his time at Union taken with President Gerald R. Ford while the 38th president was on a return visit to his hometown.

Pasteur moved on as a principal at a reform school and later Superintendent at Maxie Boys Training School for adjudicated youth. His final career stage was as consultant establishing charter schools throughout Michigan.

Daugherty's influence was a key to Pasteur's first administration job. Pasteur coveted the Grand Rapids Union job despite difficult times on the campus in the 1970s. Union, with its Dutch family neighborhoods long populating Grand Rapids, initially struggled accepting Black students through a court-ordered bussing program. The N-word and racial epithets were thrown around.

Phil Runkle, the Grand Rapids Public Schools superintendent, personally interviewed Pasteur upon receiving a letter of recommendation Daugherty wrote. Runkle, a Michigan State graduate, understood Daugherty's Spartans were a example of teamwork within fully integrated rosters.

"You're damn right my Michigan State background was important," Pasteur recalled. "Runkle told me, 'Ernie, we've got problems at Union. We need a Black assistant principal that can identify with the kids.'

"We worked hard at it. We got the parents to come in. We got the kids together. I didn't have any problems relating to kids, Black, white or whatever. We talked about Michigan State sports. Union became one of the best schools around."

Pasteur, though, admits with a laugh Runkle wanted to talk about more than the job ahead. He asked Michigan State football questions the first 30 minutes he interviewed Pasteur.

"He wanted to know about Duffy, Bubba, George Webster, Jimmy Raye," Pasteur said.

Then Runkle got down to business. He told Pasteur he had the job. Grand Rapids was another stamp in a passport Pasteur carried upon boarding Daugherty's Underground Railroad.

ERIC MARSHALL'S FAMILY

By Erica D. Marshall Lee, Ph.D, Vice Chair for Faculty Development, Emory University

When I was asked to write about my father, Eric Marshall, I was simultaneously excited and terrified. You see, I don't think there are enough words and superlatives to describe and express the impact he has had on my life and that of many others who have crossed paths with him.

He escaped segregated Oxford, Mississippi, on a football scholarship in 1963 aboard Michigan State coach Duffy Daugherty's Underground Railroad. My father instilled in me the importance of putting Heavenly Father first, the importance of discipline, the importance of education, the importance of financial literacy and the importance of being assertive. Admittedly, I embraced some guidance more so than others. We come from a family whose roots are steeped in spiritual belief and dedication. This was and is the foundation of generations in our clan. Whatever path we take and however we get there our focus is on Heavenly Father, and this is definitely reiterated by my father in every meaningful conversation.

Secondly, education was and is vital to our family history. My grandmother, Susie Marshall, graduated from Rust College, a Historically Black College and University in Holly Springs, Mississippi. She strongly encouraged my father as well as his siblings to do their best academically and well as in their civic duties. My father attended Michigan State on an athletic scholarship and received his bachelor's degree in political science.

For him, the athletic opportunity was key, but the academic opportunity was crucial. He had dreamed of attending Michigan State since the sixth grade and was discounted and mocked when he shared this goal in a speech to his class. He was undeterred. As he left for Michigan State, the University of Mississippi down the street from the family home desegregated with the admission of James Meredith, an Air Force veteran.

This was just further validation that there was nothing that he could not do if he worked hard and remained focused on his goals. He shared this passion with me and upon entry to college as an undergraduate. I had a full scholarship to Mississippi, but he was vehemently against me taking on any type of part-time job. He wanted me to remain focused on my education.

Another value he instilled was that of being assertive, speaking up for myself and expressing my voice and choice. Much to his chagrin, I did so and while I started my studies in electrical engineering, I switched my major in psychology and English. He has been proud of me. He also realized I am my father's child and would not stop there. I went on to receive my Ph.D in Clinical Psychology and become an Associate Professor at the Emory University School of Medicine.

His example of fearlessness and risk taking was not lost on me. It seems we were always on the move with his tours of duty as a U.S. Army officer. Upon graduation at the height of the Vietnam War, he was drafted. He instead enrolled in the Army's Officer Training School. He was soon enough sent to Vietnam, commanding a platoon of mixed races as a Lieutenant.

Once he decided to remain in the Army as a career choice, we explored the world, from Europe and Asia to southeastern United States. He exposed me to jumping out of planes and learning to swim (by throwing me in the pool) at a very young age.

He taught me not to accept no and to stand my ground, display persistence and the ability to regroup. There was an instance while we were in Germany involving a young white boy who rode the school bus with me. He bullied me and spit on my backpack. I was mortified and went home in tears.

When I recounted the story to my father, he listened, consoled me, and continued as usual. The next day, he accompanied me to the bus, instructed me to point out the boy and strongly advised him to steer clear of me. This was extremely brave on my father's part as the boy's father outranked my father and possessed the ability to exact career-ending repercussions for him. My father was undeterred, with the situation ending in the boy's father requiring him to apologize to me and my father. I learned the importance of valuing myself, my family and my future.

As an officer he continued his trajectory in leadership, taking him all the way to Lt. Colonel. He retired from the military and became an educational administrator and eventually a dean in the San Francisco school district. He values education and educating youth to become the next generation of inclusive, diverse and socially just leaders.

His illustration of leadership in this fashion paved the way for my intentional and purposeful career in academia and an academic medical teaching hospital. I first focused on becoming Clinical Director of a specific clinic, followed by obtaining positions in regional and national professional associations, then securing institutional appointments, and now the highest certification given to psychologists. Without him as a role model, I am not sure I would have accomplished these milestones.

My life journey experiences to date were instrumentally influenced and informed by the example set forth by my father and the opportunities he gained through his college experience. I never heard him curse, saw him drink alcohol—or any questionable substances, for that matter. I'd say his drug of choice is Pepsi and cloyingly sweet tea.

My father has always exuded confidence and commanded respect. He was and is fiercely protective of me and never misses an opportunity to share his knowledge, experiences and perspective solicited or not with me, his grandchildren and great grandchildren.

VAGAS FERGUSON'S FAMILY

By Vagas Ferguson, Richmond (Ind.) Public Schools Equity Officer

When Tom Shanahan contacted me about my Notre Dame football career playing for Dan Devine, he prompted me to revisit many thoughts I had dating to my playing days, 1976-79. It was a time when Notre Dame's campus experienced cultural change for African-American students and athletes.

I was fortunate to be the fourth person in my family to attend college, but a football scholarship eased my path to college. I was raised by my grandparents, and my grandmother always emphasized education.

So, understanding academic opportunities and diversity have been important issues to me for a long time. I've used my practical experiences

THE RIGHT THING TO DO 349

gained over the years in my job in my hometown of Richmond, Indiana. For the past 30 years, I've been in different roles as an administrator for the Richmond Public School District. My Notre Dame experience helped me to understand diversity opportunity and progress for students and athletes. We need to continue the focus that began with the civil rights movement into the 21st century.

As Tom and I talked, he informed me Devine had a track record of recruiting more Black athletes than were on the original roster he had inherited as the new head coach. This was true first at Arizona State and then at Missouri. He asked me to comment on the changes I saw at Notre Dame under Devine.

His questions sparked an interest in me to learn the numbers. When I was a high-school senior taking recruiting trips, I noticed Michigan and Ohio State had more Black athletes on the team than Notre Dame (Tom was disappointed to learn Michigan State didn't recruit me when he asked about visiting Michigan State). The difference had always been in the back of my mind but answers to such questions weren't part of the conversation in those days.

So, I volunteered to do the research. I relied on my memories and my access to old team media guides and team photos. I also talked with teammates. I broke down the numbers year by year. I wanted to replace estimates and assumptions with hard numbers.

Devine replaced famed Notre Dame coach Ara Parseghian in 1975, and I believe Ara realized he needed to address diversity at the end of his 11 years as head coach, 1964-75. It was difficult for Devine's personality to measure up to the popular Parseghian, but Dan did benefit from arriving at a time progress was underway.

Parseghian's realization dated to Notre Dame playing Michigan State coach Duffy Daugherty's Spartans in the 1966 Game of the Century. Alan Page was Notre Dame's only Black player. Michigan State had 20 Black players, 11 Black starters, two Black team captains and a Black quarterback, Jimmy Raye.

Duffy Daugherty's courage in the 1960s changed the mindset of major college football programs. When Parseghian surprised the college football world by retiring at the end of the 1974 season, the 1975 recruiting class he handed off to Devine was another step upward. Most of the contacts had been made through Parseghian by the time Devine took over as head coach.

Devine's first full year of recruiting as Notre Dame's coach was my class, 1976. The 10 Black recruits were the most in school history to that point. In my four seasons, the 24 Black players out of 100-some players on the 1976 team was at the time the most in Notre Dame's history.

However, a year later there was only one Black recruit in the Irish's 1977 class. It was the smallest in my four years. Attrition from injuries, academics, playing time or other issues also contributed to fluctuating roster totals.

In 1977, the year we won the national title, we had only 18 Black players, but the Black starters had grown to seven. My class of 10 recruits was down to nine sophomores still in the program.

In 1978, the roster regressed to 14 Black players. Three more from my class left the program to drop the total to six juniors.

In 1979, the combined Black players was 18, but there were only three Black starters: Dave Waymer (defensive back), Bobby Leopold (linebacker) and me (running back). My class held steady for its senior year with six.

The 1979 total was fewer than 1976's high mark of 24, but both numbers were far more Notre Dame had a decade earlier and represented overall upward trend from the early 1970s. The numbers continued to grow into the 1980s.

I thank Tom for spurring to me to think again about how Notre Dame's culture changed in my time on campus.

As an African-American football player, I can see how my opportunity indirectly came about through Duffy Daugherty's 1966 team playing Notre Dame to a 10-10 in their Game of the Century. Because of Duffy's commitment to developing college football's first fully integrated rosters in the 1960s, college football joined a much bigger social movement.

The result has been more opportunities and diversity for African Americans—students and athletes—at colleges and universities across the country.

WILLIE BURDEN'S FAMILY

By Willie Burden Jr., Staff Attorney, International Brotherhood of Teamsters, Washington, D.C.

Son, "would you rather soar with the eagles or hoot with the owls?"
My father, Willie James Burden, always taught me life lessons.
"To get to the place you want to be in life you are going to have to

work twice as hard as your competition. Don't compare yourself to the lesser talent around you at the current moment. There is always a bigger fish out there ready to take your spot."

They are lessons that I will never forget and still to this day shape my mentality, work ethic, and overall approach to life. I can't help but believe these lessons, and the ensuing mentality that came as a result, were adopted by my father as a direct result of his childhood and career experiences. Eventually, the same lessons and experience would lead to a similar outlook and mentality being passed down to his children, mentees and loved ones.

My father was born in a rural community in eastern North Carolina on July 12, 1951. Segregation still ruled the South when my father was growing up in the 1950s and 1960s. I understand better now than when I was younger my father accomplished so much despite growing up Black under Jim Crow laws. He was the first member of my family to attend college thanks to a North Carolina State football scholarship. He and his friend and high-school teammate, Charley Young, were N.C. State's first two Black scholarship football recruits in the fall of 1970.

My father grew up in a small household with six children—two sisters and three brothers. He was the second oldest of the bunch. When my dad discussed his childhood with me, it quickly became apparent that times weren't always easy for the Burden family. He often shared memories of long days working on the farm. His stories would feature several reoccurring events, such as cold nights huddled around the kitchen furnace and days where the only thing available to eat were my grandma's homemade biscuits. That explains why my father loved to eat biscuits and molasses so often.

Typically, it was a meal my father would enjoy on Sundays after the family came home from church. I vividly recall watching sports on Sundays with my dad, him eating a fresh plate of biscuits with molasses made by my mom, Velma, and myself there asking a million questions about whatever game or player was on TV. Of course, my father wouldn't only take these opportunities to answer my questions about the sports or competition, but also highlight any real-world considerations and consequences to take away from what we were watching. Little did I know at the time, but reflecting upon those conversations, I now understand it was during these moments my father sought to teach me how to be "intelligent," or in other words, "how to learn not only from my own mistakes, but also from the mistakes of others." When having these conversations, I could feel the passion in my dad's voice and eventually realized just how much emphasis he placed on being supportive and available to his children. Consequently, it's not surprising that I never felt the need to identify or establish a favorite role model, or mentor, outside of my own household.

My father was aware of the life struggles that potentially awaited me and my siblings. Of course, my father dealt with a very difficult childhood at times, and things certainly did not get any easier when my dad's father decided to leave the family when he was around 12 years old. Thankfully he was blessed with a strong and resilient mother, Emily, whose love and determination kept the family afloat and progressing. When discussing his early childhood my dad often recognized his mother as the foundation of the family and person who influenced him the most. I think it fair to say those same qualities he would one day use to find his wife, and my mother.

After my dad's father left the family, they moved from the rural countryside to the inner city of Raleigh, North Carolina. In order to provide for her family, Emily worked several jobs, often working day and night shifts when possible. Of course, all of this was done in an effort to allow my dad and his siblings to focus on school and staying out of trouble. I recall my dad telling me that after moving to Raleigh he would meet for the first time some of the people he would in time call his lifelong friends, and together they would navigate the late '60s and '70s as young Black men growing up in Raleigh. Jimmy Mitchell, Charley Young, a few others and my dad were an inseparable group.

They went to school, went to hangouts and parties, avoided neighborhood conflicts and fights, and frequently visited neighbors' houses for dinner or a quick snack. He would always tell me having such a profound circle of friends helped expand his interest to include sports and motivated him to purse sports while in middle school and high school. He would always say the opportunity to play sports was a foundational piece to his long-term success. Thus, it is not surprising he took a similar approach with his children.

As early as I can remember, my dad introduced me to every sport imaginable. By the time I was ten I had participated in organized football, basketball, baseball, golf, track and field, and soccer. I remember listening to my father talk about the opportunities and doors sport could open for a person during their life. He encouraged my little brother and me to participate in as many sports as we could, for as long as we could. Little did I realize at the time how much of an impact my father's advice and direction would have on my own life. Ultimately, it would also be my own familiarity and understanding of several sports that would help me obtain my first job after graduation as an Academic Advisor at Georgia Southern University for the football team, baseball team and the men's and women's golf teams.

It was only natural that my dad's Hall of Fame football career would persuade my brother and I to pursue football as a first choice. However, much like myself, my dad's favorite sport was basketball. Most of the sports stories he passed on from his childhood involved pickup basketball games with friends at the local park, or him playing for the varsity basketball team at Enloe High School.

During my adolescence years, it would be commonplace to find my family engaged in competitive games of basketball in the backyard. Me being the oldest child in the house, and oldest son, would always team up with my mom to take on my dad and little brother. During those games my skills improved drastically while playing against my dad, but more importantly I learn the lesson of sportsmanship, losing with grace, and perseverance to succeed despite the odds being against me. Still, my father never let sports cloud the bigger picture of what he needed to accomplish in life, including raising us. With the assistance of his family, friends and neighbors, he made sure we were just as prepared for success off the field and court as we were on.

When my dad was in high school, he was blessed to have as a neighbor Marjorie Debnam. She was an educator who took an interest in my dad and his friends and assembled them into a local group known as the "Men of Distinction." Together with her husband, Ms. Debnam would use her time, money and resources to ensure the young men in the group had help applying for college, looking for jobs, and learning to appreciate the community they were a part of. She would become a second mother to my dad and many of his friends.

More importantly, she served as the first example of a successful professional Black face for my father and his friends to learn from. As an educator she inspired my dad to pursue a profession that aimed to serve and help others. For my father this would only cement the belief that he could do more with his life than farm, as his parents had to for so many years.

She made education, etiquette and manners, and professional skills priorities for the group. My father was so fond of her he would always make an effort to take our family to visit her each time we were in the Raleigh area. Watching my father's appreciation towards Ms. Debnam showed me what it meant to display gratitude and the lengths one should be willing to go to give back to those who assisted you when you were in need. Watching him interact with Ms. Debnam provided an excellent example, especially considering we learned family can be just as thick, and sometimes thicker than blood, and gratitude and grace was something we should afford to any who helped us along the way, family or not, no matter how rich, famous or old we may become.

Following an outstanding high-school football career at Raleigh's William G. Enloe High School, my dad joined his high-school teammate and friend Charley Young as the first African Americans to sign athletic scholarships with the North Carolina State University football team in 1970. He would often share stories of his college experience with me and my younger brother. His stories highlighted his rewarding career and included several feats such as setting the school's single-game record with 198 rushing yards against Kent State University in 1971, becoming a member of "The Stallions"—a backfield group consisting of Burden, Young, Stan Fritts and Roland Hooks—who all went on to play pro football. In 1973, my father's senior season, N.C. State won the Atlantic Coast Conference championship, and he was the first Wolfpack player to rush for 1,000 yards in a season. He was named the ACC Player of the Year.

Most importantly, my dad would also emphasis that he graduated with a bachelor's degree in economics. Not graduating was never an option for my dad as the stakes were too high. Not only was he now representing the Black community as one of the few Black faces on a predominantly white campus freshly introduced to the concept of integration, he also was representing his family as the first person to ever attend college.

It was not always an easy path to navigate as one of the Black students on campus in the early 1970s. There was no true mentor to offer unsolicited guidance or unspecified advice. My dad accentuated the resources available to him for the first time, including study hall, a full library and access to tutors. Yet, while he never spoke of any uncomfortable, insulting or violent situations, he acknowledged there were certainly cultural differences that he had to adapt to in the classrooms and while on campus.

As stated earlier, my father would preach to me and my little brother that "to get to the place you want to be in life you are going to have to work twice as hard as your competition." I believe it was during his college years that my father truly learned to embody that message.

Hearing his stories of often being one of, if not the only Black person in the room while at N.C. State was very transferable, and certainly assisted me in gaining the confidence while on my journey to law school. Those stories gave me the confidence I needed to thrive in a space where only 5 percent of all lawyers are African American. For my brother, in similar fashion, the challenge of navigating the campus of Georgia Tech, where only 5 percent of the student population is African American.

Attending N.C. State allowed my father to maintain a close relationship with his mother and family in addition to many of his childhood friends. Consequently, he remained motivated to change the lives of those around him. Taking full advantage of the resources offered to make sure his academics did not suffer because of his football obligation. My father's graduation motivated several of his young siblings to also pursue a college education and sparked a new family trend whereby the next generation of family members, including myself, saw college as an expectation rather than a dream or mere possibility.

Once his time at N.C. State was up, my dad was selected by the Detroit Lions in the sixth round of the 1974 NFL draft and in the 17th round of the 1974 WFL Draft. However, after a knee injury in training camp brought his NFL debut with the Lions to quick end, he signed as a free agent with the Calgary Stampeders of the Canadian Football League. Although my dad landed on his feet, I distinctly recall him stressing to me that if he did not have his college degree to fall back on, it could have very easily been all over for him. Furthermore, he would always highlight the 100 percent injury rate for all athletes, especially in the sport of football. Still, the Stampeders would be my father's home for eight seasons, between 1974 and 1981. Upon his retirement in 1981, he finished with 6,234 rushing yards, fifth best in Stampeders history, and recorded 299 receptions, fourth in team history, for 2,669 yards and 16 receiving touchdowns.

He won the CFL's Most Outstanding Player Award and All Canadian All-Star honors in 1975. His jersey No. 10 was retired by the Stamps in 1982 before he was added to their Wall of Fame in 1992. A little under 10 years later, my family and I would have the great honor of traveling back to Canada in 2001 to witness his induction into the Canadian Football Hall of Fame, where he was also chosen as one of the league's 50 greatest stars. While in Canada I realized for the first time how big of a star my dad was. Everywhere we went there was someone who wanted to take a picture with him or requested he sign something. Every time someone approach him, he would smile and comply with the request. Again, I was able to witness the gratitude, patience and elegance he displayed while interacting with others. Likewise, the mutual respect and credit he would give to his fellow inductees, including the great Warren Moon. Of course, this gave me and my little brother an opportunity to interact and become comfortable being around living stars at an early age. Our trip would lead us to meeting the likes of James Parker, Bill Frank, Warren Moon, and even a nonplaying star who attended, Ice Cube, the rapper and movie star.

My father continued to build upon his educational experience, receiving his master's degree in sports administration from Ohio University while working as an assistant football coach and instructor in the Department of Physical Education and Recreation until 1984. While in Ohio my father would meet another lifelong friend who was destined to have a significant impact on his life moving forward. Drew Zwald is so close to our family I consider him to be my uncle. Drew and my dad were both assistant coaches and in the grad school program at Ohio University in the 1980s. The relationship he built with Drew and his desired career path would eventually lead to another life-altering opportunity for our family.

Similar to my dad, my mom grew up in rural North Carolina and had strong family and educational values. The two met in Raleigh in 1980 and were married five years later, on August 3, 1985. In my opinion meeting my mom certainly enhanced my dad's passion for helping others advance. My mother was a hard worker with plenty of ambitions on her own, and together the two pushed each other, my brother and I, and countless others forwards personally and professionally. After getting married both my parents would eventually receive their Ed.Ds, with my dad receiving his doctorate in Education at Tennessee State University in 1990 and my mom her Ed.D in Education Administration from Georgia Southern University in 2010.

Following the receipt of his Ed.D my dad would take on what was from my vantage point perhaps the greatest challenging jobs of his professional career, serving as the Athletic Director and as an instructor of Health and Physical Education for North Carolina A&T University from 1990 to 1999. Becoming an Athletic Director up to this point was my father's dream job. At the time he would always tell my mom, this was an opportunity to "steer my own ship." I believe what my father truly meant was, being an Athletic Director provided him the opportunity to ensure young men and women, particularly those of color navigating the college landscape without any or very little guidance, would have the same support and resources available to them that he had at N.C. State. Considering North Carolina A&T University was, and is still today, one of the most prominently known Historical Black Colleges & Universities, the opportunity was one he could not pass at the time.

After a while my father started to take me to work with him on some occasions. The demands of being an Athletic Director kept him working around the clock, with many days requiring a 6 a.m.-10 p.m. schedule. Consequently, I spent several days hanging out with various coaches, including the volleyball coach and track and field coach. I remember watching the various team practices and seeing all the administrative professionals and athletes in the hallways. Of course, this experience was unique, as I experienced firsthand the degree of hard work my dad would invest into his job. Nevertheless, it was in his next move that would again display for my brother and I to witness and learn from, an assertion of his life priorities, including his family and a passion for helping others.

While serving as Athletic Director for North Carolina A&T, my dad would often visit his friend Drew, who at the time was teaching Sport Administration at the University of North Carolina Chapel Hill. Drew would invite my dad into his classroom to teach a class every now and then as a visiting professor.

Drew moved on to Georgia Southern University in 1994 and after a few years placed a call to my dad to tell him about a GSU opening. He landed the job in 1999.

My father welcomed this new challenge despite only being a Temporary Adjunct Professor to start. He did not care about the "temporary" title and put everything into improving his instructor skills and curriculum. As the years passed by, he would eventually graduate from being a Temporary Instructor to an Associate Professor, to a fully tenured full-time Professor, to Professor Emeritus. During this time, he devoted himself to improving his craft, researching, writing and ultimately publishing his work in several academic journals.

Of course, it should be easy to discern why young Black men would frequently be some of the first to seek him out for additional guidance or wisdom. My dad once told me one of the most underrated gifts a person can benefit from is a living example or role model. Particularly for most Black men, there are still only a minuscule number of examples to follow in most prestigious professional fields. By becoming a college professor my father provided a Black face in the crowd of successful people, in a profession where most of the successful people did not look like him.

My brother and I especially were very lucky from that standpoint. We experienced most of our childhood while my dad was in the role of professor, which not only allowed for him to spend more time with us, but also allowed us to benefit from the relationships he built with others. He often introduced us to the students he mentored in hope that we could learn from them as well. Several even ended up coaching one of our Little League teams. It was during those experiences I would come to learn how impactful my father was for several of his students.

Some common quotes we would get from his students were, "Hey Junior, your dad is the man," "You and your brother are lucky to have Dr. B," and "Your Dad is one of the best professors I have had." Whenever I was around one of his students it was always a positive feeling and interaction, something I can only attribute to the way he must have treated them. I would soon learn this to be fact when I decided to stay close to home and attend Georgia Southern University myself. Naturally, at the time I wanted to pursue a career in athletic administration like my father had, so it was only a matter of time before I found myself in my father's course as not only his son, but one of his students.

To this day his students can be found across the state of Georgia and the nation with jobs in everything from coaching at the high-school level to working in the front office of professional sports franchises. The impact my father had on my life, the lives of my siblings, the people he touched, and the students he taught is evident.

He continued to rack up the accolades during this time in recognition of his career. In 2005 he was inducted into Hall of Fame for the Boys & Girls Clubs of America of Raleigh, North Carolina, for his lifetime of good works. In 2009, he was inducted into the North Carolina Sports Hall of Fame.

Sadly, my father would pass away six years later at the age of 64 from a heart condition resulting from an underlying condition that causes an abnormal buildup of protein in the body. The older I get the more and more I realize just how significant of a loss that was for me at the age of 24, and my brother who was only 21 when he passed. Little did I know at the time how much more I could have learned from him. Thankfully we were blessed with our mother, who, to this very day, does her best to help us and offer unconditional guidance and perspective whenever we need it. But, perhaps more importantly, losing my dad also made me realize just how fortunate we were to have him for the time we did. After all, one thing I am sure of is that his legacy and spirit of helping will live on through me, my siblings, and all of those he connected with.

Willie Burden Sr., Spring of 2015—"Son I won't be here forever, and when I go it will be up to you to carry on."

LEON BURTON'S FAMILY

By Lynnae Pickens, University of Chicago MBA, Wall Street executive

Editor's note: Lynnae Pickens wrote this essay on her father before he passed away on Oct. 7, 2022 at age 87.

My father Leon Burton was a young Black male in the 1950s when there weren't many opportunities open to African Americans. Truth be told, we are still fighting for equality to this day, but my dad knew he had to try. And try mightily, he did.

He was born in Flint, Michigan, to an automobile factory worker and a domestic worker. The bar wasn't set high academically or professionally. However, there was something that drove him to want better for himself. Using his talents through organized sports, he was able to earn a football scholarship to play at Arizona State. He faced down the challenging obstacles that had to be conquered along the way.

But for all the injustices that Dad may have endured, he kept his dignity, his pride and his cool. He taught us to do better, be better. And like him, follow your dream

For me, that meant getting my education and like him, opening my own doors. My education consists of a BBA from the University of Michigan and an MBA from the University of Chicago. In my career as a Wall Street executive, I've endured my own painful racial experiences and biases, but I learned from my father to persevere and gain from an opportunity.

When I joined Wall Street in the mid-1980s, there weren't many women, and even fewer Blacks, in professional positions. I have endured indescribably unbelievable racial and sexual discrimination, experienced more unpleasantness than I care to remember and cried buckets of tears (in the restroom—never let them see you cry).

Wall Street back then was seemingly an all-white boys club running rampant on hormones and illegal drugs. Unlike today, there was no sheriff, no protective laws around—at least none enforced—to stop the unmitigated debauchery as long as the trading floor was making money. But I didn't quit. Why? Because my dad had instilled in me the determination to succeed, and I knew I could.

My dad was oldest of 12 children in his family. He loved to run and play outside, and he challenged his friends to races down their street. As a student at Flint Northern High School, he excelled in football and track and field. His senior year at Flint Northern the Vikings won state titles in football and track and field. He set many records. His hurdles times were among the fastest in the nation. One of the local sportswriters wrote Dad "flew down the football field like a jet airplane!" Hence, the nickname "The Jet" was born.

Michigan State head coach Duffy Daugherty and assistant coach Dan Devine recruited my father. His parents couldn't have otherwise afforded to send him to college, and he felt this was his ticket out. He envisioned a better life for himself and his family with an education.

But as fate would have it, he was involved in a near-fatal car crash. He was one of five passengers in a car driven by a friend that collided with a semi truck. The scar bisecting his back is still visible today. He was lucky to be alive, much less ever hope to play football again.

Dreams dashed and scholarship lost, Dad had no choice but to head to the General Motors manufacturing plant to work. Like so many African Americans at that time, he headed to the Flint auto factory lines as a means of getting decent employment. Many family members were already on the line, so when he healed they helped him get a job with AC Spark Plug. The repetitive, boring nature of a line job was not his dream. He knew there had to be a better way.

Fortunately, Dan Devine remembered him. In 1955, Devine was named the head coach at Arizona State. Devine remembered my dad's athleticism prior to the accident. He took a gamble my dad could be a cornerstone to building a program.

My father developed into the school's first Black athletic star. Devine called him a "game breaker" saying, "he might have been the best running back I've ever seen." The school went from an unknown, sleepy college—not even a university until 1959—to membership in a major conference, the Pac-12. Sun Devil Stadium opened seating 30,450 fans and was expanded to nearly 75,000 until its current renovation capacity of 56,634.

Dad set many rushing and scoring records. In 1957, ASU led the nation in total offensive and scoring. He was inducted into the ASU Hall of Fame in 1978 and the ASU Ring of Honor in 2013.

Back in the late 1950s, there weren't many Blacks in Arizona. My father was easily recognized around the campus town of Tempe. He had the town's respect and adulation. He also had Dan Devine's support. My dad mentioned Devine was like a father to him. To be clear, that's not to say my dad didn't face discrimination, but it was diminished with his stature of an athlete. Everyone loves a winner.

In one awful incident after ASU defeated in-state rival Arizona, my parents were traveling with two of my dad's white teammates who also were with their wives. The two white couples were given menus but not my parents. The diner made it clear they didn't serve Negroes. All six of them left, although my dad said his two teammates considered overturning the tables.

My father played his senior year in 1958 for Frank Kush, who was promoted to head coach when Devine was hired as the new head coach at Missouri. In 1959, the San Francisco 49ers drafted him in the eighth round. He didn't make the team, but he played in the Canadian Football League with Toronto before joining the new American Football League in 1960 with the New York Titans (later renamed the Jets). He returned two kickoffs for touchdowns, including a 101-yarder. Special teams players weren't as valued as they are in modern pro football, and that led to him playing only one year in New York.

My father's career ambition was architecture, but there were few opportunities in Grand Rapids and other American cities for an African-American architect. He knew his opportunities were limited if he pursued that career path. Grand Rapids was a racially divided city at a time racial tensions were high in American cities.

With a growing family, my father began working at Meijer, a local powerhouse supermarket chain. They were the Walmart of Michigan before that company expanded nationally. My father was a manager and supervisor in their HVAC engineering department.

It pains me to know that in my dad's era, you could not always follow your passion because there was a strong possibility you wouldn't be hired nor afforded a living in certain professions. The 1960s was one of the worst times for racial tensions.

An incident that comes to mind is when he wanted to move us to a nicer neighborhood. The bank continued to delay the closing without valid reason. Eventually it was divulged that the white neighbors didn't want my parents to move there. Unfortunately, that was not uncommon situation for the era. We were not prevented from moving in, but this certainly was yet another blatant example of prejudice. The first thing people see is your skin color. Not intellect. Not personality. Not character. And nothing more if they chose not to.

In his life, I am sure there are many incidents of racism that my father faced. Racism is ugly, it is hurtful and embarrassing. It is not something easily discussed, especially when you feel like you're on a pedestal on your child's eyes.

His work ethic and tenacity had given me the road map to not only to succeed but to do it with dignity and pride. His words and his actions throughout his entire life demonstrated that with perseverance and dedication, you can achieve your goals.

Today, I have forty-plus year career on Wall Street and am currently a Managing Director in Fixed Income Sales. And although I've achieved some hard-won success in my profession, the struggle continues. I continue to experience bias on Wall Street even today. It will be a long time, perhaps centuries if ever, before racism is eradicated. Only when people of color are in positions of power and use their platforms responsibly will some of the sting from the past injustices begin to be corrected. Yes, Dad, I am following my dream.

For life's lessons, I thank him. Because of him I learned to strive for what may have been deemed unattainable. No, my dad didn't achieve NFL fame. He didn't become an architectural engineer. He wasn't able to escape the mental and physical ravages that football inflicted on his body. But what he did achieve was instilling in us the value of not giving up. To put in the effort to achieve your goal. And work like hell to follow your dream.

Football ended up being the catalyst for Dad's way out of the cycle of poverty. The scholarship not only changed the trajectory of his life, it also changed the lives of his descendants. Education is so important. Having access to it is paramount.

In reflection, I look up to my dad with an abundance of pride, respect and admiration for all the sacrifices he made so that we could enjoy a better life. I'm sure I don't know half of what he experienced as a little Black kid in 1950s America. But what I do know is the rich and abundant legacy that he leaves behind. And for that, I am eternally grateful.

Walter Leon Burton. The Jet. My Dad. My Hero.

www.ingramcontent.com/pod-product-compliance
Lightning Source LLC
Chambersburg PA
CBHW070044080526
44586CB00013B/911